A READER IN ECCLESIOLOGY

This Reader presents a diverse and ecumenical cross-section of ecclesiological statements from across the twenty centuries of the church's existence. It builds on the foundations of early Christian writings, illustrates significant medieval, reformation, and modern developments, and provides a representative look at the robust attention to ecclesiology that characterizes the contemporary period. This collection of readings offers an impressive overview of the multiple ways Christians have understood the church to be both the 'body of Christ' and, at the same time, an imperfect, social and historical institution, constantly subject to change, and reflective of the cultures in which it is found.

This comprehensive survey of historical ecclesiologies is helpful in pointing readers to the remarkable number of images and metaphors that Christians have relied upon in describing the church and to the various tensions that have characterized reflection on the church as both united and diverse, community and institution, visible and invisible, triumphant and militant, global and local, one and many. Students, clergy and all interested in Christianity and the church will find this collection an invaluable resource.

Ashgate Contemporary Ecclesiology

The field of ecclesiology has grown remarkably in the last decade, and most especially in relation to the study of the contemporary church. Recently, theological attention has turned once more to the nature of the church, its practices and proclivities, and to interpretative readings and understandings on its role, function and ethos in contemporary society.

This new series draws from a range of disciplines and established scholars to further the study of contemporary ecclesiology and publish an important cluster of landmark titles in this field. The Series Editors represent a range of Christian traditions and disciplines, and this reflects the breadth and depth of books developing in the Series. This Ashgate series presents a clear focus on the contemporary situation of churches worldwide, offering an invaluable resource for students, researchers, ministers and other interested readers around the world working or interested in the diverse areas of contemporary ecclesiology and the important changing shape of the church worldwide.

A Reader in Ecclesiology

BRYAN P. STONE
Boston University School of Theology, USA

ASHGATE

Published by
Ashgate Publishing Limited
Wey Court East
Union Road
Farnham
Surrey, GU9 7PT
England

Ashgate Publishing Company
Suite 420
101 Cherry Street
Burlington
VT 05401-4405
USA

www.ashgate.com

British Library Cataloguing in Publication Data
Stone, Bryan P., 1959–
   A reader in ecclesiology. – (Contemporary ecclesiology) 1. Church. 2. Church history.
   3. Christian literature–History and criticism.
   I. Title II. Series
   262'.009–dc22

Library of Congress Cataloging-in-Publication Data
Stone, Bryan P., 1959–
   A reader in ecclesiology / Bryan Stone.
    p. cm. – (Ashgate contemporary ecclesiology)
   Includes index.
   ISBN 978-1-4094-2855-8 (hardcover : alk. paper) – ISBN 978-1-4094-2856-5 (pbk. : alk. paper)
   – ISBN 978-1-4094-2857-2 (ebook) 1. Church–History of doctrines. I. Title.
   BV598.S67 2011
   262–dc23

2011030106

ISBN 9781409428558 (hbk)
ISBN 9781409428565 (pbk)
ISBN 9781409428572 (ebk)

Printed and bound in Great Britain by the
MPG Books Group, UK

Contents

O God, we pray for thy Church, which is set to-day amid the perplexities of a changing order, and face to face with a great new task. We remember with love the nurture she gave to our spiritual life in its infancy, the tasks she set for our growing strength, the influence of the devoted hearts she gathers, the steadfast power for good she has exerted. When we compare her with all human institutions, we rejoice, for there is none like her. But when we judge her by the mind of her Master, we bow in pity and contrition. Oh, baptize her afresh in the life-giving spirit of Jesus! Grant her a new birth, though it be with the travail of repentance and humiliation. Bestow upon her a more imperious responsiveness to duty, a swifter compassion with suffering, and an utter loyalty to the will of God. Put upon her lips the ancient gospel of her Lord. Help her to proclaim boldly the coming of the Kingdom of God and the doom of all that resist it. Fill her with the prophets' scorn of tyranny, and with a Christ-like tenderness for the heavy-laden and down-trodden. Give her faith to espouse the cause of the people, and in their hands that grope after freedom and light to recognize the bleeding hands of Christ. Bid her cease from seeking her own life, lest she lose it. Make her valiant to give her life to humanity, that like her crucified Lord she may mount by the path of the cross to a higher glory.

Walter Rauschenbusch, "For the Church" (1909)

Acknowledgments

The editor gratefully acknowledges the following permissions to reproduce copyright material. All possible attempts have been made to contact copyright holders and to acknowledge their copyright correctly.

The cover artwork is *Flores Para La Iglesia* and is used here with the gracious permission of the artist, Jan Oliver (www.janoliver.com).

The prayer at the beginning of this volume is from Walter Rauschenbusch, *Prayers of the Social Awakening* (Boston: The Pilgrim Press, 1909), pp. 119–20.

Part 1

1   All scripture quotations from the New Revised Standard Version of the Bible. Copyright © 1989 the National Council of Churches of the Churches of Christ in the USA. Used by permission. All rights reserved.

2–4, 6, 8 Excerpts from Michael W. Holmes (trans. and ed.), *The Apostolic Fathers in English*, 3rd edn. (Grand Rapids: Baker Academic, 2006), pp. 60–64, 68–9, 97–8, 104–5, 108–9, 123–4, 166–71, 206–87, 295–6. Used by permission.

5   F. Bland Tucker, "Father, We Thank You," in *The Hymnal 1982: According to the Use of the Episcopal Church* (New York: The Church Pension Fund, 1985), #382.

7   Cyril C. Richardson (trans. and ed.), *Early Christian Fathers*, Library of Christian Classics (Louisville: Westminster John Knox, 1953), pp. 247–8, 253, 287. Used by permission of Westminster John Knox Press (www.wjkbooks.com). Used by permission of Hymns Ancient & Modern.

9   Robert M. Grant, *Irenaeus of Lyons*, Early Church Fathers (New York: Routledge, 1997), pp. 70–71. Reproduced by permission of Taylor & Francis Books, UK.

10–11 Alexander Roberts and James Donaldson (eds.), *The Ante-Nicene Fathers: Translations of the Writings of the Fathers down to A.D. 325*

(Edinburgh: T. & T. Clark, 1866–72), vol. 2, pp. 220, 231, 295; vol. 3, pp. 42–3, 46–7, 49.

12   Alistair Stewart-Sykes, *Hippolytus: On the Apostolic Tradition* (Crestwood, NY: St. Vladimir's Seminary Press, 2001), pp. 97–100. Used by permission.

13   Alistair Stewart-Sykes, *The Didascalia Apostolorum: An English Version with Introduction and Annotation*, Studia Traditionis Theologiae (Turnhout: Brepols, 2009), vol. 1, pp. 178–81. Used by permission.

14   Stanley L. Greenslade (trans. and ed.), *Early Latin Theology*, Library of Christian Classics (Philadelphia: Westminster, 1956), pp. 126–9. Used by permission of Westminster John Knox Press (www.wjkbooks. com). Used by permission of Hymns Ancient & Modern.

15   Excerpt from *Commentary on the Song of Songs* from *Origen: An Exhortation to Martyrdom, Prayer and Selected Works*, trans. and intro. Rowan A. Greer (Mahwah, NJ: Paulist Press, 1979), p. 230. Copyright © 1979 Paulist Press, Inc. Reprinted by permission of Paulist Press, Inc. (www.paulistpress.com). Excerpt from *Commentary on the Song of Songs* from Hans Urs von Balthasar, *Origen: Spirit and Fire: A Thematic Anthology of His Writings*, trans. Robert J. Daly, S.J. (Washington, D.C.: Catholic University of America Press, 1984), pp. 148–9. Used by permission. Excerpt from *Homilies on Joshua* from Barbara J. Bruce (trans.) and Cynthia White (ed.), *The Fathers of the Church* (Washington, D.C.: Catholic University of America Press, 2002), pp. 46–50, 184–5. Used by permission.

16   Philip Schaff and Henry Wace (trans. and eds.), *Nicene and Post-Nicene Fathers of the Christian Church*, 2nd ser. (New York: The Christian Literature Company, 1894), vol. 7, pp. 139–40.

17   Alexander Roberts and James Donaldson (eds.), *The Ante-Nicene Fathers: Translations of the Writings of the Fathers down to A.D. 325* (Edinburgh: T. & T. Clark, 1866–72), vol. 7, pp. 421–2.

18   Philip Schaff (ed.), *The Nicene and Post-Nicene Fathers of the Christian Church*, 1st ser. (Buffalo, NY: The Christian Literature Company, 1887), vol. 4, p. 623.

19   Excerpts from *De baptismo* and *Concerning the Correction of the Donatists* from Philip Schaff (ed.), *The Nicene and Post-Nicene Fathers of the Christian Church*, 1st ser. (Buffalo, NY: The Christian Literature

Company, 1887), vol. 4, p. 453–5, 623, 640–42. Excerpt from *Tractates on the Gospel of John* from John W. Rettig (trans.), *Tractates on the Gospel of John* (Washington, D.C.: Catholic University of America Press, 1988), vol. 2, pp. 186–7. Used by permission. Excerpt from *The City of God* from Marcus Dods (trans.), *The Works of Aurelius Augustine, Bishop of Hippo: A New Translation* (Edinburgh: T. & T. Clark, 1888), vol. 1, p. 46; vol. 2, pp. 47–8, 50–51, 326–8.

20   J. H. Robinson, *Readings in European History* (Boston: Ginn & Co., 1905), pp. 72–3.

Part 2

1   Rev. J. M. Neale (trans.), *Mediaeval Hymns and Sequences*, 2nd edn. (London: Joseph Masters, 1853), pp. 18–20.

2   Ernest F. Henderson (ed. and trans.), Select Historical Documents of the Middle Ages (London: George Bell and Sons, 1892), pp. 366–7, 395–6, 401–2.

3   Kilian Walsh (trans.), *The Works of Bernard of Clairvaux* (Shannon: Irish University Press), 1971, vol. 2, pp. 86. Copyright 1971 Cistercian Publications, copyright 2008 Order of Saint Benedict. Published by the Liturgical Press, Collegeville, MN. Reprinted with permission.

4   Excerpt from Isaac of Stella from Henri de Lubac, S.J., *Catholicism: Christ and the Common Destiny of Man* (San Francisco: Ignatius Press, 1988), pp. 420–21.

5   Excerpts from Columba Hart and Jane Bishop (trans.), *Hildegard of Bingen: Scivias* (Mahwah, NJ: Paulist Press, 1990), pp. 169–73, 237–9. Copyright © 1990 Abbey of Regina Laudis: Benedictine Congregation Regina Laudis of the Strict Observance, Inc. Reprinted by permission of Paulist Press, Inc. (www.paulistpress.com).

6   Oliver J. Thatcher and Edgar Holmes McNeal, *A Source Book for Mediaeval History* (New York: Charles Scribner's Sons, 1905), p. 208.

7   H. J. Schroeder, *Disciplinary Decrees of the General Councils: Text, Translation and Commentary* (St. Louis: B. Herder, 1937), pp. 238–9.

8   Excerpt from the *Exposition on the Apostles' Creed* from Joseph B. Collins (trans.), *Catechetical Instructions of St. Thomas* (New York:

Wagner, 1939), pp. 48–53. Excerpt from the *Summa Theologica* from *The Summa Theologica of St. Thomas Aquinas*, trans. Fathers of the English Dominican Province (New York: Benzinger Bros, 1913), pp. 130, 140.

9   James H. Robinson, *Readings in European History* (Boston: Ginn & Co., 1904), pp. 346–8.

10   Oliver J. Thatcher and Edgar Holmes McNeal (eds.), *A Source Book for Mediaeval History* (New York: Charles Scribner's Sons, 1905), pp. 317–24.

11   William of Ockham, *A Short Discourse on the Tyrannical Government*, ed. Arthur Stephen McGrade; trans. John Kilcullen (Cambridge: Cambridge University Press, 1992), pp. 23–4, 30, 157. Used by permission.

12   Thomas Arnold (ed.), *Select English Works of John Wyclif* (Oxford: Clarendon Press, 1869), vol. 3, p. 339–40. Translated into modern English by the editor.

13   Jan Huss, *The Church*, trans. David S. Schaff (New York: Charles Scribner's Sons, 1915), pp. 11, 14–15, 48, 58, 66.

14, 16 Oliver J. Thatcher and Edgar Holmes McNeal, *A Source Book for Mediaeval History* (New York: Charles Scribner's Sons, 1905), pp. 328–9, 331–2.

15   Nicholas of Cusa, *The Catholic Concordance*, ed. and trans. Paul E. Sigmund (Cambridge: Cambridge University Press, 1991), pp. 97–8, 113, 194. Used by permission.

17   Excerpt from *To the Christian Nobility* from Charles M. Jacobs (trans.) and James Atkinson (rev. and ed.), *Luther's Works* (Philadelphia: Fortress, 1966), vol. 44, pp. 129–31. Used by permission. Excerpt from *The Gospel for the Early Christmas Service* from Hans J. Hillerbrand (trans. and ed.), *Luther's Works* (Philadelphia: Fortress, 1974), vol. 52, pp. 39–40. Used by permission. Excerpt from *Concerning the Ministry* from Conrad Bergendoff (trans. and ed.), *Luther's Works* (Philadelphia: Fortress, 1958), vol. 40, pp. 9, 34, 41. Used by permission. Excerpt from *Lectures on Galatians* from Jaroslav Pelikan (trans. and ed.), *Luther's Works* (St. Louis: Concordia Publishing House, 1963), vol. 26, pp. 441–2. Copyright © 1963, 1991 Concordia Publishing House (www.cph.org). Used by permission. All rights reserved. Excerpt from *The Smalcald Articles* from Theodore G. Tappert (trans. and ed.),

The Smalcald Articles, in *The Book of Concord* (Philadelphia: Fortress, 1959), p. 315. Used by permission. Excerpt from *On the Councils and the Churches* from Charles M. Jacobs (trans.), *Luther's Works*, rev. and ed. Eric W. Gritsch (Philadelphia: Fortress Press, 1966), vol. 41, pp. 143–67. Used by permission.

18   John Howard Yoder, *The Legacy of Michael Sattler* (Scottdale, PA: Herald Press, 1977), pp. 36–42. Used by permission.

19   Theodore G. Tappert (trans. and ed.), *Book of Concord* (Philadelphia: Fortress, 1959), p. 32. Used by permission.

20   G. W. Bromiley (ed.), *Zwingli and Bullinger*, Library of Christian Classics (Philadelphia: Westminster, 1953), pp. 265–6. Used by permission of Westminster John Knox Press. (www.wjkbooks.com). Used by permission of Hymns Ancient & Modern.

21   Excerpt from *Institutes* (1536) from John Calvin, *Institutes of the Christian Religion*, trans. Ford Lewis Battles (Grand Rapids: Eerdmans, 1975; rev. edn. 1986), pp. 9–10. Used by permission. Excerpt from *Reply to Sadoleto* from John C. Olin (ed.), *A Reformation Debate: Sadoleto's Letter to the Genevans and Calvin's Reply* (New York: Harper & Row, 1966), pp. 60–64, 75–6. Used by permission. Excerpt from *The Catechism of the Church of Geneva* from Henry Beveridge (trans.), *Calvin's Tracts and Treatises* (Grand Rapids: Eerdmans, 1958), vol. 2, pp. 50–2. Used by permission. Excerpt from *Institutes* (1559) from John T. McNeill (trans.) and Ford Lewis Battles (ed.), *Calvin: Institutes of the Christian Religion*, Library of Christian Classics (Louisville: Westminster John Knox, 1960), pp. 1016–31. Used by permission of Westminster John Knox Press (www.wjkbooks.com). Used by permission of Hymns Ancient & Modern.

22   G. W. Bromiley (trans.), *Zwingli and Bullinger*, Library of Christian Classics (Philadelphia: Westminster, 1953), pp. 289–304. Used by permission of Westminster John Knox Press (www.wjkbooks.com). Used by permission of Hymns Ancient & Modern.

23   J. C. Wenger (ed.) and Leonard Verduin (trans.), *The Complete Writings of Menno Simons, c. 1496–1561* (Scottdale, PA: Herald Press, 1986), p. 739–42. Used by permission.

24   John Knox, *The History of the Reformation of Religion in Scotland* (Glasgow: Blackie, Fullarton & Co., 1831), p. 215.

Maurice, *Sermons Preached in Lincoln's Inn Chapel* (London: Macmillan & Co., 1891), vol. 1, p. 251. Excerpt from Letter to Palmer from F. D. Maurice, *Three Letters to the Rev. W. Palmer*, 2nd edn. (London: John W. Parker, 1842), p. 7–8, 12–13.

10   S. J. Stone, *Hymnal According to the Use of the Protestant Episcopal Church in the United States of America* (New York: James Pott & Co., 1871), #202.

Part 4

1   Excerpt from Walter Rauschenbusch, *The Righteousness of the Kingdom*, ed. Max L. Stackhouse (Nashville, Abingdon, 1968), pp. 152, 176–7. Reprinted with permission. Excerpt from Walter Rauschenbusch, *Christianity and the Social Crisis* (London: Macmillan & Co. Ltd., 1908), pp. 185–6. Excerpt from Walter Rauschenbusch, *A Theology for the Social Gospel* (New York: The Macmillan Company, 1917), pp. 119–20, 128–30.

2   Ryūsaku Tsunoda, William Theodore de Bary, and Donald Keene (eds.), *Sources of Japanese Tradition* (New York: Columbia University Press, 1958), vol. 2, pp. 347–8. Copyright © 1958 Columbia University Press. Reprinted with permission of the publisher.

3   Ernst Troeltsch, *The Social Teaching of the Christian Churches*, trans. Olive Wyon (London: George Allen & Unwin Ltd., 1931), vol. 2, pp. 993–4, 997–9, 1006–7. Copyright © 1931. Reproduced by permission of Taylor & Francis Books, UK.

4   Excerpt from Karl Barth, *Church Dogmatics*, ed. G. W. Bromily and T. F. Torrance (Edinburgh: T. & T. Clark, 1958), vol. IV/2, pp. 620–21, 648, 719–23. Excerpt from Karl Barth, *Church Dogmatics*, ed. G. W. Bromiley and T. F. Torrance (Edinburgh: T. & T. Clark, 1962), vol. IV/3.2, pp. 795–7.

5   Walter Suckau and Krishana Suckau (trans.), "The Barmen Theological Declaration," from Alfred Burgsmüller and Rudolf Weth (eds.), *Die Barmer Theologische Erklärung: Einführung und Dokumentation* (Neukirchen-Vluyn: Neukirchener Verlag, 1983).

6   Excerpt from *The Cost of Discipleship* from Geffrey B. Kelly, John D. Godsey (eds.), Barbara Green, and Rieinhard Krauss (trans.), *Dietrich Bonhoeffer Works* (Minneapolis: Fortress, 2001), vol. 4, pp. 213–20,

236, 244, 250–51. Used by permission. Excerpt from *Life Together* from Geffrey B. Kelly (ed.) and Daniel W. Bloesch (trans.), *Dietrich Bonhoeffer Works* (Minneapolis: Fortress, 1996), vol. 5, pp. 31, 82–3. Used by permission.

7   William Temple, *Christianity and Social Order* (New York: Penguin Books, 1942), pp. 39–41, 43, 58–9.

8   Henri de Lubac, S.J., *Catholicism: Christ and the Common Destiny of Man* (San Francisco: Ignatius Press, 1988), pp. 48–9, 62–4, 74–7.

9   Tokuo Yamaguchi, "Here, O Lord, Your Servants Gather," trans. Everett M. Stowe from *The United Methodist Hymnal* (Nashville: United Methodist Publishing House, 1989). Copyright © 1958 The United Methodist Publishing House/Administered by Coltman International, 8 Marshfoot Lane, Hailsham, East Sussex, BN27 2RA, UK.

10   Excerpt from Lesslie Newbigin, *The Household of God: Lectures on the Nature of the Church* (London: SCM Press, 1953), pp. 25–6, 28–31. Used by permission. Excerpt from Lesslie Newbigin, "On Being the Church for the World," in Giles S. Ecclestone (ed.), *The Parish Church? Explorations in the Relationship of the Church and the World* (Oxford: Mowbray, 1988), pp. 30–31, 37–40. Printed with permission from the Continuum Publishing Company. Copyright © 1988 Giles Ecclestone. Excerpt from Lesslie Newbigin, *The Gospel in a Pluralistic Society* (Grand Rapids: Eerdmans, 1989), pp. 118–9. Used by permission.

11   Austin Flannery, O.P. (ed.), *Vatican Council II: The Basic Sixteen Documents* (Northport, NY: Costello Publishing Co., 1996), pp. 6–9, 12, 17–23, 36–7, 49–52, 163–5, 173–4, 206–15. Used by permission.

12   Excerpt from "Ecumenism" from Basil Christopher Butler, *The Theology of Vatican II: The Sarum Lectures 1966* (London: Darton Longman & Todd Ltd., 1967), pp. 133–5. Published and copyright 1967 by Darton Longman & Todd Ltd., London, and used by permission of the publishers. Reprinted with the kind permission of Downside Abbey.

13   Excerpt from "The Answer to a Perplexing Question" from Clayborn Carson (ed.), *The Papers of Martin Luther King, Jr.* (Berkely: University of California Press, 2007), vol. 6, pp. 549–50. Copyright 2007 in the format Textbook via Copyright Clearance Center, used by permission.

14   Excerpt from M. M. Thomas, *Towards a Theology of Contemporary Ecumenism: A Collection of Addresses to Ecumenical Gatherings (1947–1975)* (Madras: The Christian Literature Society, 1978), pp. 162–4. Used by permission. Excerpt from M. M. Thomas, *Salvation and Humanization: Some Crucial Issues of the Theology of Mission in Contemporary India* (Madras: The Christian Literature Society, 1971), pp. 58–60. Used by permission. Excerpt from M. M. Thomas, *Risking Christ for Christ's Sake: Towards an Ecumenical Theology of Pluralism* (Geneva: World Council of Churches, 1987), pp. 114–16, 119.

15   John Howard Yoder, *The Royal Priesthood*, ed. Michael G. Cartwright (Scottdale, PA: Herald Press, 1998), pp. 57, 61, 62–4, 74–5, 91. Used by permission.

16   World Council of Churches, "The Church for Others," in *The Church for Others: Two Reports on the Missionary Structure of the Congregation* (Geneva: World Council of Churches, 1967), pp. 16–20.

17   Excerpt from Hans Küng, *The Church*, trans. Ray Ockenden and Rosaleen Ockenden (London: Burns and Oates, 1967), pp. 32–3, 164–7, 285, 340–1. Printed with permission from Continuum International Publishing Company. Copyright © 1967 Hans Küng. Excerpt from Hans Küng, *The Catholic Church: A Short History*, trans. John Bowden (New York: Modern Library, 2001), pp. 203–4. Copyright © 2001 Hans Küng. Used by permission of Modern Library, a division of Random House, Inc.

18   Alexander Schmemann, "Ecclesiological Notes," *St. Vladimir's Seminary Quarterly* 11/1 (1 Jan. 1967), pp. 35–9. Reproduced by permission of St. Vladimir's Seminary Press (www.svspress.com).

19   Juan Luis Segundo, *The Community Called Church*, trans. John Drury (Maryknoll, NY: Orbis, 1973), pp. 8–11, 15. Used by permission.

20   James H. Cone, *Black Theology and Black Power* (Maryknoll, NY: Orbis, 1997), pp. 63, 65–6, 71–3, 112–13.

21   Gustavo Gutíerrez, *A Theology of Liberation*, trans. and ed. Sister Caridad Inda and John Eagleson (Maryknoll, NY: Orbis, 1988), pp. 143, 145–8. Used by permission of Hymns Ancient & Modern.

22   Jürgen Moltmann, *The Church in the Power of the Spirit: A Contribution to Messianic Ecclesiology*, trans. Margaret Kohl (Minneapolis: Fortress, 1993), pp. 196–7. Used by permission.

23   James R. Brockman, S.J. (ed. and trans.), *Oscar Romero: The Violence of Love* (Maryknoll, NY: Orbis, 2004), pp. 26, 28–9, 101–2, 125, 135–6, 186–7.

24   Leonardo Boff, *Igreja: Carisma e Poder* (Petropolis, RJ, Brazil: Editora Vozes, 1981), pp. 113–15. Original translation by Andrea Reily Rocha, Rachel Vogelzang, and the editor.

25   Stanley Hauerwas, *The Peaceable Kingdom: A Primer in Christian Ethics* (Notre Dame: University of Notre Dame Press, 1983), pp. 96–102.

26   John D. Zizioulas, *Being as Communion: Studies in Personhood and the Church* (Crestwood, NY: St. Vladimir's Seminary Press, 1985), pp. 15, 22–3, 113. Used by permission.

27   Rosemary Radford Reuther, *Women-Church: Theology and Practice of Feminist Liturgical Communities* (San Francisco: Harper & Row, 1985), pp. 57–62, 72–4, 87.

28   George A. Lindbeck, "The Church," in Geoffrey Wainwright (ed.), *Keeping the Faith: Essays to Mark the Centenary of Lux Mundi* (Philadelphia: Fortress, 1988), pp. 182–6, 192–3. Used by permission.

29   Elisabeth Schüssler Fiorenza, "Daughters of Vision and Struggle," in *Discipleship of Equals: A Critical Feminist Ekklēsia-logy of Liberation* (New York: Crossroad, 1994), pp. 328–31. Printed with permission from the Continuum International Publishing Company. Copyright © 1994 Elisabeth Schüssler Fiorenza.

30   Bénézet Bujo, *African Theology in its Social Context*, trans. John O'Donohue (Maryknoll, NY: Orbis, 1992), pp. 94–5. Used by permission. Copyright © St Paul Communications, Paulines Publications, Africa, P.O. Box 49026, 00100 Nairobi GPO (Kenya). Used by permission.

31   Wolfhart Pannenberg, *Systematic Theology*, trans. G. W. Bromiley (Grand Rapids: Eerdmans, 1998), vol. 3, pp. 32–3. Used by permission.

32   Letty M. Russell, *Church in the Round: Feminist Interpretation of the Church* (Louisville: Westminster John Knox, 1993), pp. 13, 14, 25, 42, 110. Used by permission of Westminster John Knox Press (www.wjkbooks.com).

33   Delores S. Williams, *Sisters in the Wilderness: The Challenge of Womanist God-Talk* (Maryknoll, NY: Orbis, 1993), pp. 204–6. Used by permission.

34   Miroslav Volf, *After Our Likeness: The Church as the Image of the Trinity* (Grand Rapids: Eerdmans, 1998), pp. 128–9, 137, 145, 147.

35   Elizabeth A. Johnson, *Friends of God and Prophets: A Feminist Theological Reading of the Communion of Saints* (New York: Continuum, 1999), pp. 220–23, 234–6. Printed with permission from Continuum International Publishing Company. Copyright © 1999 Elizabeth Johnson.

36   Amos Yong, *The Spirit Poured Out on All Flesh: Pentecostalism and the Possibility of Global Theology* (Grand Rapids: Baker Academic, 2005), pp. 135–8, 144–5.

Introduction

This work had its beginnings in the context of my teaching a course in ecclesiology and my disappointment that no collection of representative readings from across Christian history was to be found. Students gain much from reading book-length treatments on ecclesiology, but shorter excerpts from a greater variety of ecclesiologies can be useful for gaining perspective on the wide sweep of Christian thought and its patterns of change over time. I have tried to do justice to some of that breadth and development in the excerpts I have chosen for this volume.

Ecclesiology is a discipline that undertakes critical and constructive reflection on the Christian community as a distinct social body in the world and as a particular people in history. This community understands itself to be the "body of Christ," the "temple of God," and a living "sacrament" that, because of its union with Christ, reveals to the world something of God's very nature and purpose. At the same time, the church is also and always an imperfect, social and historical institution; constantly subject to change; reflective of the cultures in which it is to be found; and created, organized, and maintained by particular human beings in specific times and places. This dialectic shows up often in writings on the church. Indeed, one of the fascinating features of a historical survey of Christian ecclesiologies is the glimpse it affords of the ways this dialectic has been developed over time and the way a number of ecclesiological distinctions have been held in tension—for example, the church as both united and diverse, community and institution, visible and invisible, triumphant and militant, global and local, one and many. A broad survey of historical ecclesiologies is also helpful in pointing us to the remarkable number of images and metaphors that Christians have relied upon in describing the church.[1]

While this volume is a collection of excerpts on the church from throughout Christian history, it is not intended as a systematic or constructive essay that would attempt to distill some common essence or to comprehend an overall unity and trajectory. The introductions to each excerpt are deliberately brief and attempt simply to provide some sense of the context that helps explain the significance of the excerpt. The volume does not make an argument for or against a particular type of ecclesiology, nor does it seek to present only those ecclesiological reflections that the editor deems laudatory. If anything,

---

[1] Paul Minear's classic treatment of this in his *Images of the Church in the New Testament* (Philadelphia: Westminster, 1960) still remains important in this regard. Minear identified as many as 96 such images.

it implicitly argues for plurality and for the importance of context when thinking about the church's nature, mission, and relationship to the world. I have tried to restrict the number of excerpts to those that have either been influential upon or representative of the Christian movement over the last twenty centuries. I have left the excerpts in their original form as much as possible while employing a common formatting for ease of reading.

This undertaking would have been impossible without the assistance of the Center for Practical Theology at Boston University School of Theology and the good graces, advice, and support of my colleagues there. I especially wish to thank Carl Daw for his valuable counsel about ecclesiological hymns. Early on, Holly Reed and Xochitl Alvizo provided research and manuscript assistance, and I am thankful to them for their contributions. I am grateful as well to Blake Huggins, Rachel Vogelzang, Andrea Rocha, and Walter and Krishana Suckau for their assistance. The bulk of the research and editing assistance, manuscript preparation, and support in securing copyright permissions is the work of Debbie Brubaker, and I am enormously grateful to her for her efficiency, attention to detail, and theological insight.

Part 1
The Early Church

The starting point for Christian ecclesiological reflection is not as clear-cut or uncontested as it might initially seem. In describing their new communities, the first Christians took over the Greek political term ecclesia, which signified the gathering and association (literally, the "calling out") of those with citizen rights of a whole city from their private homes into a public assembly. One could, therefore, profit from exploring ancient literature that describes these assemblies. But, of course, the historical genesis of the church is not to be found primarily in Greco-Roman culture or its various social institutions, but in Judaism itself. Just as important, therefore, is the way the term ecclesia linked early Christians with Israel as a nation and as the people of God. Any fully adequate understanding of Christian ecclesiology would need, therefore, to explore Hebrew modes of community that predate Christianity and account for the church's early and ongoing relation to Judaism. Yet another way of getting at the earliest reflections on the nature of the church, and the one taken here, is to start with the earliest documents of the church itself as canonized within the New Testament.

The first five centuries of the Christian church witnessed the remarkable transformation of a small band of Jewish followers of Jesus of Nazareth into the official religion of the Roman empire. That transformation, as can be readily seen from the documents in this section, went hand in hand with distinctive attitudes about the relationship of the Christian community to the empire, to its leaders, and to its surrounding culture. This relationship is reflected in changing internal, institutional patterns as a more charismatic, messianic movement (where, for example, the roving prophet is highly respected) gives way to a more highly structured, uniform, and clericalized "church." But it is also reflected in a growing concern, especially in the context of persecution, that Christians, while distinct in terms of their character, practices, beliefs, and values, be understood nonetheless as loyal citizens of the empire.

1   The New Testament

Source: New Revised Standard Version of the Bible.

The Pauline letters to particular ecclesial communities contain some of Christianity's classic statements about the nature and mission of the church, especially in relationship to Christ, just as they also give us insight into important issues those communities faced both internally and in relation to the world of which they were a part. Likewise, the pastoral letters written under Paul's name help us understand the early church in connection with criteria for those in church leadership positions whose primary task it was to guard against disorder, false teaching, moral laxity, and improprieties of all sorts. The New Testament Gospel narratives afford us insight into the early church's understanding of itself as a continuation of the mission and ministry of Jesus, especially in its record of the activities and sayings attributed to Jesus in gathering together a community of followers and sending them into the world as witnesses. The Easter, Pentecost, and Ascension narratives of the first Christians are each, in its own way, decisive as a place to find the church's "birth." The excerpt from Acts focuses on the event of Pentecost that was decisive in creating the church as a distinct social body and as one that continues Christ's ministry and mediates his ongoing presence in the world. Lastly, the excerpt from the Revelation to John paints a portrait of the church finally gathered up with all the people of God in the heavenly courts.

Paul's First Epistle to the Corinthians (c. 54)

Now there are varieties of gifts, but the same Spirit; and there are varieties of services, but the same Lord; and there are varieties of activities, but it is the same God who activates all of them in everyone. To each is given the manifestation of the Spirit for the common good. To one is given through the Spirit the utterance of wisdom, and to another the utterance of knowledge according to the same Spirit, to another faith by the same Spirit, to another gifts of healing by the one Spirit, to another the working of miracles, to another prophecy, to another the discernment of spirits, to another various kinds of tongues, to another the interpretation of tongues. All these are activated by one and the same Spirit, who allots to each one individually just as the Spirit chooses.

For just as the body is one and has many members, and all the members of the body, though many, are one body, so it is with Christ. For in the one Spirit we were all baptized into one body—Jews or Greeks, slaves or free—and we were all made to drink of one Spirit. Indeed, the body does not consist of one member but of many. If the foot would say, "Because I am not a hand, I do not belong to the body," that would not make it any less a part of the body. And if the ear would say, "Because I am not an eye, I do not belong to the body," that would not make it any less a part of the body. If the whole body were an eye, where would the hearing be? If the whole body were hearing, where would the sense of smell be? But as it is, God arranged the members in the body, each one of them, as he chose. If all were a single member, where would the body be? As it is, there are many members, yet one body. The eye cannot say to the hand, "I have no need of you," nor again the head to the feet, "I have no need of you." On the contrary, the members of the body that seem to be weaker are indispensable, and those members of the body that we think less honorable we clothe with greater honor, and our less respectable members are treated with greater respect; whereas our more respectable members do not need this. But God has so arranged the body, giving the greater honor to the inferior member, that there may be no dissension within the body, but the members may have the same care for one another. If one member suffers, all suffer together with it; if one member is honored, all rejoice together with it.

Now you are the body of Christ and individually members of it. And God has appointed in the church first apostles, second prophets, third teachers; then deeds of power, then gifts of healing, forms of assistance, forms of leadership, various kinds of tongues. Are all apostles? Are all prophets? Are all teachers? Do all work miracles? Do all possess gifts of healing? Do all speak in tongues? Do all interpret? But strive for the greater gifts. And I will show you a still more excellent way. (12:4–31)

Paul's Epistle to the Ephesians (c. 60–62)

I pray that the God of our Lord Jesus Christ, the Father of glory, may give you a spirit of wisdom and revelation as you come to know him, so that, with the eyes of your heart enlightened, you may know what is the hope to which he has called you, what are the riches of his glorious inheritance among the saints, and what is the immeasurable greatness of his power for us who believe, according to the working of his great power. God put this power to work in Christ when he raised him from the dead and seated him at his right hand in the heavenly places, far above all rule and authority and power and dominion, and above every name that is named, not only in this age but also in the age to come. And he has put all things under his feet and has made him the head over all things for the church, which is his body, the fullness of him who fills all in all. (1:17–23)

I therefore, the prisoner in the Lord, beg you to lead a life worthy of the calling to which you have been called, with all humility and gentleness, with patience, bearing with one another in love, making every effort to maintain the unity of the Spirit in the bond of peace. There is one body and one Spirit, just as you were called to the one hope of your calling, one Lord, one faith, one baptism, one God and Father of all, who is above all and through all and in all. But each of us was given grace according to the measure of Christ's gift. … The gifts he gave were that some would be apostles, some prophets, some evangelists, some pastors and teachers, to equip the saints for the work of ministry, for building up the body of Christ, until all of us come to the unity of the faith and of the knowledge of the Son of God, to maturity, to the measure of the full stature of Christ. We must no longer be children, tossed to and fro and blown about by every wind of doctrine, by people's trickery, by their craftiness in deceitful scheming. But speaking the truth in love, we must grow up in every way into him who is the head, into Christ, from whom the whole body, joined and knit together by every ligament with which it is equipped, as each part is working properly, promotes the body's growth in building itself up in love. (4:1–16)

Paul's Epistle to the Colossians (c. 60–62)

[Christ] is the head of the body, the church; he is the beginning, the firstborn from the dead, so that he might come to have first place in everything. For in him all the fullness of God was pleased to dwell, and through him God was pleased to reconcile to himself all things, whether on earth or in heaven, by making peace through the blood of his cross. And you who were once estranged and hostile in mind, doing evil deeds, he has now reconciled in his fleshly body through death, so as to present you holy and blameless and irreproachable before him—provided that you continue securely established and steadfast in the faith, without shifting from the hope promised by the gospel that you heard, which has been proclaimed to every creature under heaven. (1:18–23a)

Paul's First Epistle to Timothy (c. 62–64)

The saying is sure: whoever aspires to the office of bishop desires a noble task. Now a bishop must be above reproach, married only once, temperate, sensible, respectable, hospitable, an apt teacher, not a drunkard, not violent but gentle, not quarrelsome, and not a lover of money. He must manage his own household well, keeping his children submissive and respectful in every way—for if someone does not know how to manage his own household, how can he take care of God's church? He must not be a recent convert, or he may be puffed up with conceit and fall into the condemnation of the devil. Moreover, he must be well thought of by outsiders, so that he may not fall into disgrace and the snare of the devil.

   Deacons likewise must be serious, not double-tongued, not indulging in much wine, not greedy for money; they must hold fast to the mystery of the faith with a clear conscience. And let them first be tested; then, if they prove themselves blameless, let them serve as deacons. Women likewise must be serious, not slanderers, but temperate, faithful in all things. Let deacons be married only once, and let them manage their children and their households well; for those who serve well as deacons gain a good standing for themselves and great boldness in the faith that is in Christ Jesus. (3:1–13)

The First Epistle of Peter (c. 62–65)

Come to him, a living stone, though rejected by mortals yet chosen and precious in God's sight, and like living stones, let yourselves be built into a spiritual house, to be a holy priesthood, to offer spiritual sacrifices acceptable to God through Jesus Christ. For it stands in scripture: "See, I am laying in Zion a stone, a cornerstone chosen and precious; and whoever believes in him will not be put to shame." To you then who believe, he is precious; but for those who do not believe, "The stone that the builders rejected has become the very head of the corner," and "A stone that makes them stumble, and a rock that makes them fall." They stumble because they disobey the word, as they were destined to do. But you are a chosen race, a royal priesthood, a holy nation, God's own people, in order that you may proclaim the mighty acts of him who called you out of darkness into his marvelous light. Once you were not a people, but now you are God's people; once you had not received mercy, but now you have received mercy. Beloved, I urge you as aliens and exiles to abstain from the desires of the flesh that wage war against the soul. Conduct yourselves honorably among the Gentiles, so that, though they malign you as evildoers, they may see your honorable deeds and glorify God when he comes to judge. (2:4–12)

The Acts of the Apostles (c. 70–85)

They devoted themselves to the apostles' teaching and fellowship, to the breaking of bread and the prayers. Awe came upon everyone, because many wonders and signs were being done by the apostles. All who believed were together and had all things in common; they would sell their possessions and goods and distribute the proceeds to all, as any had need. Day by day, as they spent much time together in the temple, they broke bread at home and ate their food with glad and generous hearts, praising God and having the goodwill of all the people. And day by day the Lord added to their number those who were being saved. (2:42–7)

Now the whole group of those who believed were of one heart and soul, and no one claimed private ownership of any possessions, but everything they owned was held in common. With great power the apostles gave their testimony to the resurrection of the Lord Jesus, and great grace was upon them all. There was not a needy person among them, for as many as owned lands or houses sold them and brought the proceeds of what was sold. They laid it at the apostles' feet, and it was distributed to each as any had need. (4:32–5)

The Gospel of Matthew (c. 75–85)

Now when Jesus came into the district of Caesarea Philippi, he asked his disciples, "Who do people say that the Son of Man is?" And they said, "Some say John the Baptist, but others Elijah, and still others Jeremiah or one of the prophets." He said to them, "But who do you say that I am?" Simon Peter answered, "You are the Messiah, the Son of the living God." And Jesus answered him, "Blessed are you, Simon son of Jonah! For flesh and blood has not revealed this to you, but my Father in heaven. And I tell you, you are Peter, and on this rock I will build my church, and the gates of Hades will not prevail against it. I will give you the keys of the kingdom of heaven, and whatever you bind on earth will be bound in heaven, and whatever you loose on earth will be loosed in heaven." (16:13–19)

"If another member of the church sins against you, go and point out the fault when the two of you are alone. If the member listens to you, you have regained that one. But if you are not listened to, take one or two others along with you, so that every word may be confirmed by the evidence of two or three witnesses. If the member refuses to listen to them, tell it to the church; and if the offender refuses to listen even to the church, let such a one be to you as a Gentile and a tax collector. Truly I tell you, whatever you bind on earth will be bound in heaven, and whatever you loose on earth will be loosed in heaven. Again, truly I tell you, if two of you agree on earth about anything you ask, it will be done for you by my Father in heaven. For where two or three are gathered in my name, I am there among them." (18:15–20)

The Gospel of John (c. 90)

After Jesus had spoken these words, he looked up to heaven and said, "Father, the hour has come; glorify your Son so that the Son may glorify you, since you have given him authority over all people, to give eternal life to all whom you have given him. And this is eternal life, that they may know you, the only true God, and Jesus Christ whom you have sent. I glorified you on earth by finishing the work that you gave me to do. So now, Father, glorify me in your own presence with the glory that I had in your presence before the world existed.

I have made your name known to those whom you gave me from the world. They were yours, and you gave them to me, and they have kept your word. Now they know that everything you have given me is from you; for the words that you gave to me I have given to them, and they have received them and know in truth that I came from you; and they have believed that you sent me. I am asking on their behalf; I am not asking on behalf of the world, but on behalf of those whom you gave me, because they are yours. All mine are yours, and yours are mine; and I have been glorified in them.

And now I am no longer in the world, but they are in the world, and I am coming to you. Holy Father, protect them in your name that you have given me, so that they may be one, as we are one. While I was with them, I protected them in your name that you have given me. I guarded them, and not one of them was lost except the one destined to be lost, so that the scripture might be fulfilled. But now I am coming to you, and I speak these things in the world so that they may have my joy made complete in themselves. I have given them your word, and the world has hated them because they do not belong to the world, just as I do not belong to the world. I am not asking you to take them out of the world, but I ask you to protect them from the evil one. They do not belong to the world, just as I do not belong to the world.

Sanctify them in the truth; your word is truth. As you have sent me into the world, so I have sent them into the world. And for their sakes I sanctify myself, so that they also may be sanctified in truth.

I ask not only on behalf of these, but also on behalf of those who will believe in me through their word, that they may all be one. As you, Father, are in me and I am in you, may they also be in us, so that the world may believe that you have sent me. The glory that you have given me I have given them, so that they may be one, as we are one, I in them and you in me, that they may become completely one, so that the world may know that you have sent me and have loved them even as you have loved me.

Father, I desire that those also, whom you have given me, may be with me where I am, to see my glory, which you have given me because you loved me before the foundation of the world. Righteous Father, the world does not know you, but I know you; and these know that you have sent me. I made your name known to them, and I will make it known, so that the love with which you have loved me may be in them, and I in them. (17:1–26)

The Revelation to John (c. 90–96)

After this I looked, and there was a great multitude that no one could count, from every nation, from all tribes and peoples and languages, standing before the throne and before the Lamb, robed in white, with palm branches in their hands. They cried out in a loud voice, saying, "Salvation belongs to our God who is seated on the throne, and to the Lamb!" And all the angels stood around the throne and around the elders and the four living creatures, and they fell on their faces before the throne and worshiped God, singing, "Amen! Blessing and glory and wisdom and thanksgiving and honor and power and might be to our God forever and ever! Amen." Then one of the elders addressed me, saying, "Who are these, robed in white, and where have they come from?" I said to him, "Sir, you are the one that knows." Then he said to me, "These are they who have come out of the great ordeal; they have washed their robes and made them white in the blood of the Lamb. For this reason they are before the throne of God, and worship him day and night within his temple, and the one who is seated on the throne will shelter them. They will hunger no more, and thirst no more; the sun will not strike them, nor any scorching heat; for the Lamb at the center of the throne will be their shepherd, and he will guide them to springs of the water of life, and God will wipe away every tear from their eyes." (7:9–17)

Then the angel showed me the river of the water of life, bright as crystal, flowing from the throne of God and of the Lamb through the middle of the street of the city. On either side of the river is the tree of life with its twelve kinds of fruit, producing its fruit each month; and the leaves of the tree are for the healing of the nations. Nothing accursed will be found there any more. But the throne of God and of the Lamb will be in it, and his servants will worship him; they will see his face, and his name will be on their foreheads. And there will be no more night; they need no light of lamp or sun, for the Lord God will be their light, and they will reign forever and ever. (22:1–5)

For further reading

Kent E. Brower and Andy Johnson (eds.), *Holiness and Ecclesiology in the New Testament* (Grand Rapids: Eerdmans, 2007).

Raymond F. Collins, *The Many Faces of the Church: A New Testament Study* (New York: Crossroad, 2003).

Frederick J. Cwiekowski, *The Beginnings of the Church* (Mahwah, NJ: Paulist Press, 1988).

Gerhard Lohfink, *Jesus and Community* (Minneapolis: Fortress, 1984).

Wayne A. Meeks, *The First Urban Christians*, 2nd edn. (New Haven: Yale University Press, 2003).

2 Clement of Rome (d. 101)

This letter from the church at Rome addresses a situation of schism in the Corinthian church in which duly appointed presbyters (local elders, or "priests") had been deposed thereby causing dissension in the community. The letter demonstrates an early concern for unity in the context of initial church growth and expansion, and it seeks to establish that unity through obedience to the bishop in accordance with a divinely ordained organizational structure that links the church to Christ through the apostles and their successors.

1 Clement (c. 96)

Source: Michael W. Holmes (trans. and ed.), *The Apostolic Fathers* in English, 3rd edn.

The apostles received the gospel for us from the Lord Jesus Christ; Jesus the Christ was sent forth from God. So then Christ is from God, and the apostles are from Christ. Both, therefore, came of the will of God in good order. Having therefore received their orders and being fully assured by the resurrection of our Lord Jesus Christ and full of faith in the word of God, they went forth with the firm assurance that the Holy Spirit gives, preaching the good news that the kingdom of God was about to come. So, preaching both in the country and in the towns, they appointed their first fruits, when they had tested them by the Spirit, to be bishops and deacons for the future believers. And this was no new thing they did, for indeed something had been written about bishops and deacons many years ago; for somewhere thus says the scripture: "I will appoint their bishops in righteousness and their deacons in faith." (42:1–5)

Our apostles likewise knew, through our Lord Jesus Christ, that there would be strife over the bishop's office. For this reason, therefore, having received complete foreknowledge, they appointed the leaders mentioned earlier and afterwards they gave the offices a permanent character; that is, if they should die, other approved men should succeed to their ministry. These, therefore, who were appointed by them or, later on, by other reputable men with the consent of the whole church, and who have ministered to the flock of Christ blamelessly, humbly, peaceably, and unselfishly, and for a long time have been well-spoken of by all—these we consider to be unjustly removed from their ministry. For it will be no small sin for us if we depose from the bishop's office those who have offered the gifts blamelessly and in holiness. Blessed are those presbyters who have gone on ahead, who took their departure at a mature and fruitful age, for they need no longer fear that someone may remove them from their established place. For we see that you have removed certain people, their good conduct notwithstanding, from the ministry that had been held in honor by them blamelessly. Be competitive and zealous, brothers, but about the things that relate to salvation. (44:1–45:1)

For further reading

Barbara Ellen Bowe, *A Church in Crisis: Ecclesiology and Paraenesis in Clement of Rome* (Minneapolis: Fortress, 1989).
James F. Jeffers, *Conflict at Rome: Social Order and Hierarchy in Early Christianity* (Minneapolis: Fortress, 1991).

3 Ignatius of Antioch (c. 35–110)

Source: Michael W. Holmes (trans. and ed.), *The Apostolic Fathers in English*, 3rd edn.

Writing to churches in Asia Minor as a prisoner on his way to martyrdom, the letters of Ignatius, bishop of Antioch, are concerned with the unity of the church understood as a transcendent harmony founded upon obedience to the church's hierarchy in its tripartite form of bishop, elders, and deacons. For Ignatius, the church's hierarchy reflects a transcendent, divine order. Thus, demonstrating respect for church authorities is a way of demonstrating respect for God.

To the Ephesians (c. 110)

I am not commanding you, as though I were someone important. For even though I am in chains for the sake of the Name, I have not yet been perfected in Jesus Christ. For now I am only beginning to be a disciple, and I speak to you as my fellow students. For I need to be trained by you in faith, instruction, endurance, and patience. But since love does not allow me to be silent concerning you, I have therefore taken the initiative to encourage you, so that you may run together in harmony with the mind of God. For Jesus Christ, our inseparable life, is the mind of the Father, just as the bishops appointed throughout the world are in the mind of Christ.

Thus it is proper for you to run together in harmony with the mind of the bishop, as you are in fact doing. For your council of presbyters, which is worthy of its name and worthy of God, is attuned to the bishop as strings to a lyre. Therefore in your unanimity and harmonious love Jesus Christ is sung. You must join this chorus, everyone of you, so that by being harmonious in unanimity and taking your pitch from God you may sing in unison with one voice through Jesus Christ to the Father, in order that he may both hear you and, on the basis of what you do well, acknowledge that you are members of his Son. It is, therefore, advantageous for you to be in perfect unity, in order that you may always have a share in God.

For if I in a short time experienced such fellowship with your bishop, which was not merely human but spiritual, how much more do I congratulate you who are united with him, as the church is with Jesus Christ and as Jesus Christ is with the Father, so that all things may be harmonious in unity. Let no one be misled: if anyone is not within the sanctuary, he lacks the bread of God. For if the prayer of one or two has such power, how much more that of the bishop together with the whole church! Therefore whoever does not meet with the congregation thereby demonstrates his arrogance and has separated himself, for it is written: "God opposes the arrogant." Let us, therefore, be careful not to oppose the bishop, in order that we may be obedient to God.

Furthermore, the more anyone observes that the bishop is silent, the more one should fear him. For everyone whom the Master of the house sends to manage his own house we must welcome as we would the one who sent him. It is obvious, therefore, that we must regard the bishop as the Lord himself. (3:1–6:1)

To the Magnesians (c. 110)

Indeed, it is right for you also not to take advantage of the youthfulness of your bishop but to give him all the respect due him in accordance with the power of God the Father, just as I know that the holy presbyters likewise have not taken advantage of his youthful appearance but defer to him as one who is wise in God; yet not really to him, but to the Father of Jesus Christ, the bishop of all. For the honor, therefore, of the one who loved you it is right to be obedient without any hypocrisy, for it is not so much a matter of deceiving this bishop who is seen but of cheating the one who is unseen. In such a case he must reckon not with the flesh but with God, who knows our secrets.

It is right, therefore, that we not just be called Christians, but that we actually be Christians, unlike some who call a man bishop but do everything without regard for him. Such people do not appear to me to act in good conscience, inasmuch as they do not validly meet together in accordance with the commandment. … Be eager to do everything in godly harmony, the bishop presiding in the place of God and the presbyters in the place of the council of the apostles and the deacons, who are especially dear to me, since they have been entrusted with the ministry of Jesus Christ, who before the ages was with the Father and appeared at the end of time. Let all, therefore, accept the same attitude as God and respect one another, and let no one regard his neighbor in merely human terms, but in Jesus Christ love one another always. Let there be nothing among you that is capable of dividing you, but be united with the bishop and with those who lead, as an example and lesson of incorruptibility.

Therefore as the Lord did nothing without the Father, either by himself or through the apostles (for he was united with him), so you must not do anything without the bishop and the presbyters. Do not attempt to convince yourselves that anything done apart from the others is right, but, gathering together, let there be one prayer, one petition, one mind, one hope, with love and blameless joy, which is Jesus Christ, than whom nothing is better. (3:1–7:1)

To the Trallians (c. 110)

For when you are subject to the bishop as to Jesus Christ, it is evident to me that you are living not in accordance with human standards but in accordance with Jesus Christ, who died for us in order that by believing in his death you might escape death. It is essential, therefore, that you continue your current practice and do nothing without the bishop, but be subject also to the council of presbyters as to the apostles of Jesus Christ, our hope, in whom we shall be found, if we so live. Furthermore, it is necessary that those who are deacons of the mysteries of Jesus Christ please everyone in every respect. For they are not merely deacons of food and drink but ministers of God's church. Therefore they must avoid criticism as though it were fire.

Similarly, let everyone respect the deacons as Jesus Christ, just as they should respect the bishop, who is a model of the Father, and the presbyters as God's council and as the band of the apostles. Without these no group can be called a church. I am sure that you agree with me regarding these matters, for I received a living example of your love and still have it with me in the person of your bishop, whose very demeanor is a great lesson and whose gentleness is his power; I think that even the godless respect him. (chs. 2–3)

To the Smyrnaeans (c. 110)

Flee from divisions as the beginning of evils. You must all follow the bishop as Jesus Christ followed the Father, and follow the council of presbyters as you would the apostles; respect the deacons as the commandment of God. Let no one do anything that has to do with the church without the bishop. Only that Eucharist which is under the authority of the bishop (or whomever he himself designates) is to be considered valid. Wherever the bishop appears, there let the congregation be; just as wherever Jesus Christ is, there is the catholic church. It is not permissible either to baptize or to hold a love feast without the bishop. But whatever he approves is also pleasing to God, in order that everything you do may be trustworthy and valid. (8:1–2)

For further reading

Virginia Corwin, *St. Ignatius and Christianity in Antioch* (New Haven: Yale University Press, 1960).

Harry O. Maier, *The Social Setting of the Ministry as Reflected in the Writings of Hermas, Clement, and Ignatius* (Waterloo, ON: Wilfrid Laurier University Press, 1991).

4   The *Didache* (c. 110)

The Didache, *or "teaching," is both an instruction in the way of holiness and a manual of church order. This excerpt focuses on the church's holiness as preserved in practices such as baptism, the Lord's Supper, fasting, fraternal correction, and the treatment of itinerant prophets—all set within the context of the rapidly approaching end of the world. While the document was likely edited early in the second century, it represents a primitive understanding of ministerial leadership as charismatically ordered (the gift of prophecy is still very important) prior to the development of a more structured church hierarchy.*

Source: Michael W. Holmes (trans. and ed.), *The Apostolic Fathers in English*, 3rd edn.

Now concerning baptism, baptize as follows: after you have reviewed all these things, baptize in the name of the Father and of the Son and of the Holy Spirit in running water. But if you have no running water, then baptize in some other water; and if you are not able to baptize in cold water, then do so in warm. But if you have neither, then pour water on the head three times in the name of Father and Son and Holy Spirit. And before the baptism let the one baptizing and the one who is to be baptized fast, as well as any others who are able. Also, you must instruct the one who is to be baptized to fast for one or two days beforehand.

But do not let your fasts coincide with those of the hypocrites. They fast on Monday and Thursday, so you must fast on Wednesday and Friday. Nor should you pray like the hypocrites. Instead, pray like this, just as the Lord commanded in his Gospel:

> "Our Father in heaven, hallowed be your name, your kingdom come, your will be done on earth as it is in heaven. Give us today our daily bread, and

forgive us our debt, as we also forgive our debtors; and do not lead us into temptation, but deliver us from the evil one; for yours is the power and the glory forever" (Matt. 6:9–13).

Pray like this three times a day.

Now concerning the Eucharist, give thanks as follows. First, concerning the cup:

> We give you thanks, our Father, for the holy vine of David your servant, which you have made known to us through Jesus, your servant; to you be the glory forever.

And concerning the broken bread:

> We give you thanks, our Father, for the life and knowledge that you have made known to us through Jesus, your servant; to you be the glory forever. Just as this broken bread was scattered upon the mountains and then was gathered together and became one, so may your church be gathered together from the ends of the earth into your kingdom; for yours is the glory and the power through Jesus Christ forever.

But let no one eat or drink of your Eucharist except those who have been baptized into the name of the Lord, for the Lord has also spoken concerning this: "Do not give what is holy to dogs" (Matt. 7:6).

And after you have had enough, give thanks as follows:

> We give you thanks, Holy Father, for your holy name, which you have caused to dwell in our hearts, and for the knowledge and faith and immortality that you have made known to us through Jesus your servant; to you be the glory forever. You, almighty Master, created all things for your name's sake, and gave food and drink to humans to enjoy, so that they might give you thanks; but to us you have graciously given spiritual food and drink, and eternal life through your servant. Above all we give thanks to you because you are mighty; to you be the glory forever. Remember your church, Lord, to deliver it from all evil and to make it perfect in your love; and from the four winds gather the church that has been sanctified into your kingdom, which you have prepared for it; for yours is the power and the glory forever. May grace come, and may this world pass away. Hosanna to the God of David. If anyone is holy, let him come; if anyone is not, let him repent. Maranatha! Amen.

But permit the prophets to give thanks however they wish.

So, if anyone should come and teach you all these things that have just been mentioned above, welcome him. But if the teacher himself goes astray and teaches a different teaching that undermines all this, do not listen to him. However, if his teaching contributes to righteousness and knowledge of the Lord, welcome him as you would the Lord.

Now concerning the apostles and prophets, deal with them as follows in accordance with the rule of the gospel. Let every apostle who comes to you be welcomed as if he were the Lord. But he is not to stay for more than one day, unless there is need, in which case he may stay another. But if he stays three days, he is a false prophet. And when the apostle leaves, he is to take nothing except bread until he finds his next night's lodging. But if he asks for money, he is a false prophet. Also, do not test or evaluate any prophet who speaks in the spirit, for every sin will be forgiven, but this sin will not be forgiven. However, not everyone who speaks in the spirit is a prophet, but only if he exhibits the Lord's ways. By his conduct, therefore, will the false prophet and the prophet be recognized. Furthermore, any prophet who orders a meal in the spirit shall not partake of it; if he does, he is a false prophet. If any prophet teaches the truth, yet does not practice what he teaches, he is a false prophet. But any prophet proven to be genuine who does something with a view to portraying in a worldly manner the symbolic meaning of the church (provided that he does not teach you to do all that he himself does) is not to be judged by you, for his judgment is with God. Besides, the ancient prophets also acted in a similar manner. But if anyone should say in the spirit, "Give me money" or anything else, do not listen to him. But if he tells you to give on behalf of others who are in need, let no one judge him.

Everyone who comes in the name of the Lord is to be welcomed. But then examine him, and you will find out—for you will have insight—what is true and what is false. If the one who comes is merely passing through, assist him as much as you can. But he must not stay with you for more than two or, if necessary, three days. However, if he wishes to settle among you and is a craftsman, let him work for his living. But if he is not a craftsman, decide according to your own judgment how he shall live among you as a Christian, yet without being idle. But if he does not wish to cooperate in this way, then he is trading on Christ. Beware of such people.

But every genuine prophet who wishes to settle among you is worthy of his food. Likewise, every genuine teacher is, like the worker, worthy of his food. Take, therefore, all the first fruits of the produce of the wine press and threshing floor, and of the cattle and sheep, and give these first fruits to the prophets, for they are your high priests. But if you have no prophet, give them to the poor. If you make bread, take the first fruit and give in accordance with the commandment. Similarly, when you open a jar of wine or oil, take the first fruit and give it to the prophets. As for money and clothes and any other possessions, take the first fruit that seems right to you and give in accordance with the commandment.

On the Lord's own day gather together and break bread and give thanks, having first confessed your sins so that your sacrifice may be pure. But let no one who has a quarrel with a companion join you until they have been reconciled, so that your sacrifice may not be defiled. For this is the sacrifice concerning which the Lord said, "In every place and time offer me a pure sacrifice, for I am a great king, says the Lord, and my name is marvelous among the nations."

Therefore appoint for yourselves bishops and deacons worthy of the Lord, men who are humble and not avaricious and true and approved, for they too carry out for you the ministry of the prophets and teachers. You must not, therefore, despise them, for they are your honored men, along with the prophets and teachers.

Furthermore, correct one another not in anger but in peace, as you find in the Gospel; and if anyone wrongs his or her neighbor, let no one speak to that person, nor let that one hear a word from you, until he or she repents. As for your prayers and acts of charity and all your actions, do them all just as you find it in the Gospel of our Lord. (7:1–15:4)

For further reading

Aaron Milavec, *The Didache: Faith, Hope, and Life of the Earliest Christian Communities*, 50–70 C.E. (New York: Newman Press, 2003).

5 "Father, We Thank You" (based on the *Didache*, c. 110)

This hymn, though it first appeared in 1939, was F. Bland Tucker's (1895–1984) translation of selected prayers from the Didache *(excerpted above): the post-communion prayer and the prayer to be used during distribution of the bread.*

Source: F. Bland Tucker, "Father, We Thank You," in *The Hymnal 1982: According to the Use of the Episcopal Church*.

Father, we thank you, for you planted
your holy name within our hearts.
Knowledge and faith and life immortal
Jesus your Son to us imparts.

Lord, you have made all for your pleasure,
and given us food for all our days,
giving in Christ the bread eternal;
yours is the power, be yours the praise.

Watch o'er your church, O Lord, in mercy,
save it from evil, guard it still;
perfect it in your love, unite it,
cleansed and conformed unto your will.

As grain, once scattered on the hill-sides,
was in the broken bread made one,
so from all lands your church be gathered
into your kingdom by your Son.

6   *Epistle to Diognetus* (c. 150–225)

*This anonymous Christian apology is one of the earliest ever written. The document
criticizes idol worship and distinguishes Christian practices from what it describes as
"the superstitions of the Jews." As a defense against objections that Christians were a
dangerous or disruptive sect, its main line of argument is its assertion of the various
ways the Christian community is "in" the world while not "of" it.*

Source: Michael W. Holmes (trans. and ed.), *The Apostolic Fathers in English*, 3rd edn.

For Christians are not distinguished from the rest of humanity by country,
language, or custom. For nowhere do they live in cities of their own, nor do
they speak some unusual dialect, nor do they practice an eccentric way of life.
This teaching of theirs has not been discovered by the thought and reflection
of ingenious people, nor do they promote any human doctrine, as some do.
But while they live in both Greek and barbarian cities, as each one's lot was
cast, and follow the local customs in dress and food and other aspects of life,
at the same time they demonstrate the remarkable and admittedly unusual
character of their own citizenship. They live in their own countries, but only as
nonresidents; they participate in everything as citizens, and endure everything
as foreigners. Every foreign country is their fatherland, and every fatherland
is foreign. They marry like everyone else, and have children, but they do not
expose their offspring. They share their food but not their wives. They are in
the flesh, but they do not live according to the flesh. They live on earth, but
their citizenship is in heaven. They obey the established laws; indeed in their
private lives they transcend the laws. They love everyone, and by everyone
they are persecuted. They are unknown, yet they are condemned; they are
put to death, yet they are brought to life. They are poor, yet they make many
rich; they are in need of everything, yet they abound in everything. They are
dishonored, yet they are glorified in their dishonor; they are slandered, yet
they are vindicated. They are cursed, yet they bless; they are insulted, yet
they offer respect. When they do good, they are punished as evildoers; when
they are punished, they rejoice as though brought to life. By the Jews they are

assaulted as foreigners, and by the Greeks they are persecuted, yet those who hate them are unable to give a reason for their hostility.

In a word, what the soul is to the body, Christians are to the world. The soul is dispersed through all the members of the body, and Christians throughout the cities of the world. The soul dwells in the body, but is not of the body; likewise Christians dwell in the world, but are not of the world. The soul, which is invisible, is confined in the body, which is visible; in the same way, Christians are recognized as being in the world, and yet their religion remains invisible. The flesh hates the soul and wages war against it, even though it has suffered no wrong, because it is hindered from indulging in its pleasures; so also the world hates the Christians, even though it has suffered no wrong, because they set themselves against its pleasures. The soul loves the flesh that hates it, and its members, and Christians love those who hate them. The soul is locked up in the body, but it holds the body together; and though Christians are detained in the world as if in a prison, they in fact hold the world together. The soul, which is immortal, lives in a mortal dwelling; similarly Christians live as strangers amid perishable things, while waiting for the imperishable in heaven. The soul, when poorly treated with respect to food and drink, becomes all the better; and so Christians when punished daily increase more and more. Such is the important position to which God has appointed them, and it is not right for them to decline it. (5:1–6:10)

For further reading

Paul Foster, "The Epistle to Diognetus," *Expository Times* 118/4 (2007), pp. 162–8.
George Weigel, "The Church's Political Hopes for the World; or, Diognetus Revisited," in Carl E. Braaten and Robert W. Jenson (eds.), *The Two Cities of God: The Church's Responsibility for the Earthly City* (Grand Rapids: Eerdmans, 1997), pp 59–77.

7   Justin Martyr (c. 100–165)

Justin was a Gentile convert to Christianity who had been influenced by Platonic philosophy. Justin's defense of Christianity centers on how Christians are both different from the rest of the empire in their character and practices while at the same time loyal citizens of the emperor. Christians do not participate in the imperial cult but rather in practices such as baptism and Eucharist. The latter can, of course, appear to be bizarre or esoteric to the uninitiated. Therefore, Justin takes care to explain these practices and to defend Christianity against charges of godlessness and incivility. The excerpts below demonstrate Justin's understanding of the relationship of church and empire and provide a brief description of a weekly Christian assembly.

Apology 1 (c. 155)

Source: Cyril C. Richardson (trans. and ed.), *Early Christian Fathers*, Library of Christian Classics.

When you hear that we look for a kingdom, you rashly suppose that we mean something merely human. But we speak of a Kingdom with God, as is clear from our confessing Christ when you bring us to trial, though we know that death is the penalty for this confession. For if we looked for a human kingdom we would deny it in order to save our lives, and would try to remain in hiding in order to obtain the things we look for. But since we do not place our hopes on the present [order], we are not troubled by being put to death, since we will have to die somehow in any case.

We are in fact of all men your best helpers and allies in securing good order, convinced as we are that no wicked man, no covetous man or conspirator, or virtuous man either, can be hidden from God, and that everyone goes to eternal punishment or salvation in accordance with the character of his actions. If all men knew this, nobody would choose vice even for a little time, knowing that he was on his way to eternal punishment by fire; every man would follow the self-restrained and orderly path of virtue, so as to receive the good things that come from God and avoid his punishments. (§§11–12)

More even than others we try to pay the taxes and assessments to those whom you appoint, as we have been taught by him. For once in his time some came to him and asked whether it were right to pay taxes to Caesar. And he answered, "Tell me, whose image is on the coin." They said, "Caesar's." And he answered them again, "Then give what is Caesar's to Caesar and what is God's to God" (Matt. 22:20–21). So we worship God only, but in other matters we gladly serve you, recognizing you as emperors and rulers of men, and praying that along with your imperial power you may also be found to have a sound mind. If you pay no attention to our prayers and our frank statements about everything, it will not injure us, since we believe, or rather are firmly convinced, that every man will suffer in eternal fire in accordance with the quality of his actions, and similarly will be required to give account for the abilities which he has received from God, as Christ told us when he said, "To whom God has given more, from him more will be required" (Luke 12:48). (§17)

After these [services] we constantly remind each other of these things. Those who have more come to the aid of those who lack, and we are constantly together. Over all that we receive we bless the Maker of all things through his Son Jesus Christ and through the Holy Spirit. And on the day called Sunday there is a meeting in one place of those who live in cities or the country, and the memoirs of the apostles or the writings of the prophets are read as long as time permits. When the reader has finished, the president in a discourse urges and invites [us] to the imitation of these noble things. Then we all stand up together and offer prayers. And, as said before, when we have finished the prayer, bread is brought, and wine and water, and the president similarly sends up prayers and thanksgivings to the best of his ability, and the congregation assents, saying the Amen; the distribution, and reception of the consecrated [elements] by each one, takes place and they are sent to the absent by the deacons. Those who prosper, and who so wish, contribute, each one as much as he chooses to. What is collected is deposited with the president, and he takes care of orphans and widows, and those who are in want on account of sickness or any other cause, and those who are in bonds, and the strangers who are sojourners among [us], and, briefly, he is the protector of all those in need. We all hold this common gathering on Sunday, since it is the first day, on which God transforming darkness and matter made the universe, and Jesus Christ our Saviour rose from the dead on the same day. (§67)

For further reading

L. W. Barnard, *Justin Martyr: His Life and Thought* (Cambridge: Cambridge University Press, 1967).

8   *Shepherd of Hermas* (c. 140)

The Shepherd of Hermas *was a popular and widely circulated collection of visions, or revelations, received by the author from an angelic figure in the form of a shepherd. It focuses on two primary issues—the possibility of post-baptismal repentance (given the early belief among some Christians that there was only one repentance) and the relationship of the wealthy to the poor within the church. Both of these themes surface in the following excerpt, a dialogue between Hermas and an elderly woman, wherein she explains his vision of a tower that is being built, which is the church.*

Source: Michael W. Holmes (trans. and ed.), *The Apostolic Fathers in English*, 3rd edn.

"Now hear about the stones that go into the building. The stones that are square and white and fit at their joints, these are the apostles and bishops and teachers and deacons who have walked according to the holiness of God and have ministered to the elect of God as bishops and teachers and deacons with purity and reverence; some have fallen asleep, while others are still living. And they always agreed with one another, and so they had peace with one another and listened to one another. For this reason their joints fit together in the building of the tower."

"But who are the ones that are dragged from the deep and placed in the building, whose joints fit together with the other stones already used in the building?"

"They are those who have suffered for the name of the Lord."

"And I wish to know who are the other stones brought from the dry land, lady."

She said, "Those going into the building without being hewn are those whom the Lord has approved because they walked in the uprightness of the Lord and rightly performed his commandments."

"And who are the ones who are being brought and placed in the building?"

"They are young in faith, and faithful; but they are warned by the angels to do good, because wickedness was not found in them."

"Who are the ones they rejected and threw away?"

"They are the ones who have sinned and wish to repent. Therefore they were not thrown far from the tower, because they will be useful for building if they repent. So, then, the ones who are about to repent, if in fact they do repent, will be strong in the faith if they repent now while the tower is still being built. But if the tower is finished, they will no longer have a place, but will be rejects. The only advantage they have is this, that they lie near the tower. And do you want to know who are the ones that are broken in pieces and thrown far away from the tower? These are the children of lawlessness; they believed hypocritically, and no wickedness escaped them. Therefore they do not have salvation, because they are not useful for building on account of their wickedness. That is why they were broken up and thrown far away, because of the Lord's wrath, for they angered him. As for the others that you saw lying around in great numbers and not going into the building, the ones that are damaged are those who have known the truth but did not abide in it, nor do they associate with the saints. Therefore they are useless."

"But who are the ones with cracks?"

"These are the ones who have something against one another in their hearts and are not at peace among themselves. Instead, they have only the appearance of peace, and when they leave one another their evil thoughts remain in their hearts. These are the cracks that the stones have. The ones that are too short are those who have believed and live for the most part in righteousness, but they have a certain amount of lawlessness; that is why they are too short and not perfect."

"And who are the white and round stones that do not fit into the building, lady?"

She answered and said to me, "How long will you be foolish and stupid, asking about everything and understanding nothing? These are the ones who have faith, but also have the riches of this world. Whenever persecution comes, they deny their Lord because of their riches and their business affairs."

And I answered her and said, "Then when, lady, will they be useful for the building?"

"When," she replied, "their riches, which lead their souls astray, are cut away, then they will be useful to God. For just as the round stone cannot become square unless it is trimmed and loses some part of itself, so also those who are rich in this world cannot become useful to the Lord unless their riches are cut away. Learn first from yourself: when you were rich, you were useless, but now you are useful and beneficial to life. Be useful to God, for you yourself are to be used as one of these stones. And the other stones that you saw thrown far from the tower, and falling onto the road and rolling off the road to wastelands, are those who have believed but because of their double-mindedness abandon their true road. Thinking that they can find a better way, they go astray and wander about in misery, trudging through the wastelands. Those falling into the fire and burning are those who have completely rebelled against the living God, and the thought no longer enters their heart to repent on account of their licentious desires and the evil deeds they do. And do you want to know who are the ones that fall near the waters but are not able to roll into the water? They are the ones who heard the word and want to be baptized in the name of the Lord. Then, when they remember the purity of the truth, they change their mind and return again to their evil desires."

So she finished the explanation of the tower. Still unabashed, I asked her whether all these stones that were rejected and do not fit into the construction of the tower have opportunity for repentance and a place in this tower.

"They have," she said, "an opportunity for repentance, but they cannot fit into this tower. But they will fit into another much inferior place, but not until they have been tormented and fulfilled the days of their sins. And they will be transferred for this reason only, that they received the righteous word. And then it will happen that they will be transferred out of their torments, if the evil deeds that they have done come into their hearts; but if their evil deeds do not come into their hearts, they will not be saved, because of their hard-heartedness." …

Then I began to ask her about the times, in particular if the consummation had already arrived. But she cried out in a loud voice, saying: "You foolish man, can you not see that the tower is still being built? When the tower is finished being built, then the end comes. But it will be built up quickly. (13:1–16:9a)

For further reading

Harry O. Maier, *The Social Setting of the Ministry as Reflected in the Writings of Hermas, Clement, and Ignatius* (Waterloo, ON: Wilfrid Laurier University Press, 1991).

Lage Pernveden, *The Concept of the Church in the Shepherd of Hermas*, Studia Theologica Lundensia, 27 (Lund: C. W. K. Gleerup, 1966).

9   Irenaeus of Lyons (c. 140–202)

In response to heretical movements such as Gnosticism and Marcionism that threatened the unity of the church, Irenaeus, the bishop of Gaul, asserted the unbroken and uniform Christian tradition deposited with the church in the form of scripture and the apostolic succession of bishops.

Against Heresies (c. 175–89)

Source: Robert M. Grant, *Irenaeus of Lyons*, Early Church Fathers.

The church, dispersed throughout the world to the ends of the earth, received from the apostles and their disciples the faith in one God the Father Almighty, "who made heaven and earth and sea and all that is in them" (Exod. 20:11), and in one Christ Jesus, the Son of God, incarnate for our salvation, and in the Holy Spirit, who through the prophets predicted the dispensations of God: the coming, the birth from the Virgin, the passion, the resurrection from the dead, and the ascension of the beloved Jesus Christ our Lord in the flesh into the heavens, and his coming from the heavens in the glory of the Father to "recapitulate all things" (Eph. 1:10) and raise up all flesh of the human race, so that to Christ Jesus our Lord and God and Savior and King, according to the good pleasure of the indivisible Father, "every knee should bow, of beings in heaven and on earth and under the earth, and that every tongue should confess him" (Phil. 2:10–11), and that he should render a just judgment on all and send to eternal fire the spiritual powers of iniquity, the lying and apostate angels, and men who are impious, unjust, iniquitous, and blasphemous, while on the contrary he should give life imperishable as a reward to the just and equitable who keep his commandments and persevere in his love (some from the beginning, others since their conversion), and surround it with eternal glory.

The church, having received this preaching and this faith, as we have just said, though dispersed in the whole world, diligently guards them as living in one house, believes them as having one soul and one heart (Acts 4:32), and consistently preaches, teaches, and hands them down as having one mouth. For if the languages in the world are dissimilar, the power of the tradition is one and the same. The churches founded in Germany believe and hand down no differently, nor do those among the Iberians, among the Celts, in the Orient, in Egypt, or in Libya, or those established in the middle of the world. As the sun, God's creature, is one and the same in the whole world, so the light, the preaching of truth, shines everywhere and illuminates all men who wish to come to the knowledge of truth. And none of the rulers of the churches, however gifted he may be in eloquence, will say anything different—for no one is above the Master (Matt. 10:24)—nor will one weak in speech damage the tradition. Since the faith is one and the same, he who can say much about it does not add to it nor does he who says little diminish it. (Book I, 10:1–2)

For further reading

Denis Minns, *Irenaeus: An Introduction* (Washington, D.C.: Georgetown University Press, 1994).
Steven Shakespeare, "Ecclesiology and Philosophy," in Gerard Mannion and Lewis Mudge (eds.), *The Routledge Companion to the Christian Church* (New York: Routledge, 2008), pp. 655–73.

10   Clement of Alexandria (c. 150–215)

In the tradition of the Alexandrian school, which developed a widely known system of Christian doctrine integrated with Greek philosophy, salvation is conceived of as a spiritual knowledge (gnosis) of God and the church as a school of formation such that we can receive this knowledge as a divine gift. Clement was the head of the school and a genius at constructive, integrative thinking in relation to the Christian faith.

Paedogogus [The Instructor] (c. 190–92)

Source: Alexander Roberts and James Donaldson (eds.), *The Ante-Nicene Fathers: Translations of the Writings of the Fathers down to A.D. 325.*

O mystic marvel! The universal Father is one, and one the universal Word; and the Holy Spirit is one and the same everywhere, and one is the only virgin mother. I love to call her the Church. This mother, when alone, had not milk, because alone she was not a woman. But she is once virgin and mother—pure as a virgin, loving as a mother. And calling her children to her, she nurses them with holy milk, viz., with the Word for childhood. Therefore she had not milk; for the milk was this child fair and comely, the body of Christ, which nourishes by the Word the young brood, which the Lord Himself brought forth in throes of the flesh, which the Lord Himself swathed in His precious blood. O amazing birth! O holy swaddling bands! The Word is all to the child, both father and mother and tutor and nurse. "Eat ye my flesh," He says, "and drink my blood." Such is the suitable food which the Lord ministers, and He offers His flesh and pours forth His blood, and nothing is wanting for the children's growth. O amazing mystery! We are enjoined to cast off the old and carnal corruption, as also the old nutriment, receiving in exchange another new regimen, that of Christ, receiving Him if we can, to hide Him within; and that, enshrining the Saviour in our souls, we may correct the affections of our flesh. (bk I, ch. 6)

Feed us, the children, as sheep. Yea, Master, fill us with righteousness, Thine own pasture; yea, O Instructor, feed us on Thy holy mountain the Church, which towers aloft, which is above the clouds, which touches heaven. (bk I, ch. 9)

O nurslings of His blessed training! Let us complete the fair face of the church; and let us run as children to our good mother. And if we become listeners to the Word, let us glorify the blessed dispensation by which man is trained and sanctified as a child of God, and has his conversation in heaven, being trained from earth, and there receives the Father, whom he learns to know on earth. The Word both does and teaches all things, and trains in all things. (bk III, ch. 12)

For further reading

Jean Daniélou, *Gospel Message and Hellenistic Culture* (Philadelphia: Westminster, 1973).
Eric Osborn, *Clement of Alexandria* (Cambridge: Cambridge University Press, 2005).
Walter H. Wagner, *After the Apostles: Christianity in the Second Century* (Minneapolis: Augsburg Fortress, 1994).

11   Tertullian of Carthage (c. 160–220)

Tertullian is a complex figure who went through significant changes in religious outlook during his lifetime. In his writings we find descriptions of early church life and practice. We also find an emphasis on the holiness of the church in terms of a marked difference from the rest of the world. Christians are no less loyal to the emperor, nor do they shrink from full participation in civic duties or the ordinary obligations of daily living. But Christians are empowered by the Spirit to live a life of moral purity that stands in radical contrast to the public entertainments and idolatrous activities of those around them.

Apology (c. 197)

Source: Alexander Roberts and James Donaldson (eds.), *The Ante-Nicene Fathers: Translations of the Writings of the Fathers down to A.D. 325.*

For we offer prayer for the safety of our princes to the eternal, the true, the living God, whose favour, beyond all others, they must themselves desire. They know from whom they have obtained their power; they know, as they are men, from whom they have received life itself; they are convinced that He is God alone, on whose power alone they are entirely dependent, to whom they are second, after whom they occupy the highest places, before and above all the gods. …

But we merely, you say, flatter the emperor, and feign these prayers of ours to escape persecution. Thank you for your mistake, for you give us the opportunity of proving our allegations. Do you, then, who think that we care nothing for the welfare of Caesar, look into God's revelations, examine our sacred books, which we do not keep in hiding, and which many accidents put into the hands of those who are not of us. Learn from them that a large benevolence is enjoined upon us, even so far as to supplicate God for our enemies, and to beseech blessings on our persecutors. Who, then, are greater enemies and persecutors of Christians, than the very parties with treason against whom we are charged? Nay, even in terms, and most clearly, the Scripture says, "Pray for kings, and rulers, and powers, that all may be peace with you." For when there is disturbance in the empire, if the commotion is felt by its other members, surely we too, though we are not thought to be given to disorder, are to be found in some place or other which the calamity affects.

There is also another and a greater necessity for our offering prayer in behalf of the emperors, nay, for the complete stability of the empire, and for Roman interests in general. For we know that a mighty shock impending over the whole earth—in fact, the very end of all things threatening dreadful woes—is only retarded by the continued existence of the Roman empire. We have no desire, then, to be overtaken by these dire events; and in praying that their coming may be delayed, we are lending our aid to Rome's duration. … We respect in the emperors the ordinance of God, who has set them over the nations. We know that there is that in them which God has willed; and to what God has willed we desire all safety, and we count an oath by it a great oath. …

I shall at once go on, then, to exhibit the peculiarities of the Christian society, that, as I have refuted the evil charged against it, I may point out its positive good. We are a body knit together as such by a common religious profession, by unity of discipline, and by the bond of a common hope. We meet together as an assembly and congregation, that, offering up prayer to God as with united force, we may wrestle with Him in our supplications. This violence God delights in. We pray, too, for the emperors, for their ministers and for all in authority, for the welfare of the world, for the prevalence of peace, for the delay of the final consummation. We assemble to read our sacred writings, if any peculiarity of the times makes either forewarning or reminiscence needful. However it be in that respect, with the sacred words we nourish our faith, we animate our hope, we make our confidence more steadfast; and no less by inculcations of God's precepts we confirm good habits. In the same place also exhortations are made, rebukes and sacred censures are administered. For with a great gravity is the work of judging carried on among us, as befits those who feel assured that they are in the sight of God; and you have the most notable example of judgment to come when any one has sinned so grievously as to require his severance from us in prayer, in the congregation and in all sacred intercourse. The tried men of our elders preside over us, obtaining that honour not by purchase, but by established character. There is no buying and selling of any sort in the things of God. Though we have our treasure-chest, it is not made up of purchase-money, as of a religion that has its price. On the monthly day, if he likes, each puts in a small donation; but only if it be his pleasure, and only if he be able: for there is no compulsion; all is voluntary. These gifts are, as it were, piety's deposit fund. For they are not taken thence and spent on feasts, and drinking-bouts, and eating-houses, but to support and bury poor people, to supply the wants of boys and girls destitute of means and parents, and of old persons confined now to the house; such, too, as have suffered shipwreck; and if there happen to be any in the mines, or banished to the islands, or shut up in the prisons, for nothing but their fidelity to the cause of God's Church, they become the nurslings of their confession. But it is mainly the deeds of a love so noble that lead many to put a brand upon us. See, they say, how they love one another, for themselves are animated by mutual hatred; how they are ready even to die for one another, for they themselves will sooner put to death. And they are wroth with us, too, because we call each other brethren; for no other reason, as I think, than because among themselves names of consanguinity are assumed in mere pretence of affection. But we are your brethren as well, by the law of our common mother nature, though you are hardly men, because brothers so unkind. At the same time, how much more fittingly they are called and counted brothers who have been led to the knowledge of God as their common Father, who have drunk in one spirit of holiness, who from the same womb of a common ignorance have agonized into the same light of truth! But on this very account, perhaps, we are regarded as having less claim to be held true brothers, that no tragedy makes a noise about our brotherhood, or that the family possessions, which generally destroy brotherhood among you, create fraternal bonds among us. One in mind and soul, we do not hesitate to share our earthly goods with one another. All things are common among us but our wives. ... Our feast explains itself by its name. The Greeks call it agapè, i.e., affection. Whatever it costs, our outlay in the name of piety is gain, since with the good things of the feast we benefit the needy; not as it is with you, do parasites aspire to the glory of satisfying their licentious propensities, selling themselves for a belly-feast to all disgraceful treatment, —but as it is with God himself, a peculiar respect is shown to the lowly. If the object of our feast be good, in the light of that consider its further regulations. As it is an act of religious service, it permits no vileness or immodesty. The participants, before reclining, taste first of prayer to God. As much is eaten as satisfies the cravings of hunger; as much is drunk as befits the chaste. They say it is enough, as those who remember that even during the night they have to worship God; they talk as those who know that the Lord is one of their auditors. After manual ablution, and the bringing in of lights, each is asked to stand forth and sing, as he can, a hymn to God, either one from the holy Scriptures or one of his own composing, —a proof of the measure of our drinking. As the feast commenced with prayer, so with prayer it is closed. We go from it, not like troops of mischief-doers, nor bands of vagabonds, nor to break out into licentious acts, but to have as much care of our modesty and chastity as if we had been at a school of virtue rather than a banquet. Give the congregation of the Christians its due, and hold it unlawful, if it is like assemblies of the illicit sort: by all means let it be condemned, if any complaint can be validly laid against it, such as lies against secret factions. But who has ever suffered harm from our assemblies? We are in our congregations just what we are when separated from each other; we are as a community what we are individuals; we injure nobody, we trouble nobody. When the upright, when the virtuous meet together, when the pious, when the pure assemble in congregation, you ought not to call that a faction, but a curia—[i.e., the court of God.]

But we are called to account as harm-doers on another ground, and are accused of being useless in the affairs of life. How in all the world can that be the case with people who are living among you, eating the same food, wearing the same attire, having the same habits, under the same necessities of existence? We are not Indian Brahmins or Gymnosophists, who dwell in woods and exile themselves from ordinary human life. We do not forget the debt of gratitude we owe to God, our Lord and Creator; we reject no creature of His hands, though certainly we exercise restraint upon ourselves, lest of any gift of His we make an immoderate or sinful use. So we sojourn with you in the world, abjuring neither forum, nor shambles, nor bath, nor booth, nor workshop, nor inn, nor weekly market, nor any other places of commerce. We sail with you, and fight with you, and till the ground with you; and in like manner we unite with you in your traffickings—even in the various arts we make public property of our works for your benefit. How it is we seem useless in your ordinary business, living with you and by you as we do, I am not able to understand. (30–32, 39, 42)

For further reading

Eric Osborn, *Tertullian: First Theologian of the West* (Cambridge: Cambridge University Press, 1997).

David Ivan Rankin, *Tertullian and the Church* (Cambridge: Cambridge University Press, 1995).

12   Hippolytus (c. 170–236)

The Apostolic Tradition *is a document attributed to the second-century church leader Hippolytus, who broke with the bishop of Rome over what he took to be ecclesiastical and liturgical innovations incompatible with proper Christian tradition. In the following excerpt from his sketch of the correct procedure for initiation rites,*

Hippolytus paints a picture of a church that is set over against the worldliness of the surrounding society.

The Apostolic Tradition (c. 215)

Source: Alistair Stewart-Sykes, *Hippolytus: On the Apostolic Tradition.*

Those who come to hear the word for the first time should be brought to the teachers in the house, before the people come in. And they should enquire concerning the reason why they have turned to the faith. And those who brought them shall bear witness whether they have the ability to hear the word. They might be questioned about their state of life, whether he has a wife, or whether he is a slave. If he is the slave of a believer and his master encourages him, let him hear the word. If his master does not bear witness to him, that he is good, he should be rejected. If his master is a pagan, teach him to please his master, that there should be no scandal. If there is somebody who has a wife, or if a woman has a husband, so should they be taught that the man be contented with his wife and the wife with her husband. If there is somebody who does not live with a wife he should be taught not to fornicate but that he should either take a wife in accordance with the law or should remain [as he is] in accordance with the law. But if there is one who has a demon, let him not hear the word of teaching until he be purified.

Enquiry should be made concerning the crafts and occupations of those who are brought to be instructed. If any is a pimp or procurer of prostitutes he should desist or he should be rejected. If any is a sculptor or a painter he should be instructed not to make idols; he should desist or be rejected. If any is an actor, or makes presentations in the theater, he should desist, or he should be rejected. If somebody teaches children it is better that he desist; if he have no other trade let him be allowed. Likewise a charioteer who competes, or anyone who goes to the races, should desist or be rejected. If any is a gladiator, or trains gladiators in fighting, or one who fights with beasts in the games, or a public official engaged in gladiatorial business should desist, or he should be rejected. If any is a priest of idols, or a guardian of idols, he should desist, or he should be rejected. A soldier in command must be told not to kill people; if he is ordered so to do, he shall not carry it out. Nor should he take the oath. If he will not agree, he should be rejected. Anyone who has the power of the sword, or who is a civil magistrate wearing the purple, should desist, or he should be rejected. If a catechumen or a believer wishes to become a soldier they should be rejected, for they have despised God. A prostitute or a wastrel or any who has been castrated, or any who has performed any other unspeakable deed, should be rejected, for they are impure. A magician should not be brought for a decision. A maker of spells or an astrologer or a soothsayer or an interpreter of dreams or a rabble-rouser or somebody who cuts fringes on clothes (that is to say scissor-users) or any who makes amulets, should desist, or they should be rejected. Somebody's concubine, if she is his slave, if she has raised his children and holds to him alone, should hear; otherwise she should be rejected. A man who has a concubine should desist, and take a wife in accordance with the law. If he does not wish to do so he should be rejected. If a believing women consort with a slave she should desist, or she should be rejected. If we have omitted any other matter the works will instruct your eyes. For we all have the spirit of God.

For further reading

Paul Bradshaw, *Early Christian Worship: A Basic Introduction to Ideas and Practice* (Collegeville, MN: The Liturgical Press, 1996).
Burton Scott Easton, *The Apostolic Tradition of Hippolytus* (New York: The Macmillan Company, 1934).
Adolf Hamel, *Kirche bei Hippolyt von Rom* (Gütersloh: Bertelsmann, 1951).

13   *Didascalia Apostolorum* (c. 200–250)

The Didascalia Apostolorum *or* Teaching of the Apostles *purports to be a consensus of the first-century apostolic council in Jerusalem (mentioned in Acts 15), but was likely composed in the first part of the third century in Syria. Very much like the* Didache, *the document is a manual of church order that provides instruction on moral purity for men, women, widows, children, and clergy and the proper authority and duties of the overseer ("bishop") of the congregation. In this excerpt, instruction is given regarding the importance of the church's assembling itself regularly.*

Source: Alistair Stewart-Sykes, *The Didascalia Apostolorum: An English Version with Introduction and Annotation*, Studia Traditionis Theologiae.

When you are teaching you are to command and exhort the people that they should gather in church, and come together always, that none should be absent and so reduce the church through their withdrawal, so as to make the body of Christ defective in a limb. People should not simply be thinking of others, but of themselves, since it is said: "Whoever does not gather with me, is a scatterer" (Matt. 12:20). Since you are members of Christ you should not scatter yourselves from the church by failing to gather with others. Since, as he promised, you have Christ as your head, present with you and communicating himself to you, do not neglect yourselves, nor distance the Savior from his own members, and do not tear or scatter his body, not lend precedence to worldly affairs over the word of God, but put them aside each Lord's day and hurry to the church; for she is your glory. For what excuse shall they who do not assemble on that day to hear the saving word and to be nourished with divine and everlasting food, give to God?

You are concerned to gain things which are temporary, lasting a day or an hour, but neglect those which are eternal. You are concerned about bathing and the nourishment of food and drink for the belly, and for things, but there is no concern for things eternal; rather you are neglectful of your souls and have no interest in the church, for hearing and receiving the word of God.

What excuse do you have, by comparison to those who are astray? For every day the pagans go in the morning to worship and serve their idols when they rise from sleep, and before any work or business they go first to worship their idols; likewise they do not absent themselves from their feasts and festivals but are faithful in their attendance, not only from those from the locality but those who attend from afar. And likewise they all assemble and attend the spectacle of their theatre. The same is true of those who vainly are called Jews; after six days they remain idle for a day, and assemble in their synagogue. They do not absent themselves, and do not neglect their synagogue and do not neglect their idleness. They are denuded of the meaning of the word, of the name, Jew, by which they call themselves, since they do not believe. For "Jew" is to be interpreted as "confession," but these are no confessors, for they do not confess the murder of Christ, which they brought about through transgressing the law, and so repent and be saved. Thus if they who are not saved are attentive at all times to things which bring them no profit and which help them in nothing, what excuse before the Lord God shall the one who absents himself from the assembly of the church have? He does not even imitate the gentiles, but through failing to assemble grows neglectful and scornful and distances himself and does evil. He it is whom the Lord addresses by means of Jeremiah: "You have not kept my laws, you have not even acted in accordance with the laws of the gentiles; you have nearly surpassed them in wickedness" (Ezek. 5:7). And "Do the gentiles exchange their gods, which are not gods. But my people have exchanged their honour for what is worthless" (Jer. 2:11). How then shall anyone who is neglectful, and who has no concern for the assembly of the church of God, excuse himself?

And if there is anyone who is delayed in by worldly work, and becomes hindered, he should know that the trades of the faithful are termed unnecessary works; for their true works are religion. Pursue your trades, therefore, as unnecessary works, for your support, but let your true work be religion.

So you should be concerned never to withdraw from the assembly of the church. If anyone should leave the church and go to the assembly of the gentiles, what shall he say, what excuse should he give to God, on the day of judgment? He has deserted the holy church, and the words of the living God, which are living and lifegiving, which are able to redeem, to deliver from fire, and to save alive, and has gone to the assembly of the gentiles through craving for the spectacle of the theatre. He shall, on this account, be reckoned as one of those who went into it out of craving to hear and to receive the words of their stories which are of dead men, and the spirit of Satan. They are dead and they are deathly, turning away from the faith and leading on to everlasting fire. Yet your care is for this world, and your concern for material matters, whilst disdaining to attend to the catholic church, for the beloved daughter of the Lord, God most high, where you may receive the teaching of God, which endures for ever, and which is capable of saving those who receive the word of life.

Be constant, therefore, in assembling with those faithful who are being saved, in your mother, the church.

Be careful not to assemble with those who are perishing in the theatre, which is the assembly of the pagans, of error and destruction, for anyone who enters the assembly of the gentiles shall be counted as one of them and shall receive the woe. For the Lord God speaks by means of Isaiah to those who are such: "Woe, woe to them that come from the spectacle" (Deut. 28:9). And again he says: "Come, you women who are coming from the spectacle, since it is a people without understanding" (Isa. 27:11). So it is that he refers to the church as women, whom he called and rescued and brought forth from the theatre. He kept hold of them and received them and taught us to go there no more. For he says through Jeremiah: "You shall not learn in accordance with the ways of the gentiles" (Jer. 10:2). And again he says, in the Gospel: "You shall not go in the way of the gentiles" (Matt. 10:5), thus warning us in demanding that we shun every heresy, which are the "towns of the Samaritans," and go furthermore that we stay far away from the assemblies of the gentiles and that we enter not any gathering of strangers, and that we should stay far away from the theatre, and from their festivals, because of the idols. A believer should go nowhere near a festival, except to buy nourishment for his body and soul. So avoid any idolatrous spectacle, and the festivals of their feasts. (ch. 13)

For further reading

Paul F. Bradshaw, *The Search for the Origins of Christian Worship: Sources and Methods for the Study of Early Liturgy*, 2nd edn. (Oxford: Oxford University Press, 2002).
See also the Introduction to Stewart-Sykes, *The Didascalia Apostolorum*.

14   Cyprian of Carthage (c. 200–258)

In the wake of the Decian persecution that divided the church and led to martyrdoms as well as defections from the faith, Cyprian, bishop of Carthage, asserted the priority of Peter (and thus Rome), the indivisibility of the church, and the necessity of the church for salvation. Cyprian is famous for claiming that "there is no salvation outside of the church" (Epistle 72, §21), and in his writings we find a greater institutionalization of church structure and governance legitimated by an ecclesiology in which authority is traced back through episcopal succession to the apostles and ultimately to Christ himself. Without the church as mother, one does not have God as father.

The Unity of the Catholic Church (c. 251)

Source: Stanley L. Greenslade (trans. and ed.), *Early Latin Theology*, Library of Christian Classics.

The Lord says to Peter: "I say unto thee that thou art Peter, and upon this rock I will build my Church; and the gates of hell shall not prevail against it. I will give unto thee the keys of the kingdom of heaven: and whatsoever thou shalt bind on earth shall be bound in heaven; and whatsoever thou shalt loose on earth shall be loosed also in heaven" (Matt. 16:18–19). He builds the Church upon one man. True, after the resurrection he assigned the like power to all the apostles, saying: "As the Father hath sent me, even so send I you. Receive ye the Holy Ghost: whose soever sins ye remit, they shall be remitted unto him; whose soever ye retain, they shall be retained" (John 20:21–3). Despite that, in order to make unity manifest, he arranged by his own authority that this unity should, from the start, take its beginning from one man. Certainly the rest of the apostles were exactly what Peter was; they were endowed with an equal share of office and power. But there was unity at the beginning before any development, to demonstrate that the Church of Christ is one. This one Church is also intended in the Song of Songs, when the Holy Spirit says, in the person of the Lord: "My dove, my perfect one, is but one; she is the only one of her mother, the choice one of her that bare her" (6:9). Can one who does not keep this unity of the Church believe that he keeps the faith? Can one who resists and struggles against the Church be sure that he is in the Church? For the blessed apostle Paul gives the same teaching and declares the same mystery of unity when he says: "There is one body and one Spirit, one hope of your calling, one Lord, one faith, one baptism, one God" (Eph. 4:4).

It is particularly incumbent upon those of us who preside over the Church as bishops to uphold this unity firmly and to be its champions, so that we may prove the episcopate also to be itself one and undivided. Let no one deceive the brotherhood with lies or corrupt the true faith with faithless treachery. The episcopate is a single whole, in which each bishop's share gives him a right to, and a responsibility for, the whole. So is the Church a single whole, though she spreads far and wide into a multitude of churches as her fertility increases. We may compare the sun, many rays but one light, or a tree, many branches but one firmly rooted trunk. When many streams flow from one spring, although the bountiful supply of water welling out has the appearance of plurality, unity is preserved in the source. Pluck a ray from the body of the sun, and its unity allows no division of the light. Break a branch from the tree, and when it is broken off it will not bud. Cut a stream off from its spring, and when it is cut off it dries up. In the same way the Church, bathed in the light of the Lord, spreads her rays throughout the world, yet the light everywhere diffused is one light and the unity of the body is not broken. In the abundance of her plenty she stretches her branches over the whole earth, far and wide she pours her generously flowing streams. Yet there is one head, one source, one mother boundlessly fruitful. Of her womb are we born, by her milk we are nourished, by her breath we are quickened.

The bride of Christ cannot be made an adulteress. She is undefiled and chaste. She knows but one home, she guards with virtuous chastity the sanctity of one bed-chamber. It is she who keeps us for God and seals for the kingdom the sons she has borne. If you abandon the Church and join yourself to an adulteress, you are cut off from the promises of the Church. If you leave the Church of Christ you will not come to Christ's rewards, you will be an alien, an outcast, an enemy. You cannot have God for your father unless you have the Church for your mother. If you could escape outside Noah's ark, you could escape outside the Church. The Lord warns us, saying: "He that is not with me is against me; and he that gathereth not with me, scattereth" (Matt. 12:30). To break the peace and concord of Christ is to go against Christ. To gather somewhere outside the Church is to scatter Christ's Church. The Lord says: "I and the Father are one" (John 10:30), and again, of Father, Son, and Holy Spirit it is written: "And the three are one" (1 John 5:7). Can you believe that this unity, which originates in the immutability of God and coheres in heavenly mysteries, can be broken in the Church and split by the divorce of clashing wills? He who does not keep this unity does not keep the law of God, nor the faith of the Father and the Son—nor life and salvation. (4–6)

For further reading

Allen Brent, *Cyprian and Roman Carthage* (Cambridge: Cambridge University Press, 2010).
J. Patout Burns, *Cyprian the Bishop* (London and New York: Routledge, 2002).
John Meyendorff (ed.), *The Primacy of Peter: Essays in Ecclesiology and the Early Church* (Crestwood, NY: St. Vladimir's Seminary Press, 1992).

15   Origen of Alexandria (c. 185–254)

For Origen, a student of Clement of Alexandria, the church is a mysterious reality bound up with the mystery of Christ. For this reason, we must rely on images in describing it, especially images drawn from the allegorical reading of scripture—bride, temple, ark, Jerusalem, city, vine, vineyard, etc.[1] In the excerpts from his Commentary

---

[1]   See also F. Ledegang, *Mysterium Ecclesiae: Images of the Church and its Members in Origen* (Leuven: Leuven University Press, 2001).

on the Song of Songs, Origen uses the image of a bride to emphasize the purity of the church and to characterize its burning love for Christ, the eternal logos made flesh. The transcendence of the church is further underscored by Origen's belief in its pre-existence. In the excerpt from his homilies on Joshua, Origen comments on Rahab, the prostitute who hung a scarlet cord out her window so that it could be identified by Joshua's troops and provide salvation to those within. Rahab's action anticipates and provides a "type" of the church, which is made up of former sinners but now is the house of God and a place of salvation marked by the scarlet of Christ's blood. Only those inside that house will be saved. At the same time, as the second excerpt from a later homily on Joshua demonstrates, Origen recognizes that the church is always a mixture of purity and impurity, saintliness and sinfulness.

Commentary on the Song of Songs (c. 240)

Source: Rowan A. Greer (trans.), *Origen: An Exhortation to Martyrdom, Prayer and Selected Works.*

The present book of Scripture, then, speaks of this love with which the blessed soul burns and is on fire in regard to the Word of God. And she sings this wedding song through the Spirit, by which the Church is joined and united with its heavenly bridegroom Christ, desiring to be mingled with Him through the Word so that she may conceive from Him and be enabled to be saved through this chaste bearing of children (cf. 1 Tim. 2:15). And this will happen when the children continue in faith and holiness with modesty as they were conceived of the seed of the Word of God and brought forth and born either by the spotless Church or by the soul that seeks nothing corporeal, nothing material, but is on fire with love only for the Word of God. (Prologue, 2:46)

Source: Hans Urs von Balthasar, *Origen: Spirit and Fire: A Thematic Anthology of His Writings*, trans. Robert J. Daly.

You are not to think that it is only since the coming of Christ in the flesh that it has been called bride or church, but from the beginning of the human race and the very foundation of the world, or rather, to follow Paul's lead in seeking the origin of the mystery even earlier, even "before the foundation of the world." For his words are: "Even as he chose us in him before the foundation of the world, that we should be holy and blameless before him. He destined us in love to be his sons" (Eph. 1:4–5). In the Psalms too it is written: "Remember your congregation which you have gathered from the beginning" (Ps. 74:2). For the first foundations of the congregation of the church were laid right "from the beginning," which is why the Apostle says that the church "is built" not only "on the foundation of the apostles," but also on that of "the prophets" (Eph. 2:20). But among the prophets is also counted Adam who prophesied a great mystery in Christ and in the church. This is found in the words: "Therefore a man leaves his father and his mother and cleaves to his wife, and they become one flesh" (Gen. 2:24). For it is obviously about these words that the Apostle says that "this is a great mystery, and I take it to mean Christ and the church" (Eph. 5:32). And when the same apostle says: "Christ loved the church and gave himself up for her, that he might sanctify her … by the washing of water" (Eph. 5:25–6), he is by no means pointing out that the church did not exist before that. For how would he have loved her if she did not exist? … But she was in all the saints who have lived from the beginning of the world. (bk II:8)

Homilies on Genesis (c. 230)

Source: Hans Urs von Balthasar, *Origen: Spirit and Fire: A Thematic Anthology of His Writings*, trans. Robert J. Daly.

And so, just as that Noah at that time was told to build an ark and bring into it with him not only his sons and relatives but also animals of different kinds, so too was our Noah, the Lord Jesus Christ, who alone is truly just and who alone is perfect, told by the Father at the end of the ages to build for himself an ark … and fill it with heavenly mysteries. (Homily II:3)

Homilies on Joshua (c. 250)

Source: Barbara J. Bruce (trans.) and Cynthia White (ed.), *The Fathers of the Church*.

Meanwhile, the spies are sent by [Joshua] to Jericho and are received by the prostitute Rahab. … She is called Rahab, but Rahab means "breadth." What is breadth, therefore, if not this Church of Christ, which is gathered together from sinners as if from prostitution? She says, "That place is too narrow for me. Make me a place where I may dwell. Yet who has nurtured these for me?" And again, it is said to her, "Lengthen your stakes and enlarge your tents." Therefore, that one is "breadth," the one who received the spies of [Joshua]. …

Therefore, even this prostitute who received the spies of [Joshua] … stations those she has received in the higher places and deposits them in the high and lofty mysteries of faith. For no one who is sent by [Joshua] is found down below lying on the ground, but remains in the higher places. Not only that person persists in the higher places and summits, but also the prostitute who receives them becomes, instead of a prostitute, a prophet. For she says, "I know that the Lord your God has delivered this land to you." You see how that one who was once a prostitute and impious and unclean, is now filled with the Holy Spirit: She makes confession of past things, has faith in present things, prophesies and foretells future things. Thus Rahab, whose name means "breadth," is extended and goes forward to where "his sound goes forth into all the earth." …

Also this commandment is given to the person who was once a prostitute: "All," it says, "who will be found in your house will be saved. But concerning those who go out from the house, we ourselves are free of them by your oath." Therefore, if anyone wants to be saved, let him come into the house of this one who was once a prostitute. Even if anyone from that people wants to be saved, let him come in order to be able to attain salvation. Let him come to this house in which the blood of Christ is the sign of redemption. For among those who said, "His blood be upon us and upon our children," the blood of Christ is for condemnation. For Jesus had been appointed "for the ruin and the resurrection of many." Therefore, for those refuting his sign, his blood effects punishment; for those who believe, salvation.

Let no one persuade himself, let no one deceive himself. Outside this house, that is, outside the Church, no one is saved. If anyone goes outside, he is responsible for his own death. … In that the sign hangs in a window I think this is indicated: A window is that which illumines the house and through which we receive light, not wholly but enough, enough to suffice for the eye and for the vision. Even the incarnation of the Savior did not give us pure wine and the whole aspect of divinity, but through his incarnation, just as through the window, he makes us behold he splendor of the divinity. For that reason, so it seems to me, the sign of salvation was given through a window.

By that sign, all persons attain salvation, all those who are found in the house of the one who was once a prostitute, all those cleansed in the water and by the Holy Spirit and in the blood of our Lord and Savior Jesus Christ, "to whom is the glory and the dominion forever and ever. Amen!" (3:3–5)

But let us understand these verses spiritually, claiming the parable of the Gospel, which says concerning the weeds, "Let them grow up together, lest perhaps when you wish to pluck up the weeds, you also pluck up the wheat with them" (Matt. 13:29). Therefore, just as the weeds are permitted in the Gospel to grow up together with the wheat, in the same manner even here in Jerusalem—that is, in the Church—there are certain Jebusites who lead an ignoble and degenerate life, and who are perverse not only in their faith, but in their actions, and in every manner of living. For while the Church is on earth, it is not possible to cleanse it to such purity that neither an ungodly person nor any sinner seems to reside in it, where everyone is holy and blessed and no blot of sin is found in them. But just as it is said concerning the weeds, "lest perhaps plucking up the weeds, at the same time you may also pluck up the wheat with them," so it can also be said of those in whom there are either doubtful or secret sins. For we are not saying that those who are clearly and plainly sinful should not be expelled from the Church. … Therefore, since we cannot cast out those who trample upon us, let us at least drive out those whom we can, those whose sins are evident. For when a sin is not plain, we cannot expel someone from the Church lest by chance, plucking up the weeds, we also pluck up at the same time the wheat with them. (21:1)

For further reading

William G. Rusch, "Some Comments on the Ecclesiology of Origen of Alexandria," in F. Young, M. Edwards, and P. Parvis (eds.), *Studia Patristica,* 16 (Louvain: Peeters, 2006), pp. 253–8.

F. Ledegant, *Mysterium Ecclesiae: Images of the Church and Its Members in Origen* (Leuven: Peeters, 2001).

V. D. Verbrugge, "Origen's Ecclesiology and the Biblical Metaphor of the Church as the Bride of Christ," in Charles Kannengiesser and William L. Petersen (eds.), *Origen of Alexandria: His World and His Legacy* (Notre Dame: University of Notre Dame Press, 1988), pp 277–94.

16   Cyril of Jerusalem (c. 315–386)

Here in the only remaining set of prebaptismal instructions we have inherited from the early church,[2] Cyril, a high-ranking bishop in Jerusalem, argues for the importance of referring to the church as fully "catholic." Cyril's was a major voice during the Arian controversy asserting the divinity of Christ and affirming Nicene orthodoxy.

Catechetical Lecture 18 (c. 347)

Source: Philip Schaff and Henry Wace (trans. and eds.), *Nicene and Post-Nicene Fathers of the Christian Church*, 2nd ser.

[The church] is called Catholic then because it extends over all the world, from one end of the earth to the other; and because it teaches universally and completely one and all the doctrines which ought to come to men's knowledge, concerning things both visible and invisible, heavenly and earthly; and because it brings into subjection to godliness the whole race of mankind, governors and governed, learned and unlearned; and because it universally treats and heals the whole class of sins, which are committed by soul or body, and possesses in itself every form of virtue which is named, both in deeds and words, and in every kind of spiritual gifts. (23)

But since the word Ecclesia is applied to different things ... and since one might properly and truly say that there is a *Church of evil doers,* I mean the meetings of the heretics, the Marcionists and Manichees, and the rest, for this cause the Faith has securely delivered to thee now the Article, "And in one Holy Catholic Church;" that thou mayest avoid their wretched meetings, and ever abide with the Holy Church Catholic in which thou wast regenerated. And if ever thou art sojourning in cities, inquire not simply where the Lord's

---

[2]   Jan William Drijvers, *Cyril of Jerusalem: Bishop and City* (Leiden: E. J. Brill, 2004), p. xi.

House is (for the other sects of the profane also attempt to call their own dens houses of the Lord), nor merely where the Church is, but where is the Catholic Church. For this is the peculiar name of this Holy Church, the mother of us all, which is the spouse of our Lord Jesus Christ, the Only-begotten Son of God. (26)

For further reading

Alexis James Doval, *Cyril of Jerusalem, Mystagogue: The Authorship of the Mystagogic Catecheses*, Patristic Monographs 17 (Washington, D.C.: Catholic University of America Press, 2001).
Edward Yarnold, S.J., *Cyril of Jerusalem* (London and New York: Routledge, 2000).

17   The *Apostolic Constitutions* (c. 375)

The Apostolic Constitutions *are a fourth-century compilation, or manual, of ecclesiastical polity pertaining to liturgy, doctrine, and morality. Though the exhortations are attributed to the Apostles as handed down through Clement of Rome, they are clearly of a much later origin. They are generally agreed upon to have originated in Syriac Christianity and thus provide insight into ecclesiastical practice and organization of that period and place, including great detail about seating arrangements and church architecture, all of which have ecclesiological significance.*

Source: Alexander Roberts and James Donaldson (eds.), *The Ante-Nicene Fathers: Translations of the Writings of the Fathers down to A.D. 325.*

But be thou, O bishop, holy, unblameable, no striker, not soon angry, not cruel; but a builder up, a converter, apt to teach, forbearing of evil, of a gentle mind, meek, long-suffering, ready to exhort, ready to comfort, as a man of God.

When thou callest an assembly of the Church as one that is the commander of a great ship, appoint the assemblies to be made with all possible skill, charging the deacons as mariners to prepare places for the brethren as for passengers, with all due care and decency. And first, let the building be long, with its head to the east, with its vestries on both sides at the east end, and so it will be like a ship. In the middle let the bishop's throne be placed, and on each side of him let the presbytery sit down; and let the deacons stand near at hand, in close and small girt garments, for they are like the mariners and managers of the ship: with regard to these, let the laity sit on the other side, with all quietness and good order. And let the women sit by themselves, they also keeping silence. In the middle, let the reader stand upon some high place: let him read the books of Moses, of Joshua the son of Nun, of the Judges, and of the Kings and of the Chronicles, and those written after the return from the captivity; and besides these, the books of Job and of Solomon, and of the sixteen prophets. But when there have been two lessons severally read, let some other person sing the hymns of David, and let the people join at the conclusions of the verses. Afterwards let our Acts be read, and the Epistles of Paul our fellow-worker, which he sent to the churches under the conduct of the Holy Spirit; and afterwards let a deacon or a presbyter read the Gospels, both those which I Matthew and John have delivered to you, and those which the fellow-workers of Paul received and left to you, Luke and Mark. And while the Gospel is read, let all the presbyters and deacons, and all the people, stand up in great silence; for it is written: "Be silent, and hear, O Israel" (Deut. 27:9). And again: "But do thou stand there, and hear" (Deut. 5:31). In the next place, let the presbyters one by one, not all together, exhort the people, and the bishop in the last place, as being the commander. Let the porters stand at the entries of the men, and observe them. Let the deaconesses also stand at those of the women, like shipmen. For the same description and pattern was both in the tabernacle of the testimony and in the temple of God. But if any one be found sitting out of his place, let him be rebuked by the deacon, as a manager of the foreship, and be removed into the place proper for him; for the Church is not only like a ship, but also like a sheepfold. For as the shepherds place all the brute creatures distinctly, I mean goats and sheep, according to their kind and age, and still every one runs together, like to his like; so is it to be in the Church. Let the young persons sit by themselves, if there be a place for them; if not, let them stand upright. But let those that are already stricken in years sit in order. For the children which stand, let their fathers and mothers take them to them. Let the younger women also sit by themselves, if there be a place for them; but if there be not, let them stand behind the women. Let those women which are married, and have children, be placed by themselves; but let the virgins, and the widows, and the elder women, stand or sit before all the rest; and let the deacon be the disposer of the places, that every one of those that comes in may go to his proper place, and may not sit at the entrance. In like manner, let the deacon oversee the people, that nobody may whisper, nor slumber, nor laugh, nor nod; for all ought in the church to stand wisely, and soberly, and attentively, having their attention fixed upon the word of the Lord. After this, let all rise up with one consent, and looking towards the east, after the catechumens and penitents are gone out, pray to God eastward, who ascended up to the heaven of heavens to the east; remembering also the ancient situation of paradise in the east, from whence the first man, when he had yielded to the persuasion of the serpent, and disobeyed the command of God, was expelled. As to the deacons, after the prayer is over, let some of them attend upon the oblation of the Eucharist, ministering to the Lord's body with fear. Let others of them watch the multitude, and keep them silent. But let that deacon who is at the high priest's hand say to the people, Let no one have any quarrel against another; let no one come in hypocrisy. Then let the men give the men, and the women give the women, the Lord's kiss. But let no one do it with deceit, as Judas betrayed the Lord with a kiss. After this let the deacon pray for the whole Church, for the whole world, and the several parts of it, and the fruits of it; for the priests and the rulers, for the high priest and the king, and the peace of the universe. After this let the high priest pray for peace upon the people, and bless them, as Moses commanded the priests to bless the people, in these words: "The Lord bless thee, and keep thee: the Lord make His face to shine upon thee, and give thee peace" (Num. 6:24). Let the bishop pray for the people, and say: "Save Thy people, O Lord, and bless Thine inheritance, which Thou hast obtained with the precious blood of Thy Christ, and hast called a royal priesthood, and an holy nation." After this let the sacrifice follow, the people standing, and praying silently; and when the oblation has been made, let every rank by itself partake of the Lord's body and precious blood in order, and approach with reverence and holy fear, as to the body of their king. Let the women approach with their heads covered, as is becoming the order of women; but let the door be watched, lest any unbeliever, or one not yet initiated, come in (bk II, 7:57).

For further reading

R. H. Cresswell, *The Liturgy of the Eighth Book of "The Apostolic Constitutions": Commonly Called The Clementine Liturgy*, 2nd edn. (London: SPCK, 1924).

18   Petilian of Citra (born c. 365)

During the great persecution of the Emperor Diocletian (303–305), a number of Christians, including some bishops and priests, renounced the Christian faith. After the persecution, those who refused to accept the sacramental and spiritual authority of these lapsed Christians came to be known as the Donatists (named for the bishop Donatus), insisting that the validity of the sacraments depends upon the holiness (understood as moral purity) of the clergy who administer them. Augustine argued against the Donatists, and in his response to a letter from Petilian, the Donatist bishop of Citra, we find quotations that provide us the substance of the Donatist position as understood by Augustine.

Answer to Petilian the Donatist (c. 400)

Source: Philip Schaff (ed.), *The Nicene and Post-Nicene Fathers of the Christian Church*, 1st ser.

"The conscience," [Petilian] says, "of one that gives in holiness is what we look for to cleanse the conscience of the recipient; for he who has received his faith from one that is faithless, receives not faith but guilt." And as though some one had said to him, Whence do you derive your proof of this? He goes on to say, "For everything has its existence from a source and root; and if anything has not a head, it is nothing; nor does anything well confer a new birth, unless it be born again of good seed. And this being so, brethren, what perversity must it be to maintain that he who is guilty by reason of his own offenses should make another free from guilt; whereas our Lord Jesus Christ says, 'A good tree bringeth forth good fruit: do men gather grapes of thorns?' And again, 'A good man, out of the good treasure of his heart, bringeth forth good things; and an evil man, out of the evil treasure, brings forth evil things.'" (bk III, §52:64)

For further reading

W. H. C. Frend, *The Donatist Church: A Movement of Protest in Roman North Africa* (Oxford: Clarendon Press, 1952).
G. G. Willis, *Saint Augustine and the Donatist Controversy* (London: SPCK, 1950).

19   Augustine of Hippo (354–430)

As with all ecclesiologies, Augustine's reflects something of the historical situation out of which it was born. With the empire now officially Christian, Christian identity became less and less a matter of visible, even deviant, behavior associated with obedience to Jesus' teachings. Theologians such as Augustine could now even suggest that the true church is not the same as the visible church, and that it is therefore more accurate to speak of the true church as "invisible" (a claim that is revived in the Protestant Reformation). The Donatist schism represents one of Christianity's earliest, most significant, and long-lasting ecclesiological controversies focused precisely on this question of how and where we are to locate the holiness of the church when its members are increasingly only nominally Christian. While the Donatists argued that the validity of the sacraments was dependent upon the lived holiness of the clergy, Augustine rejected this as perfectionism and defended the objective holiness of the sacraments based on the church as the body of Christ and the bride of Christ. In his Tractates on the Gospel of John *and* De baptismo, *for example, Augustine insists that the church really is Christ's body, objectively, rather than conditionally. This intimate union, performed sacramentally, rather than the church's exemplary exercise of moral virtue, guarantees the church's holiness. The church's holiness is a participation in the holiness of Christ. Augustine's realism about the sinfulness of the church and the holiness of Christ as the source of the church's holiness did not lead him to be unconcerned about the holiness of individual members. The church's mission was to offer ministries of healing, restoration, and moral guidance, but Augustine could also insist on the use of coercive measures, imperially administered, to deal with wayward Christians.*

De baptismo (c. 400)

Source: Philip Schaff (ed.), *The Nicene and Post-Nicene Fathers of the Christian Church*, 1st ser.

Since it is clearly possible that in those who belong to the devil's party, Christ's sacrament may yet be holy … and that not only if they are led astray after they have been baptized, but even if they were such in heart when they received the sacrament … the sacrament is not to be again administered which they received when they were astray; so far as I can see, the case is already clear and evident, that in the question of baptism we have to consider, not who gives, but what he gives; not who receives, but what he receives; not who has, but what he has. …

Accordingly, neither without, any more than within, can any one who is of the devil's party, either in himself or in any other person, stain the sacrament which is of Christ. … When baptism is given in the words of the gospel, however great be the perverseness of understanding on the part either of him through whom, or of him to whom it is given, the sacrament itself is holy in itself on account of Him whose sacrament it is. And if any one, receiving it at the hands of a misguided man, yet does not receive the perversity of the minister, but only the holiness of the mystery, being closely bound to the unity of the Church in good faith and hope and charity, he receives remission of his sins, — not by the words which do eat as doth a canker, but by the sacraments of the gospel flowing from a heavenly source. But if the recipient himself be misguided, on the one hand, what is given is of no avail for the salvation of the misguided man; and yet, on the other hand, that which is received remains holy in the recipient, and is not renewed to him if he be brought to the right way. (bk IV, §§17, 19)

Concerning the Correction of the Donatists (c. 417)

Source: Philip Schaff (ed.), *The Nicene and Post-Nicene Fathers of the Christian Church*, 1st ser.

But as to the argument of those men who are unwilling that their impious deeds should be checked by the enactment of righteous laws, when they say that the apostles never sought such measures from the kings of the earth, they do not consider the different character of that age, and that everything comes in its own season. For what emperor had as yet believed in Christ, so as to serve Him in the cause of piety by enacting laws against impiety? … Seeing, then, that the kings of the earth were not yet serving the Lord in the time of the apostles, but were still imagining vain things against the Lord and against His Anointed, that all might be fulfilled which was spoken by the prophets, it must be granted that at that time acts of impiety could not possibly be prevented by the laws, but were rather performed under their sanction. (5:19–20)

It is indeed better (as no one ever could deny) that men should be led to worship God by teaching, than that they should be driven to it by fear of punishment or pain; but it does not follow that because the former course produces the better men, therefore those who do not yield to it should be neglected. For many have found advantage (as we have proved, and are daily proving by actual experiment), in being first compelled by fear or pain, so that they might afterwards be influenced by teaching, or might follow out in act what they had already learned in word. … But while those are better who are guided aright by love, those are certainly more numerous who are corrected by fear. …

Why, therefore, should not the Church use force in compelling her lost sons to return, if the lost sons compelled others to their destruction? Although even men who have not been compelled, but only led astray, are received by their loving mother with more affection if they are recalled to her bosom through the enforcement of terrible but salutary laws, and are the objects of far more deep congratulation than those whom she had never lost. Is it not a part of the care of the shepherd, when any sheep have left the flock, even though not violently forced away, but led astray by tender words and coaxing blandishments, to bring them back to the fold of his master when he has found them, by the fear, or even the pain of the whip? (6:21, 23)

Tractates on the Gospel of John (c. 418)

Source: John W. Rettig (trans.), *Tractates on the Gospel of John*.

Therefore, let us rejoice and give thanks, not only that we have been made Christians, but that we have been made Christ. Do you understand, brothers, do you comprehend the grace of God upon us? Be in awe. Rejoice. We have been made Christ. For his is the head, we are the members — a whole man, he and we. This is what the Apostle Paul says, "that we may be now no longer children, tossed to and fro and beset by every wind of doctrine" (Eph. 4:14). But just previously he had said, "until we all attain to the unity of the faith, and to the knowledge of the Son of God, to a perfect man, to the mature measure of the age of the fullness of Christ" (Eph. 4:13).

The fullness of Christ, therefore, head and members. What does it mean, head and members? Christ and the Church. For we would proudly claim this for ourselves if he had not deigned to promise this who says through the same Apostle, "Now you are the body and members of Christ" (1 Cor. 12:27). (tractate 21, 8:1–2)

City of God (c. 426)

Augustine's immense City of God *is at once a comprehensive philosophy of history, an ecclesiology, and a commentary on his own historical situation in the final days of the Roman empire just following the invasion of Rome in 410. The metaphor of the city (with unmistakable reference to Rome itself) frames his understanding of the church and the multiple senses in which he uses the word "church." The church is the heavenly city, which includes the angels and reaches back to the beginning of history. The church can also be understood as that part of the heavenly city that is on pilgrimage in the world. The visible church on earth is neither perfect nor is it simply to be equated with the heavenly city. Rather, the visible church includes both sinners and saints. The true church is an eschatological communion of angels and the elect, and known only on the day of judgment. While Augustine's situation is that of a church which has become increasingly accommodated to the surrounding culture, his view of the world and of culture is ambivalent. On the one hand, the earthly city is idolatrous, a "life of captivity," and born in rebellion against God. On the other hand, life in the earthly city can be good and the job of the church is to defend, seek, and make use of whatever earthly peace is possible, even if that peace is always fragmentary and partial, ever directing the peace of the earthly city to peace of the city of God.*

Source: Marcus Dods (trans.), *The Works of Aurelius Augustine, Bishop of Hippo: A New Translation*.

Let [the pilgrim city of King Christ] bear in mind, that among her enemies lie hid those who are destined to be fellow-citizens, that she may not think it a fruitless labour to bear what they inflict as enemies until they become confessors of the faith. So, too, as long as she is a stranger in the world, the city of God has in her communion, and bound to her by the sacraments, some who shall not eternally dwell in the lot of the saints. Of these, some are not now recognised; others declare themselves, and do not hesitate to make common cause with our enemies in murmuring against God, whose sacramental badge they wear. These men you may to-day see thronging the churches with us, to-morrow crowding the theatres with the godless. But we have the less reason to despair of the reclamation even of such persons, if among our most declared enemies there are now some, unknown to themselves, who are destined to become our friends. In truth, these two cities are entangled together in this world, and intermixed until the last judgment effect their separation. (1:35)

Two cities have been formed by two loves: the earthly by the love of self, even to the contempt of God; the heavenly by the love of God, even to the contempt of self. The former, in a word, glories in itself, the latter in the Lord. For the one seeks glory from men; but the greatest glory of the other is God, the witness of conscience. The one lifts up its head in its own glory; the other says to its God, "Thou art my glory, and the lifter up of mine head." In the one, the princes and the nations it subdues are ruled by the love of ruling; in the other, the princes and the subjects serve one another in love, the latter obeying, while the former take thought for all. The one delights in its own strength, represented in the persons of its rulers; the other says to its God, "I will love Thee, O Lord, my strength." And therefore the wise men of the one city, living according to man, have sought for profit to their own bodies or souls, or both, and those who have known God "glorified Him not as God, neither were thankful, but became vain in their imaginations, and their foolish heart was darkened; professing themselves to be wise,"—that is, glorying in their own wisdom, and being possessed by pride,—"they became fools, and changed the glory of the incorruptible God into an image made like to corruptible man, and to birds, and four-footed beasts, and creeping things." For they were either leaders or followers of the people in adoring images, "and worshipped and served the creature more than the Creator, who is blessed forever." But in the other city there is no human wisdom, but only godliness, which offers due worship to the true God, and looks for its reward in the society of the saints, of holy angels as well as holy men, "that God may be all in all." (14:28)

Of these two first parents of the human race, then, Cain was the first-born, and he belonged to the city of men; after him was born Abel, who belonged to the city of God. For as in the individual the truth of the apostle's statement is discerned, "that is not first which is spiritual, but that which is natural, and afterward that which is spiritual," whence it comes to pass that each man, being derived from a condemned stock, is first of all born of Adam evil and carnal, and becomes good and spiritual only afterwards, when he is grafted into Christ by regeneration: so was it in the human race as a whole. When these two cities began to run their course by a series of deaths and births, the citizen of this world was the first-born, and after him the stranger in this world, the citizen of the city of God, predestinated by grace, elected by grace, by grace a stranger below, and by grace a citizen above. By grace,—for so far as regards himself he is sprung from the same mass, all of which is condemned in its origin; but God, like a potter (for this comparison is introduced by the apostle judiciously, and not without thought), of the same lump made one vessel to honour, another to dishonour. But first the vessel to dishonour was made, and after it another to honour. For in each individual, as I have already said, there is first of all that which is reprobate, that from which we must begin, but in which we need not necessarily remain; afterwards is that which is well-approved, to which we may by advancing attain, and in which, when we have reached it, we may abide. Not, indeed, that every wicked man shall be good, but that no one will be good who was not first of all wicked; but the sooner any one becomes a good man, the more speedily does he receive this title, and abolish the old name in the new. Accordingly, it is recorded of Cain that he built a city, but Abel, being a sojourner, built none. For the city of the saints is above, although here below it begets citizens, in whom it sojourns till the time of its reign arrives, when it shall gather together all in the day of the resurrection; and then shall the promised kingdom be given to them, in which they shall reign with their Prince, the King of the ages, time without end. (15:1)

The families which do not live by faith seek their peace in the earthly advantages of this life; while the families which live by faith look for those eternal blessings which are promised, and use as pilgrims such advantages of time and of earth as do not fascinate and divert them from God, but rather aid them to endure with greater ease, and to keep down the number of those burdens of the corruptible body which weigh upon the soul. Thus the things necessary for this mortal life are used by both kinds of men and families alike, but each has its own peculiar and widely different aim in using them. The earthly city, which does not live by faith seeks an earthly peace, and the end it proposes, in the well-ordered concord of civic obedience and rule, is the combination of men's wills to attain the things which are helpful to this life. The heavenly city, or rather the part of it which sojourns on earth and lives by faith, makes use of this peace only because it must, until this mortal condition which necessitates it shall pass away. Consequently, so long as it lives like a captive and a stranger in the earthly city, though it has already received the promise of redemption, and the gift of the Spirit as the earnest of it, it makes no scruple to obey the laws of the earthly city, whereby the things necessary for the maintenance of this mortal life are administered; and thus, as this life is common to both cities, so there is a harmony between them in regard to what belongs to it. But, as the earthly city has had some philosophers whose doctrine is condemned by the divine teaching, and who, being deceived either by their own conjectures or by demons, supposed that many gods must be invited to take an interest in human affairs, and assigned to each a separate function and a separate department … and as the celestial city, on the other hand, knew that one God only was to be worshipped, and that to Him alone was due that service which the Greeks call λατρεία, and which can be given only to a god, it has come to pass that the two cities could not have common laws of religion, and that the heavenly city has been compelled in this matter to dissent, and to become obnoxious to those who think differently, and to stand the brunt of their anger and hatred and persecutions, except in so far as the minds of their enemies have been alarmed by the multitude of the Christians and quelled by the manifest protection of God accorded to them. This heavenly city, then, while it sojourns on earth, calls citizens out of all nations, and gathers together a society of pilgrims of all languages, not scrupling about diversities in the manners, laws, and institutions whereby earthly peace is secured and maintained, but recognising that, however various these are, they all tend to one and the same end of earthly peace. It therefore is so far from rescinding and abolishing these diversities, that it even preserves and adopts them, so long only as no hindrance to the worship of the one supreme and true God is thus introduced. Even the heavenly city, therefore, while in its state of pilgrimage, avails itself of the peace of earth, and, so far as it can without injuring faith and godliness, desires and maintains a common agreement among men regarding the acquisition of the necessaries of life, and makes this earthly peace bear upon the peace of heaven; for this alone can be truly called and esteemed the peace of the reasonable creatures, consisting as it does in the perfectly ordered and harmonious enjoyment of God and of one another in God. When we shall have reached that peace, this mortal life shall give place to one that is eternal, and our body shall be no more this animal body which by its corruption weighs down the soul, but a spiritual body feeling no want, and in all its members subjected to the will. In its pilgrim state the heavenly city possesses this peace by faith; and by this faith it lives righteously when it refers to the attainment of that peace every good action towards God and man; for the life of the city is a social life. (19:17)

For further reading

David C. Alexander, *Augustine's Early Theology of the Church: Emergence and Implications, 386–391* (New York: Peter Lang, 2008).
Pasquale Borgomeo, *L'Eglise de ce temps dans the predication de saint Augustin* (Paris: Etudes Augustiniennes, 1972).
Peter Brown, *Augustine of Hippo* (Berkeley: University of California Press, 1969)
Yves Congar, *L'Eglise: De saint Augustin à l'époque moderne* (Paris: Editions du Cerf, 1970).
Michael A. Fahey, "Augustine's Ecclesiology Revisited," in Joanne McWilliam (ed.), *Augustine: From Rhetor to Theologian* (Waterloo, ON: Wilfrid Laurier University Press, 1992), pp. 173–81
Eugene TeSelle, *Augustine the Theologian* (London: Burns and Oats, 1970).

20   Gelasius I (d. 496)

By the end of the fifth century, Christianity was present throughout the Roman empire, and especially entrenched in the east. Whereas emperors had previously taken it upon themselves to direct the affairs of the church, call councils, and appoint bishops, the Roman papacy had grown increasingly powerful. In the following correspondence to the eastern emperor Anastasius, Pope Gelasius asserts two separate spheres according to which the world is to be governed and, accordingly, two powers, or "swords," responsible for that governance. Together these two spheres constitute a unity of Christian society.

Letter of Gelasius I to Emperor Anastasius (494)

Source: J. H. Robinson, *Readings in European History*.

There are two powers, august Emperor, by which this world is chiefly ruled, namely, the sacred authority of the priests and the royal power. Of these that of the priests is the more weighty, since they have to render an account for even the kings of men in the divine judgment. You are also aware, dear son, that while you are permitted honorably to rule over human kind, yet in things divine you bow your head humbly before the leaders of the clergy and await from their hands the means of your salvation. In the reception and proper disposition of the heavenly mysteries you recognize that you should be subordinate rather than superior to the religious order, and that in these matters you depend on their judgment rather than wish to force them to follow your will.

If the ministers of religion, recognizing the supremacy granted you from heaven in matters affecting the public order, obey your laws, lest otherwise they might obstruct the course of secular affairs by irrelevant considerations, with what readiness should you not yield them obedience to whom is assigned the dispensing of the sacred mysteries of religion. Accordingly, just as there is no slight danger in the case of the priests if they refrain from speaking when the service of the divinity requires, so there is no little risk for those who disdain—which God forbid—when they should obey. And if it is fitting that the hearts of the faithful should submit to all priests in general who properly administer divine affairs, how much the more is obedience due to the bishop of that see which the Most High ordained to be above, ill others, and which is consequently dutifully honored by the devotion of the whole Church.

For further reading

Roger Collins, "The Two Swords," in *Keepers of the Keys: A History of the Papacy* (New York: Basic Books, 2009), pp. 77–97.
Justin Taylor, "The Early Papacy at Work: Gelasius I (492–6)," *Journal of Religious History* 8/4 (Dec. 1975), pp. 317–32.
Aloysius K. Ziegler, "Pope Gelasius I and His Teaching on the Relation of Church and State," *Catholic Historical Review* 27/4 (Jan 1942), pp. 412–37.

Part 2
The Middle Ages and the Reformation

By the eleventh century, we find a thorough clericalization of the Western church such that papal supremacy came to define the church as an institution. It is not surprising, therefore, that ecclesiological reflection frequently turned to questions of how ecclesial power and authority are to be related to that of secular rulers and temporal authorities. With the now central role that the church played in all of Western life and culture, we find an elaborate institutional and political infrastructure, but also a belief in and devotion to the church as a mystical reality—as salvation itself—expressed in hymns, art, architecture, liturgies, prayers, sermons, and mystical visions such as those of Hildegard. With the rise of the universities, we also find the beginnings of more systematic expositions on the nature of the church and eventually full-scale treatises on canon law that govern the organization of the church and its rituals.

By the fourteenth century, opposition to clerical and papal authority over temporal affairs increased (Marsilius of Padua is important in this regard) as did attacks on the opulence and power of the church. Renaissance humanism motivated the flowering of Western art, culture, and learning and, at the same time, generated appeals to the dignity of the individual conscience and to the free consent of those ruled as the basis of the authority of those who rule. Ecclesiologically, the ground was ripe for the conciliar movement, which pressed for the subordination of the authority of popes to that of councils, and thus a more representative form of ecclesial governance. By the late fourteenth century, more radical reforming voices such as those of Wyclif and Hus began to make themselves heard and to gather significant groups of followers until at last occurred the deepest rift the church had seen since the break between East and West in the eleventh century—the Protestant Reformation.

The readings in this section attempt to do justice to some of the more important and consistent ecclesiological dimensions of the Reformation—the priesthood of believers, the distinction between an invisible and visible church, the rejection of papal authority and infallibility, the priority of faith in salvation rather than reliance on one's nominal membership in the church. At the same time, there are important differences among the reformers to be highlighted, especially between more radical visions of the church's faithfulness to the gospel and independence from secular rule (such as we find in the Anabaptists), on the one hand, and the various visions of a reformed Christian culture enacted by the so-called "magisterial" reformers who continued to emphasize the role of secular magistrates, princes, and rulers in the maintenance of a Christian culture and civilization.

1   *Urbs beata Jerusalem* (eighth century)

This hymn is better known today as "Christ is Made the Sure Foundation"—words taken from the second part of the original Latin text and translated into English by the eminent Anglican priest, translator, and hymn-writer John Mason Neale. The hymn has been used throughout history in church dedication liturgies, and is an exalted statement of the church's relationship to God, founded on Christ, using the metaphor and symbolism of a city or building.

Source: Rev. J. M. Neale (trans.), *Mediaeval Hymns and Sequences*, 2nd edn.

Blessed City, Heavenly Salem,
    Vision dear of Peace and Love,
Who, of living stones upbuilded,
    Art the joy of Heav'n above,
And, with angel cohorts circled,
    As a Bride to earth dost move!

From celestial realms descending,
    Ready for the nuptial bed,
To His presence, deck'd with jewels,
    By her Lord shall she be led:
All her streets, and all her bulwarks,
    Of pure gold are fashioned.

Bright with pearls her portal glitters;
    It is open evermore;
And, by virtue of His merits,
    Thither faithful souls may soar,
Who for Christ's dear Name, in this world
    Pain and tribulation bore.

Many a blow and biting sculpture
    Polish'd well those stones elect,
In their places now compacted
    By the Heavenly Architect,
Who therewith hath will'd for ever
    That His Palace should be deck'd.

Christ is made the sure Foundation,
    And the precious Corner-stone,
Who, the twofold walls surmounting,
    Binds them closely into one:

Holy Sion's help for ever,
    And her confidence alone.

All that dedicated City,
    Dearly lov'd by God on high,
In exultant jubilation
    Pours perpetual melody;
God the One, and God the Trinal,
    Singing everlastingly.

To this temple, where we call Thee,
    Come, O Lord of Hosts, to-day!
With Thy wonted loving-kindness
    Hear Thy people as they pray;
And Thy fullest benediction
    Shed within its walls for aye.

Here vouchsafe to all Thy servants
    That they supplicate to gain:
Here to have and hold for ever
    Those good things their pray'rs obtain;
And hereafter, in Thy Glory
    With Thy blessed ones to reign.

Laud and honour to the FATHER;
    Laud and honour to the SON;
Laud and honour to the SPIRIT;
    Ever Three and Ever ONE:
Consubstantial, Co-eternal,
    While unending ages run. Amen.

2   Gregory VII (c. 1020–1085)

Just as with Gelasius, Pope Gregory VII (Hildebrand) supposed that there is one universal and united Christendom throughout Europe with two spheres of government — temporal and spiritual. For Gregory, the former is absolutely subordinate to the latter. While this understanding of the church further advanced a hierarchical and institutional understanding of the church, it was also the basis of the "Gregorian reforms," which sought to restore the dignity and freedom of the episcopacy, to eliminate the purchase of clerical offices (simony) and clerical marriages, and to regulate the functioning of the church through a uniform system of law. These reforms and the ecclesiology that undergirds them are outlined in 27 theses of papal supremacy called the Dictatus papae *("The Dictates of the Pope"), a papal bull called*

Libertas ecclesiae ("Freedom of the Church"), and a letter from Gregory to Bishop Hermann of Metz, in which he argues for papal supremacy and defends his famous deposition of King Henry IV.

Source: Ernest F. Henderson (ed. and trans.), *Select Historical Documents of the Middle Ages.*

Dictatus papae (1075)

That the Roman church was founded by God alone.

That the Roman pontiff alone can with right be called universal.

That he alone can depose or reinstate bishops.

That, in a council, his legate, even if a lower grade, is above all bishops, and can pass sentence of deposition against them.

That the pope may depose the absent.

That, among other things, we ought not to remain in the same house with those excommunicated by him.

That for him alone is it lawful, according to the needs of the time, to make new laws, to assemble together new congregations, to make an abbey of a canonry; and, on the other hand, to divide a rich bishopric and unite the poor ones.

That he alone may use the imperial insignia.

That of the pope alone all princes shall kiss the feet.

That his name alone shall be spoken in the churches.

That this is the only name in the world.

That it may be permitted to him to depose emperors.

That he may be permitted to transfer bishops if need be.

That he has power to ordain a clerk of any church he may wish.

That he who is ordained by him may *preside* over another church, but may not hold a subordinate position; and that such a one may not receive a higher grade from any bishop.

That no synod shall be called a general one without his order.

That no chapter and no book shall be considered canonical without his authority.

That a sentence passed by him may be retracted by no one; and that he himself, alone of all, may retract it.

That he himself may be judged by no one.

That no one shall dare to condemn one who appeals to the apostolic chair.

That to the latter should be referred the more important cases of every church.

That the Roman church has never erred; nor will it err to all eternity, the Scripture bearing witness.

That the Roman pontiff, if he have been canonically ordained, is undoubtedly made a saint by the merits of St. Peter. ...

That, by his command and consent, it may be lawful for subordinates to bring accusations.

That he may depose and reinstate bishops without assembling a synod.

That he who is not at peace with the Roman church shall not be considered catholic.

That he may absolve subjects from their fealty to wicked men.

Letter of Gregory VII to Bishop Hermann of Metz (1081).

Who does not know the words of our Lord and Saviour Jesus Christ who says in the gospel: "Thou art Peter and upon this rock will I build my church, and the gates of hell shall not prevail against it; and I will give unto thee the keys of the kingdom of Heaven; and whatsoever thou shalt bind upon earth shall be bound also in Heaven, and whatsoever thou shalt loose upon earth shall be loosed also in Heaven"? Are kings excepted here, or do they not belong to the sheep which the Son of God committed to St. Peter? Who, I ask, in this universal concession of the power of binding and loosing, can think that he is withdrawn from the authority of St. Peter, unless, perhaps, that unfortunate man who is unwilling to bear the yoke of the Lord and subjects himself to the burden of the devil, refusing to be among the number of Christ's sheep? It will help him little to his wretched liberty, indeed, that he shake from his proud neck the divinely granted power of Peter. For the more any one, through pride, refuses to bear it, the more heavily shall it press upon him unto damnation at the judgment.

The holy fathers, indeed, as well in general councils as otherwise in their writings and doings, have called the holy Roman church the universal mother, accepting and serving with great veneration this institution founded by the divine will, this pledge of a dispensation to the church, this privilege handed over in the beginning and confirmed to St. Peter the chief of the apostles. And even as they accepted its proofs in confirmation of their faith and of the doctrines of holy religion, so also they received its judgments—consenting in this, and agreeing as it were with one spirit and one voice: that all greater matters and exceptional cases, and judgments over all churches, ought to be referred to it as to a mother and a head; that from it there was no appeal; that no one should or could retract or refute its decisions. ...

Since it belongs to our office to distribute exhortation to each person according to the rank or dignity which he adorns, we take care, God impelling us, to provide weapons of humility just for emperors and kings and other princes, that they may be able to subdue the risings of the sea and the waves of pride. For we know that mundane glory and worldly cares usually do induce to pride, especially those who are in authority. They, in consequence, neglecting humility and seeking their own glory, always desire to dominate over their brothers. Wherefore to kings and emperors especially it is of advantage, when their mind tends to exalt itself and to delight in its own particular glory, to find out a means of humbling themselves and to be brought to realize that what they have been rejoicing in is the thing most to be feared. Let them, therefore, diligently consider how dangerous and how much to be feared the royal or imperial dignity is. For in it the fewest are saved; and those who, through the mercy of God, do come to salvation are not glorified in the holy church and in the judgment of the Holy Spirit to the same extent as many poor people. For, from the beginning of the world until these our own times, in the whole of authentic history we do not find seven emperors or kings whose lives were as distinguished for religion and as beautified by significant portents as those of an innumerable multitude who despised the world—although we believe many of them to have found mercy in the presence of God Almighty.

For further reading

Klaus Schatz, "The Gregorian Reform and the Beginning of a Universal Ecclesiology," *The Jurist* 57 (1997), pp. 123–36.
Brian Tierney (ed.), *The Crisis of Church and State, 1050–1300* (Englewood Cliffs, NJ: Prentice-Hall, 1980).

3   Bernard of Clairvaux (1090–1153)

Bernard, the Abbot of Clairvaux, had tremendous influence during his lifetime and wrote a number of books, letters, and sermons that have become spiritual classics. Among his most important contributions to the ecclesiology of the Middle Ages is the development of the metaphor of the church as "bride." His exploitation of this metaphor was not merely the expression of an other-worldly mysticism emphasizing the ecstatic, spiritual union that exists between the soul and God and between Christ and the church, but an important and influential response to the ecclesiastical politics and theological controversies of his time. Bernard was concerned, for example, that the power held by the pope had become wholly administrative and institutional without attention to sanctity, contemplation, and virtue. Bernard's Christocentrism and his emphasis on love undergird an ecclesiology that focuses on holiness, spirituality, and the church's participation in and response to God's initiatives rather than being preoccupied with ecclesiastical law, rule, uniformity, and institution.

Sermons on the Song of Songs (c. 1136)

Source: Kilian Walsh (trans.), *The Works of Bernard of Clairvaux.*

The man whose speech intoxicates and whose good deeds radiate may take as addressed to himself the words: "Your breasts are better than wine, redolent of the best ointments." (Song 1:2–3). Now who is worthy of such a commendation? Which of us can live uprightly and perfectly even for one hour, an hour free from fruitless talk and careless work? Yet there is one who truthfully and unhesitatingly can glory in this praise. She is the Church, whose fullness is a never-ceasing fount of intoxicating joy, perpetually fragrant. For what she lacks in one member she possesses in another according to the measure of Christ's gift (Eph. 4:7) and the plan of the Spirit who distributes to each one just as he chooses (1 Cor. 12:11). The Church's fragrance is radiated by those who use their money, tainted though it be, to win themselves friends (Luke 16:9); she intoxicates by the words of her preachers, who drench the earth and make it drunk (Ps. 64:10) with the wine of spiritual gladness, and yield a harvest through their perseverance (Luke 8:15). With the bold assurance of one confident that her breasts are better than wine and redolent of the choicest perfumes (Song 1:2–3), she lays claim to the title of bride. And although none of us will dare arrogate for his own soul the title of bride of the Lord, nevertheless we are members of the Church which rightly boasts of this title and of the reality that it signifies, and hence may justifiably assume a share in this honor. For what all of us simultaneously possess in a full and perfect manner, that each single one of us undoubtedly possesses by participation. Thank you, Lord Jesus, for your kindness in uniting us to the Church you so dearly love, not merely that we may be endowed with the gift of faith, but that like brides we may be one with you in an embrace that is sweet, chaste and eternal, beholding with unveiled faces (2 Cor. 3:18) that glory which is yours in union with the Father and the Holy Spirit for ever and ever. Amen. (Sermon 12)

For further reading

G. R. Evans, *The Mind of Bernard of Clairvaux* (Oxford: Clarendon Press, 1983).
J. W. Gray, "The Problem of Papal Power in the Ecclesiology of St. Bernard," *Transactions of the Royal Historical Society* 24 (1974), pp. 1–17.
John R. Sommerfeldt, *On the Spirituality of Relationship* (Mahwah, NJ: Paulist Press, 2004).

4   Isaac of Stella (c. 1100–1169)

For much of Catholic ecclesiology, Mary has functioned imaginatively in ways that mediate fundamental beliefs about the nature of the church. Indeed, she is frequently treated as an archetype for the church so that what is said of her is also said of the church, and vice-versa, as demonstrated by this excerpt from Isaac of Stella. Isaac lived during the reforms of Bernard of Clairvaux and was a philosopher and Cistercian abbot of Etoile ("Stella" in Latin). In the twentieth century, Vatican II would explicitly link Mariology and ecclesiology in ways that recall Isaac's words as it sought to avoid a purely institutional notion of the church and instead highlight its more human and personal dimensions.

Sermon 61, "On the Assumption"

Source: Henri de Lubac, S.J., *Catholicism: Christ and the Common Destiny of Man.*

Head and Body: one single whole, Christ: of one God in heaven and one mother on earth. Sons both many and one: for as the head and members are one son, as well as more than one, so Mary and the Church are one mother and more than one, one virgin and more than one.

Each of the two is mother, each of the two is virgin. Each conceives by the same spirit without carnal attraction, each without sin brings forth an offspring to God the Father. Mary without sin provides the head for the body: the Church by the remission of all sins provides the body for the head. Each is the mother of Christ, but neither gives birth to the whole without the other.

Therefore, in the divinely inspired Scripture, what is said universally of the Church, virgin and mother, is also said individually of Mary; and what is said in a special way of Mary, virgin and mother, is understood by right, but in a general way, of the Church, virgin and mother: so that, when the Scripture is understood to be speaking of either, it can be applied to one or the other almost indifferently and in a mixed manner.

Also each faithful soul is the spouse of the Word of God, the mother, daughter, and sister of Christ. Each faithful soul is understood in its own sense to be virgin and fruitful.

The same thing is therefore said universally for the Church, in a special way for Mary, individually for the faithful soul: and it is the Wisdom of God who speaks, the Word of the Father.

… It is also said: "And I shall dwell in the heritage of the Lord." For the heritage of the Lord, in a universal sense, is the Church, in a special sense, Mary, in an individual sense, each faithful soul.

Christ dwelt for nine months in the tabernacle of Mary's womb. He dwells till the end of the world in the tabernacle of the Church's faith. He will dwell forever and ever in the knowledge and love of the faithful soul.

For further reading

Anglican–Roman Catholic International Commission, *Mary: Grace and Hope in Christ* (Ottawa, ON: Novalis, 2005).

Dániel Deme, *The Selected Works of Isaac of Stella: A Cistercian Voice from the Twelfth Century* (Aldershot: Ashgate, 2007).

Elizabeth Johnson, *Truly Our Sister: A Theology of Mary in the Communion of Saints* (New York: Continuum, 2003).

Hans Küng and Jürgen Moltmann (eds.), *Mary in the Churches* (New York: Seabury, 1983).

Rosemary Radford Ruether, *Mary, the Feminine Face of the Church* (Philadelphia: Westminster, 1977).

Hans Urs von Balthasar, *Mary for Today* (San Francisco: Ignatius Press, 1988).

Hans Urs von Balthasar and Joseph Cardinal Ratzinger (Pope Benedict XVI), *Mary: The Church at the Source*, trans. Adrian Walker (San Francisco: Ignatius Press, 2005).

5   Hildegard of Bingen (1098–1179)

Hildegard was the German founder and abbess of a Benedictine community. She gained considerable renown as a public preacher and writer, leaving behind a wide range of visionary, prophetic, speculative, and even scientific works. Both ecclesiastical and secular rulers consulted with her. Her Scivias *(shortened from the Latin* Scito vias Domini, *"Know the Ways of the Lord") are a three-part collection of visions experienced by Hildegard that contain allegories of the Christian faith followed by theological interpretation and commentary. The two visions excerpted here are among her most ecclesiological and rely heavily on marital, maternal, and birth imagery to paint a picture of the church's majesty, sanctity, inviolability, and relationship to Christ her spouse.*

Scivias (1152)

Source: Columba Hart and Jane Bishop (trans.), *Hildegard of Bingen: Scivias, Classics of Western Spirituality.*

Book II, vision 3

After this I saw the image of a woman as large as a great city, with a wonderful crown on her head and arms from which a splendor hung like sleeves, shining from Heaven to earth. Her womb was pierced like a net with many openings, with a huge multitude of people running in and out. She had no legs or feet, but stood balanced on her womb in front of the altar that stands before the eyes of God, embracing it with her outstretched hands and gazing sharply with her eyes throughout all of Heaven. I could not make out her attire, except that she was arrayed in great splendor and gleamed with lucid serenity, and on her breast shone a red glow like the dawn; and I heard a sound of all kinds of music singing about her, "Like the dawn, greatly sparkling."

And that image spreads out its splendor like a garment, saying, "I must conceive and give birth!" And at once, like lightning, there hastened to her a multitude of angels, making steps and seats within her for people, by whom the image was to be perfected.

Then I saw black children moving in the air near the ground like fishes in water, and they entered the womb of the image through the openings that pierced it. But she groaned, drawing them upward to her head, and they went out by her mouth, while she remained untouched. And behold, that serene light with the figure of a man in it, blazing with a glowing fire, which I had seen in my previous vision, again appeared to me, and stripped the black skin off each of them and threw it away; and it clothed each of them in a pure white garment and opened to them the serene light, saying to them one by one:

"Cast off the old injustice, and put on the new sanctity. For the gate of your inheritance is unlocked for you. Consider, therefore, how you have been taught, that you may know your Father Whom you have confessed. I have received you, and you have confessed Me. Now, therefore, behold the two paths, one to the East and the other to the North. If you will diligently contemplate Me with your inner vision, as in faith you have been taught, I will receive you into My kingdom. And if you love Me rightly, I will do whatever you shall wish. But if you despise Me and turn away from Me, looking backward and not seeking to know or understand Me, Who am recalling you by pure penitence though you are filthy with sin, and if you run back to the Devil as to your father, then perdition will take you; for you will be judged according to your works, since when I gave you the good you did not choose to know Me."

But the children who had passed through the womb of the image walked in the splendor that surrounded her. And she, benignly gazing on them, said in a sad voice, "These children of mine will return again to dust. I conceive and bear many who oppress me, their mother, by heretical, schismatic and useless battles, by robberies and murders, by adultery and fornication, and by many such errors. Many of these rise again in true penitence to eternal life, but many fall in false obduracy to eternal death."

And again I heard the voice from Heaven saying to me: "The great edifice of living souls, which is constructed in Heaven from living stones, is adorned with the immense beauty of its children's virtues, encircling them as a great city encircles its immense throngs of people, or as a wide net does a multitude of fishes; and however much the work of the faithful thrives in the Christian name, by so much does it blossom with celestial virtues."

1. The building of the church, who redeems her children by Spirit and water

Wherefore now you *see the image of a woman as large as a great city*; this designates the Bride of my Son, who always bears her children by regeneration in the Spirit and in water, for the strong Warrior founded her on a wide base of virtue, that she might hold and perfect the great crowd of His elect; and no enemy can conquer or storm her. She expels unbelief and expands belief, by which it should be understood that in the mortal world each of the faithful is an example to his neighbor, and so they do great works of virtue in Heaven. And when the just, one by one, shall come to join the children of light, the good they have worked will appear in them, which cannot be seen here among mortal ashes, concealed as it is by the shadow of trouble. ...

4. On the maternal kindness of the church

Her womb is pierced like a net with many openings, with a huge multitude of people running in and out; that is, she displays her maternal kindness which is so clever at capturing faithful souls by diverse goads of virtue, and in which the trusting peoples devoutly lead their lives by the faith of their true belief. But He Who casts the net to capture the fishes is My Son, the Bridegroom of His beloved Church, whom He betrothed to Himself in His blood to repair the fall of lost humanity.

5. The church, not yet perfected, will be brought to perfection near the end

She does not yet have legs or feet, for she has not yet been brought to the full strength, of her constancy or the full purity of her fulfillment for when the son of perdition comes to delude the world she will suffer; fiery and bloody anguish in all her members from his cruel wickedness. By this calamity, with bleeding wounds, she will be brought to perfection; then let her run swiftly into the heavenly Jerusalem, where she will sweetly rise anew as a bride in the blood of My Son, entering into life with ardor in the joy of her offspring.

12. Those regenerated by the church their mother in the faith of the Trinity

Then you see black children moving in the air near the ground like fishes in water, and they enter the womb of the image through the openings that pierce it. This signifies the blackness of those foolish people who are not yet washed in the bath of salvation, but love earthly things and run about doing them, building their dwelling on their unsteadiness; they come at last to the mother of holiness, contemplate the dignity of her secrets and receive her blessing, by which they are snatched from the Devil and restored to God. Thus they enter the confines of the churchly order in which the faithful person is blessed by salvation, when he says within himself, "I believe in God," and the rest of the articles of faith.

But she groans, drawing them upward to her head, and they go out by her mouth, while she remains untouched. For this blessed mother sighs inwardly when baptism is celebrated by the sacred anointing of the Holy Spirit, because the person is renewed by the true circumcision of the Spirit and water, and thus offered to the Supreme Beatitude Who is the Head of all, and made a member of Christ, regenerated unto salvation by invocation of the Holy Trinity. But in this that mother suffers no hurt, for she will remain forever in the wholeness of virginity, which is the Catholic faith; for she arose in the blood of the true Lamb, her intimate Bridegroom, Who was born of the untouched Virgin without any corruption of integrity. So too that Bride will remain untouched, so that no schism can corrupt her. ...

And thus the Church is the virginal mother of all Christians, since by the mystery of the Holy Spirit she conceives and bears them, offering them to God so that they are called the children of God. And as the Holy Spirit overshadowed the Blessed Mother, so that she miraculously conceived and painlessly bore the Son of God and yet remained a virgin, so does the Holy Spirit illumine the Church, happy mother of believers, so that without any corruption she conceives and bears children naturally, yet remains a virgin.

Book II, vision 6

And after these things I saw the Son of God hanging on the cross, and the aforementioned image of a woman coming forth like a bright radiance from the ancient counsel. By divine power she was led to Him, and raised herself upward so that she was sprinkled by the blood from His side; and thus, by the will of the Heavenly Father, she was joined with Him in happy betrothal and nobly dowered with His body and blood.

And I heard the voice from Heaven saying to Him: "May she, O Son, be your Bride for the restoration of My people; may she be a mother to them, regenerating souls through the salvation of the Spirit and water."

1. The Church was joined to Christ in His Passion and dowered with His Blood

When Jesus Christ, the true Son of God, hung on the tree of His passion, the Church, joined to Him in the secret mysteries of heaven, was dowered with His crimson blood; as she herself shows when she often approaches the altar and reclaims her wedding gift, carefully noting with what degree of devotion her children receive it when they come to the divine mysteries. Therefore you see *the Son of God hanging on the cross, and the aforementioned image of a woman coming forth like a bright radiance from the ancient counsel; and by divine power she is led to Him.* For when the innocent Lamb was lifted up on the altar of the cross for human salvation, the Church suddenly appeared in Heaven by a profound mystery, in purity of faith and all the other virtues; and by the Supreme majesty she was joined to the Only-Begotten of God. What does this mean? That when blood flowed from the wounded side of My Son, at once salvation of souls came into being; for the glory from which the Devil and his followers were driven out was given to humanity when my Only-Begotten suffered temporal death on the cross, despoiled Hell and led the faithful souls to Heaven. Therefore, in His disciples and their sincere followers faith began to increase and strengthen, so that they became heirs of the celestial Kingdom. Hence that image *raises herself upward so that she is sprinkled by the blood from His side; and thus, by the will of the heavenly Father, she is joined with Him in happy betrothal.* For when the strength of the Passion of the Son of God flows burningly forth and rises to the height of the celestial mysteries, as the perfume of the spices diffuses itself upward, the Church, fortified by that strength in the pure heirs of the eternal Kingdom, is faithfully joined by the high Father's decision to the Only-Begotten of God. How? As a bride, subjected to her bridegroom in her offering of subordination and obedience, receives from him a gift of fertility and a pact of love for procreating children, and educates them as to their inheritance. So too the Church, joined to the Son of God in the exercise of humility and charity, receives from Him the regeneration of the Spirit and water to save souls and restore life, and sends those souls to heaven.

Therefore *she is nobly dowered with His body and blood*; for the Only-Begotten of God conferred His body and blood in surpassing glory on His faithful, who are the Church and her children, that through Him they may have life in the celestial city.

For further reading

Catherine of Siena, *The Dialogue*, trans. Suzanne Noffke (New York: Paulist Press, 1980).

Sabina Flanagan, *Hildegard of Bingen: A Visionary Life* (London: Routledge, 1998).

Barbara Newman, *St. Hildegard's Theology of the Feminine* (Berkeley: University of California Press, 1989).

Barbara Newman (ed.), *Voice of the Living Light: Hildegard of Bingen and Her World* (Berkeley: University of California Press, 1998).

6 Innocent III (1160–1216)

Under Innocent III, the papacy reached enormous power, authority, and wealth through international diplomacy, excommunication, and violent campaigns against heresy and infidelity. The decree from which the following excerpt is taken is a prime example of the theologically rationalized relationship between church and state in the High Middle Ages.

Sicut universitatis conditor (1198)

Source: Oliver J. Thatcher and Edgar Holmes McNeal, *A Source Book for Mediaeval History*.

As God, the creator of the universe, set two great lights in the firmament of heaven, the greater light to rule the day, and the lesser light to rule the night (Gen. 1:15–16), so He set two great dignities in the firmament of the universal church … the greater to rule the day, that is, souls, and the lesser to rule the night, that is, bodies. These dignities are the papal authority and the royal power. And just as the moon gets her light from the sun, and is inferior to the sun in quality, quantity, position, and effect, so the royal power gets the splendor of its dignity from the papal authority.

For further reading

Brenda Bolton, *Innocent III: Studies on Papal Authority and Pastoral Care* (Aldershot: Ashgate, 1995).

John C. Moore, *Pope Innocent III (1160/61–1216): To Root Up and To Plant* (Notre Dame: University of Notre Dame Press, 2009).

James M. Powell, *Innocent III: Vicar of Christ or Lord of the World?* 2nd edn. (Washington, D.C.: Catholic University of America Press, 1994).

7   Fourth Lateran Council (1215)

Convoked by Innocent III, the Fourth Lateran Council is considered the twelfth ecumenical council and widely viewed as the most significant of the medieval councils, attended as it was by numerous bishops and patriarchs. In Canon I, from which the following excerpt is taken, we find a thorough presentation of medieval catholic ecclesiology including, notably, the doctrine of transubstantiation, which taught that the wine and bread are literally transformed into the body and blood of Christ.

Canon I: The Creed, The Church, The Sacraments, and Transubstantiation

Source: H. J. Schroeder, *Disciplinary Decrees of the General Councils: Text, Translation and Commentary.*

There is one Universal Church of the faithful, outside of which there is absolutely no salvation. In which there is the same priest and sacrifice, Jesus Christ, whose body and blood are truly contained in the sacrament of the altar under the forms of bread and wine; the bread being changed (*transubstantiatis*) by divine power into the body, and the wine into the blood, so that to realize the mystery of unity we may receive of Him what He has received of us. And this sacrament no one can effect except the priest who has been duly ordained in accordance with the keys of the Church, which Jesus Christ Himself gave to the Apostles and their successors.

But the sacrament of baptism, which by the invocation of each Person of the Trinity, namely of the Father, Son, and Holy Ghost, is effected in water, duly conferred on children and adults in the form prescribed by the Church by anyone whatsoever, leads to salvation. And should anyone after the reception of baptism have fallen into sin, by true repentance he can always be restored. Not only virgins and those practicing chastity, but also those united in marriage, through the right faith and through works pleasing to God, can merit eternal salvation.

For further reading

Henri de Lubac, S.J., *Corpus Mysticum: The Eucharist and the Church in the Middle Ages* (Notre Dame: University of Notre Dame Press, 2006).
Joseph F. Kelly, *The Ecumenical Councils of the Catholic Church* (Collegeville, MN: The Liturgical Press, 2009).
Terence Nichols, "Transubstantiation and Eucharistic Presence," *Pro Ecclesia* 11/1 (2002), pp. 57–75.

8 Thomas Aquinas (1225–1274)

Aquinas left no systematic account of the church as such. Yet his ecclesiological vision pervades his theology and rests on a grand synthesis of the spiritual, soteriological, and sacramental dimensions of the church with its institutional and hierarchical dimensions. That synthesis both exemplified the scholastic approach of the medieval universities and would influence the church's self-understanding for generations. In the excerpts below, Aquinas employs two of his most commonly used terms to describe the church: the mystical body of Christ and a congregation of believers.[1] For Aquinas, because of Christ's headship and the church's animation by the Holy Spirit, the church is a means of grace, with its many diverse members having been formed into a united body characterized by universality, equality, love, holiness, growth in grace, unfaltering strength, and unerring truth.

Exposition on the Apostles' Creed (c. 1273)

Source: Joseph B. Collins (trans), *Catechetical Instructions of St. Thomas.*

We see that in a man there are one soul and one body; and of his body there are many members. So also the Catholic Church is one body and has different members. The soul which animates this body is the Holy Spirit. Hence, after confessing our faith in the Holy Ghost, we are bid to believe in the Holy Catholic Church. Thus, in the [Creed] it is said, "the Holy Catholic Church."

It must be known that "church" is the same as assembly. So, the Holy Church is the same as the assembly of the faithful, and every Christian is a member of this Church, of which it is written: "Draw near to Me, ye unlearned; and gather yourselves together into the house of discipline" (Ecclus. 51:31). The Church has four essential conditions, in that she is one, holy, catholic, and strong and firm.

The unity of the church
Of the first, it must be known that the Church is one. Although various heretics have founded various sects, they do not belong to the Church, since they are but so many divisions. Of her it is said: "One is My dove; My perfect one is but one" (Song 6:9). The unity of the Church arises from three sources:

1. *The unity of faith.* All Christians who are of the body of the Church believe the same doctrine. "I beseech you … that you all speak the same thing and that there be no schisms among you" (1 Cor. 1:10). And: "One Lord, one faith, one baptism" (Eph. 4:5);

---

[1]   Joseph P. Wawrykow, *The Westminster Handbook to Thomas Aquinas* (Louisville: Westminster John Knox, 2005), p. 25.

2. *The unity of hope.* All are strengthened in one hope of arriving at eternal life. Hence, the Apostle says: "One body and one Spirit, as you are called in one hope of your calling" (Eph. 4:4);

3. *The unity of charity.* All are joined together in the love of God, and to each other in mutual love: "And the glory which Thou hast given Me, I have given them; that they may be one, as We also are one" (John 17:22). It is clear that this is a true love when the members are solicitous for one another and sympathetic towards each other: "We may in all things grow up in Him who is the head, Christ. From whom the whole body, being compacted, and fitly joined together, by what every joint supplieth, according to the operation in the measure of every part, maketh increase of the body unto the edifying of itself in charity" (Eph. 4:15–16). This is because each one ought to make use of the grace God grants him, and be of service to his neighbor. No one ought to be indifferent to the Church, or allow himself to be cut off and expelled from it; for there is but one Church in which men are saved, just as outside of the ark of Noah no one could be saved.

The holiness of the church

Concerning the second mark, holiness, it must be known that there is indeed another assembly, but it consists of the wicked: "I hate the assembly of the malignant" (Ps. 25:5). But such a one is evil; the Church of Christ, however, is holy: "For the temple of God is holy, which you are" (1 Cor. 3:16). Hence, it is said: "the Holy Church." The faithful of this Church are made holy because of four things:

1. Just as a church is cleansed materially when it is consecrated, so also the faithful are washed in the blood of Christ: "Jesus Christ ... who hath loved us and washed us from our sins in His own blood" (Rev. 1:5). And: "That He might sanctify the people by his blood, suffered without the gate" (Heb. 13:12).

2. Just as there is the anointing of the church, so also the faithful are anointed with a spiritual unction in order to be sanctified. Otherwise they would not be Christians, for Christ is the same as Anointed. This anointing is the grace of the Holy Spirit: "He that confirmeth us with you in Christ and that hath anointed us, is God" (2 Cor. 1:21–2). And: "You are sanctified ... in the name of our Lord Jesus Christ" (1 Cor. 6:11).

3. The faithful are made holy because of the Trinity who dwells in the Church; for wheresoever God dwells, that place is holy. "The place whereon thou standest is holy" (Jos. 5:15). And: "Holiness becometh Thy house, O Lord" (Ps. 93:5).

4. Lastly, the faithful are sanctified because God is invoked in the Church: "But Thou, O Lord, art among us, and Thy name is called upon by us; forsake us not." (Jer. 14:9). Let us, therefore, beware, seeing that we are

thus sanctified, lest by sin we defile our soul which is the temple of God: "Know you not that you are the temple of God and that the Spirit of God dwelleth in you? But if any man violate the temple of God, him shall God destroy" (1 Cor. 3:17).

The catholicity or universality of the church

The Church is Catholic, that is, universal. Firstly, it is universal in place, because it is worldwide. This is contrary to the error of the Donatists. For the Church is a congregation of the faithful; and since the faithful are in every part of the world, so also is the Church: "Your faith is spoken of in the whole world" (Rom. 1:8). And also: "Go ye into the whole world and preach the gospel to every creature" (Mark 16:15). Long ago, indeed, God was known only in Judea; now, however, He is known throughout the entire world. The Church has three parts: one is on earth, one is in heaven, and one is in purgatory. Secondly, the Church is universal in regard to all the conditions of mankind; for no exceptions are made, neither master nor servant, neither man nor woman: "Neither bond nor free; there is neither male nor female" (Gal. 3:28). Thirdly, it is universal in time. Some have said that the Church will exist only up to a certain time. But this is false, for the Church began to exist in the time of Abel and will endure up to the end of the world: "Behold, I am with you all days, even to the consummation of the world" (Matt. 28:20). Nay more, even after the end of the world, it will continue to exist in heaven.

The apostolicity of the church

The Church is firm. A house is said to be firm if it has a solid foundation. The principal foundation of the Church is Christ: "For other foundation no men can lay but that which is laid, which is Christ Jesus" (1 Cor. 3:11). The secondary foundation, however, is the Apostles and their teaching. Therefore, the Church is firm. It is said in the Apocalypse that the city has "twelve foundations," and therein were "written the names of the twelve Apostles" (Rev. 21:14). From this the Church is called Apostolic. Likewise, to indicate this firmness of the Church St. Peter is called the crowning head.

The firmness of a house is evident if, when it is violently struck, it does not fall. The Church similarly can never be destroyed, neither by persecution nor by error. Indeed, the Church grew during the persecutions, and both those who persecuted her and those against whom she threatened completely failed: "And whosoever shall fall upon this stone, shall be broken; but on whomsoever it shall fall, it shall grind him to powder" (Matt. 21:44). As regards errors, indeed, the more errors arise, the more surely truth is made to appear: "Men corrupt in mind, reprobate in faith; but they shall proceed no further" (2 Tim. 3:8–9).

Nor shall the Church be destroyed by the temptations of the demons. For she is like a tower towards which all flee who war against the devil: "The name of the Lord is a strong tower" (Prov. 18:10). The devil, therefore, is chiefly intent on destroying the Church, but he will not succeed, for the Lord has said: "The gates of hell shall not prevail against it" (Matt. 16:18).

This is as if He said: "They shall make war against thee, but they shall not overcome thee." And thus it is that only the Church of Peter (to whom it was given to evangelize Italy when the disciples were sent to preach) was always firm in faith. On the contrary, in other parts of the world there is either no faith at all or faith mixed with many errors. The Church of Peter flourishes in faith and is free from error. This, however, is not to be wondered at, for the Lord has said to Peter: "But I have prayed for thee, that thy faith fail not; and thou, being once converted, confirm thy brethren" (Luke 22:32).

Summa Theologica (c. 1273)

Source: *The Summa Theologica of St. Thomas Aquinas*, trans. Fathers of the English Dominican Province.

As the whole Church is termed one mystic body from its likeness to the natural body of a man, which in divers members has divers acts, as the Apostle teaches (Rom. 12; 1 Cor. 12), so likewise Christ is called the Head of the Church from a likeness with the human head, in which we may consider three things, viz. order, perfection, and power: *Order*, indeed; for the head is the first part of man, beginning from the higher part; and hence it is that every principle is usually called a head. ... *Perfection*, inasmuch as in the head dwell all the senses, both interior and exterior, whereas in the other members there is only touch. ... *Power*, because the power and movement of the other members, together with the direction of them in their acts, is from the head, by reason of the sensitive and motive power there ruling. ... (III.8, art. 1)

The head influences the other members in two ways. First, by a certain intrinsic influence, inasmuch as motive and sensitive force flow from the head to the other members; secondly, by a certain exterior guidance, inasmuch as by sight and the senses, which are rooted in the head, man is guided in his exterior acts. Now the interior influx of grace is from no one save Christ, Whose manhood, through its union with the Godhead, has the power of justifying; but the influence over the members of the Church, as regards their exterior guidance, can belong to others; and in this way others may be called heads of the Church, according to Amos 6:1, "Ye great men, heads of the people"; differently, however, from Christ. (III.8, art. 6)

For further reading

Yves Congar, "The Idea of the Church in St. Thomas Aquinas," in *The Mystery of the Church*, trans. A. V. Littledale, rev. edn. (Baltimore: Helicon Press, 1965), pp. 53–74.

Avery Dulles, "The Church According to Thomas Aquinas," in *A Church to Believe In: Discipleship and the Dynamics of Freedom* (New York: Crossroad, 1982), pp. 149–69.

George Sabra, *Thomas Aquinas' Vision of the Church: Fundamentals of an Ecumenical Ecclesiology* (Mainz: Matthias Grünewald, 1987).

9   Unam Sanctam (1302)

In this bull, Pope Boniface VIII asserted the rights of the papacy against secular authority and in doing so makes some of the strongest assertions ever recorded about the unity of the church and the pope as the supreme head of the church, most notably as regards salvation. The bull was issued in the context of a conflict between the pope and Philip IV, the king of France, which began over the authority of the king to levy taxes from the church and its clergy.

Source: J. H. Robinson, *Readings in European History*.

That there is one holy Catholic and apostolic Church we are impelled by our faith to believe and to hold—this we do firmly believe and openly confess—and outside of this there is neither salvation nor remission of sins, as the bridegroom proclaims in Canticles, "My dove, my undefiled is but one; she is the only one of her mother, she is the choice one of her that bare her" (Song 6:9). The Church represents one mystic body, and of this body Christ is the head; of Christ, indeed, God is the head. In it is one Lord, and one faith, and one baptism. In the time of the flood there was one ark of Noah, prefiguring the one Church, finished in one cubit, having one Noah as steersman and commander. Outside of this all things upon the face of the earth were, as we read, destroyed. This Church we venerate and this alone. … It is that seamless coat of the Lord, which was not rent but fell by lot. Therefore, in this one and only Church there is one body and one head—not two heads as if it were a monster—namely, Christ and Christ's vicar, Peter and Peter's successor; for the Lord said to Peter himself, "Feed my sheep" (John 21:17). "*My* sheep," he said using a general term and not designating these or those sheep, so that we must believe that all the sheep were committed to him. If, then, the Greeks, or others, shall say that they were not entrusted to Peter and his successors, they must perforce admit that they are not of Christ's sheep, as the Lord says in John, "there is one fold, and one shepherd" (John 10:16).

In this Church and in its power are two swords, to wit, a spiritual and a temporal, and this we are taught by the words of the Gospel; for when the apostles said, "Behold, here are two swords" (Luke 22:38) (in the Church, namely, since the apostles were speaking), the Lord did not reply that it was too many, but enough. And surely he who claims that the temporal sword is not in the power of Peter has but ill understood the word of our Lord when he said, "Put up again thy sword into his place" (Matt. 26:52). Both the spiritual and the material swords, therefore, are in the power of the Church, the latter indeed to be used for the Church, the former by the Church, the one by the priest, the other by the hand of kings and soldiers, but by the will and sufferance of the priest.

It is fitting, moreover, that one sword should be under the other, and the temporal authority subject to the spiritual power. For when the apostle said, "there is no power but of God: the powers that be are ordained of God," they would not be ordained unless one sword were under the other, and one, as inferior, was brought back by the other to the highest place. ... Therefore, if the earthly power shall err, it shall be judged by the spiritual power; if the lesser spiritual power err, it shall be judged by the higher. But if the supreme power err, it can be judged by God alone and not by man, the apostles bearing witness saying, "The spiritual man judges all things, but he himself is judged by no one." Hence this power, although given to man and exercised by man, is not human, but rather a divine power, given by the divine lips to Peter, and founded on a rock for him and his successors in him (Christ) whom he confessed, the Lord saying to Peter himself, "Whatsoever thou shalt bind," etc.

Whoever, therefore shall resist this power, ordained by God, resists the ordination of God, unless there should be two beginnings [i.e. principles], as the Manichaean imagines. But this we judge to be false and heretical, since, by the testimony of Moses, not in the *beginnings*, but in the *beginning*, God created the heaven and the earth. We, moreover, proclaim, declare, and pronounce that it is altogether necessary to salvation for every human being to be subject to the Roman pontiff.

For further reading

Roger Collins, "False Guilt-Ridden Babylon," in *Keepers of the Keys: A History of the Papacy* (New York: Basic Books, 2009), pp. 272–96.
Brian Tierney, *The Crisis of Church and State, 1050–1300* (Englewood Cliffs, NJ: Prentice-Hall, 1964).

10   Marsilius of Padua (1324)

Defensor pacis ("Defender of the Peace") was a tremendously significant and controversial document, when it appeared early in the fourteenth century, having been drawn up by Marsilius of Padua, an Italian physician and theologian. Censured by popes and hailed by monarchs and emperors, the document divides sharply between the authority and power of the secular state, which is the defender of peace, and the authority of the church along with its popes, bishops, and clergy. Marsilius argues his position on theological grounds, for according to him, Christ rejected wealth, property, and temporal things, and excluded both himself and his apostles from "every office of rulership, contentious jurisdiction, government, or coercive judgment in this world" (IV: 4). *Likewise the church and its leaders should submit themselves to lawful secular authority and to the will of the people, who are the source of all governing authority. Only in this way can peace and tranquility obtain in the world. The following is a listing of Marsilius's conclusions.*

Defensor pacis

Source: Oliver J. Thatcher and Edgar Holmes McNeal (eds.), *A Source Book for Mediaeval History*.

1. The one divine canonical Scripture, the conclusions that necessarily follow from it, and the interpretation placed upon it by the common consent of Christians, are true, and belief in them is necessary to the salvation of those to whom they are made known.
2. The general council of Christians or its majority alone has the authority to define doubtful passages of the divine law, and to determine those that are to be regarded as articles of the Christian faith, belief in which is essential to salvation; and no partial council or single person of any position has the authority to decide these questions.
3. The gospels teach that no temporal punishment or penalty should be used to compel observance of divine commandments.
4. It is necessary to salvation to obey the commandments of the new divine law [the New Testament] and the conclusions that follow necessarily from it and the precepts of reason; but it is not necessary to salvation to obey all the commandments of the ancient law [the Old Testament].
5. No mortal has the right to dispense with the commands or prohibitions of the new divine law; but the general council and the Christian "legislator" alone have the right to prohibit things which are permitted by the new law, under penalties in this world or the next, and no partial council or single person of any position has that right.
6. The whole body of citizens or its majority alone is the human "legislator."
7. Decretals and decrees of the bishop of Rome, or of any other bishops or body of bishops, have no power to coerce anyone by secular penalties or punishments, except by the authorization of the human "legislator."
8. The "legislator" alone or the one who rules by its authority has the power to dispense with human laws.
9. The elective principality or other office derives its authority from the election of the body having the right to elect, and not from the confirmation or approval of any other power.
10. The election of any prince or other official, especially one who has the coercive power, is determined solely by the expressed will of the "legislator."
11. There can be only one supreme ruling power in a state or kingdom.

12. The number and the qualifications of persons who hold state offices and all civil matters are to be determined solely by the Christian ruler according to the law or approved custom.

13. No prince, still more, no partial council or single person of any position, has full authority and control over other persons, laymen or clergy, without the authorization of the "legislator."

14. No bishop or priest has coercive authority or jurisdiction over any layman or clergyman, even if he is a heretic.

15. The prince who rules by the authority of the "legislator" has jurisdiction over the persons and possessions of every single mortal of every station, whether lay or clerical, and over every body of laymen or clergy.

16. No bishop or priest or body of bishops or priests has the authority to excommunicate anyone or to interdict the performance of divine services, without the authorization of the "legislator."

17. All bishops derive their authority in equal measure immediately from Christ, and it cannot be proved from the divine law that one bishop should be over or under another, in temporal or spiritual matters.

18. The other bishops, singly or in a body, have the same right by divine authority to excommunicate or otherwise exercise authority over the bishop of Rome, having obtained the consent of the "legislator," as the bishop of Rome has to excommunicate or control them.

19. No mortal has the authority to permit marriages that are prohibited by the divine law, especially by the New Testament. The right to permit marriages which are prohibited by human law belongs solely to the "legislator" or to the one who rules by its authority.

20. The right to legitimatize children born of illegitimate union so that they may receive inheritances, or other civil or ecclesiastical offices or benefits, belongs solely to the "legislator."

21. The "legislator" alone has the right to promote to ecclesiastical orders, and to judge of the qualifications of persons for these offices, by a coercive decision, and no priest or bishop has the right to promote anyone without its authority.

22. The prince who rules by the authority of the laws of Christians has the right to determine the number of churches and temples, and the number of priests, deacons, and other clergy who shall serve in them.

23. "Separable" ecclesiastical offices [those not essential to the clergy] may be conferred or taken away only by the authority of the "legislator"; the same is true of ecclesiastical benefices and other property devoted to pious purposes.

24. No bishop or body of bishops has the right to establish notaries or other civil officials.

25. No bishop or body of bishops may give permission to teach or practice in any profession or occupation, but this right belongs to the Christian "legislator" or to the one who rules by its authority.

26. In ecclesiastical offices and benefices those who have received consecration as deacons or priests, or have been otherwise irrevocably dedicated to God, should be preferred those who have not been thus consecrated.

27. The human "legislator" has the right to use ecclesiastical temporalities for the common public good and defense after the needs of the priests and clergy, the expenses of divine worship, and the necessities of the poor have been satisfied.

28. All properties established for pious purposes or for works of mercy, such as those that are left by will for the making of a crusade, the redeeming of captives, or the support of the poor, and similar purposes, may be disposed of by the prince alone according to the decision of the "legislator" and the purpose of the testator or giver.

29. The Christian "legislator" alone has the right to forbid or permit the establishment of religious orders or houses.

30. The prince alone, acting in accordance with the laws of the "legislator," has the authority to condemn heretics, delinquents, and all others who should endure temporal punishment, to inflict bodily punishment upon them, and to exact fines from them.

31. No subject who is bound to another by a legal oath may be released from his obligation by any bishop or priest, unless the "legislator" has decided by a coercive decision that there is just cause for it.

32. The general council of all Christians alone has the authority to create a metropolitan bishop or church, and to reduce him or it from that position.

33. The Christian "legislator" or the one who rules by its authority over Christian states, alone has the right to convoke either a general or local council of priests, bishops, and other Christians, by coercive power; and no man may be compelled by threats of temporal or spiritual punishment to obey the decrees of a council convoked in any other way.

34. The general council of Christians or the Christian "legislator" alone has the authority to ordain fasts and other prohibitions of the use of food; the council or "legislator" alone may prohibit the practice of mechanical arts or teaching which divine law permits to be practiced on any day, and the "legislator" or the one who rules by its authority alone may constrain men to obey the prohibition by temporal penalties.

35. The general council of Christians alone has the authority to canonize anyone or to order anyone to be adored as a saint.

36. The general council of Christians alone has the authority to forbid the marriage of priests, bishops, and other clergy, and to make other laws concerning ecclesiastical discipline, and that council or the one to whom it delegates its authority alone may dispense with these laws.

37. It is always permitted to appeal to the "legislator" from a coercive decision rendered by a bishop or priest with the authorization of the "legislator."

38. Those who are pledged to observe complete poverty may not have in their possession any immovable property, unless it be with the fixed intention of selling it as soon as possible and giving the money to the poor; they

may not have such rights in either movable or immovable property as would enable them, for example, to recover them by a coercive decision from any person who should take or try to take them away.

39. The people as a community and as individuals, according to their several means, are required by divine law support the bishops and other clergy authorized by the gospel, so that they may have food and clothing and the other necessaries of life; but the people are not required to pay tithes or other taxes beyond the amount necessary for such support.

40. The Christian "legislator" or the one who rules by its authority has the right to compel bishops and other clergy to live in the province under its control and whom it supplies with the necessities of life, to perform divine services and administer the sacrament.

41. The bishop of Rome and any other ecclesiastical or spiritual minister may be advanced to a "separable" ecclesiastical office only by the Christian "legislator" or the one who rules by its authority, or by the general council of Christians; and they may be suspended from or deprived of office by the same authority.

For further reading

George Garnett, *Marsilius of Padua and "the Truth of History"* (Oxford: Oxford University Press, 2006).

Alan Gewirth, *Marsilius of Padua: The Defender of Peace*, 2 vols. (New York: Columbia University Press, 1951).

Gerson Moreno-Riano (ed.), *The World of Marsilius of Padua* (Tunhout: Brepols, 2006).

11   William of Ockham (1285–1347)

William of Ockham and others broke with Pope John XXII, whom they took to be a pseudo-pope and guilty of heresy. Ockham was excommunicated in 1328. Ockham does not go as far as Marsilius in subordinating the authority of the pope to the secular rulers; indeed, he affirms the divine authority and origin of the offices of bishop and pope.[2] At the same time, he argues for a limited and relativized understanding of papal and episcopal offices, power, and structures in relationship to the faith of the church as a whole and as accumulated throughout the ages. It is this church as the mystical body (corpus mysticum) of Christ to which God has given authority, and what God has "promised to the whole ... should not be attributed to any part, even the more important." Therefore, church law, the pope, bishops, and councils are always subject to the judgment of the universal church, and no one individual or group of

---

[2]   See John J. Ryan, *The Nature, Structure, and Function of the Church in William of Ockham* (Missoula, MT: Scholar's Press, 1979).

individuals in the church is above error or incapable of heresy. Ockham is not entirely a "conciliarist" (those who held that the pope is subordinate to councils in matters of faith). But his ecclesiology both represents and shapes views that were increasingly becoming prominent at the time.

Short Discourse Concerning the Tyrannical Government (c. 1343)

Source: William of Ockham, *A Short Discourse on the Tyrannical Government*, ed. Arthur Stephen McGrade; trans. John Kilcullen.

But if the pope had by Christ's precept and ordinance such fullness of power that in temporal and spiritual matters he could by right do without exception anything not against divine or natural law, then Christ's law would involve a most horrendous servitude, incomparably greater than that of the Old Law. For all Christians—emperors and kings, and absolutely all their subjects— would be in the strictest sense of the term the pope's slaves, because there never was nor will be by right anyone with more power over any man whatever than power over him in respect of all things not against natural or divine law. ... The above assertion must therefore be regarded as heretical. And it is also dangerous to all Christendom. For if the pope had such fullness of power in temporal matters he could by right despoil all kings and rulers of their kingdoms and lordships and confer them on his relatives or any other low persons he pleased, or keep them for himself; this could easily give rise to schisms, dissensions, and wars dangerous to all Christendom. ...

The pope is the spouse of the Church. But a spouse or husband does not have fullness of power over his spouse, because she is not a maidservant, and in many things is judged to be entitled to equality. Therefore, neither does the pope have such fullness of power over the Church. ...

[Christ] gave blessed Peter the right to receive unbelievers by baptism into the Church militant, and also the right of "feeding" the Church militant, but not of being its lord. In respect of the Church triumphant, also, he did not give him lordship, but in a certain way gave him a certain right relating to it, for he gave him the right of in some way absolving from sins, and one absolved from sin is worthy of being led into the Church triumphant. He gave him also a right of teaching and training members of the Church militant in good works, by which ... the gates of the Church triumphant are opened.

For further reading

John J. Ryan, *The Nature, Structure, and Function of the Church in William of Ockham* (Missoula, MT: Scholars Press, 1979).

John B. Morrall, "Ockham and Ecclesiology," in John A. Watt, John B. Morrall, and F. X. Martin, O.S.A., *Medieval Studies Presented to Aubrey Gwynn* (Dublin: Colm O Lochlainn, 1961), pp. 481–92.

William of Ockham, *The Letter to the Friars Minor and Other Writings*, ed. Arthur Stephen McGrade and John Kilcullen; trans. John Kilcullen (Cambridge: Cambridge University Press, 1995).

12 John Wyclif (1328–1384)

As a forerunner to the Protestant Reformation, John Wyclif is of enormous ecclesiological significance. Wyclif attacked the wealth, incompetence, and low moral standards of the clergy. He also became an outspoken critic of the papacy, transubstantiation, worship of relics, and prayers to the saints. In the following excerpt from his treatise on the church, Wyclif offers his tripartite understanding of the church and argues that no one, not even the pope, can know with certainty if he or she is among those who will be saved.

The Church and Her Members (c. 1384)

Source: Thomas Arnold (ed.), *Select English Works of John Wyclif.*

Christ's church is his spouse and has three parts. The first part is in bliss with Christ, head of the church, and contains angels and blessed ones who are now in heaven. The second part of the church is the saints in purgatory, and these do not commit new sins, but purge their old sins. Many errors have arisen from praying for these saints, and since they all are dead in body, Christ's words may be applied to them: "we follow Christ as our life, and let the dead bury the dead." The third part of the church is composed of the true ones who live here, who shall afterwards be saved in heaven, and who live here the life of the Christian. The first part is called the over-coming, the middle is called the sleeping, and the third is called the Church militant. And all these make one church, and the head of this church is Jesus Christ, both God and human. This church is mother to everyone who shall be saved, and contains no other members except those who shall be saved.

For as Christ vouchsafes to call this Church his spouse, so he calls those cursed who are devils, as was Iscariot. And far be it from Christians to grant that Christ has wedded the devil; since Paul says, in our belief, that Christ does not commune with Belial. And here we take it as a matter of belief that each member of holy Church shall be saved with Christ, just as each member of the devil is damned. Therefore, while we are fighting here and do not know whether we shall be saved, we do not know whether we are members of holy Church. For just as it is God's will concerning these three parts of the Church, that we cannot distinguish them with certainty, so with good reason he wills that we do not know whether we are of the Church. But as each of us may hope that we shall be saved in bliss, so we should suppose that we are limbs of holy Church; and thus should love holy Church and worship it as our mother.

And because of this hope, which does not rise to the level of belief, two sins should be put to flight: pride and covetousness, which arise because of a confidence in being members of holy Church. For no pope that lives knows whether he is a member of the Church or whether he is a limb of the devil, to be damned with Lucifer. And thus it is a blind folly that people should fight for the pope more than they fight for the faith; for they are actually fighting for the devil. And we take this as a matter of faith, or at least consonant with the faith, that none of us living knows whether he or she shall be saved or damned, although we may hope, short of belief, that we shall be saved in heaven.

For further reading

William E. Farr, "Wyclif's Emerging Ecclesiology," in *John Wyclif as Legal Reformer* (Leiden: E. J. Brill, 1974), pp 22–41.
Stephen E. Lahey, *John Wyclif* (Oxford: Oxford University Press, 2009).
Herbert B. Workman, *John Wyclif: A Study of the English Medieval Church*, 2 vols. (Oxford: Clarendon Press, 1926).
John Wyclif, "The Pastoral Office," in *Advocates of Reform: From Wyclif to Erasmus*, ed. Matthew Spinka (Philadelphia: Westminster, 2006).

13   Jan Hus (1369–1415)

Jan Hus was a Czech priest and theologian who was influenced by the teachings of Wyclif and likewise preached on the need for reform in the church. Hus, who was especially critical of the sale of indulgences and the moral laxity of the clergy, wrote his treatise on the church in 1413, some two years prior to his arrest, imprisonment, and execution at the Council of Constance. In De Ecclesia (On the Church)*, Hus distinguishes between those who merely belong to the church and those who are true members of the church and conform to Christ's law. True membership in the church will only be revealed after death. He asserts the priority of scripture over later ecclesiastical tradition in defining the nature of the church and focuses on Christ as the head of the church as well as the rock upon which it is built. If Peter or a pope has pre-eminence and authority in the church, it is because of their moral virtue and faithfulness. The legitimacy of the pope or bishops can thus become undermined by their infidelity. The church's unity rests not on the pope or the sacraments but on predestinating grace.*

On the Church (1413)

Source: Jan Huss, *The Church*, trans. David S. Schaff.

It having been said what the holy universal church is—that she is only one just as the number of all the predestinate is one, and also that she is distributed in her members throughout all the word—it must be known that this holy universal church is tripartite, that is, divided into the church triumphant, militant and dormient.

The church militant is the number of the predestinate now on its pilgrimage to the heavenly country, and is called militant because it wages Christ's warfare against the flesh, the world and the devil.

The church dormient is the number of the predestinate suffering in purgatory. It is called dormient because being there she does not enjoy the blessedness which in the present life through God's prevenient and assisting grace she merited that she might get her reward in the heavenly country after the satisfaction made in purgatory.

The church triumphant consists of the blessed at rest in the heavenly country who kept up Christ's warfare against Satan and have finally triumphed. There will, however, be one great church on the day of judgment, made up of all these. ...

But this universal church is a virgin, the bride of Christ—who is a virgin—from whom as from a true mother we are spiritually born. A virgin, I say, all beautiful and in whom there is no spot (Song 4:7), "having neither spot nor wrinkle" (Eph. 5:27), holy and immaculate, and so most chaste even as she is in the heavenly country. Nevertheless by fornicating with the adulterant devil and with many of his children she is partially corrupt by wrong-doing. However, she is never received as the bride to be embraced, beatifically at the right hand and in the bed of the bridegroom, until she has become a pure virgin, altogether without wrinkle. For Christ is the bridegroom of virginity, who, as he lives forever, can not allow the bride to desert him and fornicate spiritually. ... Therefore, the whole of Christian doctrine is involved in that prayer of the church in which we pray the bridegroom, by his coming into the flesh, that he may teach us to despise earthly things and love heavenly things—to despise, that is, to subordinate, terrestrial things in our affections and to love Christ the bridegroom above all things.

The unity of the catholic church consists in the unity of predestination, inasmuch as her separate members are one by predestination and in the unity of blessedness, and inasmuch as her separate sons are finally united in bliss. For, in the present time, her unity consists in the unity of faith and the Christian virtues and in the unity of love. ... To this unity the apostle refers, [in] Eph. 4:3: "endeavoring to keep the unity of the Spirit in the bond of peace. There is one body, one Spirit, one Lord, one faith, one baptism, one God and Father of all." Nor is it to be doubted that without this union, as indicated before, is there any salvation. ...

But we know imperfectly and indistinctly enough those who are now pilgrims and those who are sleeping. But when that which is perfect is come that which is in part shall vanish away, because in heaven we shall distinguish our mother clearly and also her individual members. And let not the faithful [Christian] complain but rejoice in the truth that holy mother church is to so great a degree unknown to him here on the way, because over him stands the merit of Christian faith. ...

If we put aside the church, nominally so called and as she is generally esteemed to be, then the church is said to be threefold. In one sense it is the congregation or company of the faithful in respect to what is for a time or in respect to present righteousness alone, and in this sense the reprobate are of the church for the time in which they are in grace. But this church is not Christ's mystical body nor the holy catholic church nor any part of it. In the second sense the church is taken to be the admixture of the predestinate and the reprobate while they are in grace in respect to present righteousness. And this church is in part but not in whole identical with God's holy church. And this church is called mixed in character — grain and chaff, wheat and tares — the kingdom of heaven like unto a net cast into the sea and gathering fish of every kind and the kingdom of heaven like unto ten virgins, of whom five were foolish and five wise, as was said above. ...

In the third sense the church is taken for the company of the predestinate, whether they are in grace in respect to present righteousness or not. In this sense the church is an article of faith, about which the apostle was speaking when he said, [in] Eph. 5:26: "Christ loved the church and gave himself for it, cleansing it by the washing of water in the word of life, that he might present it to himself a glorious church not having spot or wrinkle or any such thing, but that it might be holy and without spot." ...

Neither is the pope the head nor are the cardinals the whole body of the holy, universal, catholic church. For Christ alone is the head of that church, and his predestinate are the body and each one is a member, because his bride is one person with Jesus Christ.

For further reading

Daniel DiDomizio, "Jan Hus's *De Ecclesia*, Precursor of Vatican II?" *Theological Studies* 60 (1999), pp. 247–60.

John Hus, *The Letters of John Hus*, trans. Matthew Spinka (Manchester: Manchester University Press, 1972).

Matthew Spinka, *John Hus' Concept of the Church* (Princeton: Princeton University Press, 1966).

14   Council of Constance (1414–1418)

The Council of Constance ended the papal schism that had produced two popes, each commanding the loyalty of different populations. Ecclesiologically, the council was a high point in the reforming movement that came to be known as "conciliarism," based on the belief that a general council is the highest authority in the church. If the council's document Haec sancta *(also known as* Sacrosancta*) put this belief into words, its later document* Frequens *built in a schedule for regularizing the process of calling for councils.*

Source: Oliver J. Thatcher and Edgar Holmes McNeal, *A Source Book for Mediaeval History*.

Haec sancta (1415)

This holy synod of Constance, being a general council, and legally assembled in the Holy Spirit for the praise of God and for ending the present schism, and for the union and reformation of the church of God in its head and in its members, in order more easily, more securely, more completely, and more fully to bring about the union and reformation of the church of God, ordains, declares, and decrees as follows: And first it declares that this synod, legally assembled, is a general council, and represents the catholic church militant and has its authority directly from Christ; and everybody, of whatever rank or dignity, including also the pope, is bound to obey this council in those things which pertain to the faith, to the ending of this schism, and to a general reformation of the church in its head and members. Likewise it declares that if anyone, of whatever rank, condition, or dignity, including also the pope, shall refuse to obey the commands, statutes, ordinances, or orders of this holy council, or of any other holy council properly assembled, in regard to the ending of the schism and to the reformation of the church, he shall be subject to the proper punishment; and unless he repents, he shall be duly punished; and if necessary, recourse shall be had to other aids of justice.

Frequens (1417)

A good way to till the field of the Lord is to hold general councils frequently, because by them the briers, thorns, and thistles of heresies, errors, and schisms are rooted out, abuses reformed, and the way of the Lord made more fruitful. But if general councils are not held, all these evils spread and flourish. We therefore decree by this perpetual edict that general councils shall be held as follows: The first one shall be held five years after the close of this council, the second one seven years after the close of the first, and forever thereafter one shall be held every ten years. One month before the close of each council the pope, with the approval and consent of the council, shall fix the place for holding the next council. If the pope fails to name the place the council must do so.

For further reading

Francis Oakley, *Council Over Pope? Towards a Provisional Ecclesiology* (New York: Herder and Herder, 1969).
Brian Tierney, *Foundations of the Conciliar Theory: The Contribution of the Medieval Canonists from Gratian to the Great Schism* (Cambridge: Cambridge University Press, 1955).

15   Nicholas of Cusa (1401–1464)

Nicholas of Cusa was a cardinal, philosopher, theologian, papal legate, and a significant defender of the conciliarist cause, as is clear from this excerpt from his work of political theory, The Catholic Concordance. *The work is one of the most important political and ecclesiological treatises of the fifteenth century and was written during the Council of Basel, which dealt with questions of papal supremacy along with the reform movement surrounding Jan Hus. Nicholas wanted to preserve the authority and power of the papacy, which he argued is derived from the free consent and election of humans through the vehicle of councils. Nicholas grounded the relationship between rulers and ruled in a doctrine of human rights based on natural law.*

The Catholic Concordance (1433)

Source: Nicholas of Cusa, *The Catholic Concordance*, ed. and trans. Paul E. Sigmund.

And although we insist that the pope is not the universal bishop but the first over the others, and we base the force of the holy councils not on the pope but on the consent of all, at the same time since we defend truth and maintain the rights of everyone, we rightly give honor to the pope. ...

All legislation is based on natural law and any law which contradicts it cannot be valid. ... Hence since natural law is naturally based on reason, all law is rooted by nature in the reason of man. The wiser and more outstanding men are chosen as rulers by the others to draw up just laws by the clear reason, wisdom, and prudence given them by nature and to rule the others by these laws and to decide controversies for the maintenance of peace. ... From this we conclude that those better endowed with reason are the natural lords and masters of the others but not by any coercive law or judgment imposed on someone against his will. For since all are by nature free, every governance whether it consists in a written law or is living law in the person of a prince— by which subjects are compelled to abstain from evil deeds and their freedom directed towards the good through fear of punishment can only come from the agreement and consent of the subjects. For if by nature men are equal in power and equally free, the true properly ordered authority of one common ruler who is their equal in power cannot be naturally established except by the election and consent of the others and law is also established by consent. ... (bk 2:126–7)

But because those who sit in that see are human beings subject to error and sin, and especially because at present with the world moving towards its end and evil on the increase they abuse their power using what was granted for the building up [of the church] to destroy it, who of sound mind can doubt that without any diminution of the true power and privilege of that see the universal council has power both over abuses and over the one who commits them—to act for the preservation and the well-ordered rule of the whole church? I believe that it is wrong to say that the universal council also cannot take judicial cognizance of, and make decisions concerning the primacy of the Roman church for we read in the records that the Council of Chalcedon expressly involved itself in this and passed judgment on it. Hence it can be said in general that a universal council that represents the Catholic church has power directly from Christ and is in every respect over both the pope and the Apostolic See. ... (bk 2:148)

It is true that the universal council of the Catholic church has supreme power in all things over the Roman pontiff himself. And thus it was necessary to ask what was the authority of the Roman pontiff both as to rulership and as to the power to command and to legislate. And although I have used many arguments, I have emphasized this one—that although according to writings of many of the holy Fathers the power of the Roman pontiff is from God and according to others it comes from man and the universal council, it seems that in fact the intermediate position demonstrable in the Scriptures finally comes to this, that the power of the Roman pontiff as to preeminence, priority, and rulership, is from God by way of man and the councils; namely, by means of elective consent. (bk 2:249)

For further reading

Christopher M. Bellito, Thomas M. Izbicki, and Gerald Christianson (eds.), *Introducing Nicholas of Cusa: A Guide to a Renaissance Man* (New York: Paulist Press, 2004).

Henry Bett, *Nicholas of Cusa* (Merrick, NY: Richwood Publishing, 1976).

Nicholas of Cusa, *Selected Spiritual Writings*, trans. H. Lawrence Bond, Classics of Western Spirituality (Mahwah, NJ: Paulist Press, 1997).

———— *Writings on Church and Reform*, trans. Thomas M. Izbicki, I Tatti Renaissance Library, 33 (Cambridge, MA: Harvard University Press, 2008).

Gerald Christianson and Thomas M. Izbicki, *Nicholas of Cusa on Christ and the Church: Essays in Memory of Chandler McCuskey Brooks for the American Cusanus Society* (Leiden: E. J. Brill, 1996).

16   *Execrabilis* (1460)

Aeneas Silvius was a controversial but influential voice at the Council of Basel and was later made bishop of Siena and then cardinal prior to his election as Pope Pius II in 1458. As a way of putting an end to conciliarism, Pius issued the bull Execrabilis, *in which he condemns both the doctrine that councils are superior to popes and appeals to a council. Opponents of various councils ever since have cited the document.*

Source: Oliver J. Thatcher and Edgar Holmes McNeal, *A Source Book for Mediaeval History*.

The execrable and hitherto unknown abuse has grown up in our day, that certain persons, imbued with the spirit of rebellion, and not from a desire to secure a better judgment, but to escape the punishment of some offence which they have committed, presume to appeal from the pope to a future council, in spite of the fact that the pope is the vicar of Jesus Christ and to him, in the person of St Peter, the following was said: "Feed my sheep" (John 21:16) and "Whatsoever thou shalt bind on earth shall be bound in heaven" (Matt. 16:18). Wishing therefore to expel this pestiferous poison from the church of Christ and to care for the salvation of the flock entrusted to us, and to remove every cause of offence from the fold of our Saviour, with the advice and consent of our brothers, the cardinals of the holy Roman church, and of all the prelates, and of those who have been trained in the canon and civil law, who are at our court, and with our own sure knowledge, we condemn all such appeals and prohibit them as erroneous and detestable.

For further reading

Gerald Christianson, Thomas M. Izbicki, and Christopher M. Bellito, *The Church, The Councils, and Reform* (Washington, D.C.: Catholic University of America Press, 2008).
Thomas M. Izbicki, *Reform, Ecclesiology, and the Christian Life in the Late Middle Ages* (Aldershot: Ashgate, 2008).

17   Martin Luther (1483–1546)

Few individuals have had as large an impact on the modern church as Martin Luther. A German priest and theologian, Luther began by railing against the sale of indulgences (granting remission of sins) to raise money for St. Peter's Basilica in Rome. Luther's theological reflections often stress the inwardness of personal faith in contrast to the mere keeping of church tradition, mechanical performance of ritual, or blind trust of ecclesiastical authorities. Yet Luther believed strongly in the church as the locus of salvation. While his doctrine of justification by faith conditions and re-orients his understanding of the church, the following excerpts reveal the centrality of the church for Luther as a spiritual fellowship with a priesthood made up of all Christians. Luther's emphasis is on the local congregation, and he identifies seven outward practices, or marks, that make the church what it is and render it visible to the world.

To the Christian Nobility of the German Nation Concerning the Reform of the Christian Estate (1520)

Source: Charles M. Jacobs (trans.) and James Atkinson (rev. and ed.), *Luther's Works*.

There is no true, basic difference between laymen and priests, princes and bishops, between religious and secular, except for the sake of office and work, but not for the sake of status. They are all of the spiritual estate, all are truly priests, bishops, and popes. But they do not all have the same work to do. Just as all priests and monks do not have the same work. This is the teaching of St. Paul in Romans 12:4–5 and 1 Corinthians 12:12 and in 1 Peter 2:9, as I have said above, namely, that we are all one body of Christ the Head, and all members one of another. Christ does not have two different bodies, one temporal, the other spiritual. There is but one Head and one body.

Therefore, just as those who are now called "spiritual," that is, priests, bishops, or popes, are neither different from other Christians nor superior to them, except that they are charged with the administration of the word of God and the sacraments, which is their work and office, so it is with the temporal authorities. They bear the sword and rod in their hand to punish the wicked and protect the good. A cobbler, a smith, a peasant—each has the work and office of his trade, and yet they are all alike consecrated priests and bishops. Further, everyone must benefit and serve every other by means of his own work or office so that in this way many kinds of work may be done for the bodily and spiritual welfare of the community, just as all the members of the body serve one another (1 Cor. 12:14–26).

The Gospel for the Early Christmas Service, Luke 2:15–20 (1522)

Source: Hans J. Hillerbrand (trans. and ed.), *Luther's Works*.

It was not without intention that Luke writes: "They found Mary and Joseph and the babe in the manger," mentioning Mary before Joseph and both of them before the infant. As we said above, Mary is the Christian church and Joseph the servant of the church, and this is exactly what the position of the bishops and priests should be when they preach the gospel. The church comes before the prelates of the church, as Christ, too, says in Luke 22:26: "He who wishes to be the greatest among you, must be the least." Nowadays this has been reversed, and one need not be astonished about it because they have rejected the gospel and exalted the babblings of men. The Christian church, on the contrary, keeps all the words of God in her heart and ponders them, compares one with the other and with Holy Scripture. Therefore he who wants to find Christ, must first find the church. How would one know Christ and faith in him if one did not know where they are who believe in him? He who would know something concerning Christ, must neither trust in himself nor build his bridge into heaven by means of his own reason, but he should go to the church; he should attend it and ask his questions there.

The church is not wood and stone but the assembly of people who believe in Christ. With this church one should be connected and see how the people believe, live, and teach. They certainly have Christ in their midst, for outside the Christian church there is no truth, no Christ, no salvation. It follows that the pope or a bishop erroneously claims that he alone should be believed, posing as master; for all of them are in error and may be in error. Their teaching should rather be subject to the assembly of believers. What they teach, should be subject to the judgment and verdict of the congregation; to this judgment one should defer, so that Mary may be found ahead of Joseph and the Church preferred to the preachers. For it is not Joseph but Mary who keeps these words in her heart, who ponders them and keeps them or compares them. (52:39–40)

Concerning the Ministry (1523)

Source: Conrad Bergendoff (trans. and ed.), *Luther's Works.*

First, regard as an unmovable rock that the New Testament knows of no priest who is or can be anointed externally. If there are such, they are imitators and idols. There is neither example nor command nor a simple word in Gospels or Epistles of the apostles in support of this vanity. They are established and brought in only by the kind of human invention of which Jeroboam once was guilty in Israel's history (1 Kgs 12:32–3.). For a priest, especially in the New Testament, was not made but was born. He was created, not ordained. He was born not indeed of flesh, but through a birth of the Spirit, by water and Spirit in the washing of regeneration (John 3:6–7; Tit. 3:5–6). Indeed, all Christians are priests, and all priests are Christians. Worthy of anathema is any assertion that a priest is anything else than a Christian. For such an assertion has no support in the Word of God and is based only on human opinions, on ancient usage, or on the opinions of the majority, any one of which is ineffectual to establish an article of faith without sacrilege and offense, as I have sufficiently shown elsewhere.

Here we take our stand: There is no other Word of God than that which is given all Christians to proclaim. There is no other baptism than the one which any Christian can bestow. There is no other remembrance of the Lord's Supper than that which any Christian can observe and which Christ has instituted. There is no other kind of sin than that which any Christian can bind or loose. There is no other sacrifice than of the body of every Christian. No one but a Christian can pray. No one but a Christian may judge of doctrine. These make the priestly and royal office. Let therefore the papists either prove other functions of the priesthood or let them resign their own. Shaving, anointing, putting on of vestments, and other rites arising out of human superstition, do not convince us otherwise, even were they given by angels from heaven. Much less are we affected by the arguments of ancient use, the opinion of the majority, or of the authority which has been recognized. … In this view of the ministry, the so-called "indelible character" vanishes and the perpetuity of the office is shown to be fictitious. A minister may be deposed if he proves unfaithful. On the other hand he is to be permitted in the ministry as long as he is competent and has the favor of the church as a whole, just as in civil matters any administrator is treated as an equal among his brethren. In fact a spiritual minister is more readily removable than any civil administrator, since if he is unfaithful he should be less tolerable than a civil officer. The latter can be harmful only in matters of this life, whereas the former can be destructive of eternal possessions. Therefore, it is a privilege of the other brethren to excommunicate such a one and substitute someone else.

Such is the firm and dependable foundation of Scripture, if we are to believe the Word of God. … In this Word we see more clearly and surely than by any light or assurance whence priests or ministers of the Word are to be sought, namely, from the flock of Christ alone, and nowhere else. We have clearly shown that to each one is given the right of ministering in the Word, and indeed that he is commanded to do so if he sees that teachers are lacking or if those in office are not teaching correctly, as Paul affirmed in 1 Cor. 14:28–9, so that the power of God might be proclaimed by us all. How much more, then, does not a certain community as a whole have both right and command to commit by common vote such an office to one or more, to be exercised in its stead. With the approval of the community these might then delegate the office to others.

If you are troubled and anxious as to whether or not you are truly a church of God, I would say to you, that a church is not known by customs but by the Word. In 1 Cor. 14:24–5, Paul says that if an unbeliever comes into the church and finds those disclosing the secrets of his heart, he will fall on his face and declare that God is really present there. Of this you can be sure, that the Word of God and knowledge of Christ are richly present among you. And wherever the Word of God and knowledge of Christ are, they are not in vain, however deficient those who have the Word may be in external customs. The church indeed is weak because of its sins. But its fault is not in the Word. It sins indeed, but it does not deny or ignore the Word. We may not, therefore, reject those who accept and confess the Word, even though they do not shine in any splendid sanctity, as long as they do not persist in manifest sins. There is then no reason for you to doubt that the church of God is among you, even if there are only ten or six who have the Word. What such would do, along with others who do not yet have the Word but who would give their consent, certainly may be considered the work of Christ if they act, as we have said, in humility and in the spirit of prayer.

Lectures on Galatians (1535)

Source: Jaroslav Pelikan (trans. and ed.), *Luther's Works*.

Therefore Sarah, or Jerusalem, our free mother, is the church, the bride of Christ who gives birth to all. She goes on giving birth to children without interruption until the end of the world, as long as she exercises the ministry of the Word, that is, as long as she preaches and propagates the Gospel; for this is what it means for her to give birth. Now she teaches the Gospel in such a way that we are set free from the curse of the Law, from sin, death, and other evils, not through the Law and works but through Christ. Therefore the Jerusalem that is above, that is, the church, is not subject to the Law and works; but she is free and is a mother without Law, sin, or death. And as the mother is, so are the children to whom she gives birth.

Therefore this allegory teaches in a beautiful way that the church should not do anything but preach the Gospel correctly and purely and thus give birth to children. In this way we are all fathers and children to one another, for we are born of one another. I was born of others through the Gospel, and now I am a father to still others, who will be fathers to still others; and so this giving birth will endure until the end of the world. ... Therefore just as Isaac has the inheritance from his father solely on the basis of the promise and of his birth, without the Law or works, so we are born as heirs by Sarah, the free woman, that is, by the church. She teaches, cherishes, and carries us in her womb, her bosom, and her arms; she shapes and perfects us to the form of Christ, until we grow into perfect manhood (Eph. 4:13). Thus everything happens through the ministry of the Word. It is the duty of a free woman to go on giving birth to children endlessly, that is, to sons who know that they are justified by faith, not by the Law.

Smalcald Articles (1537)

Source: Theodore G. Tappert (trans. and ed.), *The Book of Concord*.

We do not concede to the papists that they are the church, for they are not. Nor shall we pay any attention to what they command or forbid in the name of the church, for, thank God, a seven-year-old child knows what the church is, namely, holy believers and sheep who hear the voice of their Shepherd. So children pray, "I believe in one holy Christian church." Its holiness does not consist of surplices, tonsures, albs, or other ceremonies of theirs which they have invented over and above the Holy Scriptures, but it consists of the Word of God and true faith.

On the Councils and the Church (1539)

Source: Charles M. Jacobs (trans.), *Luther's Works*, rev. and ed. Eric W. Gritsch.

Now there are many peoples in the world; the Christians, however, are a people with a special call and are therefore called not just *ecclesia*, "church," or "people," but *sancta catholica Christiana*, that is, "a Christian holy people" who believe in Christ. That is why they are called a Christian people and have the Holy Spirit, who sanctifies them daily, not only through the forgiveness of sin acquired for them by Christ (as the Antinomians foolishly believe), but also through the abolition, the purging, and the mortification of sins, on the basis of which they are called a holy people. Thus the "holy Christian church" is synonymous with a Christian and holy people or, as one is also wont to express it, with "holy Christendom," or "whole Christendom." The Old Testament uses the term "God's people."

If the words, "I believe that there is a holy Christian people," had been used in the Children's Creed, all the misery connected with this meaningless and obscure word ("church") might easily have been avoided. For the words "Christian holy people" would have brought with them, dearly and powerfully, the proper understanding and judgment of what is, and what is not, church. Whoever would have heard the words "Christian holy people" could have promptly concluded that the pope is no people, much less a holy Christian people. So too the bishops, priests, and monks are not holy, Christian people, for they do not believe in Christ, nor do they lead a holy life, but are rather the wicked and shameful people of the devil. He who does not truly believe in Christ is not Christian or a Christian. He who does not have the Holy Spirit against sin is not holy. Consequently, they cannot be "a Christian holy people," that is, *sancta et catholica ecclesia*. …

But how will or how can a poor confused person tell where such Christian holy people are to be found in this world? … First, the holy Christian people are recognized by their possession of the holy word of God. To be sure, not all have it in equal measure, as St. Paul says (1 Cor. 3:12–14). Some possess the word in its complete purity, others do not. Those who have the pure word are called those who "build on the foundation with gold, silver, and precious stones"; those who do not have it in its purity are the ones who "build on the foundation with wood, hay, and straw," and yet will be saved through fire. … This is the principal item, and the holiest of holy possessions, by reason of which the Christian people are called holy; for God's word is holy and sanctifies everything it touches; it is indeed the very holiness of God, "It is the power of God for salvation to every one who has faith" (Rom. 1:16), and "Everything is consecrated by the word of God and prayer" (1 Tim. 4:5). …

But we are speaking of the external word, preached orally by men like you and me, for this is what Christ left behind as an external sign, by which his church, or his Christian people in the world, should be recognized. We also speak of this external word as it is sincerely believed and openly professed before the world, as Christ says, "Every one who acknowledges me before men, I also will acknowledge before my Father and his angels" (Matt. 10:32). There are many who know it in their hearts, but will not profess it openly. Many possess it, but do not believe in it or act by it, for the number of those who believe in and act by it is small—as the parable of the seed in Matthew 13:4–8 says that three sections of the field receive and contain the seed, but only the fourth section, the fine and good soil, bears fruit with patience.

Now, wherever you hear or see this word preached, believed, professed, and lived, do not doubt that the true *ecclesia sancta catholica*, "a Christian holy people" must be there, even though their number is very small. For God's word "shall not return empty" (Isa. 55:11), but must have at least a fourth or a fraction of the field. And even if there were no other sign than this alone, it would still suffice to prove that a Christian, holy people must exist there, for God's word cannot be without God's people, and conversely, God's people cannot be without God's word. Otherwise, who would preach or hear it preached, if there were no people of God? And what could or would God's people believe, if there were no word of God? …

Second, God's people or the Christian holy people are recognized by the holy sacrament of baptism, wherever it is taught, believed, and administered correctly according to Christ's ordinance. That too is a public sign and a precious, holy possession by which God's people are sanctified. It is the holy bath of regeneration through the Holy Spirit (Tit. 3:5), in which we bathe and with which we are washed of sin and death by the Holy Spirit, as in the innocent holy blood of the Lamb of God. Wherever you see this sign you may know that the church, or the holy Christian people, must surely be present, even if the pope does not baptize you or even if you know nothing of his holiness and power. … Indeed, you should not even pay attention to who baptizes, for baptism does not belong to the baptizer, nor is it given to him, but it belongs to the baptized. It was ordained for him by God, and given to him by God, just as the word of God is not the preacher's (except in so far as he too hears and believes it) but belongs to the disciple who hears and believes it; to him is it given.

Third, God's people, or Christian holy people, are recognized by the holy sacrament of the altar, wherever it is rightly administered, believed, and received, according to Christ's institution. This too is a public sign and a precious, holy possession left behind by Christ by which his people are sanctified so that they also exercise themselves in faith and openly confess that they are Christian, just as they do with the word and with baptism. And here too you need not be disturbed if the pope does not say mass for you, does not consecrate, anoint, or vest you with a chasuble. Indeed, you may, like a patient in bed, receive this sacrament without wearing any garb, except that outward decency obliges you to be properly covered. Moreover, you need not ask whether you have a tonsure or are anointed. In addition, the question of whether you are male or female, young or old, need not be argued—just as little as it matters in baptism and the preached word. It is enough that you are consecrated and anointed with the sublime and holy chrism of God, with the word of God, with baptism, and also this sacrament; then you are anointed highly and gloriously enough and sufficiently vested with priestly garments.

Moreover, don't be led astray by the question of whether the man who administers the sacrament is holy, or whether or not he has two wives. The sacrament belongs to him who receives it, not to him who administers it, unless he also receives it. In that case he is one of those who receives it, and thus it is also given to him. Wherever you see this sacrament properly administered, there you may be assured of the presence of God's people. For, as was said above of the word, wherever God's word is, there the church must be; likewise, wherever baptism and the sacrament are, God's people must be, and vice versa. No others have, give, practice, use, and confess these holy possessions save God's people alone, even though some false and unbelieving Christians are secretly among them. They, however, do not profane the people of God because they are not known; the church, or God's people, does not tolerate known sinners in its midst, but reproves them and also makes them holy. Or, if they refuse, it casts them out from the sanctuary by means of the ban and regards them as heathen (Matt. 18:17).

Fourth, God's people or holy Christians are recognized by the office of the keys exercised publicly. That is, as Christ decrees in Matthew 18:15–20, if a Christian sins, he should be reproved; and if he does not mend his ways, he should be bound in his sin and cast out. If he does mend his ways, he should be absolved. That is the office of the keys. Now the use of the keys is twofold, public and private. There are some people with consciences so tender and despairing that even if they have not been publicly condemned, they cannot find comfort until they have been individually absolved by the pastor. On the other hand, there are also some who are so obdurate that they neither recant in their heart and want their sins forgiven individually by the pastor, nor desist from their sins. Therefore the keys must be used differently, publicly and privately. Now where you see sins forgiven or reproved in some persons, be it publicly or privately, you may know that God's people are there. If God's people are not there, the keys are not there either; and if the keys are not present for Christ, God's people are not present. Christ bequeathed them as a public sign and a holy possession, whereby the Holy Spirit again sanctifies the fallen sinners redeemed by Christ's death, and whereby the Christians confess that they are a holy people in this world under Christ. And those who refuse to be converted or sanctified again shall be cast out from this holy people, that is, bound and excluded by means of the keys, as happened to the unrepentant Antinomians.

You must pay no heed here to the two keys of the pope, which he converted into two skeleton keys to the treasure chests and crowns of all kings. If he does not want to bind or reprove sin, whether it be publicly or privately (as he really does not), let it be reproved and bound in your parish. If he will not loose, or forgive it, let it be loosed and forgiven in your parish, for his retaining or binding, his remitting or releasing, makes you neither holy nor unholy, since he can only have skeleton keys, not the true keys. The keys belong not to the pope (as he lies) but to the church, that is, to God's people, or to the holy Christian people throughout the entire world, or wherever there are Christians. They cannot all be in Rome, unless it be that the whole world is there first—which will not happen in a long time. The keys are the pope's as little as baptism, the sacrament, and the word of God are, for they belong to the people of Christ and are called "the church's keys" not "the pope's keys."

Fifth, the church is recognized externally by the fact that it consecrates or calls ministers, or has offices that it is to administer. There must be bishops, pastors, or preachers, who publicly and privately give, administer, and use the aforementioned four things or holy possessions in behalf of and in the name of the church, or rather by reason of their institution by Christ, as St. Paul states in Ephesians 4:8, "He received gifts among men …"—his gifts were that some should be apostles, some prophets, some evangelists, some teachers and governors, etc. The people as a whole cannot do these things, but must entrust or have them entrusted to one person. Otherwise, what would happen if everyone wanted to speak or administer, and no one wanted to give way to the other? It must be entrusted to one person, and he alone should be allowed to preach, to baptize, to absolve, and to administer the sacraments. The others should be content with this arrangement and agree to it. Wherever you see this done, be assured that God's people, the holy Christian people, are present. …

Now wherever you find these offices or officers, you may be assured that the holy Christian people are there; for the church cannot be without these bishops, pastors, preachers, priests; and conversely, they cannot be without the church. Both must be together.

Sixth, the holy Christian people are externally recognized by prayer, public praise, and thanksgiving to God. Where you see and hear the Lord's Prayer prayed and taught; or psalms or other spiritual songs sung, in accordance with the word of God and the true faith; also the creed, the Ten Commandments, and the catechism used in public, you may rest assured that a holy Christian people of God are present. For prayer, too, is one of the precious holy possessions whereby everything is sanctified, as St. Paul says (1 Tim. 4:5). The psalms too are nothing but prayers in which we praise, thank, and glorify God. The creed and the Ten Commandments are also God's word and belong to the holy possession, whereby the Holy Spirit sanctifies the holy people of Christ. However, we are now speaking of prayers and songs which are intelligible and from which we can learn and by means of which we can mend our ways. The clamor of monks and nuns and priests is not prayer, nor is it praise to God; for they do not understand it, nor do they learn anything from it; they do it like a donkey, only for the sake of the belly and not at all in quest of any reform or sanctification or of the will of God.

Seventh, the holy Christian people are externally recognized by the holy possession of the sacred cross. They must endure every misfortune and persecution, all kinds of trials and evil from the devil, the world, and the flesh (as the Lord's Prayer indicates) by inward sadness, timidity, fear, outward poverty, contempt, illness, and weakness, in order to become like their head, Christ. And the only reason they must suffer is that they steadfastly adhere to Christ and God's word, enduring this for the sake of Christ, "Blessed are you when men persecute you on my account" (Matt. 5:11). They must be pious, quiet, obedient, and prepared to serve the government and everybody with life and goods, doing no one any harm. No people on earth have to endure such bitter hate; they must be accounted worse than Jews, heathen, and Turks. In summary, they must be called heretics, knaves, and devils, the most pernicious people on earth, to the point where those who hang, drown, murder, torture, banish, and plague them to death are rendering God a service. No one has compassion on them; they are given myrrh and gall to drink when they thirst. And all of this is done not because they are adulterers, murderers, thieves, or rogues, but because they want to have none but Christ, and no other God. Wherever you see or hear this, you may know that the holy Christian church is there, as Christ says in Matthew 5:11–12, "Blessed are you when men revile you and utter all kinds of evil against you on my account. Rejoice and be glad, for your reward is great in heaven." This too is a holy possession whereby the Holy Spirit not only sanctifies his people, but also blesses them.

Meanwhile, pay no heed to the papists' holy possessions from dead saints, from the wood of the holy cross. For these are just as often bones taken from a carrion pit as bones of saints, and just as often wood taken from gallows as wood from the holy cross. There is nothing but fraud in this. The pope thus tricks people out of their money and alienates them from Christ. Even if it were a genuine holy possession, it would nonetheless not sanctify anyone. But when you are condemned, cursed, reviled, slandered, and plagued because of Christ, you are sanctified. It mortifies the old Adam and teaches him patience, humility, gentleness, praise and thanks, and good cheer in suffering. That is what it means to be sanctified by the Holy Spirit and to be renewed to a new life in Christ; in that way we learn to believe in God, to trust him, to love him, and to place our hope in him, as Romans 5:1–5 says, "Suffering produces hope," etc.

These are the true seven principal parts of the great holy possession whereby the Holy Spirit effects in us a daily sanctification and vivification in Christ, according to the first table of Moses. By this we obey it, albeit never as perfectly as Christ. But we constantly strive to attain the goal, under his redemption or remission of sin, until we too shall one day become perfectly holy and no longer stand in need of forgiveness. Everything is directed toward that goal. I would even call these seven parts the seven sacraments, but since that term has been misused by the papists and is used in a different sense in Scripture, I shall let them stand as the seven principal parts of Christian sanctification or the seven holy possessions of the church.

In addition to these seven principal parts there are other outward signs that identify the Christian church, namely, those signs whereby the Holy Spirit sanctifies us according to the second table of Moses; when he assists us in sincerely honoring our father and mother, and conversely, when he helps them to raise their children in a Christian way and to lead honorable lives; when we faithfully serve our princes and lords and are obedient and subject to them, and conversely, when they love their subjects and protect and guard them; also when we bear no one a grudge, entertain no anger, hatred, envy, or vengefulness toward our neighbors, but gladly forgive them, lend to them, help them, and counsel them; when we are not lewd, not drunkards, not proud, arrogant, overbearing, but chaste, self-controlled, sober, friendly, kind, gentle, and humble; when we do not steal, rob, are not usurious, greedy, do not overcharge, but are mild, kind, content, charitable; when we are not false, mendacious, perjurers, but truthful, trustworthy, and do whatever else is taught in these commandments—all of which St. Paul teaches abundantly in more than one place. We need the Decalogue not only to apprise us of our lawful obligations, but we also need it to discern how far the Holy Spirit has advanced us in his work of sanctification and by how much we still fall short of the goal, lest we become secure and imagine that we have now done all that is required. Thus we must constantly grow in sanctification and always become new creatures in Christ. This means "grow" and "do so more and more" (2 Pet. 3:18).

However, these signs cannot be regarded as being as reliable as those noted before since some heathens too practice these works and indeed at times appear holier than Christians; yet their actions do not issue from the heart purely and simply, for the sake of God, but they search for some other end because they lack a real faith in and a true knowledge of God. But here is the Holy Spirit, who sanctifies the heart and produces these fruits from "an honest and good heart," as Christ says in the parable recorded in Matthew 13 (Luke 8:15). Since the first table is greater and must be a holier possession, I have summarized everything in the second table. Otherwise, I could have divided it too into seven holy possessions or seven principal parts, according to the seven commandments.

Now we know for certain what, where, and who the holy Christian church is, that is, the holy Christian people of God; and we are quite certain that it cannot fail us. Everything else may fail and surely does.

For further reading

Paul Althaus, *The Theology of Martin Luther*, trans. Robert C. Schultz (Philadelphia: Fortress, 1966).

Carl E. Braaten and Robert W. Jenson (eds.), *Marks of the Body of Christ* (Grand Rapids: Eerdmans, 1999).

Bernhard Lohse, *Martin Luther: An Introduction to His Life and Work* (Philadelphia: Fortress, 1986).

Martin Luther, "The Babylonian Captivity of the Church" (1520), in Helmut T. Lehmann (ed.), *Luther's Works*, vol. 36 (Philadelphia: Muhlenberg Press, 1959), pp. 11–126.

——— "The Blessed Sacrament of the Holy and True Body of Christ, and the Brotherhoods" (1519), in E. Theodore Bachmann (ed.), *Luther's Works*, vol. 35 (Philadelphia: Muhlenberg Press, 1960), pp. 49–73.

——— "The Holy and Blessed Sacrament of Baptism" (1519), in E. Theodore Bachmann (ed.), *Luther's Works*, vol. 35, pp. 29–43.

——— "The Misuse of the Mass" (1521), in Helmut T. Lehmann (ed.), *Luther's Works*, vol. 36, pp. 133–230.

——— "On the Papacy in Rome against the Most Celebrated Romanist in Leipzig" (1520), in Eric W. Gritsch (ed.), *Luther's Works*, vol. 39 (Philadelphia: Fortress, 1970), pp. 55–104.

——— "That a Christian Assembly or Congregation has the Right and Power to Judge All Teaching and to Call, Appoint, and Dismiss Teachers, Established and Proven by Scripture" (1523), in Eric W. Gritsch (ed.), *Luther's Works*, vol. 39, pp. 305–14.

——— "The Sacrament of Penance" (1519), in E. Theodore Bachmann (ed.), *Luther's Works*, vol. 35, pp. 9–22.

18   The *Schleitheim Confession* (1527)

The Anabaptists ("re-baptizers") were a radical reform movement in and around what are now Germany, Austria, Switzerland, the Netherlands, and the Czech Republic. They subscribed to a "free church" or "believers' church" that rejected infant baptism and defied the Constantinian model whereby the church either controlled or was controlled by the emperor, king, magistrates, princes, or other secular powers. They held that the other reformers had not gone far enough in moving the church toward reform and an identity based on the gospel alone. Because of their radical beliefs and way of life, they were persecuted, tortured, and killed by Catholics and Protestants alike. The Schleitheim Confession is a statement of early Anabaptist beliefs and practices, authored largely by Michael Sattler, a former monk who gave leadership to the movement. The confession was ratified on 24 February 1527 in the Swiss village of Schleitheim.

Source: John Howard Yoder, *The Legacy of Michael Sattler*.

Article 1   Notice concerning baptism

Baptism shall be given to all those who have been taught repentance and the amendment of life and [who] believe truly that their sins are taken away through Christ, and to all those who desire to walk in the resurrection of Jesus

Christ and be buried with Him in death, so that they might rise with Him; to all those who with such an understanding themselves desire and request it from us; hereby is excluded all infant baptism, the greatest and first abomination of the pope. For this you have the reasons and the testimony of the writings and the practice of the apostles (Matt. 28:19; Mark 16:6; Acts 2:38; 8:36; 16:31–3; 19:4). We wish simply yet resolutely and with assurance to hold to the same.

Article 2 We have been united as follows concerning the ban

We have been united as follows concerning the ban. The ban shall be employed with all those who have given themselves over to the Lord, to walk after [Him] in His commandments; those who have been baptized into the one body of Christ, and let themselves be called brothers or sisters, and still somehow slip and fall into error and sin, being inadvertently overtaken. The same [shall] be warned twice privately and the third time be publicly admonished before the entire congregation according to the command of Christ (Matt. 18). But this shall be done according to the ordering of the Spirit of God before the breaking of bread so that we may all in one spirit and in one love break and eat from one bread and drink from one cup.

Article 3 Concerning the breaking of bread

Concerning the breaking of bread, we have become one and agree thus: all those who desire to break the one bread in remembrance of the broken body of Christ and all those who wish to drink of one drink in remembrance of the shed blood of Christ, they must beforehand be united in the one body of Christ, that is the congregation of God, whose head is Christ, and that by baptism. For as Paul indicates (1 Cor. 10:21), we cannot be partakers at the same time of the table of the Lord and the table of devils. Nor can we at the same time partake and drink of the cup of the Lord and the cup of devils. That is: all those who follow the devil and the world, have no part with those who have been called out of the world unto God. All those who lie in evil have no part in the good. …

Article 4 We have been united concerning the separation that shall take place

We have been united concerning the separation that shall take place from the evil and the wickedness which the devil has planted in the world, simply in this; that we have no fellowship with them, and do not run with them in the confusion of their abominations. So it is; since all who have not entered into the obedience of faith and have not united themselves with God so that they will to do His will, are a great abomination before God, therefore nothing else can or really will grow or spring forth from them than abominable things. Now there is nothing else in the world and all creation than good or evil, believing and unbelieving, darkness and light, the world and those who are [come] out of the world, God's temple and idols. Christ and Belial, and none will have part with the other.

To us, then, the commandment of the Lord is also obvious, whereby He orders us to be and to become separated from the evil one, and thus He will be our God and we shall be His sons and daughters (2 Cor. 6:17).

Further, He admonishes us therefore to go out from Babylon and from the earthly Egypt, that we may not be partakers in their torment and suffering, which the Lord will bring upon them. (Rev. 18:4–8).

From all this we should learn that everything which has not been united with our God in Christ is nothing but an abomination which we should shun. By this are meant all popish and repopish works and idolatry, gatherings, church attendance, winehouses, guarantees and commitments of unbelief, and other things of the kind, which the world regards highly, and yet which are carnal or flatly counter to the command of God, after the pattern of all the iniquity which is in the world. From all this we shall be separated and have no part with such, for they are nothing but abominations, which cause us to be hated before our Christ Jesus, who has freed us from the servitude of the flesh and fitted us for the service of God and the Spirit whom He has given us.

Thereby shall also fall away from us the diabolical weapons of violence— such as sword, armor, and the like, and all of their use to protect friends or against enemies—by virtue of the word of Christ: "you shall not resist evil" (Matt. 5:39).

Article 5   We have been united as follows concerning shepherds in the church of God

We have been united as follows concerning shepherds in the church of God. The shepherd in the church shall be a person according to the rule of Paul, fully and completely, who has a good report of those who are outside the faith. The office of such a person shall be to read and exhort and teach, warn, admonish, or ban in the congregation, and properly to preside among the sisters and brothers in prayer, and in the breaking of bread, and in all things to take care of the body of Christ, that it may be built up and developed, so that the name of God might be praised and honored through us, and the mouth of the mocker be stopped.

He shall be supported, wherein he has need, by the congregation which has chosen him, so that he who serves the gospel can also live therefrom, as the Lord has ordered (1 Cor. 9:14). But should a shepherd do something worthy of reprimand, nothing shall be done with him without the voice of two or three witnesses. If they sin they shall be publicly reprimanded, so that others might fear.

But if the shepherd should be driven away or led to the Lord by the cross at the same hour another shall be ordained to his place, so that the little folk and the little flock of God may not be destroyed, but be preserved by warning and be consoled.

Article 6   We have been united as follows concerning the sword

We have been united as follows concerning the sword. The sword is an ordering of God outside the perfection of Christ. It punishes and kills the wicked and guards and protects the good. In the law the sword is established over the wicked for punishment and for death and the secular rulers are established to wield the same.

But within the perfection of Christ only the ban is used for the admonition and exclusion of the one who has sinned, without the death of the flesh, simply the warning and the command to sin no more.

Now many, who do not understand Christ's will for us, will ask; whether a Christian may or should use the sword against the wicked for the protection and defense of the good, or for the sake of love.

The answer is unanimously revealed: Christ teaches and commands us to learn from Him, for He is meek and lowly of heart and thus we shall find rest for our souls (Matt. 11:29). Now Christ says to the woman who was taken in adultery (John 8:11), not that she should be stoned according to the law of His Father (and yet He says, "What the Father commanded me, that I do") (John 8:22) but with mercy and forgiveness and the warning to sin no more, says: "Go, sin no more." Exactly thus should we also proceed, according to the rule of the ban.

Second, is asked concerning the sword: whether a Christian shall pass sentence in disputes and strife about worldly matters, such as the unbelievers have with one another. The answer: Christ did not wish to decide or pass judgement between brother and brother concerning inheritance, but refused to do so (Luke 12:13). So should we also do.

Third, is asked concerning the sword: whether the Christian should be a magistrate if he is chosen thereto. This is answered thus: Christ was to be made King, but He fled and did not discern the ordinance of His Father. Thus we should also do as He did and follow after Him, and we shall not walk in darkness. For He Himself says: "Whoever would come after me, let him deny himself and take up his cross and follow me" (Matt. 16:24). He Himself further forbids the violence of the sword when He says: "The princes of this world lord it over them etc., but among you it shall not be so" (Matt. 20:25). Further Paul says, "Whom God has foreknown, the same he has also predestined to be conformed to the image of his Son," etc. (Rom. 8:30). Peter also says: "Christ has suffered (not ruled) and has left us an example, that you should follow after in his steps" (1 Pet. 2:21).

Lastly, one can see in the following points that it does not befit a Christian to be a magistrate: the rule of the government is according to the flesh, that of the Christians according to the spirit. Their houses and dwelling remain in this world, that of the Christians is in heaven. Their citizenship is in this world, that of the Christians is in heaven (Phil. 3:20). The weapons of their battle and warfare are carnal and only against the flesh, but the weapons of Christians are spiritual, against the fortification of the devil. The worldly are armed with steel and iron, but Christians are armed with the armor of God, with truth, righteousness, peace, faith, salvation, and with the Word of God. In sum: as Christ our Head is minded, so also must be minded the members of the body of Christ through Him, so that there be no division in the body, through which it would be destroyed. Since then Christ is as is written of Him, so must His members also be the same, so that His body may remain whole and unified for its own advancement and upbuilding. For any kingdom which is divided within itself will be destroyed (Matt. 12:25).

Article 7 We have been united as follows concerning the oath

We have been united as follows concerning the oath. The oath is a confirmation among those who are quarreling or making promises. In the law it is commanded that it should be done only in the name of God, truthfully and not falsely. Christ, who teaches the perfection of the law, forbids His [followers] all swearing, whether true or false; neither by heaven nor by earth, neither by Jerusalem nor by our head; and that for the reason which He goes on to give: "For you cannot make one hair white or black." You see, thereby all swearing is forbidden. We cannot perform what is promised in the swearing, for we are not able to change the smallest part of ourselves (Matt. 5:34–7). ... Christ taught us similarly when He says: Your speech shall be yea, yea; and nay, nay; for what is more than that comes of evil. He says, your speech or your word shall be yes and no, so that no one might understand that He had permitted it. Christ is simply yea and nay, and all those who seek Him simply will understand His Word. Amen.

For further reading

Guy F. Hershberger (ed.), *The Recovery of the Anabaptist Vision* (Scottdale, PA: Herald Press, 1957).
"Sattler, Michael," in *Mennonite Encyclopedia* (Scottdale, PA: Mennonite Publishing House, 1955–1959), vol. 4, pp. 427–34.
C. Arnold Snyder, *The Life and Thought of Michael Sattler* (Scottdale, PA: Herald Press, 1984).

19   The *Augsburg Confession* (1530)

In 1530 Charles V, holy Roman emperor, convened an imperial diet to discuss religious differences within his realm. The Lutherans prepared a united statement, which has since been held as one of the primary confessions of the Lutheran faith. Note the two marks of the church—pure teaching (or preaching) of the gospel and right administration of the sacraments—a hallmark of the Reformation.

Source: Theodore G. Tappert (trans. and ed.), *Book of Concord*.

VII The church

Our churches also teach that one holy church is to continue forever. The church is the assembly of saints in which the Gospel is taught purely and the sacraments are administered rightly. For the true unity of the church it is enough to agree concerning the teaching of the Gospel and the administration of the sacraments. It is not necessary that human traditions or rites and ceremonies, instituted by men, should be alike everywhere. It is as Paul says, "One faith, one baptism, one God and Father of all," etc. (Eph. 4:5–6).

VIII What is the church?

Properly speaking, the church is the assembly of saints and true believers. However, since in this life many hypocrites and evil persons are mingled with believers, it is allowable to use the sacraments even when they are administered by evil men, according to the saying of Christ, "The scribes and Pharisees sit on Moses' seat," etc. (Matt. 23:2). Both the sacraments and the Word are effectual by reason of the institution and commandment of Christ even if they are administered by evil men.

Our churches condemn the Donatists and others like them who have denied that the ministry of evil men may be used in the church and who have thought the ministry of evil men to be unprofitable and without effect.

For further reading

Leif Grane, *The Augsburg Confession: A Commentary*, trans. John H. Rasmussen (Minneapolis: Augsburg, 1987).

20 Huldrych Zwingli (1484–1531)

Zwingli was another of the great reformers of the sixteenth century and the "people's priest" in Zurich, where many of his reforms were implemented. Zwingli called for strict obedience to the teachings of scripture regardless of church tradition and was in agreement with other reformers such as Luther on most principles of the reformation except for their notable disagreement about the presence of Christ in the Lord's Supper (Zwingli held that the practice is a symbolic memorial). While Zwingli's views were in many ways as radical as the Anabaptists, he contested their separation of the church from secular authority and believed strongly that civil government stands united with the local Christian assembly under the lordship of Christ, with the former having responsibility for enforcing church discipline. Zwingli's An Exposition of the Faith *was written to the French court as a defense of the reformation and a statement of his own principles in an attempt to secure its support.*

An Exposition of the Faith (1531)

Source: G. W. Bromiley (ed.), *Zwingli and Bullinger*, Library of Christian Classics.

The church
We also believe that there is one holy, catholic, that is, universal Church, and that this Church is either visible or invisible. According to the teaching of Paul, the invisible Church is that which came down from heaven, that is to say, the Church which knows and embraces God by the enlightenment of the Holy Spirit. To this Church belong all who believe the whole world over. It is not called invisible because believers are invisible, but because it is concealed from the eyes of men who they are: for believers are known only to God and to themselves. And the visible Church is not the Roman pontiff and others who bear the mitre, but all who make profession of faith in Christ the whole world over. In this number there are those who are called Christians falsely, seeing they have no inward faith. Within the visible Church, therefore, there are some who are not members of the Church elect and invisible. For in the Supper there are some who eat and drink to their own condemnation, although their brethren do not know who they are. Consequently the visible Church contains within itself many who are insolent and hostile, thinking nothing of it if they are excommunicated a hundred times, seeing they have no faith. Hence there arises the need of government for the punishment of flagrant sinners, whether it be the government of princes or that of the nobility. For the higher powers do not bear the sword in vain. Seeing, then, that there are shepherds in the Church, and amongst these we may number princes, as may be seen from Jeremiah, it is evident that without civil government a Church is maimed and impotent. Far from undermining authority, most pious king, or advocating its dissolution, as we are accused of doing, we teach that authority is necessary to the completeness of the body of the Church.

For further reading

Bruce Gordon, *The Swiss Reformation* (Manchester: Manchester University Press, 2002).
W. P. Stephens, *The Theology of Huldrych Zwingli* (Oxford: Clarendon Press, 1988).

21   John Calvin (1509–1564)

Calvin's ecclesiology focuses on the church as a community of believers who hear the Word of God and by the power of the Spirit respond in faith. As with the other Protestant reformers, Calvin criticizes any simple identification of the true church with the Roman church and its hierarchy. This ecclesiology finds one of its earliest statements in his major theological work, the Institutes of the Christian Religion, *first published in 1536 and revised several times thereafter. The following excerpts from the* Institutes *emphasize the invisibility of the true church and highlight the two classic marks of the reformed church—"the pure preaching of God's word" and "the lawful administration of the sacraments." In Geneva (1536–1538), Calvin's more academic ecclesiological positions were given practical shape by his first, and relatively unsuccessful, attempts at organizing a reforming church. After two years of steady controversy with civil authorities, Calvin went to Strasbourg where his pastoral experience helped him further refine his understanding of church discipline and liturgy as well as the relationship between church and civil polity. After Cardinal Sadoleto wrote to the Genevans urging their return to the Roman church, Calvin sent a reply, which provides a revealing picture of his basic understanding of the church. Calvin's return in 1541 to Geneva, where he would spend the rest of his life, initiated a full-scale Reformation experiment in the city. The "Catechism of the Church of Geneva," with its question-and-answer format between a minister and a child, provides the broad outlines of Calvin's ecclesiology.*

Institutes of the Christian Religion (1536)

Source: John Calvin, *Institutes of the Christian Religion*, trans. Ford Lewis Battles.

"Prefatory address to King Francis I of France"
                6   Errors about the nature of the church
By their double-horned argument they do not press us so hard that we are forced to admit either that the church has been lifeless for some time or that we are now in conflict with it. Surely the church of Christ has lived and will live so long as Christ reigns at the right hand of his Father. It is sustained by his hand; defended by his protection; and is kept safe through his power. For he will surely accomplish what he once promised: that he will be present with his own even to the end of the world (Matt. 28:20). Against this church we now have no quarrel. For, of one accord with all believing folk, we worship and adore one God, and Christ the Lord (1 Cor. 8:6), as he has always been adored by all godly men. But they stray very far from the truth when they do not recognize the church unless they see it with their very eyes, and try to keep it within limits to which it cannot at all be confined.

Our controversy turns on these hinges: first, they contend that the form of the church is always apparent and observable. Secondly, they set this form in the see of the Roman Church and its hierarchy. We, on the contrary, affirm that the church can exist without any visible appearance, and that its appearance is not contained within that outward magnificence which they foolishly admire. Rather, it has quite another mark: namely, the pure preaching of God's Word and the lawful administration of the sacraments. They rage if the church cannot always be pointed to with the finger. But among the Jewish people how often was it so deformed that no semblance of it remained? What form do we think it displayed when Elijah complained that he alone was left (1 Kgs 19:10, 14)? How long after Christ's coming was it hidden without form? How often has it since that time been so oppressed by wars, seditions, and heresies that it did not shine forth at all? If they had lived at that time, would they have believed that any church existed? But Elijah heard that there still remained seven thousand men who had not bowed the knee before Baal. And we must not doubt that Christ has reigned on earth ever since he ascended into heaven. But if believers had then required some visible form, would they not have straightway lost courage? Since the Lord alone "knows who are his" (2 Tim. 2:19), let us therefore leave to him the fact that he sometimes removes from men's sight the external notion of his church.

Reply to Sadoleto (1539)

Source: John C. Olin (ed.), *A Reformation Debate: Sadoleto's Letter to the Genevans and Calvin's Reply*.

You either labor under a delusion as to the term *church*, or, at least, knowingly and willingly give it a gloss. I will immediately show the latter to be the case, though it may also be that you are somewhat in error. First, in defining the term, you omit what would have helped you, in no small degree, to the right understanding of it. When you describe it as that which in all parts, as well as at the present time, in every region of the earth, being united and consenting in Christ, has been always and everywhere directed by the one Spirit of Christ, what comes of the Word of the Lord, that clearest of all marks, and which the Lord himself, in pointing out the Church, so often recommends to us? For seeing how dangerous it would be to boast of the Spirit without the Word, he declared that the Church is indeed governed by the Holy Spirit, but in order that that government might not be vague and unstable, He annexed it to the Word. For this reason Christ exclaims, that those who are of God hear the Word of God—that his sheep are those which recognize his voice as that of their Shepherd, and any other voice as that of a stranger (John 10:27). For this reason the Spirit, by the mouth of Paul, declares that the Church is built upon the foundation of the Apostles and Prophets (Eph. 2:20). Also, that the Church is made holy to the Lord, by the washing of water in the Word of life. The same thing is declared still more clearly by the mouth of Peter, when he teaches that people are regenerated to God by that incorruptible seed (1 Pet. 1:23). In short, why is the preaching of the gospel so often styled the kingdom of God, but because it is the sceptre by which the heavenly King rules His people?

... Had you known, or been unwilling to disguise the fact, that the Spirit goes before the Church, to enlighten her in understanding the Word, while the Word itself is like the Lydian Stone, by which she tests all doctrines, would you have taken refuge in that most perplexing and thorny question? Learn, then, by your own experience, that it is no less unreasonable to boast of the Spirit without the Word, than it would be absurd to bring forward the Word itself without the Spirit. Now, if you can bear to receive a truer definition of the Church than your own, say, in future, that it is the society of all the saints, a society which, spread over the whole world, and existing in all ages, yet bound together by the one doctrine, and the one Spirit of Christ, cultivates and observes unity of faith and brotherly concord. With this Church we deny that we have any disagreement. Nay, rather, as we revere her as our mother, so we desire to remain in her bosom. ...

Since there are three things on which the safety of the Church is founded, viz., doctrine, discipline, and the sacraments, and to these a fourth is added, viz., ceremonies, by which to exercise the people in offices of piety, in order that we may be most sparing of the honor of your Church, by which of these things would you have us to judge her? The truth of Prophetical and Evangelical doctrine, on which the Church ought to be founded, has not only in a great measure perished in your Church, but is violently driven away by fire and sword. Will you obtrude upon me, for the Church, a body which furiously persecutes everything sanctioned by our religion, both as delivered by the oracles of God, and embodied in the writings of holy Fathers, and approved by ancient Councils? Where, pray, exist among you any vestiges of that true and holy discipline, which the ancient bishops exercised in the Church? Have you not scorned all their institutions? Have you not trampled all the Canons under foot? Then, your nefarious profanation of the sacraments I cannot think of without the utmost horror.

Of ceremonies, indeed, you have more than enough, but, for the most part, so childish in their import, and vitiated by innumerable forms of superstition, as to be utterly unavailing for the preservation of the Church. ... In the Sacraments, all we have attempted is to restore the native purity from which they had degenerated, and so enable them to resume their dignity. Ceremonies we have in a great measure abolished, but we were compelled to do so, partly because by their multitude they had degenerated into a kind of Judaism, partly because they had filled the minds of the people with superstition, and could not possibly remain without doing the greatest injury to the piety which it was their office to promote. Still we have retained those which seemed sufficient for the circumstances of the times. ...

But what arrogance, you will say, to boast that the Church is with you alone, and to deny it to all the world besides! We, indeed, Sadoleto, deny not that those over which you preside are Churches of Christ, but we maintain that the Roman Pontiff, with his whole herd of pseudo-bishops, who have seized upon the pastor's office, are ravening wolves, whose only study has hitherto been to scatter and trample upon the kingdom of Christ, filling it with ruin and devastation. Nor are we the first to make the complaint. ... For iniquity has reached its height, and now those shadowy prelates, by whom you think the Church stands or perishes, and by whom we say that she has been cruelly torn and mutilated, and brought to the very brink of destruction, can bear neither their vices nor the cure of them. Destroyed the Church would have been, had not God, with singular goodness, prevented. For in all places where the tyranny of the Roman Pontiff prevails, you scarcely see as many stray and tattered vestiges as will enable you to perceive that there Churches lie half buried. Nor should you think this absurd, since Paul tells you (2 Thess. 2:4) that antichrist would have his seat in no other place than in the midst of God's sanctuary. Ought not this single warning to put us on our guard against tricks and devices which may be practiced in the name of the church?

The Catechism of the Church of Geneva (1545)

Source: Henry Beveridge (trans.), *Calvin's Tracts and Treatises*.

Master   What is the Church?

Scholar   The body and society of believers whom God hath predestined to eternal life.

Master   Is it necessary to believe this article also?

Scholar   Yes, verily, if we would not make the death of Christ without effect, and set at nought all that has hitherto been said. For the one effect resulting from all is, that there is a Church.

Master   You mean then that we only treated of the cause of salvation, and showed the foundation of it when we explained that by the merits and intercession of Christ, we are taken into favour by God, and that this grace is confirmed in us by virtue of the Spirit. Now, however, we are explaining the effect of all these things, that by facts our faith may be made more firm?

Scholar   It is so.

Master   In what sense do you call the Church holy?

Scholar   All whom God has chosen he justifies, and forms to holiness and innocence of life (Rom. 8:30), that his glory may be displayed in them. And this is what Paul means when he says that Christ sanctified the Church which he redeemed, that it might be a glorious Church, free from all blemish (Eph. 5: 25).

Master   What is meant by the epithet Catholic or Universal?

Scholar   By it we are taught, that as all believers have one head, so they must all be united into one body, that the Church diffused over the whole world may be one—not more (Eph. 4:15; 1 Cor. 12:12).

Master   And what is the purport of what immediately follows concerning the communion of saints?

Scholar   That is put down to express more clearly the unity which exists among the members of the Church. It is at the same time intimated, that whatever benefits God bestows upon the Church, have a view to the common good of all; Seeing they all have communion with each other.

Master   But is this holiness which you attribute to the Church already perfect?

Scholar   Not yet, that is as long as she has her warfare in this world. For she always labours under infirmities, and will never be entirely purged of the remains of vice, until she adheres completely to Christ her head, by whom she is sanctified.

Master   Can this Church be known in any other way than when she is believed by faith?

Scholar   There is indeed also a visible Church of God, which he has described to us by certain signs and marks, but here we are properly speaking of the assemblage of those whom he has adopted to salvation by his secret election. This is neither at all times visible to the eye nor discernible by signs.

Institutes of the Christian Religion (1559)

Source: John T. McNeill (trans.) and Ford Lewis Battles (ed.), *Calvin: Institutes of the Christian Religion*, Library of Christian Classics.

The visible church as mother of believers

But because it is now our intention to discuss the visible church, let us learn even from the simple title "mother" how useful, indeed how necessary, it is that we should know her. For there is no other way to enter into life unless this mother conceive us in her womb, give us birth, nourish us at her breasts, and lastly, unless she keep us under her care and guidance until, putting off mortal flesh, we become like the angels (Matt. 22:30). Our weakness does not allow us to be dismissed from her school until we have been pupils all our lives. Furthermore, away from her bosom one cannot hope for any forgiveness of sins or any salvation, as Isaiah (Isa. 37:32) and Joel (Joel 2:32) testify. Ezekiel agrees with them when he declares that those whom God rejects from heavenly life will not be enrolled among God's people (Ezek. 13:9). On the other hand, those who turn to the cultivation of true godliness are said to inscribe their names among the citizens of Jerusalem (cf. Isa. 56:5; Ps. 87:6). For this reason, it is said in another psalm: "Remember me, O Jehovah, with favor toward thy people; visit me with salvation: that I may see the well-doing of thy chosen ones, that I may rejoice in the joy of thy nation, that I may be glad with thine inheritance" (Ps. 106:4–5). By these words God's fatherly favor and the especial witness of spiritual life are limited to his flock, so that it is always disastrous to leave the church. (IV:1:4)

Invisible and visible church

How we are to judge the church visible, which falls within our knowledge, is, I believe, already evident from the above discussion. For we have said that Holy Scripture speaks of the church in two ways. Sometimes by the term "church" it means that which is actually in God's presence, into which no persons are received but those who are children of God by grace of adoption and true members of Christ by sanctification of the Holy Spirit. Then, indeed, the church includes not only the saints presently living on earth, but all the elect from the beginning of the world. Often, however, the name "church" designates the whole multitude of men spread over the earth who profess to worship one God and Christ. By baptism we are initiated into faith in him; by partaking in the Lord's Supper we attest our unity in true doctrine and love; in the Word of the Lord we have agreement, and for the preaching of the Word the ministry instituted by Christ is preserved. In this church are mingled many hypocrites who have nothing of Christ but the name and outward appearance. There are very many ambitious, greedy, envious persons, evil speakers, and some of quite unclean life. Such are tolerated for a time either because they cannot be convicted by a competent tribunal or because a vigorous discipline does not always flourish as it ought. Just as we must believe, therefore, that the former church, invisible to us is visible to the eyes of God alone, so we are commanded to revere and keep communion with the latter, which is called "church" in respect to men. (IV:1:7)

The marks of the church and our application of them to judgment
From this the face of the church comes forth and becomes visible to our eyes. Wherever we see the Word of God purely preached and heard, and the sacraments administered according to Christ's institution, there, it is not to be doubted, a church of God exists (cf. Eph. 2:20). For his promise cannot fail: Wherever two or three are gathered in my name, there I am in the midst of them" (Matt. 18:20).

But that we may clearly grasp the sum of this matter, we must proceed by the following steps: the church universal is a multitude gathered from all nations; it is divided and dispersed in separate places, but agrees on the one truth of divine doctrine, and is bound by the bond of the same religion. Under it are thus included individual churches, disposed in towns and villages according to human need, so that each rightly has the name and authority of the church. Individual men who, by their profession of religion, are reckoned within such churches, even though they may actually be strangers to the church, still in a sense belong to it until they have been rejected by public judgment.

There is, however, a slightly different basis for judgment concerning individual men and churches. For it may happen that we ought to treat like brothers and count as believers those whom we think unworthy of the fellowship of the godly, because of the common agreement of the church by which they are borne and tolerated in the body of Christ. We do not by our vote approve such persons as members of the church, but we leave to them such place as they occupy among the people of God until it is lawfully taken from them.

But we must think otherwise of the whole multitude itself. If it has the ministry of the Word and honors it, if it has the administration of the sacraments, it deserves without doubt to be held and considered a church. For it is certain that such things are not without fruit. In this way we preserve for the universal church its unity, which devilish spirits have always tried to sunder; and we do not defraud of their authority those lawful assemblies which have been set up in accordance with local needs. (IV:1:9)

Marks and authority of the church
We have laid down as distinguishing marks of the church the preaching of the Word and the observance of the sacraments. These can never exist without bringing forth fruit and prospering by God's blessing. I do not say that wherever the Word is preached there will be immediate fruit; but wherever it is received and has a fixed abode, it shows its effectiveness. However it may be, where the preaching of the gospel is reverently heard and the sacraments are not neglected, there for the time being no deceitful or ambiguous form of the church is seen; and no one is permitted to spurn its authority, flout its warnings, resist its counsels, or make light of its chastisements—much less to desert it and break its unity. For the Lord esteems the communion of his church so highly that he counts as a traitor and apostate from Christianity anyone who arrogantly leaves any Christian society, provided it cherishes the true ministry of Word and sacraments. He so esteems the authority of the church that when it is violated he believes his own diminished.

It is of no small importance that it is called "the pillar and ground of the truth" and "the house of God" (1 Tim. 3:15). By these words Paul means that the church is the faithful keeper of God's truth in order that it may not perish in the world. For by its ministry and labor God willed to have the preaching of his Word kept pure and to show himself the Father of a family, while he feeds us with spiritual food and provides everything that makes for our salvation. It is also no common praise to say that Christ has chosen and set apart the church as his bride, "without spot or wrinkle" (Eph. 5:27), "his body and ... fullness" (Eph. 1:23). From this it follows that separation from the church is the denial of God and Christ. Hence, we must even more avoid so wicked a separation. For when with all our might we are attempting the overthrow of God's truth, we deserve to have him hurl the whole thunderbolt of his wrath to crush us. Nor can any more atrocious crime be conceived than for us by sacrilegious disloyalty to violate the marriage that the only-begotten Son of God deigned to contract with us (cf. Eph. 5:23–32). (IV:1:10)

Scandal in the church no occasion for leaving it
In bearing with imperfections of life we ought to be far more considerate. For here the descent is very slippery and Satan ambushes us with no ordinary devices. For there have always been those who, imbued with a false conviction of their own perfect sanctity, as if they had already become a sort of airy spirits, spurned association with all men in whom they discern any remnant of human nature. The Cathari of old were of this sort, as well as the Donatists,

who approached them in foolishness. Such today are some of the Anabaptists who wish to appear advanced beyond other men.

There are others who sin more out of ill-advised zeal for righteousness than out of that insane pride. When they do not see a quality of life corresponding to the doctrine of the gospel among those to whom it is announced, they immediately judge that no church exists in that place. This is a very legitimate complaint, and we give all too much occasion for it in this most miserable age. And our cursed sloth is not to be excused, for the Lord will not allow it to go unpunished, seeing that he has already begun to chastise it with heavy stripes. Woe to us, then, who act with such dissolute and criminal license that weak consciences are wounded because of us! But on their part those of whom we have spoken sin in that they do not know how to restrain their disfavor. For where the Lord requires kindness, they neglect it and give themselves over completely to immoderate severity. Indeed, because they think no church exists where there are not perfect purity and integrity of life, they depart out of hatred of wickedness from the lawful church, while they fancy themselves turning aside from the faction of the wicked.

They claim that the church of Christ is holy (Eph. 5:26). But in order that they may know that the church is at the same time mingled of good men and bad, let them hear the parable from Christ's lips that compares the church to a net in which all kinds of fish are gathered and are not sorted until laid out on the shore (Matt. 13:47–58). Let them hear that it is like a field sown with good seed which is through the enemy's deceit scattered with tares and is not purged of them until the harvest is brought into the threshing floor (Matt. 13:24–30). Let them hear finally that it is like a threshing floor on which grain is so collected that it lies hidden under the chaff until, winnowed by fan and sieve, it is at last stored in the granary (Matt. 3:12). But if the Lord declares that the church is to labor under this evil—to be weighed down with the mixture of the wicked—until the Day of Judgment, they are vainly seeking a church besmirched with no blemish. (IV:1:13)

The holiness of the church
Because they also allege that the church is not without basis called holy, it is fitting to examine in what holiness it excels lest, if we are not willing to admit a church unless it be perfect in every respect, we leave no church at all. True, indeed, is Paul's statement: "Christ … gave himself up for the church that he might sanctify her; he cleansed her by the washing of water in the word of life, that he might present her to himself as his glorious bride, without spot or wrinkle," etc. (Eph. 5:25–7). Yet it also is no less true that the Lord is daily at work in smoothing out wrinkles and cleansing spots. From this it follows that the church's holiness is not yet complete. The church is holy, then, in the sense that it is daily advancing and is not yet perfect: it makes progress from day to day but has not yet reached its goal of holiness, as will be explained more fully elsewhere. (IV:1:17)

For further reading

Jane Dempsey Douglass, "Calvin and the Church Today: Ecclesiology as Received, Changed, and Adapted," *Theology Today* 66/2 (2009), pp. 135–53.

Gerard Mannion and Eduardus Van der Borght, *John Calvin's Ecclesiology: Ecumenical Perspectives* (London: T & T Clark International).

Charles Partee, *The Theology of John Calvin* (Louisville: Westminster John Knox, 2008).

Amy Platinga Pauw, "The Continuing Relevance of Calvin's Ecclesiology," *Journal of Presbyterian History* 87/2 (2009), pp. 66–9.

22   Heinrich Bullinger (1504–1575)

Upon the death of Zwingli, Heinrich Bullinger took up the cause of defending and leading the reform begun by Zwingli in Zurich, though inclining towards Calvin's positions over time. Largely responsible for the Second Helvetic Confession *(see below), Bullinger was incredibly influential throughout Europe, and his sermons and writings became standards among second and later generation reformers. In the following excerpt, we find a clear distinction not only between the visible and invisible church so characteristic of Protestant reformers, but also between the church militant and church triumphant. As with Calvin, Bullinger focuses on only two visible marks — Word and sacraments — of the church militant, thus dropping Zwingli's third mark — discipline. This is consistent with his view that the church militant (the visible church) includes hypocrites until that day when God's judgment would reveal the true and invisible church.*

Of the Holy Catholic Church (1551)

Source: G. W. Bromiley (trans.), *Zwingli and Bullinger*, Library of Christian Classics.

The Church is the whole company and multitude of the faithful, as it is partly in heaven and partly remains still upon earth: and as it agrees plainly in unity of faith or true doctrine, and in the lawful partaking of the sacraments: for it is not divided, but united and joined together as it were in one house and fellowship.

This Church is usually called catholic, that is to say, universal. For it sends out its branches into all places of the wide world, in all times and all ages; and it comprehends generally all the faithful the whole world over. For the Church of God is not tied to any one region, nation, or kindred; to condition, age, sex, or kind: all the faithful generally and each one in particular wherever they may be, are citizens and members of this Church. St. Paul the apostle says: "There is neither Jew nor Greek, neither bondman nor free, neither man nor woman: for ye be all one in Christ Jesus" (Gal. 3:28).

The Church is distinguished into the two parts, the Church triumphant and the Church militant. The Church triumphant is the great company of holy spirits in heaven, triumphing because of the victory which has now been won against the world, and sin and the devil, and enjoying the vision of God, In which there consists the fulness of all kinds of joy and pleasure, and concerning which they set forth God's glory and praise his goodness for ever. ...

And therefore all the saints in heaven belong to our company, or rather, we belong to their fellowship; for we are companions and fellow-heirs with the saints from Adam unto the end of all worlds and God's household. And this contains the greatest comfort in all human life, and moves above all things to the study of virtue: for what more worthy thing is there, than to be of God's household? Or what may be thought more sweet to us, than to think ourselves fellows with the patriarchs, prophets, apostles and martyrs, of all angels and blessed spirits? This benefit, I say, Christ has bestowed on us. To him therefore be praise, glory, and thanks for ever and ever. Amen.

The Church militant is a congregation of men upon earth, professing the name and religion of Christ, and still fighting in the world against the devil, sin, the flesh and the world, in the camp and tents and under the banner of our Lord Christ. This Church again must be taken in two ways. For either it must be taken strictly, in which case it comprises only those who are not only called but are in actual fact the Church, the faithful and elect of God, lively members, knit unto Christ not merely with outward bands or marks but in spirit and faith, and often by the latter without the former, of which we shall speak later. This inward and invisible Church of God may well be termed the elect bride of Christ, known only to God, who alone knows who are his. It is this Church especially which we confess when we say as we are instructed in the Apostles' Creed: "I believe in the holy Catholic Church, the Communion of Saints." In these few words we understand that there is a Church, what that Church is, and what kind of a Church it is. For first we confess that there always has been and is a Church of God, and that it shall continue for ever. Then professing what it is, we add: "The Communion of Saints." That is to say: We believe the Church to be simply the company of all those saints who are and have been and shall be both in this present age and in the world to come who enjoy in common all the good things granted to them by God. And we also express what is the nature of this Church, that is, holy, the bride of Christ, cleansed and blessed. For St. Paul calls holy those who are cleansed with the Spirit and blood of our God of whom a large number have received crowns of glory, and the rest labour here upon earth, hoping to receive them in heaven. And certainly, in our consideration of the Church, the most important thing is that through the grace of God we are members of Christ's body and partakers of all heavenly gifts with all the saints; for we confess none more than ourselves to be holy.

Or the Church in the wider sense comprises not only those who are truly faithful and holy, but also those who although they have no true or unfeigned faith and are not clean and holy in the conversation of their lives do acknowledge and profess true religion together with true believers and holy men of God, approving and accepting virtues and reproving evil, and not as yet separating themselves from the unity of this holy Church militant. From this standpoint not even the wicked and hypocrites (as we find that there were in the Church of the time of Christ and the apostles, such as Judas, Ananias and Sapphira, Simon Magus, and also Demas, Hymenaeus, Alexander and many others) are excluded and put out of the Church, which Church may well be described as the outward and visible Church. ...

Now since we have said that the Church militant upon earth is marked by God with certain tokens and marks by which it may be known in this world, it follows that we must now speak of those outward marks of the Church of God. And there are two particular and principal marks, the sincere preaching of the Word of God, and the lawful partaking of the sacraments of Christ. There are some who add to these the study of godliness and unity, patience in affliction and the calling on the name of God by Christ, but we include these in the two already mentioned. St. Paul writing to the Ephesians says: "Christ gave himself for the congregation, that he might sanctify it, and cleanse it in the fountain of water through the word" (Eph. 5:25–6). In this testimony of the apostle you have the marks of the Church, that is, the Word and the sacrament by which Christ makes to himself a Church. For with his grace he calls, with the blood of Christ he purifies: and he proclaims this by his Word to be received with faith, and seals it with sacraments, in order that the faithful should have no doubts concerning their salvation obtained through Christ. Now these things properly belong to the faithful and holy members. If hypocrites are not purified, the fault is in themselves and not in God or his holy ministry: they are certainly sanctified visibly, and for that reason they are counted holy amongst men; but these things do not properly belong to them. ...

On this point, for the sake of perspicuity, having treated of the marks of the Church, we must now add that it is as a common rule that these marks declare and note the members of the Church. For there are certain special members who although they lack these marks are not excluded from the society and communion of the true Church of Christ. For it is most certain that there are many in the world who do not hear the ordinary preaching of God's Word, or come into the company of those that call upon God, or receive the sacraments: not because they despise them, or find pleasure in being absent from sermons and the preaching of God's Word, but because through necessity, such as imprisonment or sickness or the constraint of other evils, they cannot attain to that which they earnestly desire; and yet for all that they are true and lively members of Christ and of the catholic Church. ...

What we have said concerning the Word of God has necessarily to be understood of the use of the sacraments as well: for unless they are used orderly and lawfully, in the order in which the Lord himself instituted them, they are not marks or signs of the Church of God. Jeroboam sacrificed truly, indeed he sacrificed to God, but because he did not sacrifice lawfully he was reckoned a stranger and an apostate from the true Church of God. Indeed, David himself brought the ark of Lord with great devotion and much joy and melody, but because he did not carry it lawfully on the shoulders of priests, at once instead of great joy the great sorrow which followed declared that it is not enough to use the sacraments and ordinances of God unless you use them lawfully; and if you do, God will acknowledge you as his. Moreover those who formerly were baptized by heretics were not baptized again by the old catholics, because the heretics did not baptize into the name of any man, or into the society of their errors or heresies, but baptized "in the name of the Father, and of the Son, and of the Holy Ghost," and they did not invocate their own name or the name of arch-heretics, but of Jesus Christ. It was not the baptism of heretics which they did not refuse, but the baptism of the Church administered by heretics. Therefore they did not allow that the churches of heretics may be recognized as true by true signs, but they acknowledged that heretics use things which properly belong to the true Church. And it does not in any way derogate or take from a good thing simply because a wicked or evil man administers it. Today we do not acknowledge the upstart Romish church of the pope (we are not speaking now of the old apostolic Church) to be the true Church of Christ, but we do not rebaptize those who were baptized by priests imbrued with popish corruption, for we know that they are baptized with the baptism of Christ's Church and not of the pope, in the name of the Holy Trinity, to the articles of the catholic faith, not to the errors and superstitions and papastical impieties. Finally we confess that today the unworthiness of the minister cannot derogate at all from the service of God. Similarly we do not refuse the Lord's Prayer or the Apostles' Creed or finally the canonical Scriptures themselves simply because the Romish church also uses them, for that church does not have them of itself, but received them from the true Church of God. Hence we use them in common with it, not for the Romish church's sake, but we use them because they came from the true Church of Christ.

Apart from these outward marks of the Church which true believers have in common with hypocrites, there are certain inward marks which belong specially to the godly alone: or if you prefer, call them rather bonds or peculiar gifts. It is these which make the outward marks to be fruitful and make men worthy and acceptable in the sight of God if for some necessary cause the outward marks are absent. For without them no man can please God. Therefore in them we have the true mark of God's children. They are the fellowship of God's Spirit, a sincere faith, and twofold charity, for by these the faithful, as true and lively members of Christ, are united and knit together, first to their head Christ, and then to all members of the body ecclesiastical. And the consideration of this point belongs chiefly to the knowledge of the true Church of God, which although it tolerates rotten members is not defiled by them through their outward conjunction, for by continual study it labours by all means to keep itself undefiled to God.

For further reading

J. Wayne Baker, *Heinrich Bullinger and the Covenant: The Other Reformed Tradition* (Athens: Ohio University Press, 1980).

Bruce Gordon, "Heinrich Bullinger (1504–1575)," in Carter Lindberg (ed.), *The Reformation Theologians: An Introduction to Theology in the Early Modern Period* (Oxford: Blackwell, 2002), pp. 170–83.

Bruce Gordon and Emidio Campi (eds.), *Architect of Reformation: An Introduction to Heinrich Bullinger, 1504–1575* (Grand Rapids: Baker Academic, 2004).

23   Menno Simons (1496–1561)

Menno Simons (whose followers came to be known as Mennonites) was a Catholic priest who converted to the Anabaptist cause thereby rejecting his priesthood and submitting to rebaptism at around the age of 40. His leadership of Anabaptism was well known as were his writings that focused on the purity of the church (often using bridal imagery) and on the church's commitment to peacefulness. In this letter to Gellius Faber, a Reformed priest who criticized the Anabaptists, Menno describes and defends the Anabaptist church, its calling, its practices, and its ministers.

Reply to Gellius Faber (1544)

Source: J. C. Wenger (ed.) and Leonard Verduin (trans.), *The Complete Writings of Menno Simons, c. 1496–1561.*

The signs by which both churches may be known
1. In the first place, the sign by which the church of Christ may be known is the salutary and unadulterated doctrine of His holy and divine Word. … Where the church of Christ is, there His Word is preached purely and rightly. But where the church of Antichrist is, there the Word of God is falsified. There we are pointed to an earthly and unclean Christ and to foreign means of salvation which the Scriptures do not know. There we are taught a broad and easy way. There the great are coddled, and truth is perverted into falsehood. There easy things are taught, such as the poor, ignorant people gladly hear. In short, there they are consoled in their predicament so that they may underrate it, and say, "Peace, peace, when there is no peace" (Jer. 8:11). They promise life to the impenitent, whereas the Scriptures say that they shall not inherit the kingdom of God (1 Cor. 6:10; Gal. 5:21).

2. The second sign is the right and Scriptural use of the sacraments of Christ, namely, the baptism of those who, by faith, are born of God, who sincerely repent, who bury their sins in Christ's death, and arise with Him in newness of life; who circumcise the foreskin of their hearts with the circumcision of Christ, done without hands; who put on Christ, and have a clear conscience: moreover the participation in the Lord's Holy Supper by the penitent, who are flesh of Christ's flesh, and expect grace, reconciliation, and the remission of their sins in the merits of the death and blood of the Lord, who walk with their brethren in love, peace, and unity, who are led by the Spirit of the Lord into all truth and righteousness, and who prove by their fruits that they are the church and people of Christ.

But where they baptize without the command and Word of God, as they do who not only baptize without faith, but also without reason and intelligence; where the power and thing signified in baptism, namely, dying unto sin, the new life, the circumcision of the heart, are not only not practiced but also hated by those who come to years of discretion; and where the bread and wine are dispensed to the avaricious, the showy, and impenitent persons; where salvation is sought in mere elements, words, and ceremonies, and where a life is led contrary to all love, there is the church of Antichrist. This all intelligent persons must admit. For it is manifest that they reject Christ, the Son of God, His Word and ordinance, and place in its stead their own ordinance and performed works, and so establish an abomination and an idolatry.

3. The third sign is obedience to the holy Word, or the pious, Christian life which is of God. ... But how holy the church of Antichrist is, how her light shines, how unblamably and purely they walk, and how their life agrees with Christ's life, may, alas, be seen from their words and works on every hand.

4. The fourth sign is the sincere and unfeigned love of one's neighbor. For Christ says, "By this shall all men know that ye are my disciples, if ye love one another" (John 13:35). Yes, reader, wherever sincere, brotherly love is found without hypocrisy, with its fruits, there we find the church of Christ. ... But where brotherly love is rejected, where they hate, defame, strike, and beat each other, where everyone seeks his own interests, where they treat each other deceitfully and faithlessly, where they curse, swear, and vituperate, where they defile their neighbor's maids, daughters, and wives; deprive each other of honor, possessions, and life; commit all manner of willfulness, abomination, and malice against each other, as may, alas, be seen on every hand: all intelligent persons may judge according to the Scriptures, whether there is not the church of Antichrist.

5. The fifth sign is that the name, will, Word, and ordinance of Christ are confidently confessed in the face of all cruelty, tyranny, tumult, fire, sword, and violence of the world, and sustained unto the end. Christ says,

"Whosoever therefore shall confess me before men, him will I confess also before my Father which is in heaven" (Matt. 10:32). ... But where the papists stick with the papists, Lutherans with the Lutherans, Interimists stick with the Interimists, etc., now build up, and anon demolish and act the hypocrite in keeping with the magistracy's wishes, everyone who is enlightened by the truth and taught by the Spirit may judge what kind of church that is.

6. The sixth sign is the pressing cross of Christ, which is borne for the sake of His testimony and Word. Christ says unto all His disciples, "Ye shall be hated of all nations for my name's sake" (Matt. 24:9). All that will live godly in Christ Jesus shall suffer persecution (2 Tim. 3:12). Sirach says, "My son, if thou come to serve the Lord, prepare thy soul for temptation. Set thy heart aright, and constantly endure, and make not haste in time of trouble. Cleave unto him, and depart not away, that thou mayest be increased at thy last end. Whatsoever is brought upon thee, take cheerfully, and be patient when thou art changed to a low estate. For gold is tried in the fire, and acceptable men in the furnace of adversity" (Ecclus 2:1–5).

This very cross is a sure indicator of the church of Christ, and has been testified not only in olden times by the Scriptures, but also by the example of Jesus Christ, of the holy apostles and prophets, the first and unfalsified church, and also by the present pious, faithful children, especially in these our Netherlands.

On the other hand, the ungodly, heathenish lying; the hating, envying, reviling, blaspheming; the unmerciful apprehending, the exiling, confiscating, and murdering, and the sentencing to water, fire, sword, and stake, seen in various localities, are plain signs of the church of Antichrist. ... Yes, my reader, this is the very way and work of the church of Antichrist, to hate, persecute, and put to the sword those whom she cannot enchant with the golden cup of her abominations.

O Lord! Dear Lord! Grant that the wrathful dragon may not entirely devour Thy poor little flock, but that we, by Thy grace, may in patience conquer by the sword of Thy mouth; and may leave an abiding seed, which shall keep Thy commandments, preserve Thy testimony, and eternally praise Thy great and glorious name. Amen, dear Lord. Amen.

For further reading

Harold S. Bender, *The Anabaptist Vision* (Scottdale, PA: Herald Press, 1944).
Donald Durnbaugh, *The Believers' Church: The History and Character of Radical Protestantism* (Scottdale, PA: Herald Press, 1985).
Paul M. Ledarach, *A Third Way* (Scottdale, PA: Herald Press, 1980).
Franklin H. Littell, *The Free Church* (Boston: Star King Press, 1957).

24   John Knox (1510–1572)

Considered the founder of Presbyterianism, John Knox was a Scottish priest and reformer who, after having met Calvin in Geneva, spread Reformed theology and practice throughout Scotland. With the help of the Scottish nobility, he led the Protestant Reformation there and a newly founded and reformed "Kirk" based on the Confession *excerpted below.*

Scots Confession (1560)

Source: John Knox, *The History of the Reformation of Religion in Scotland.*

The notes, therefore, of the true kirk of God, we believe, confess, and avow to be, *first*, the true preaching of the Word of God; [in which] God hath revealed Himself to us, as the writings of the prophets and apostles do declare. *Secondly*, the right administration of the sacraments of Christ Jesus, which must be annexed to the word and promise of God, to seal and confirm the same in our hearts. *Lastly*, ecclesiastical discipline uprightly ministered, as God's Word prescribed, whereby vice is repressed, and virtue nourished. [Wherever] then these former notes are seen, and of any time continue—be the number never so few above two or three—[there without all doubt] is the true kirk of Christ: who according to his promise is in the midst of them. (XVIII)

For further reading

Richard L. Greaves, *Theology and Revolution in the Scottish Reformation* (Washington D.C.: Christian University, 1980).
Richard G. Kyle, *The Mind of John Knox* (Lawrence, KS: Coronado Press, 1984).
―――― "The Nature of the Church in the Thought of John Knox," *Scottish Journal of Theology* 37 (1984), pp. 485–501.
Rosalind K. Marshall, *John Knox* (Edinburgh: Birlinn Publishers, 2008).

25   Robert Bellarmine (1542–1621)

Bellarmine was a Jesuit theologian who was one of the most influential Catholic ecclesiologists of the Catholic Reformation. Bellarmine opposed the notion of the Protestant reformers that there were two churches—one visible and the other invisible. For him, the church is a political entity in its own right alongside other social bodies. It is a "perfect society" with regard to its own distinct spiritual ends, while those spiritual ends are always served by its temporal and visible polity.

Disputations Concerning the Controversies of the Christian Faith (1586–93)

Source: Bernard P. Prusak, *The Church Unfinished: Ecclesiology Through the Centuries.*

The one true Church is the community of humans brought together by profession of the true faith and communion in the same sacraments, under the rule of recognized pastors and especially of the sole vicar of Christ on earth, the Roman pontiff. ... The Church is indeed a community [*coetus*] of humans, as visible and palpable as the community of the Roman people, or the kingdom of France, or the republic of Venice. (bk 3, 2)

For further reading

Stefania Tutino, *Empire of Souls: Robert Bellarmine and the Christian Commonwealth* (Oxford: Oxford University Press, 2010).

26   Richard Hooker (1554–1600)

A priest in the Church of England, Richard Hooker has had a commanding and lasting influence on the worldwide Anglican communion. In his Of the Laws of Ecclesiastical Polity, *Hooker lays out Anglicanism's famous via media between Protestantism (especially Puritanism) and Catholicism by distinguishing between the mystical and visible church. The church thus has a kind of double existence, or two natures (like Christ), even though it must be seen as a unity of those who profess Christ. Membership in the mystical church is only possible through membership in the visible church, but that visible mediation is not identical with the company of the elect. In this way, Hooker counters a radial spiritualizing of the church, on the one side, while countering any confidence in the external, visible church as the true church, on the other.*

Of the Laws of Ecclesiastical Polity (1594)

Source: John Keble (ed.), *The Works of that Learned and Judicious Divine, Mr. Richard Hooker: With an Account of His Life and Death by Isaac Walton.*

That Church of Christ, which we properly term his body mystical, can be but one; neither can that one be sensibly discerned by any man, inasmuch as the parts thereof are some in heaven already with Christ, and the rest that are on earth (albeit their natural persons be visible) we do not discern under this property, whereby they are truly and infallibly of that body. Only our minds by intellectual conceit are able to apprehend, that such a real body there is: a body collective, because it containeth an huge multitude; a body mystical, because the mystery of their conjunction is removed altogether from sense. Whatsoever we read in Scripture concerning the endless love and the saving mercy which God sheweth towards his Church, the only proper subject thereof is this Church. Concerning this flock it is that our Lord and Saviour hath promised, "I give unto them eternal life, and they shall never perish, neither shall any pluck them out of my hands" (John 10:28). They who are of this society have such marks and notes of distinction from all others, as are not object unto our sense; only unto God, who seeth their hearts and understandeth all their secret cogitations, unto him they are clear and manifest. ...

And as those everlasting promises of love, mercy, and blessedness belong to the mystical Church; even so on the other side when we read of any duty which the Church of God is bound unto, the Church whom this doth concern is a sensibly known company. And this visible Church in like sort is but one, continued from the first beginning of the world to the last end. Which company being divided into two moieties, the one before, the other since the coming of Christ; that part, which since the coming of Christ partly hath embraced and partly shall hereafter embrace the Christian Religion, we term as by a more proper name the Church of Christ. And therefore the Apostle affirmeth plainly of all men Christian, that be they Jews or Gentiles, bond or free, they are all incorporated into one company, they all make but *one body.* The unity of which visible body and Church of Christ consisteth in that uniformity which all several persons thereunto belonging have, by reason of that *one Lord* whose servants they all profess themselves, that *one Faith* which they all acknowledge, that *one Baptism* wherewith they are all initiated.

The visible Church of Jesus Christ is therefore one, in outward profession of those things, which super-naturally appertain to the very essence of Christianity, and are necessarily required in every particular Christian man. ... But our naming of Jesus Christ as Lord is not enough to prove us Christians, unless we also embrace that faith, which Christ hath published unto the world. ... (bk 3, 1:2–4)

Is it then possible, that the selfsame men should belong both to the synagogue of Satan and to the Church of Jesus Christ? Unto that Church which is his mystical body, not possible; because that body consisteth of none but only true Israelites, true sons of Abraham, true servants and saints of God. Howbeit of the visible body and Church of Jesus Christ those may be and oftentimes are, in respect of the main parts of their outward profession, who in regard of their inward disposition of mind, yea, of external conversation, yea, even of some parts of their very profession, are most worthily both hateful in the sight of God himself, and in the eyes of the sounder parts of the visible Church most execrable. Our Saviour therefore compareth the kingdom of heaven to a net, whereunto all which cometh neither is nor seemeth fish: his Church he compareth unto a field, where tares manifestly known and seen by all men do grow intermingled with good corn, and even so shall continue till the final consummation of the world. God hath had ever and ever shall have some Church visible upon earth. … (bk 3, 1:8)

By the Church … we understand no other than only the visible Church. For preservation of Christianity there is not any thing more needful, than that such as are of the visible Church have mutual fellowship and society one with another. In which consideration, as the main body of the sea being one, yet within divers precincts hath divers names; so the Catholic Church is in like sort divided into a number of distinct Societies, every of which is termed a Church within itself. In this sense the Church is always a visible society of men; not an assembly, but a society. For although the name of the Church be given unto Christian assemblies, although any multitude of Christian men congregated may be termed by the name of a Church, yet assemblies properly are rather things that belong to a Church. Men are assembled for performance of public actions; which actions being ended, the assembly dissolveth itself and is no longer in being, whereas the Church which was assembled doth no less continue afterwards than before. … But a Church, as now we are to understand it, is a Society; that is, a number of men belonging unto some Christian fellowship, the place and limits whereof are certain. … As therefore they that are of the mystical body of Christ have those inward graces and virtues, whereby they differ from all others, which are not of the same body; again, whosoever appertain to the visible body of the Church, they have also the notes of external profession, whereby the world knoweth what they are. (bk 3, 1:14)

For further reading

W. J. Torrance Kirby (ed.), *A Companion to Richard Hooker* (Leiden: E. J. Brill, 2008).

Philip Bruce Secor, *Richard Hooker: Prophet of Anglicanism* (Burns and Oats, 1999; repr. Toronto: Anglican Book Centre, 2000).

27   The *Second Helvetic Confession* (1566)

The First Helvetic Confession was drawn up in Basel in 1536 by Heinrich Bullinger, and represented the beliefs of the Swiss Reformed churches. It was the first such national Reformed creed. The Second Helvetic Confession expands on the first and was eventually adopted by Reformed churches throughout Europe. Characteristic stress is placed on Christ as the sole head of the church.

Chapter 17   "Of the Catholic and Holy Church of God, and of the Only Head of the Church"

Source: Philip Schaff, *The Creeds of Christendom*.

Since God willed from the beginning that men should be saved and come to the knowledge of truth, it follows of necessity that there always was, and now is, and shall be to the end of time, a Church or an assembly of believers and a communion of saints, called and gathered from the world, who know and worship the true God in Christ our Saviour, and partake by faith of all the benefits freely offered through Christ. They are fellow-citizens of the same household of God (Eph. 2:19). To this refers the article in the Creed: "I believe the holy catholic Church, the communion of saints."

And as there is but one God, one Mediator between God and man, Jesus the Messiah, one pastor of the whole flock, one head of this body, one Spirit, one salvation, one faith, one testament or covenant, there must needs be but one Church, which we call catholic, that is, universal, spread throughout all parts of the world and all ages.

We therefore condemn the Donatists, who confined the Church to some corners of Africa, and also the Roman exclusiveness, which pretends that the Roman Church alone is the catholic Church.

The Church is divided, not in itself, but on account of the diversity of its members. There is a Church militant on earth struggling against the flesh, the world, and the devil, and a Church triumphant in heaven rejoicing in the presence of the Lord; nevertheless there is a communion between the two. The Church militant is again divided into particular Churches. It was differently constituted among the Patriarchs, then under Moses, then under Christ in the gospel dispensation; but there is only one salvation in the one Messiah, in whom all are united as members of one body, partaking of the same spiritual food and drink. We enjoy a greater degree of light and more perfect liberty.

This Church is called the house of the living God (1 Tim. 3:15), built of lively and spiritual stones (1 Pet. 2:5), resting on an immovable rock, the only foundation (1 Cor. 3:11), the ground and pillar of the truth (1 Tim. 3:15). It can not err as long as it rests on the rock Christ, on the foundation of the Prophets and Apostles; but it errs as often as it departs from him who is the truth. The Church is also called a virgin, the bride of Christ, the only and beloved (2 Cor. 11:2), and the body of Christ, because the believers are living members of Christ under him the head (Eph. 1:23, etc.).

The Church can have no other head than Christ. He is the one universal pastor of his flock, and has promised his presence to the end of the world. He needs, therefore, no vicar; for this would imply his absence.

But by rejecting the Roman head we do not introduce disorder and confusion into the Church of Christ, since we adhere to the government delivered by the

Apostles before there was any Pope. The Roman head preserves the tyranny and corruption in the Church, and opposes and destroys all just reformation.

They object that since our separation from Rome all sorts of controversies and divisions have arisen. As if there had never been any sects and dissensions in the Roman Church, in the pulpits, and among the people! God is indeed a God of order and peace (1 Cor. 14:33); nevertheless there were parties and divisions even in the Apostles' Church (Acts 15; 1 Cor. 3; Gal. 2). God overrules these divisions for his glory and for the illustration of truth.

Communion with the true Church of Christ we highly esteem, and deny that those who separate from it can live before God. As there was no salvation out of the ark of Noah, so there is no certain salvation out of Christ, who exhibits himself to the elect in the Church for their nourishment.

But we do not so restrict the Church as to exclude those who from unavoidable necessity and unwillingly do not partake of the sacraments, or who are weak in faith, or still have defects and errors. God had friends even outside of the Jewish people. We know what happened to Peter, and to chosen believers from day to day, and we know that the Apostle censured the Christians in Galatia and Corinth for grave offenses, and yet calls them holy churches of Christ. Yea, God may at times by a righteous judgment allow the Church to be so obscured and shaken as to appear almost annihilated, as in the days of Elijah (1 Kgs 19:18; cf. Rev. 7:4, 9); but even then he has his true worshipers, even seven thousand and more; for "the foundation of God standeth sure, having this seal, the Lord knoweth them that are his" (2 Tim. 2:19). Hence the Church may be called *invisible*, not that the men composing it are invisible, but because they are known only to God, while we are often mistaken in our judgment. There are also many hypocrites in the Church, who outwardly conform to all the ordinances, but will ultimately be revealed in their true character and be cut off (1 John 2:19; Matt. 13:24, 47).

The true unity of the Church is not to be sought in ceremonies and rites, but in the truth and in the catholic faith, as laid down in the Scriptures and summed up in the Apostles' Creed. Among the ancients there was a great diversity of rites without dissolving the unity of the Church.

For further reading

Karl Barth, *The Theology of the Reformed Confessions*, trans. Darrell L. Guder and Judith J. Guder (Louisville: Westminster John Knox, 2002).

Jan Rohls, *Reformed Confessions: Theology from Zurich to Barmen* (Louisville: Westminster John Knox, 1998).

Part 3
The Modern Period

What is here being called the "modern period" refers to the period following the Reformation, from roughly the seventeenth century through to the nineteenth century and the beginnings of the Industrial Revolution. Politically and economically, this is the time when we see the rise of independent nation-states, new discoveries and global trading patterns, the creation of European colonies throughout the New World, and an increasingly urban civilization. As the Protestant Reformation extended, so also various forms of puritanism and pietism had begun to place emphasis on a personal appropriation of the gospel not only in one's outward manner of life but also in relation to inner spiritual experience. Thus, the time was ripe not only for the kind of intense spiritual self-examination and discipline associated with the Jesuit order, but also for the revivalism associated with the Great Awakenings. The importance of the church is not diminished in this period, but it becomes reconfigured as, to put it in Schleiermacher's words, a "society of the pious," such that it is both an instrument and result of personal spiritual awakening and consciousness.

1 John Smyth (c. 1570–1612)

Baptist ecclesiology first emerged from within English Puritanism in separatist communities in England and Holland (where many of the English dissenters exiled themselves) in the early seventeenth century. John Smyth was an early and influential leader of the Baptists, so-called because of their opposition to infant baptism and practice of believers-only baptism. Ordained a priest in the Church of England, Smyth left the Church of England and led a separatist covenanting congregation before eventually leaving for Amsterdam in 1608, where he ministered and wrote during the few years before his death. As with most Protestants, Smyth believed in an invisible communion of the elect with Christ, but the visible church is the necessary ordinance given by God to humans for their salvation. The theological and practical glue that creates and sustains the visible church is a solemn covenant into which believers enter with God and one another, which shapes virtually every aspect of their lives. In his Principles and Inferences concerning the Visible Church *Smyth discusses the nature of this visible church and provides a guide for receiving church members and officers, for order in worship, and for church discipline. In his* Propositions and Conclusions, *a collection of 100 articles that may have been written by Smyth or collected posthumously by his followers, we find what is "probably the first Christian confession of faith to affirm and prescribe religious liberty, or freedom of conscience, vis-à-vis civil government and the first such claim in the English language."*[1] *The articles excerpted also affirm the incompatibility of the Christian life with the use of violent force. For ease of reading, the translations provided do not include the numerous proof texts contained throughout the documents, but it should be noted that every point Smyth makes is meticulously associated with Scripture.*

Source: W. T. Whitley (ed.), *The Works of John Smyth, Fellow of Christ's College, 1594–1598.*

Principles and Inferences concerning the Visible Church (1607)

A visible communion of saints is of two, three, or more saints joined together by covenant with God and themselves, freely to use all the holy things of God, according to the word, for their mutual edification and God's glory.

This visible communion of saints is a visible church. The visible church is the only religious society that God has ordained for persons on earth. … The visible church is God's ordinance and a means to worship god. No religious communion is to be had but with members of a visible church. … The true visible church is the narrow way that leads to life which few find. Other religious communions are the broad way that leads to destruction, which many find. …

To a true visible church three things are required: (1) true matter, (2) true form, and (3) true properties.

The true matter of a true visible church are saints—those who are separated from all known sin, practicing the whole will of God known unto them, growing in grace and knowledge, continuing to the end.

The true form of a true visible Church is partly inward and partly outward. The inward part of the form consists in three things: the Spirit, faith, and love. The Spirit is the soul animating the whole body. Faith unites the members of the body to the head Christ. Love unites the members of the body each to other.

The outward part of the true form of the true visible church is a vow, promise, oath, or covenant between God and the saints by proportion from the inward form. This covenant has two parts: that between God and the faithful and that among the faithful mutually.

The first part of the covenant with respect to God is either from God to the faithful or from the faithful to God. That which is from God to the faithful is summed up, "I will be their God." To be God to the faithful is, first, to give Christ and, second, with Christ all things else. That part of the covenant from the faithful to God is summed up in being God's people, that is obeying all the

---

[1]   James Leo Garrett, *Baptist Theology: A Four-Century Study* (Macon, GA: Mercer University Press, 2009), p. 31.

commandments of God. The second part of the covenant with regard to the faithful mutually contains all the duties of love whatsoever.

The true properties of a true Church visible are two: communion in all the holy things of God and the power of our Lord Jesus Christ.

The holy things of God are Christ and benefits by Christ. The true church has title, possession, and use of Christ. The benefits which the true church has by Christ are the means of salvation and alms. The means of salvation are the word, sacraments, prayers, censures, and the ordinances of Christ for the dispensing of them all. Alms are the works of mercy yielded to the saints in distress.

The power that the Lord Jesus Christ gave to the church has three parts: to receive, to preserve and keep within, and to cast out.

Propositions and Conclusions, Concerning True Christian Religion, Containing a Confession of Faith of Certain English People, Living at Amsterdam (c. 1612)

We believe:

82. That Christ hath set in his outward church the vocation of master and servant, parents and children, husband and wife and has commanded every soul to be subject to the higher powers not because of wrath only, but for conscience sake; that we are to give them their duty as tribute, custom, honor, and fear, not speaking evil of them that are in authority, but praying and giving thanks for them, for that is acceptable in the sight of God even our savior.

84. That the magistrate is not by virtue of office to meddle with religion, or matters of conscience, to force and compel persons to this or that form of religion, or doctrine; but to leave Christian religion free to every person's conscience and to handle only civil transgressions, injuries, and wrongs of persons against each other, in murder, adultery, theft etc. For Christ only is the king and lawgiver of the church and conscience.

85. That if the magistrate will follow Christ and be His disciple, he must deny himself, take up his cross, and follow Christ. He must love his enemies and not kill them, he must pray for them and not punish them, he must feed them and give them drink, not imprison them, banish them, dismember them, and spoil their goods. He must suffer persecution and affliction with Christ and be slandered, reviled, blasphemed, scourged, buffeted, spit upon, imprisoned and killed with Christ, and that by the authority of magistrates. These things he cannot possibly do, however, and retain the revenge of the sword.

86. That the disciples of Christ, the members of the outward church, are to judge all their causes of difference among themselves and they are not to go to law before the magistrates and that all their differences must be ended by "yea" and "nay" without an oath.

87. That the disciples of Christ, the members of the outward church, may not marry any of the profane or wicked, godless people of the world, but that everyone is to marry in the Lord—every man only one wife and every woman only one husband.

For further reading

James R. Coggins, *John Smyth's Congregation: English Separatism, Mennonite, Influence, and the Elect Nation* (Waterloo, ON: Herald Press, 1991).
Jason K. Lee, *The Theology of John Smyth: Puritan, Separatist, Baptist, Mennonite* (Macon, GA: Mercer University Press, 2003).
Miroslav Volf, *After Our Likeness: The Church as the Image of the Trinity* (Grand Rapids: Eerdmans, 1998).

2   The *Westminster Confession of Faith* (1643)

During the English Civil Wars (1642–1651), the Westminster Assembly of Divines was convened by the "Long Parliament" called by Charles I to address the reformation of the Church of England. Scottish representation was pressed on the assembly both for wider political reasons and so that the Church of England and the Church of Scotland would have nearer agreement. Though the Confession of Faith *produced by the Assembly was later revoked during the Restoration of 1660, the document became the foundation of Presbyterian and other Reformed communions worldwide and with various adaptations has been in use since that time. The following is the* Confession of Faith's *article on the church.*

Source: Philip Schaff, The Creeds of Christendom.

Chapter XXV—Of the Church

I.   The catholic or universal Church, which is invisible, consists of the whole number of the elect, that have been, are, or shall be gathered into one, under Christ the head thereof; and is the spouse, the body, the fullness of him that filleth all in all.

II. The visible Church, which is also catholic or universal under the gospel (not confined to one nation as before under the law) consists of all those, throughout the world, that profess the true religion, and of their children; and is the kingdom of the Lord Jesus Christ, the house and family of God, out of which there is no ordinary possibility of salvation.

III. Unto this catholic visible Church Christ hath given the ministry, oracles, and ordinances of God, for the gathering and perfecting of the saints, in this life, to the end of the world: and doth by his own presence and Spirit, according to his promise, make them effectual thereunto.

IV. This catholic Church hath been sometimes more, sometimes less visible. And particular churches, which are members thereof, are more or less pure, according as the doctrine of the gospel is taught and embraced, ordinances administered, and public worship performed more or less purely in them.

V. The purest churches under heaven are subject both to mixture and error; and some have so degenerated as to become no churches of Christ, but synagogues of Satan. Nevertheless, there shall be always a Church on earth to worship God according to his will.

VI. There is no other head of the Church but the Lord Jesus Christ: nor can the Pope of Rome, in any sense be head thereof; but is that Antichrist, that man of sin and son of perdition, that exalteth himself in the Church against Christ, and all that is called God.

For further reading

R. D. Anderson Jr., "*Of the Church*: An Historical Overview of the *Westminster Confession of Faith*, Chapter 25," *Westminster Theological Journal* 59/2 (1997), pp. 177–99.

S. R. Jones, "The Invisible Church of the Westminster Confession of Faith," *Westminster Theological Journal* 59/1 (1997), pp. 71–85.

3   John Owen (1616–1683)

John Owen could well be considered the greatest theologian of the Puritan movement. Deeply influenced by Reformed theology and an advocate of a congregationalist ecclesiology, Owen held that the church was constituted by individual believers, morally pure and distinct from the world, regenerated by God, and thus transferred into the kingdom of Christ. These visible saints covenant together in congregations to observe Christ's commandments and ordinances, and Christ has given to these local assemblies all that is necessary for that purpose.

The True Nature of a Gospel Church (1689)

Source: William H. Goold (ed.), *The Works of John Owen*.

Our first inquiry being concerning what sort of persons our Lord Jesus Christ requireth and admitteth to be the visible subjects of his kingdom, we are to be regulated in our determination by respect unto his honour, glory, and the holiness of his rule. To reckon such persons to be subjects of Christ, members of his body, such as he requires and owns (for others are not so), who would not be tolerated, at least not approve, in a well-governed kingdom or commonwealth of the world, is highly dishonourable unto him (Pss. 15:1–5, 24:3–4, 43:5; 2 Cor. 8:23; Eph. 5:27). But it is so come to pass, that men be never so notoriously and flagitiously wicked, until they become pests of the earth, yet are they esteemed to belong to the church of Christ; and not only so, but it is thought little less than schism to forbid them the communion of the church in all its sacred privileges. Howbeit, the Scripture doth in general represent the kingdom or church of Christ to consist of persons called *saints*, separated from the world, with many other things of an alike nature, as we shall see immediately. And if the honour of Christ were of such weight with us as it ought to be,—if understood aright the nature and ends of his kingdom, and that the peculiar glory of it above all the kingdoms in the world consists in the holiness of its subjects, such a holiness as the world in its wisdom knoweth not,—we would duly consider whom we avow to belong thereunto. Those who know aught of these things will not profess that persons openly profane, vicious, sensual, wicked, and ignorant, are approved and owned of Christ as the subjects of his kingdom, or that it is his will that we should receive them into the communion of the church (2 Tim. 3:1–5). But an old opinion of the unlawfulness of separation from a church on the account of the mixture of wicked men in it is made a scare-crow to frighten men from attempting the reformation of the greatest evils, and a covert for the composing churches of such members only.

Some things, therefore, are to be premised unto what shall be offered unto the right stating of this inquiry; as:

1. That if there be no more required of any, as unto *personal qualifications*, in a visible, uncontrollable profession, to constitute them subjects of Christ's kingdom and members of his church (Ezek. 22:26), but what is required by the most righteous and severe laws of men to constitute a good subject or citizen, the distinction between his visible kingdom and the kingdoms of the world, as unto the principal causes of it, is utterly lost. Now, all negative qualifications, as, that men are not oppressors, drunkards, revilers, swearers, adulterers, etc., are required hereunto; but yet it is so fallen out that generally more is required to constitute such a citizen as shall represent the righteous laws he liveth under than to constitute a member of the church of Christ.

2. That whereas *regeneration* is expressly required in the gospel to give a right and privilege unto an entrance into the church or kingdom of Christ (John 3:3, Tit. 3:3–5), whereby that kingdom of his is distinguished from all other kingdoms in and of the world, unto an interest wherein never any such thing was required, it must of necessity be something better, more excellent and sublime, than any thing the laws and polities of men pretend unto or prescribe. Wherefore it cannot

consist in any outward rite, easy to be observed by the worst and vilest of men. Besides, the Scripture gives us a description of it in opposition unto its consisting in any such rite (1 Pet. 3:21); and many things required unto good citizens are far better than the mere observation of such a rite.

3. Of this regeneration baptism is the symbol, the sign, the expression, and representation (John 3:5; Acts 2:38; 1 Pet. 3:21). Wherefore, unto those who are in a due manner partakers of it, it giveth all the external rights and privileges which belong unto them that are regenerate, until they come unto such seasons wherein the personal performance of those duties whereon the continuation of the estate of visible regeneration doth depend is required of them. Herein if they fail, they lose all privilege and benefit by their baptism ….

4. God alone is judge concerning this regeneration, as unto its *internal, real principle and state* in the souls of men (Acts 15:8; Rev. 2:23), whereon the participation of all the spiritual advantages of the covenant of grace doth depend. The church is judge of its evidences and fruits in their external demonstration, as unto a participation of *the outward privileges of a regenerate state*, and no farther (Acts 8:13). And we shall hereon briefly declare what belongs unto the forming of a right judgment herein, and who are to be esteemed fit members of any gospel church-state, or have a right so to be:

1. Such as from whom we are obliged to *withdraw* or *withhold communion* can be no part of the matter constituent of a church, or are not meet members for the first constitution of it (1 Cor. 6:9–11; Phil. 3:18, 19; 2 Thess. 3:6; 2 Tim. 3:5; Rom. 9:6, 7; Tit. 1:16). But such are all habitual sinners, those who, having prevalent habits and inclinations unto sins of any kind unmortified, do walk according unto them. Such are profane swearers, drunkards, fornicators, covetous, oppressors, and the like, "who shall not inherit the kingdom of God" (1 Cor. 6:9–11; Phil. 3:18–19; 2 Thess. 3:6; 2 Tim. 3:5). As a man living and dying in any known sin, that is, habitually, without repentance, cannot be saved, so a man known to live in sin cannot regularly be received into any church. To compose churches of habitual sinners, and that either as unto sins of commission or sins of omission, is not to erect temples to Christ, but chapels unto the devil.

2. Such as, being in the fellowship of the church, are to be *admonished of any scandalous sin*, which if they repent not of they are to be cast out of the church, are not meet members for the original constitution of a church (Matt. 18:15–18; 1 Cor. 5:11). This is the state of them who abide obstinate in any known sin, whereby they have given offence unto others, without a professed repentance thereof, although they have not lived in it habitually.

3. They are to be such as *visibly answer* the description given of gospel churches in the Scripture, so as the titles assigned therein unto the members of such churches may on good grounds be appropriated unto

them. To compose churches of such persons as do not visibly answer the character given of what they were of old, and what they were always to be by virtue of the law of Christ or gospel constitution, is not church edification but destruction. And those who look on the things spoken of all church-members of old, as that they were saints by calling, lively stones in the house of God, justified and sanctified, separated from the world, etc., as those which were in them, and did indeed belong unto them, but even deride the necessity of the same things in present church-members, or the application of them unto those who are so, are themselves no small part of that [woeful] degeneracy which Christian religion is fallen under. ... Wherefore, I say, to suppose churches regularly to consist of such persons, for the greater part of them, as no way answer the description given of church members in their original institution, nor capable to discharge the duties prescribed unto them, but giving evidence of habits and actions inconsistent therewithal is not only to disturb all church-order, but utterly to overthrow the ends and being of churches. Nor is there any thing more scandalous unto Christian religion than what Bellarmine affirms to be the judgment of the Papists, in opposition unto all others, namely, "That no internal virtue or grace is required unto the constitution of the church in its members" (*De Eccles.* bk 3, ch. 2).

4. They must be such as do *make an open profession of the subjection of their souls and consciences unto the authority of Christ in the gospel, and their readiness to yield obedience unto all his commands* (Rom. 10:10; 2 Cor. 8:5, 9:13; Matt. 10:32–3; Luke 9:26; 2 Tim. 2:12; Rom. 15:9; John 12:42; 1 John 4:2–3, 15). This I suppose, will not be denied; for not only doth the Scripture make this profession necessary unto the participation of any benefit or privilege of the gospel, but the nature of the things themselves requires indispensably that so it should be: for nothing can be more unreasonable than that men should be taken into the privileges attending obedience unto the laws and commands of Christ without avowing or professing that obedience.

For further reading

Kelly M. Kapic, *Communion with God: The Divine and Human in the Theology of John Owen* (Grand Rapids: Baker Academic, 2007).

Carl R. Trueman, *John Owen: Reformed Catholic, Renaissance Man* (Aldershot: Ashgate, 2007).

4 Charles Wesley (1707–1788)

If John Wesley was the acknowledged leader and architect of the Methodist movement, his younger brother Charles was no less influential as the movement's poet and hymnwriter. The following hymn emphasizes the sense in which the church is a community of virtue as it is formed into Christ and thereby made by a sacrament of care and healing.

"Jesus, Lord, We Look to Thee" (1749)

Source: Charles Wesley, *Hymns and Sacred Poems*.

Jesu, Lord, we look to Thee,
Let us in thy Name agree,
Shew Thyself the Prince of Peace,
Bid our Jars[2] forever cease.

By thy reconciling Love
Every Stumbling block remove,
Each to Each unite, indear,
Come, and spread thy Banner here.

Make us of one Heart and Mind,
Courteous, pitiful, and kind,
Lowly, meek in Thought and Word,
Altogether like our Lord.

Let us Each for Other care,
Each his Brother's Burthen bear,
To thy Church the Pattern give,
Shew how true Believers live.

Free from Anger, and from Pride,
Let us thus in God abide,
All the Depth of Love express,
All the Height of Holiness.

Let us then with Joy remove
To thy Family above,
On the Wings of Angels fly,
Shew how true Believers die.

---

[2] Or "strife."

For further reading

S. T. Kimbrough Jr., "Wesleyan Ecclesiology: Charles Wesley's Understanding of the Nature of the Church," in S. T. Kimbrough Jr. (ed.), *Orthodox and Wesleyan Ecclesiology* (Crestwood, NY: St. Vladimir's Seminary Press, 2007), pp. 129–48.

J. Ernest Rattenbury, *The Eucharistic Hymns of John and Charles Wesley* (London: Epworth, 1948).

5   John Fawcett (1740–1817)

John Fawcett was a convert of George Whitefield who eventually became a Baptist minister. The story of this particular hymn, one of the most popular of all modern ecclesiological hymns, is that Fawcett had accepted a pastoral appointment to a congregation in London much larger and more prominent than the tiny one he was leading in Wainsgate, in northern England. As his sad congregants gathered around the wagons loaded with his belongings on the day of his departure, he and his wife were so moved that they decided to stay and there remained for over fifty years. Fawcett wrote the hymn to express the love and mutuality he felt with his congregation.[3]

"Blest be the Tie that Binds" ["Brotherly Love"] (1772)

Source: John Fawcett, *Hymns Adapted to the Circumstances of Public Worship and Private Devotion.*

Blest be the tie that binds
Our hearts in Christian love;
The fellowship of kindred minds
Is like to that above.

Before our Father's throne
We pour are ardent pray'rs;
Our fears, our hopes, our aims are one,
Our comforts and our cares.

We share our mutual woes,
Our mutual burdens bear;
And often for each other flows
The sympathizing tear.

---

[3]   This account follows that given by Kenneth W. Osbeck, *101 Hymn Stories* (Grand Rapids: Kregel, 1982), pp. 100–101.

When we asunder part,
It give us inward pain;
But we shall still be join'd in heart,
And hope to meet again.

This glorious hope revives
Our courage by the way;
While each in expectation lives,
And longs to see the day.

From sorrow, toil, and pain,
And sin, we shall be free;
And perfect love and friendship reign
Thro' all eternity.

6   John Wesley (1703–1791)

As an Anglican priest and scholar, John Wesley never intended his "Methodists" to be anything other than a reforming movement within the Church of England, despite the separation that occurred after his death. In this sermon, "Of the Church," Wesley attempts to define the church while arguing for the agreeability of his definition with official Anglican ecclesiology. At the same time, in keeping with his distinctive emphasis on holiness of life, he holds that the true church is neither institutionally defined nor is it primarily (as with the Anglican "Articles of Faith") marked by preaching of "the pure Word of God" and right administration of the sacraments. Above all, the church is marked by the holiness of its members, whose distinctive walk is a visible witness to a faith that works by love.

"Of the Church" (1785)

Source: Albert Outler (ed.), *The Works of John Wesley.*

How many wonderful reasons have been found out for giving [the church] this appellation [namely, "holy"]! One learned man informs us, "The church is called holy because Christ the head of it is holy." Another eminent author affirms, "It is so called because all its ordinances are designed to promote holiness"; and yet another, "Because our Lord intended that all the members of the church should be holy." Nay, the shortest and the plainest reason that can be given, and the only true one, is: the church is called "holy" because it is holy; because every member thereof is holy, though in different degrees, as he that called them is holy. How clear is this! If the church, as to the very essence of it, is a body of believers, no man that is not a Christian believer can be a member of it. If this whole body be animated by one spirit, and endued with one faith and one hope of their calling; then he who has not that spirit, and faith, and hope, is no member of this body. It follows that not only no common swearer, no sabbath-breaker, no drunkard, no whoremonger, no thief, no liar, none that lives in any outward sin; but none that is under the power of anger or pride, no lover of the world—in a word, none that is dead to God—can be a member of his church.

Can anything then be more absurd than for men to cry out, "the Church! the Church!" and to pretend to be very zealous for it, and violent defenders of it; while they themselves have neither part nor lot therein, nor indeed know what the church is? And yet the hand of God is in this very thing! Even in this his wonderful wisdom appears, directing their mistake to his own glory, and causing "the earth to help the woman." Imagining that they are members of it themselves, the men of the world frequently defend the church. Otherwise the wolves that surround the little flock on every side would in a short time tear them in pieces. And for this very reason it is not wise to provoke them more than is unavoidable. Even on this ground let us, if it be possible, as much as lieth in us, live peaceably with all men. Especially as we know not how soon God may call them too out of the kingdom of Satan into the kingdom of his dear Son.

In the meantime let all those who are real members of the church see that they walk holy and unblameable in all things. "Ye are the light of the world!" Ye are "a city set upon a hill, and cannot be hid. O let your light shine before men!" Show them your faith by your works. Let them see by the whole tenor of your conversation that your hope is all laid up above! Let all your words and actions evidence the spirit whereby you are animated! Above all things, let your love abound. Let it extend to every child of man; let it overflow to every child of God. By this let all men know whose disciples ye are, because you love one another.

For further reading

David Carter, *Love Bade Me Welcome: A British Methodist Perspective on the Church* (Peterborough: Epworth, 2002).

S. T. Kimbrough Jr. (ed.), *Orthodox and Wesleyan Ecclesiology* (Crestwood, NY: St. Vladimir's Seminary Press, 2007).

Dow Kirkpatric (ed.), *The Doctrine of the Church* (Nashville: Abingdon Press, 1964), esp. Albert Outler, "Do Methodists Have a Doctrine of the Church?" pp. 11–28.

Gwang Seok Oh, *John Wesley's Ecclesiology: A Study in Its Sources and Development* (Metuchen, NJ: The Scarecrow Press, 2007).

7   John Newton (1725–1807)

Anglican clergyman John Newton is most well known for composing "Amazing Grace," which was published along with the following hymn, "Glorious Things of Thee Are Spoken." Newton, who had been involved in the slave-trade early in his life, was converted in 1764 and became a fervent supporter of the movement to abolish slavery. Over the years, "Glorious Things of Thee Are Spoken" has become an enormously popular hymn in the English language with its affirmation of God's sovereignty over, protection of, and provision for the church.

"Glorious Things of Thee are Spoken" (1779)

Source: John Newton, *Olney Hymns in Three Books*.

Glorious things of thee are spoken,
Zion, city of our God!
He, whose word cannot be broken,
Form'd thee for his own abode:
On the rock of ages founded,
What can shake thy sure repose?
With salvation's walls surrounded
Thou may'st smile at all thy foes.

See! the streams of living waters
Springing from eternal love;
Well supply thy sons and daughters,
And all fear of want remove:
Who can faint while such a river
Ever flows their thirst t' assuage?
Grace, which like the Lord, the giver,
Never fails from age to age.

Round each habitation hov'ring
See the cloud and fire appear!
For a glory and a cov'ring,
Shewing that the LORD is near:
Thus deriving from their banner
Light by night and shade by day;
Safe they feed upon the manna
Which he gives them when they pray.

Blest inhabitants of Zion,
Washed in the Redeemer's blood!
Jesus, whom their souls rely on,

Makes them kings and priests to God:
'Tis his love his people raises
Over self to reign as kings,
And as priests, his solemn praises
Each for a thank-offering brings.

Savior, if of Zion's city
I thro' grace a member am;
Let the world deride or pity,
I will glory in thy name:
Fading is the worldling's pleasure,
All his boasted pomp and show;
Solid joys and lasting treasure,
None but Zion's children know.

8   Friedrich Schleiermacher (1768–1834)

In Schleiermacher, one can readily detect the rejection of traditional ecclesiastical authority and the "turn to the subject" characteristic of modern theology. In Schleiermacher, however, this subjectivity and individualism is less rationalistic and instead more deeply pietistic, locating the "essence" of Christianity in the affective dimensions of human existence ("feeling," intuition, mystical experience of the infinite whole and of transcendence). In his Speeches on Religion to Its Cultured Despisers, *the form of Schleiermacher's apologetic is an appeal to those who had rejected Christianity in the name of modern humanistic ideals and an argument that authentic Christianity is the highest expression of the true religious spirit and is, in fact, the fulfillment of our deepest human aspirations. The true church, far from being an authoritarian imposition that negates the freedom and dignity of the individual, instead corresponds to a deep-seated sociality in the human and the need to communicate the noblest elements and experiences of our shared nature with one another.*

On Religion: Speeches to Its Cultured Despisers (1799)

Source: Friedrich Schleiermacher, *On Religion: Speeches to Its Cultured Despisers*, trans. John Oman.

Those of you who are accustomed to regard religion simply as a malady of the soul, usually cherish the idea that if the evil is not to be quite subdued, it is at least more endurable, so long as it only infects individuals here and there. On the other hand, the common danger is increased and everything put in jeopardy by too close association among the patients. So long as they are isolated, judicious treatment, due precautions against infection and a healthy spiritual atmosphere may allay the paroxysms and weaken, if they do not destroy, the virus, but in the other case the only remedy to be relied on is the curative influence of nature. The evil would be accompanied by the most dangerous symptoms and be far more deadly being nursed and heightened by the proximity of the infected. Even a few would then poison the whole atmosphere; the soundest bodies would be infected; all the canals in which the processes of life are carried on would be destroyed; all juices would be decomposed; and, after undergoing such a feverish delirium, the healthy spiritual life and working of whole generations and peoples would be irrecoverably ruined. Hence your opposition to the church, to every institution meant for the communication of religion is always more violent than your opposition to religion itself, and priests, as the supports and specially active members of such institutions are for you the most hated among men.

But those of you who have a somewhat milder view of religion, regarding it rather as an absurdity than as an absolute distraction, have an equally unfavourable idea of all organizations for fellowship. Slavish surrender of everything characteristic and free, spiritless mechanism and vain usages are, you consider, the inseparable consequences of every such institution. It is the skilful work of persons who with incredible success make great gain from things that are nothing, or which at least every other person could have done equally well. ...

If there is religion at all, it must be social, for that is the nature of man, and it is quite peculiarly the nature of religion. You must confess that when an individual has produced and wrought out something in his own mind, it is morbid and in the highest degree unnatural to wish to reserve it to himself. He should express it in the indispensable fellowship and mutual dependence of action. And there is also a spiritual nature which he has in common with the rest of his species which demands that he express and communicate all that is in him. The more violently he is moved and the more deeply he is impressed, the stronger that social impulse works. And this is true even if we regard it only as the endeavour to find the feeling in others, and so to be sure that nothing has been encountered that is not human.

You see that this is not a case of endeavouring to make others like ourselves, nor of believing that what is in one man is indispensable for all. It is only the endeavour to become conscious of and to exhibit the true relation of our own life to the common nature of man.

But indisputably the proper subjects for this impulse to communicate are the conscious states and feelings in which originally man feels himself passive. He is urged on to learn whether it may not be an alien and unworthy power that has produced them. Those are the things which mankind from childhood are chiefly engaged in communicating. His ideas, about the origin of which he can have no doubts, he would rather leave in quiet. Still more easily he resolves to reserve his judgments. But of all that enters by the senses and stirs the feelings he will have witnesses and participators. How could he keep to himself the most comprehensive and general influences of the world when they appear to him the greatest and most irresistible? How should he wish to reserve what most strongly drives him out of himself and makes him conscious that he cannot know himself from himself alone? If a religious view become clear to him, or a pious feeling stir his soul, it is rather his first endeavour to direct others to the same subject and if possible transmit the impulse. …

Of such a nature is the influence of religious men upon each other. Thus their natural and eternal union is produced. It is a heavenly bond, the most perfect production of the spiritual nature of man, not to be attained till man, in the highest sense, knows himself. Do not blame them if they value it more highly than the civil union which you place so far above all else, but which nevertheless will not ripen to manly beauty. Compared with that other union, it appears far more forced than free, far more transient than eternal.

But where, in all that I have said of the congregation of the pious, is that distinction between priests and laity to which you are accustomed to point as the source of so many evils? You have been deluded; this is no distinction of persons, but only of office and function. Every man is a priest, in so far as he draws others to himself in the field he has made his own and can show himself master in; every man is a layman, in so far as he follows the skill and direction of another in the religious matters with which he is less familiar. That tyrannical aristocracy which you describe as so hateful does not exist, but this society is a priestly nation, a complete republic, where each in turn is leader and people, following in others the same power that he feels in himself and uses for governing others. …

Whence then, if not from pure misunderstanding, is the wild mania for converting to single definite forms of religion that you denounce, and the awful watchword, "No salvation save with us"?

The society of the pious, as I have exhibited it and as from its nature it must be, is occupied purely with mutual communication, and subsists only among persons already having religion of some kind. How can it be their business to change the minds of those who already profess to have a definite religion, or to introduce and initiate persons who have none at all? The religion of this society as such is simply the collective religion of all the pious. As each one sees it in others it is infinite, and no single person can fully grasp it, for it is in no one instance a unity, not even when highest and most cultivated. If a man, therefore, has any share in religion, it matters not what, would it not be a mad proceeding for the society to rend from him that which suits his nature, for this element also it should embrace and therefore someone must possess it? And how would they cultivate persons to whom religion generally is still strange? Their heritage, the infinite Whole they cannot communicate to them, and any particular communication must proceed from an individual and not the society. …

Allow yourselves to be led once more to the exalted fellowship of truly religious souls. It is dispersed and almost invisible, but its spirit rules everywhere, even where but few are gathered in the name of the Deity. What is there in it that should not fill you with admiration and esteem, ye friends and admirers of the good and beautiful? They are among themselves an academy of priests. The exhibition of the holy life, which for them is the highest, is treated by everyone as his art and study, and the Deity out of His endless riches apportions to each one his own lot. To a universal sense for everything belonging to the sacred sphere of religion, every man joins as artists should, the endeavour to perfect himself in some one department. A noble rivalry prevails, and a longing to produce something worthy of such an assembly makes everyone with faithfulness and diligence master all that belongs to his special section. In a pure heart it is preserved, with concentrated mind it is arranged, by heavenly art it is moulded and perfected. Thus in every way and from every source, acknowledgment and praise of the Infinite resound, everyone bringing, with joyous heart, the ripest fruit of his thinking and examining, of his comprehending and feeling. They are also among themselves a choir of friends. Everyone knows that he is both a part and a work of the Universe, in him also its divine life and working being revealed. He, therefore, regards himself as an object worthy of the attention of others. With sacred reserve, yet with a ready openness that all may enter and behold, he lays bare everything of the relations of the Universe of which he is conscious and what of the elements of humanity takes individual shape in him. Why should they hide anything from one another? All that is human is holy, for all is divine. Again, they are among themselves a band of brothers — or have you perhaps an intenser expression for the entire blending of their natures, not in respect of existence and working, but in respect of sense and understanding? The more everyone approaches the Universe and the more they communicate to one another, the more perfectly they all become one. No one has a consciousness for himself, each has also that of his neighbour. They are no longer men, but mankind also. Going out of themselves and triumphing over themselves, they are on the way to true immortality and eternity.

If in any other department of life, or in any other school of wisdom, you have found anything nobler than this, impart it to me; mine I have given you.

For further reading

Friedrich Schleiermacher, *The Christian Faith* (Edinburgh: T & T Clark, 1976).

9   F. D. Maurice (1805–1872)

F. D. Maurice was an Anglican theologian and "Christian socialist" whose thought was formed in response to questions of the relationship of church and state along with the vitality and relevance of the church in the face of modern patterns of social organization. For Maurice, God's work of reconciliation and communion with human beings is established in the life and death of Christ and realized in the universal, spiritual society made possible by Christ. Though Maurice argued that the Anglican church preserved the relationship between the outward form and the inner meaning of the sacraments better than other Christian traditions, he was attracted by Quaker theology and held that this "universal church" transcends national and other human divisions and corresponds to that which Quakers had sought to establish. The unity and catholicity of that church are to be found in God's universal work in Christ—"the kingdom of Christ"—rather than in this or that human institution, creed, or system of belief. Maurice pushes against any ontological dualism between church and world, for Christ is the head of the human race and not just the church.

"On the Unity of the Church" (1853)

Source: F. D. Maurice, *Theological Essays*, 2nd edn.

St. John said there were many Antichrists in his day. It is no stumbling-block to our faith if there are many in ours. But it would be the utter uprooting of our faith if we found that there was no such body as the Apostles told us there should be, with which all lying and contention should be at war,—if there was no Spirit dwelling in that body against which these heresies and corruptions and Antichrists are fighting, and which will at last prevail against them. Romanists, Protestant nations, all sects, declare that there is such a body, and that there is such a Spirit. Their words bear witness of it; their crimes, which outrage those words, bear witness of it still more.

And thus we are enabled to understand better than by all artificial definitions how a Church differs from a world. "The Comforter," our Lord says, "shall convince the world." When He speaks to the disciples, He says, "He shall come and dwell in you." The world contains the elements of which the Church is composed. In the Church these elements are penetrated by a uniting, reconciling power. The Church is, therefore, human society in its normal state; the World, that same society irregular and abnormal. The world is the Church without God; the Church is the world restored to its relation with God, taken back by Him into the state for which He created it. Deprive the Church of its Centre, and you make it into a world. If you give it a false Centre, as the Romanists have done, still preserving the sacraments, forms, creeds, which speak of the true Centre, there necessarily comes out that grotesque hybrid which we witness, a world assuming all the dignity and authority of a Church,—a Church practising all the worst fictions of a world;

the world assuming to be heavenly,—a Church confessing itself to be of the earth, earthly.

"The World and the Church" (1857)

Source: F. D. Maurice, *Sermons Preached in Lincoln's Inn Chapel.*

The Universal Church, constituted in its Universal Head, exists to protest against a world which supposes itself to be a collection of incoherent fragments without a centre, which, where it reduces its practice to a maxim, treats every man as his own centre. The Church exists to tell the world of its true Centre, of the law of mutual sacrifice by which its parts are bound together. The Church exists to maintain the order of the nation and the order of the family, which this selfish practice and selfish maxim are continually threatening. And as the Church, following man's guidance, and re-constituted according to man's conception, has been enslaving, corrupting, destroying the world, and misrepresenting its Creator; so the Church, under God's guidance, obeying the principle upon which He has formed it, has been the instrument of freeing and renovating the world. The Church, exalting itself, has raised the selfishness of the world into a law, and has stamped it with divinity. The Church, humbling itself, has borne witness to the world of One who gave up Himself that He might take away its sin.

Letter to Rev. W. Palmer: "Catholicism and Protestantism" (1842)

Source: F. D. Maurice, *Three Letters to the Rev. W. Palmer*, 2nd edn.

I believe then, that our Lord came into this world to set up His Church or Kingdom in the midst of it; that this kingdom is universal, unfettered by the limits of Nation or Age, of Space, or Time. I believe that this universal Church is founded on the union established between Manhood and Godhead, in the Person of JESUS CHRIST, and upon all those acts of birth, death, burial, descent into hell, resurrection, and ascension, in which His union with our race was realized, and His union with God manifested. I believe that as this union of Godhead and manhood rests, so the Church itself rests ultimately upon the name of the Father and the Son and the Holy Ghost, wherein is expressed that highest, deepest, most perfect unity, which the spirit of men in all ages has been seeking after and longing to find.

I believe that this universal Church is the only true society for men, as men—the only body which declares to us what Humanity is, and what a false, spurious, anomalous thing that *World* is, which is based upon individual selfishness, in which each man is his own centre. I believe that this spiritual and universal body was not made by Christ to depend upon the feelings, or faith of men, because these feelings and faith are nothing, unless they have something to rest on—because it is a contradiction and absurdity to suppose that they create that without which they would have no existence. I believe that He meant His Church to stand in certain permanent and universal institutions; upon a sacrament by which men should be taken into a real and not fictitious union with Him; upon another sacrament in which they might enjoy real and not fictitious communion with Him; upon creeds in which they should assert and claim their actual relationship to Him; in forms of worship wherein they should realize the highest perfection of their being, and the greatest fellowship with each other in confessing their sins to Him, glorifying His name, and asking His help; in a permanent ministry through which He should declare His will, and dispense his blessings to the whole body, and the main office in which should be that apostolic office which belongs characteristically to the new dispensation, seeing that it expresses the general oversight of Him, who no longer confines Himself to any particular nation, but has ascended up on high, that He might fill all things. Finally, in His written scripture, wherein the whole progress and development of His kingdom, is in an orderly manner set forth; its nature and constitution explained; the meaning of its ordinances, and their inseparable and eternal connection with Himself, made intelligible. ...

I believe ... that the nations of the Continent which became Protestant, became witnesses for the distinctness of nations and the distinctness of persons, but ceased to be witnesses for the existence of a universal body or family; that the nations which remained subject to the Pope of Rome continued to bear a kind of witness for the existence of such a family, but ceased altogether to be witnesses for the moral distinctness of each man, for the moral distinctness of each nation. I believe, however, that each of these witnesses was for its own purpose most weak and unsatisfactory. ... I believe that it is God's will that we should now present these great truths to men, not merely as dogmas derived from the earliest ages (though we may thank God with all our hearts that they have been so derived to us;) but in that more practical and real form in which they were presented to the men of the first ages themselves; as the solution for mysteries, for which there is no other solution; as the answers given by heaven to cries which have been sent up from earth. And I believe that this being the case, the Church, as embodied in those permanent institutions which belong to no age or nation, and which have in so wonderful a manner been preserved through so many variations of national customs and periods, may now come forth and present herself, not as a mere utterer of dogmas, which men must not dispute because they are afraid, but as the witness and embodier of those permanent realities, which earnest hearts feel that they need, and which they have been willing by God's spirit in the day of His power to receive, and which when so set forth, will be denied at last only by those who deny their own moral being and responsibility; that she may present herself not as a body, whose chief function is to banish and anathematise, but as one from which none are excluded but those who exclude themselves, because they prefer division to unity, and the conditions of a party to the freedom of an universe.

I believe, that when any part of the Church is able to assert this position, grounding its own existence simply on the Incarnation of Christ, and putting forth all those institutions and ordinances which it has in common with Christendom, as the declaration of this Incarnation and of Christ's Headship over the Church, that part of it may be blessed by God, to be the restorer of unity to the East and to the West, to the Church in France, in Spain, in Italy, in Greece, in Syria, and in Russia.

For further reading

F. D. Maurice, *The Kingdom of Christ; Or, Hints Respecting the Principles, Constitution and Ordinances of the Catholic Church*, 2 vols. (New York: D. Appleton & Co., 1863).

Jeremy Morris, *F. D. Maurice and the Crisis of Christian Authority* (Oxford: Oxford University Press, 2005).

Jeremy Morris (ed.), *To Build Christ's Kingdom: An F. D. Maurice Reader, Canterbury Studies in Spiritual Theology* (Norwich: Canterbury Press, 2007).

10 "The Church's One Foundation" (1866)

This hymn, one of the most famous of all hymns written about the church, was composed by Anglican clergyman Samuel J. Stone (1839–1900) in response to a controversy generated by the publication of a book by John W. Colenso, bishop of Natal, South Africa. Bishop Colenso was a supporter of F. D. Maurice and an advocate of newly developing historical-critical approaches to scripture. Colenso was widely accused of heresy (and was even excommunicated by a rival bishop) for refusing to support the Bible's infallibility within a literalist framework. One can readily detect in Stone's hymn explicit references to what he and others perceived as attacks on the historic Christian faith.

Source: S. J. Stone, *Hymnal According to the Use of the Protestant Episcopal Church in the United States of America.*

The Church's one Foundation
Is Jesus Christ her Lord;
She is His new creation
By water and the word:
From heaven He came and sought her
To be His holy Bride;
With His own blood He bought her,
And for her life He died.

Elect from every nation,
Yet one o'er all the earth,
Her charter of salvation
One Lord, one faith, one birth;
One Holy Name she blesses,
Partakes one holy food,
And to one hope she presses,
With every grace endued.

Though with a scornful wonder
Men see her sore opprest,
By schisms rent asunder,
By heresies distrest,
Yet saints their watch are keeping,
Their cry goes up, "How long?"
And soon the night of weeping
Shall be the morn of song.

'Mid toil and tribulation,
And tumult of her war,
She waits the consummation
Of peace for evermore;
Till with the vision glorious
Her longing eyes are blest,
And the great Church victorious
Shall be the Church at rest.

Yet she on earth hath union
With God the Three in One,
And mystic sweet communion
With those whose rest is won:
O happy ones and holy!
Lord, give us grace that we,
Like them, the meek and lowly,
On high may dwell with Thee.

Part 4

The Twentieth Century

Yale historian Jaroslav Pelikan once said that "the doctrine of the church became, as it had never quite been before, the bearer of the whole Christian message for the twentieth century, as well as the recapitulation of the entire doctrinal tradition from preceding centuries."[1] Likewise, in 1926, Otto Dibelius called the twentieth century *das Jahrhundert der Kirche*, "the century of the church." Dibelius had in mind the fact that after centuries of having been tied to imperial or state power, the church might now gain some measure of independence and freedom, forced to "make it on its own," we might say, without the support of a nominally Christian culture or the administrative apparatus of the state. As the church found itself needing to radically re-negotiate its relationship to nations, cultures, and empires in an increasingly post-Christendom world—not to mention needing to do so in contexts like that of Nazi Germany—ecclesiology took on new urgency and importance.

The missionary movement also picked up steam in the twentieth century generating the need for reflection on what it means to be the church in non-Western contexts, often over against those Western forms of Christianity that came with the missionaries themselves (it was often the missionaries who instigated this critical reflection, it should be noted). Movements for liberation and independence throughout the world provoked new indigenous, feminist, socially transformative, and revolutionary ecclesiologies that sought to re-imagine a more inclusive, participatory, and liberative church that would challenge rather than mirror the hierarchical, patriarchal, and colonial social structures that had for centuries shaped the church.

Lastly, a truly global Christianity had emerged by the twentieth century so that new concerns with the unity of the church along with its missionary existence came to be prominent. These ecumenical and missionary concerns gave rise to new associations such as the World Council of Churches and provided motivation for Vatican II, which also sought to re-think the nature and mission of the church in a new world. Then, too, hand-in-hand with a global Christianity came the urgency to re-think the relationship of the church to other religions, ideologies, and political and economic structures. All in all, and as attested to by the breadth of readings in the following pages, the twentieth century witnessed the remarkable proliferation of ecclesiologies ranging from feminism to evangelicalism, from those influenced by the social

---

[1] Jaroslav Pelikan, *The Christian Tradition: A History of the Development of Doctrine* (Chicago: University of Chicago Press, 1989), vol. 5, p. 282.

gospel to those influenced by the Black Power movement, from the non-church movement in Japan to the confessing church in Germany, from the ecumenical interests of the World Council of Churches to ancestor-based churches in Africa.

1   Walter Rauschenbusch (1861–1918)

The Social Gospel Movement of the early twentieth century came on the heels of an intense period of industrialization in North America and as a response to it. The prophets of the social gospel, such as Walter Rauschenbusch and Shailer Matthews, criticized social conditions characterized by unemployment, poverty, and economic inequities, while emphasizing the social character of the gospel as summed up in Jesus' preaching of "the kingdom of God." Rauschenbusch emphasized the social and systemic nature of sin and stressed the incredible power of social institutions both for good and for evil. For social gospellers, however, the gospel of Jesus is just as social and systemic as is sin. When understood properly, the gospel demands transformation at the deepest levels of human existence. By re-thinking Christian doctrine in social terms, Rauschenbusch offered a challenging new lens for reading the world, re-thinking the mission of Jesus, and doing theology and ethics that was to inspire a renewal of the church's relationship to society throughout the twentieth century. For Rauschenbusch, the church is called corporately to side with the poor and the unemployed thereby allowing its mission, spirituality, and institutional life to be revolutionized by its social service to humanity.

The Righteousness of the Kingdom (c. 1892)

Source: Walter Rauschenbusch, *The Righteousness of the Kingdom*, ed. Max L. Stackhouse.

Christianity therefore is not a new philosophy which a man may entertain in isolation. Christ's purpose was the establishment and extension of the Kingdom of God, the regeneration of human society. To this end he established an organization which was to be at the same time a realization of the Kingdom within its own limits and the instrument for its propagation. Within this society Christ reigns, here his laws prevail, and his Spirit is the governing force. And from this society in turn his assimilating and conquering forces go out to extend the territory of his dominion. If Christ's purpose had been merely the conversion of individuals, the formation of the church would have been useful but not essential. Because his purpose was the immediate establishment and extension of a Kingdom, a society was absolutely essential. ...

Christ initiated the revolution, marked out its direction, warned against the dangers, organized his army, carried the revolutionary standard before them, and consecrated the cause with his blood.

Through his Spirit he is still invisibly but powerfully present with his army. His Spirit strikes the shackles of baseness and superstition from their limbs and puts them on their feet as freemen. It removes old prejudices and infuses love and a common enthusiasm. It works among them a constant renewal of energy and sacrifice to carry the struggle to the end.

Every man who has promised allegiance to Christ and has his Spirit within him is a revolutionary element, carrying on a guerilla warfare, if no more. But in spite of apparent disjointedness there is a secret unity among them. Recruits are sought, filled with the enthusiasm of the army, and instructed in the warfare. The army resists the present Prince of this world by word and deed, levies the authority of his laws, refuses to submit to his officers, levels his entrenchments, and builds others where the flag of the true King is kept flying, and whence the conquered territory is maintained and extended.

Christianity and the Social Crisis (1908)

Source: Walter Rauschenbusch, *Christianity and the Social Crisis.*

Religion demands social expression like all other great human impulses. Without an organization to proclaim it, to teach it, to stimulate it, the religious life would probably be greatly weakened in the best, and in many would be powerless and unknown. The mischief begins when the Church makes herself the end. She does not exist for her own sake; she is simply a working organization to create the Christian life in individuals and the kingdom of God in human society. She is an agent with large powers, and like all other agents she is constantly tempted to use her powers for herself. Our modern political parties were organized to advocate certain political principles and realize them in public life. Gradually they have come to regard their perpetuation as an end in itself, and public welfare is subordinated to party victory. Our public-service corporations exist for the public, but we know how these our servants have become our masters, so that the public exists for their dividends. This slow, historical embezzlement of public powers, this tendency of organizations and institutions to aggrandize themselves at the expense of the ends for which they were called into existence, is one of the most important phenomena in moral life. There is no permanent institution but has succumbed to this temptation. The organization of the Church is simply one sinner among many, and not the worst by any means. Her history is the story of how she fell by rising, and rose by falling. No one who loves her can serve her better than by bringing home to her that by seeking her life she loses it, and that when she loses her life to serve the kingdom of God, she will gain it.

A Theology for the Social Gospel (1917)

Source: Walter Rauschenbusch, *A Theology for the Social Gospel*.

The Church is the social factor in salvation. It brings social forces to bear on evil. It offers Christ not only many human bodies and minds to serve as ministers of his salvation, but its own composite personality, with a collective memory stored with great hymns and Bible stories and deeds of heroism, with trained aesthetic and moral feelings, and with a collective will set on righteousness. A super-personal being organized around an evil principle and set on predatory aims is the most potent breeder of sin in individuals and in other communities. What, then, might a super-personal being do which would be organized around Jesus Christ as its impelling power, and would have for its sole or chief object to embody his spirit in its life and to carry him into human thought and the conduct of affairs?

If there had never been such an organization as the Christian Church, every great religious mind would dream of the possibility of creating something like it. He would imagine the happy life within it where men shared the impulses of love and the convictions about life which Jesus imparted to humanity. If he understood psychology and social science, he would see the possibilities of such a social group in arousing and guiding the unformed spiritual aspirations of the young and reinforcing wayward consciences by the approval or disapproval of the best persons, and its power of reaching by free loyalty springs of action and character lying too deep for civil law and even for education to stir. He might well imagine too how the presence of such a social group would quicken and balance the civil and political community.

How far the actualities of church life fall short of such an ideal forecast, most of us know but too well. But even so, the importance of the social factor in salvation is clear from whatever angle we look at it. What chance would a disembodied spirit of Christianity have, whispering occasionally at the key-hole of the human heart? Nothing lasts unless it is organized, and if it is organized of human life, we must put up with the qualities of human life in it. ...

The saving power of the Church does not rest on its institutional character, on its continuity, its ordination, its ministry, or its doctrine. It rests on the presence of the Kingdom of God within her. The Church grows old; the Kingdom is ever young. The Church is a perpetuation of the past; the Kingdom is the power of the coming age. Unless the Church is vitalized by the ever nascent forces of the Kingdom within her, she deadens instead of begetting.

For further reading

Christopher H. Evans, *The Kingdom is Always but Coming: A Life of Walter Rauschenbusch* (Grand Rapids: Eerdmans, 2004).

Walter Rauschenbusch, *Christianizing the Social Order* (Baylor University Press, 2010).

Walter Rauschenbusch, *Christianity and the Social Crisis in the 21st Century: The Classic that Woke Up the Church*, ed. Paul Rauschenbusch (New York: HarperOne, 2007). See especially the responses from contemporary ethicists.

Walter Rauschenbusch, *The Social Principles of Jesus* (New York: The Woman's Press, 1917).

2   Kanzo Uchimura (1861–1930)

Founded by the prolific Kanzo Uchimura in Japan at the beginning of the twentieth century, the non-church movement (Mukyōkai) focused attention away from the mediation of ecclesial institutions, liturgies, denominations, clergy, etc. and instead onto God and the Christian encounter with the gospel itself. The movement was in many ways an effort at indigenization and a rejection of what was taken to be an overly Westernized Christianity brought to Japan by the missionaries. Non-church Christianity seeks to transcends national boundaries and is characterized by a counter-cultural faithfulness to Christ that, for example, is pacifist in many of its expressions.

The Non-Church Movement (1901)

Source: Ryūsaku Tsunoda, William Theodore de Bary, and Donald Keene (eds.), *Sources of Japanese Tradition.*

Mukyōkai does not have the negative meaning one sees in anarchism or nihilism; it does not attempt to overthrow anything. "Non-church" is the church for those who have no church. It is the dormitory for those who have no home, the orphanage or foundling home for the spirit. The negative character in the word *mukyōkai* should be read *nai*—without—rather than *mu ni suru*—destroy—or *mushi suru*—despise. Are not those without money, without parents, without houses to be pitied? We believe there to be many sheep without shepherds, many Christians without churches. ...

The true form of the church is *Mukyōkai*. There is no organized church in heaven. The Revelation of John says, "I saw no temple (church) within the city (heaven)" (Rev. 21:22). Bishops, deacons, preachers, and teachers exist only here on earth. In heaven, there is neither baptism nor communion; neither teachers nor students; "Then I saw a new heaven and a new earth, for the first heaven and the first earth had passed away, and there was no longer any sea. And I saw the new Jerusalem, the holy city, come down out of heaven from God, like a bride dressed and ready to meet her husband" (Rev. 21:1–2). *Mukyōkai* hopes to introduce this sort of church to the world.

Naturally, however, as long as we remain on this earth, we need churches. Some people will join churches constructed by the hands of men: there they will praise God, and there they will hear his word. Some churches will be made of stone, others of brick, and still others of wood. But not all of us need churches of this sort. That there are many Christians who do not belong to organized Christianity is similar to the fact that there are many homeless children. But even those of us who do not belong to organized Christianity need some sort of church while we exist on this earth. Where is our church and what is it like?

It is God's universe—nature. Its ceiling is the blue sky, with stars bejeweling its boards; its floor is the green fields, and its carpets the multicolored flowers; its musical instruments are pine twigs and its musicians the small birds of the forest; its pulpit is the mountain peaks and its preacher is God himself. This is our church. No church, whether in Rome or in London, can approximate it. In this sense, *Mukyōkai* has a church. Only those who have no church as conceived in conventional terms have the true church.

For further reading

Kanzo Uchimura, *The Diary of a Japanese Convert* (Gloucester: Dodo Press, 2009).

Hiroshi Miura, *The Life and Thought of Kanzo Uchimura 1861–1930* (Grand Rapids: Eerdmans, 1996).

Veli-Matti Kärkkäinen, "The Non-Church Movement in Asia," in *An Introduction to Ecclesiology: Ecumenical, Historical and Global Perspectives* (Downers Grove, IL: InterVarsity Press, 2002), pp. 167–74.

Emil Brunner, "A Unique Christian Mission: The Mukyokai ('Non-Church') Movement in Japan," in *Religion and Culture: Essays in Honor of Paul Tillich* (New York: Harper, 1959), pp. 287–90.

Akio Dohi, "The Historical Development of the Non-Church Movement in Japan," *Journal of Ecumenical Studies* 2 (1965), pp. 452–68.

3 Ernst Troeltsch (1865–1923)

Ernst Troeltsch's formulation of three sociological types (church, sect, and mysticism) developed in The Social Teaching of the Christian Churches *has been widely influential in ongoing thinking about the church. While, for Troeltsch, each of these types can be traced back to various impulses within primitive Christianity, history shows that the Christian community's interaction with the social, political, economic, and cultural contexts in which it found itself led it to develop into one of these predominant forms, thereby lending to the relative strength and success of the*

Christian movement in that situation. Troeltsch believed, however, that the modern emphasis on individual freedom and the corresponding loss of social unity and cohesion posed enormous challenges for nurturing and sustaining Christian social ideals in any one of these three types. While the church type is superior to the other two because it can sustain community in the context of fragmentation, it relies on an understanding of authority and the use of compulsion that is out of step with the modern spirit. Troeltsch's inclusion here signals the importance that sociology would come to play in twentieth century ecclesiology.

The Social Teaching of the Christian Churches (1912)

Source: Ernst Troeltsch, *The Social Teaching of the Christian Churches*, trans. Olive Wyon.

It has become clear how little the Gospel and the Primitive Church shaped the religious community itself from a uniform point of view. The Gospel of Jesus was a free personal piety, with a strong impulse towards profound intimacy and spiritual fellowship and communion, but without any tendency towards the organization of a cult, or, towards the creation of a religious community. Only when faith in Jesus, the Risen and Exalted Lord, became the central point of worship in a new religious community did the necessity for organization arise. From the very beginning there appeared the three main types of the sociological development of Christian thought: the Church, the sect, and mysticism.

The Church is an institution which has been endowed with grace and salvation as the result of the work of Redemption; it is able to receive the masses, and to adjust itself to the world, because, to a certain extent, it can afford to ignore the need for subjective holiness for the sake of the objective treasures of grace and of redemption.

The sect is a voluntary society, composed of strict and definite Christian believers bound to each other by the fact that all have experienced "the new birth." These "believers" live apart from the world, are limited to small groups, emphasize the law instead of grace, and in varying degrees within their own circle set up the Christian order, based on love; all this is done in preparation for and expectation of the coming Kingdom of God.

Mysticism means that the world of ideas which had hardened into formal worship and doctrine is transformed into a purely personal and inward experience; this leads to the formation of groups on a purely personal basis, with no permanent form, which also tend to weaken the significance of forms of worship, doctrine, and the historical element.

From the beginning these three forms were foreshadowed, and all down the centuries to the present day, wherever religion is dominant, they still appear alongside of one another, while among themselves they are strangely and variously interwoven and interconnected. The churches alone have the power to stir the masses in any real and lasting way. When mass movements take place the sects draw closer to the churches. Mysticism has an affinity with the autonomy of science, and it forms a refuge for the religious life of the cultured classes; in sections of the population which are untouched by science it leads to extravagant and emotional forms of piety, but in spite of that it forms a welcome complement to the Church and the Sects. ...

The diversity of ideas which the Christian conception of truth contains is evident in these three different types of religion, and this explains the complicated and inconsistent relation of Christianity to the authority of the State and to the idea of toleration.

The aim of the Church is to be the Church of the people and of the masses; it therefore transfers all divine and sacred character from individuals to the objective organ of redemption, with its divine endowment of grace and truth. The Church possesses a redeeming energy which is directly miraculous, and in contrast to all other kinds of human power. Thus it possesses an absolute directly divine truth and doctrinal authority over against all human subjectivity. In its very nature such truths must be uniform and universally authoritative. Thus in the Church itself this unchangeable truth is justified, and indeed bound to maintain its supremacy over pastors and teachers, and also over the laity. Every idealistic attempt to ascribe this development of the truth to the inward miraculous power of the Church itself, without compulsion, breaks down in the practical impossibility of carrying it through, and simply results in a return to compulsion. This attitude of compulsion must, however, finally express itself externally, because errors and customs which dishonour God ought not to be tolerated, and because it is not right that people who have been born into the membership of the Church should be allowed to fall a prey to temptation. Finally, the Church must see to it that the whole nation shall hear the message of salvation, and that everyone shall have at least contact with divine salvation. Mercy requires it, and the absolute divine origin of the truth of salvation justifies this procedure. Here it is permissible to force people for their own good. This, however, demands the co-operation of the material power of the State, without which neither the inner uniformity of the Church, nor the building up of popular and territorial churches, would ever have come into existence. In all this the Church is only fulfilling its duty towards Divine Truth. This line of argument explains the rise of the complicated question of the relation between Church and State.

The point of view of the sects, however, is quite different. They do not wish to be popular churches, but Christian denominations composed of "saints." The sects are small groups which exist alongside of the State and Society. They also maintain that they possess the absolute truth of the Gospel, but they claim that this truth is far beyond the spiritual grasp of the masses and of the State, and therefore they desire to be free from the State. Further, since it is precisely this absolute Gospel which forbids them to use force, authority, or law, they also must renounce forcing their opinions upon anyone, either within or without their community. Hence they demand external toleration, the religious neutrality of the State. Within their own borders, however, they practise a spiritual discipline of doctrine and of morals. They possess the tolerance of an idealism which believes in its own cause, and they forbid their followers to deduce from the absolute character of Truth the right to use violence in order to enforce it upon others. They do not expect to see the Truth permeating the masses before the Last Day. Where various sectarian groups exist alongside of each other, they permit the exercise of purely spiritual controversy and merely ethical rivalry without losing faith in the absolute character of the truth they possess. This truth is not meant for the masses, or for humanity in general; and it will only attain its final consummation at the Last Day. Their conception of toleration and freedom of conscience is of a toleration extended to groups like their own by the churches and the ruling powers; within their own borders, however, they had very little idea of toleration, since here Scriptural law prevails. Since, however, in order to uphold this unity they renounce State aid, and at the most can exercise the method of social boycott, endless divisions arise among them. It is a fact that real conformity can only be secured with the aid of the State and the exercise of compulsion.

Finally, the point of view of spiritual idealism and mysticism differs entirely from that of the churches or the sects. From its standpoint the truth of salvation is inward and relative, a personal possession which is unutterable, and lies unspoken beneath all literal forms. The merely relative significance of the Biblical, dogmatic, or ritual form in which Truth is expressed makes mysticism independent of all historic forms, and the inner Unity of the Spirit quite naturally unites all souls in the common truth which is purely spiritual, and impossible to formulate. From this point of view, and from it alone, are toleration and freedom of conscience also possible within the religious community, since the organization becomes merely a method of ecclesiastical administration, while the religious life itself can move freely under various forms of expression which are relatively justified. This however led to difficulties, for from this point of view it was very difficult to decide by what authority it was possible to determine the standard of what constituted Christianity in general. The usual answer, "the Spirit recognizes the Spirit," was found to be useless in practice. Hence this standpoint easily led to the giving up of all and every kind of organized fellowship, or to a withdrawal into private groups of a purely personal character composed of kindred souls. As well as conformity mysticism threatens to sacrifice fellowship altogether, and it easily falls into a comparative individualism. The problem of Christian toleration and liberty of conscience in relation to the conditions of the formation of religious fellowship belongs to this group of ideas. There is no escape from it. There are only varying practical suggestions of approximate utility which emerge out of this tragic interplay of forces. ...

These social and ethical ideas and energies spring out of the Christian religion. To enable them to do this it is necessary to maintain the vitality and to extend the scope of these religious energies; again, in order to achieve both these ends, an organization is needed which will lead them forward and continually produce them afresh.

This leads us to the question: What does our present inquiry teach us about this problem, which is a question of vital importance, about the formation of the religious community itself and its incorporation into the other great movements? Can we not learn something from a large work of this kind to help us to overcome our miserable ecclesiastical situation, which is daily becoming worse?

Here also the yield is a rich one, although it is more a matter of free insight into what is expedient than a scientific proof. The first thing we learn is, that the religious life—on the plane of spiritual religion—needs an independent organization, in order to distinguish it from other organizations of a natural kind. It strives after this from the moment it conceives of an independent existence, and this always remains one of its most important problems. Public worship forms the centre of such an organization; the derivation of comprehensive energies from it, or the organic attachment of them to it, is the great problem. Unless it is organized into a community with a settled form of worship, Christianity cannot be either expansive or creative. Every kind of reaction to a mere "freedom of the Spirit" in the hope that it will grow and thrive without organization, is a Utopian ideal which is out of touch with the actual conditions of life, and its only effect is to weaken the whole.

Secondly, so far as the form of this organization is concerned, it has become evident that the Church-type is obviously superior to the sect-type and to mysticism. The Church-type preserves inviolate the religious elements of grace and redemption; it makes it possible to differentiate between Divine grace and human effort; it is able to include the most varied degrees of Christian attainment and maturity, and therefore it alone is capable of fostering a popular religion which inevitably involves a great variety in its membership. In this respect the Church-type is superior to the sect-type and also to mysticism. This is why the main current of historical Christianity becomes the "History of the Church," and this is why the first result of the missionary work of the Early Church was "the universal Christian Church." At the same time, however, it cannot be denied that this does mean a modification of Christian thought in order to bring it down to the average level, to the level of practical possibility; and it is a principle of far-reaching adjustment and compromise.

For further reading

Lori K. Pearson, *Beyond Essence: Ernst Troeltsch as Historian and Theorist of Christianity*, Harvard Theological Studies, 58 (Cambridge, MA: Harvard University Press, 2008).

Ernst Troeltsch, *The Absoluteness of Christianity and the History of Religions* (Louisville: Westminster John Knox, 1971).

———— *The Christian Faith*, trans. Garrett E. Paul (Minneapolis: Fortress, 1991).

4   Karl Barth (1886–1968)

It is unlikely that any theologian of the twentieth century has had more influence than Karl Barth, a Swiss Reformed theologian who rejected theological liberalism and emphasized the sovereignty of God and God's Word as revealed in Christ. One of the ecclesiological implications of this sovereignty finds its expression in the "Barmen Declaration" (see below), which refuses the subordination of the church to the interests and authority of nation-states or political convictions. The church is a community of response to God's revelation in Christ and it is this responsive mission in the power of the Spirit that drives Barth's ecclesiology and pervades his massive Church Dogmatics. For Barth, "the church is not a church if it is not a missionary church."[2]

Source: Karl Barth, *Church Dogmatics*, ed. G. W. Bromily and T. F. Torrance.

Church Dogmatics IV/2

The existence of the true Church is not an end in itself. The divine operation by which it is vivified and constituted makes it quite impossible that its existence as the true Church should be understood as the goal of God's will for it. The divine operation in virtue of which it becomes and is a true Church makes it a movement in the direction of an end which is not reached with the fact that it exists as a true Church, but merely indicated and attested by this fact. On the way, moving in the direction of this goal, it can and should serve its Lord. For this reason it will not be the true Church at all to the extent that it tries to express itself rather than the divine operation by which it is constituted. As such it will reveal itself, or be revealed in glory at this goal; yet only as the Church which does not try to seek and express and glorify itself, but absolutely to subordinate itself and its witness, placing itself unreservedly in the service and under the control of that which God wills for it and works within it.

The goal in the direction of which the true Church proceeds and moves is the revelation of the sanctification of all humanity and human life as it has already taken place *de iure* in Jesus Christ. In the exaltation of the one Jesus, who as the Son of God became a servant in order as such to become the Lord of all men, there has been accomplished already in powerful archetype, not only the cancellation of the sins and therefore the justification, but also the elevation and establishment of all humanity and human life and therefore its sanctification. That this is the case is the theme and content of the witness with which His community is charged. It comes from the first revelation (in the resurrection of Jesus Christ) of the reconciliation of the

---

[2]   Karl Barth, "Gespräche mit Methodisenpredigern, 1961," in Eberhard Busch (ed.), *Gespräche, 1959–1962, Gesamtausgabe* (Zürich: Theologischer Verlag, 1995), p. 203.

world with God as it has taken place in this sense too. And it moves towards its final manifestation in the coming again of Jesus Christ. Christianity, or Christendom, is the holy community of the intervening period; the congregation or people which knows this elevation and establishment, this sanctification, not merely *de iure* but already *de facto*, and which is therefore a witness to all others, representing the sanctification which has already come upon them too in Jesus Christ. This representation is provisional. It is provisional because it has not yet achieved it, nor will it do so. It can only attest it "in the puzzling form of a reflection" (1 Cor. 13:12). And it is provisional because, although it comes from the resurrection of Jesus Christ, it is only on the way with others to His return, and therefore to the direct and universal and definitive revelation of His work as it has been accomplished for them and for all men. The fact that it is provisional means that it is fragmentary and incomplete and insecure and questionable; for even the community still participates in the darkness which cannot apprehend, if it also cannot overcome, the light (John 1:5). But the fact that it is provisional means also— for in this provisional way it represents the sanctification of humanity as it has taken place in Jesus Christ—that divine work is done within it truly and effectively, genuinely and invincibly, and in all its totality, so that even though it is concealed in many different ways it continually emerges and shines out from this concealment in the form of God's people. It is with this provisional representation that we have to do on the way and in the movement of the true Church. It is to accomplish it that it is on its way and in this movement. It is in order that it may accomplish it that its time is given; the time between the times, between the first and the final revelation of the work of God accomplished in Jesus Christ. The meaning and content of our time—the last time—is the fulfilment of this provisional representation as the task of the community of Jesus Christ. ...

What the Christian community owes to the world is not a law or ideal, not an exactment or demand, but the Gospel: the good news about the actuality of Jesus Christ in which it is helped, its sins are overcome and its misery ended; the word of hope in the great coming light in which its reconciliation with God will be manifested. ... The decisive contribution which the Christian community can make to the upbuilding and work and maintenance of the civil consists in the witness which it has to give to it and to all human societies in the form of the order of its own upbuilding and constitution. It cannot give in the world a direct portrayal of Jesus Christ, who is also the world's Lord and Saviour, of the peace and freedom and joy of the kingdom of God. For it is itself only a human society moving like all others to His manifestation. But in the form in which it exists among them it can and must be to the world of men around it a reminder of the law of the kingdom of God already set up on earth in Jesus Christ, and a promise of its future manifestation. *De facto* whether they realise it or not, it can and should show them that there is already on earth an order which is based on that great alteration of the human situation and directed towards its manifestation. In relation to those who are without it can and should demonstrate, as well as say, that worldly law, in the form in which they regard it as binding and outside which they believe that they cannot know any other or regard any other as practicable, has already ceased to be the last word and cannot enjoy unlimited authority and force; that there are other possibilities, not merely in heaven but on earth, not merely one day but already, than those to which it thinks that it must confine itself in the formation and administration of its law. It cannot produce any perfect or definitive thinking or action on this question of law. It can produce only a thinking and action which are defective because provisional. But for all the fact that they are defective and provisional, they can and should be different, corrected, pointing beyond themselves, and to that extent higher and better. The limits, the severity and weakness, the impossibility and inadequacy, the vulnerability and peril of a *ius humanum* drawn up in ignorance of the lordship of Jesus Christ will not be concealed from it. It knows that if there is to be right and order and peace and freedom on earth even in the defective and provisional forms of the present time, there is needed a recognition and acknowledgment of the law of the One who has reconciled them with God and in whom the sanctification of humanity has already taken place. The law of the Church is the result of its attempt to think and act in recognition and acknowledgment of the law of Jesus Christ—this human attempt which is so defective and provisional. On this basis and in this respect it has a relative—although not an absolute—advantage over all human law. On this basis and in this respect it attests the Gospel of the kingdom of God to all human law, whether it be common or statute law, civil or criminal, the law of property or the law of contract. The community knows perfectly well that it is itself in greatest need of hearing, and continually hearing, this Gospel. But this must not hinder it from causing it to be heard in the world, even in the form of its canonical order. In fact, it makes this all the more obligatory. Again, the community knows perfectly well that it cannot exemplify the law of God directly, but only in the broken form of its human law in which it can only point to the law of God. But it cannot and must not refuse to point to it in this way. Even though the world may not recognise the origin and basis of this indication, in the form of its relatively higher and better law it may be helpful and salutary to it, and therefore good news in this concealed form: the proffering of possibilities which it had never even considered; the invitation to revise or correct its own legal thought and action at least in the direction of the possibilities suggested, clarifying here and deepening there, simplifying in one case and differentiating in another, loosening at one point and strengthening at another.

Church Dogmatics IV/3.2

The Christian community is not sent into the world haphazardly or at random, but with a very definite task. It does not exist before its task and later acquire it. Nor does it exist apart from it, so that there can be no question whether or not it might have or execute it. It exists for the world. Its task constitutes and fashions it from the very outset. If it had not been given it, it would not have come into being. If it were to lose it, it would not continue. It is not, then, a kind of imparted dignity. It exists only as it has it, or rather only as the task has it. Nor is it a kind of burden laid upon it. It is the inalienable foundation which bears it. Every moment of its history it is measured by it. It stands or falls with it in all its expressions, in all its action or abstention. It either understands itself in the light of its task or not at all. It either takes itself seriously with regard to it, or it cannot do so. Even to the world it can either be respectable in relation to it, or not at all—though it may perhaps make a false impression in virtue of qualities and achievements which it shares with other historical constructs and which have nothing whatever to do with its true and distinctive being. The Christian community lives by and with its task. ...

We begin (1) by defining and describing its content. The community is given its task by Jesus Christ, and it is He who continually entrusts it to it, impresses it upon it and sees to it that it does not slip from it and that the community, deprived of it, does not sink into the abyss—He who, as He declares Himself to it, enlightens it in the power of His Holy Spirit, and whom, as it is enlightened by Him, it may know. As He gave and gives Himself to be known by many different men, they ceased and cease to be an uncoordinated mass of so many different individuals with different gifts and interests and views and convictions and aspirations. He calls them together. He calls them to the community. He makes of them His people, His body, and makes them its members. As the origin and content of their common knowledge which binds them to the community, however, He is also the origin and content of their commonly given task. As He thus constitutes and fashions them as His community, He awakens them—this is the origin of their task—as a community to *confess* Him. And He gives Himself to be known by the community— this is the content of their task—in order that they may and should confess *Him.* He who gives the community its task, who continually entrusts it to it and impresses it upon it, who in so doing causes it to become and be the community, who preserves and renews it as such, He, Jesus Christ, is *in nuce* but in totality and fulness the content of its task. His person, His work, His revealed name, the prophetic Word by which He proclaims Himself within it, is the matter at issue in its task. To use the simplest and biblical formulation: "Ye shall be witnesses unto me" (Acts 1:8). It will be seen already that we are concerned here with something which is quite definite and clear-cut, which is protected on all sides against confusion with anything else, being defined and delimited by the concreteness and uniqueness of His person, work and name.

The matter includes a great deal, indeed, a whole cosmos of distinctive reality and truth: the true and living God and true and living man; their encounter, co-existence and history with its commencement, centre and goal; the grace of God triumphant *in* judgment, His life triumphant in death and His light in darkness. But all these things are enclosed first and properly in Jesus Christ. Anything not revealed in His self-declaration and knowledge has nothing whatever to do with what is at issue in its task. We shall have to remember this. For here we have the supreme and decisive criterion in the question of the purity of its task, i.e., of the content of its task.

For further reading

Karl Barth, *The Church and the Churches* (Grand Rapids: Eerdmans, 2005).
Kimlyn J. Bender, *Karl Barth's Christological Ecclesiology* (Aldershot: Ashgate, 2005).
Wessel Bentley, *The Notion of Mission in Karl Barth's Ecclesiology* (Newcastle upon Tyne: Cambridge Scholars Publishing, 2010).
Nicholas M. Healy, "The Logic of Karl Barth's Ecclesiology: Analysis, Assessment and Proposed Modifications," *Modern Theology* 10/3 (July 1994), pp. 253–70.
Tracey Mark Stout, *A Fellowship of Baptism: Karl Barth's Ecclesiology in Light of His Understanding of Baptism* (Eugene, OR: Pickwick Publications, 2010).

5 "The Barmen Theological Declaration" (1934)

As churches throughout Germany were bowing to the pressure to conform themselves to the theological claims of National Socialism and to the ecclesial and social practices entailed by these claims, with many Christians openly proclaiming Hitler's Nazi party as a gift from God, an emerging confederation of "confessing churches" published this document drafted largely by Reformed theologian Karl Barth and Lutheran theologian Hans Asmussen. "The Barmen Declaration" protests the subordination of the church to the authority of the nation and rejects the interpretation of the Nazi seizure of power in 1933 as ordained by God. It stresses the centrality of Christ as the source of God's revelation.

Source: Walter Suckau and Krishana Suckau (trans.) "The Barmen Theological Declaration."

Preamble
According to the opening words of its constitution of July 11, 1933, the German Evangelical Church is a federation of confessional churches that grew out of the Reformation, which have equal standing with one another. The theological premise of the association of these churches is stated in

Article 1 and Article 2.1 of the constitution of the German Evangelical Church, recognized by the national government on July 14, 1933:

Article 1: The inalienable foundation of the German Evangelical Church is the gospel of Jesus Christ, as attested to us in the Holy Scripture and brought to light again through the confessions of the Reformation. In this way the authorities, which the church needs for her mission, are determined and restricted.

Article 2: The German Evangelical Church is comprised of churches (State Churches).

We, the Confessing Synod representatives of the Lutheran, Reformed, United Churches, independent synods, *Kirchentage*, and local church groups, declare that we stand together on the foundation of the German Evangelical Church as a union of German confessional churches. We are held together by confession to the one Lord of the one, holy, catholic and apostolic church.

We publically declare before all Protestant churches of Germany that the unity of this confession, and thus the unity of the German Evangelical Church, is severely threatened. In the first year of the existence of the German Evangelical Church it is threatened by the more and more visible teachings and actions of the ruling ecclesiastical party of the German Christians and the church government they support. The threat is that the theological premise by which the German Evangelical Church is united is constantly and fundamentally opposed and rendered ineffective through foreign propositions, both by the leaders and spokesmen of the German Christians and by the church government. If they are valid, the church, to those of us who stand in the power of its confessions, ceases to be the church. If so, the validity of the German Evangelical Church as a federal union of confessional churches is intrinsically impossible.

Together as members of Lutheran, Reformed, and United Churches we may and must speak today on this issue. Especially because we want to remain true to our different beliefs, we must not remain silent, because we believe that in a time of common need and temptation (*Anfechtung*) a common word has been placed in our mouth. We leave up to God what this may mean for the relationship of the confessional churches with each other.

In view of the errors of the German Christians and of the current national church government, which are devastating the Church and at the same time destroying the unity of the German Evangelical Church, we confess the following evangelical truths:

Theses

Jesus Christ said: I am the way and the truth and the life; no one comes to the Father except through me (John 14:6).

Truly, truly I say to you: he who does not enter the sheepfold through the door but climbs in somewhere else, is a thief and a robber. I am the door; if anyone enters through me, he will be saved (John 10:1, 9).

Jesus Christ, as he is attested to in Holy Scripture, is the one Word of God that we listen to, that we have to trust and obey in life and in death.

We reject the false doctrine that the Church could and should recognize as the source of its proclamation, apart from and besides this one Word of God, yet other events and powers, figures and truths, as God's revelation.

Through God you are in Jesus Christ, whom God has made our wisdom, our righteousness, our sanctification and our redemption (1 Cor. 1:30).

As Jesus Christ is God's assurance of the forgiveness of all our sins, so, with equal seriousness, he is also God's mighty claim upon our whole life; through him befalls us joyful deliverance from the godless fetters of this world for free, grateful serve to his creatures.

Let us, however, truly be in love and grow in all things into him, who is the head, into Christ, through whom the whole body is joined together (Eph. 4:15–16).

The Christian Church is the community of brethren in which Jesus Christ, in Word and Sacrament, through the Holy Spirit, acts as the Lord in the present. It has to testify with its faith and its obedience, with its message and with its order, as the Church of pardoned sinners in the midst of a sinful world, that it belongs to him alone, and lives and would like to live by his comfort and direction alone, in anticipation of his appearing.

We reject the false doctrine that the Church can abandon the form of its message and order to whatever it wishes or to changes in prevailing ideological and political beliefs.

Jesus Christ said: "You know that the rulers oppress their people and those in power do violence to them. So shall it not be among you; but whosoever wants to be great among you, he will be your servant" (Matt. 20:25–26).

The various offices in the Church do not constitute the rule of some over others; on the contrary, they are for the ministry with which the whole church has been entrusted and commanded to practice.

We reject the false doctrine that, apart from this particular ministry, the church could, and is allowed to, give or allow itself to be given appointed leaders with ruling authority.

Fear God, honor the King (1 Pet. 2:17).

The Scripture says to us that by divine order the state has the task in the not yet redeemed world, in which the Church also exists, to maintain justice and peace, to the degree this is possible according to human understanding and capacity, through threat and the use of force. The Church recognizes with gratitude and reverence toward God the benefit of this, his arrangement. It is a reminder of God's Kingdom (*Reich*), God's commandment and righteousness, and thereby of the responsibilities of rulers and those who are being ruled. It trusts and obeys the power of the Word, by which God upholds all things.

We reject the false doctrine that the state should and could, beyond its special commission, become the only and total order of human life, and thereby also fulfill the mission of the Church. We reject the false doctrine that the Church should and could, beyond its special commission, take on the appropriate characteristics, functions, and dignity of the state, thereby becoming an organ of the state.

Jesus Christ said: See, I am with you always, until the end of the world (Matt. 28:20).
God's Word is not fettered (2 Tim. 2:9).

The mission of the church, in which its freedom is founded, consists of this—in Christ's stead, and therefore in the service of his own Word and work, to deliver to all people the message of the free grace of God through preaching and sacrament.

We reject the false doctrine that through human self-glorification the Church could put the Word and work of the Lord in the service of any arbitrarily chosen human desires, purposes, and plans.

The Confessional Synod of the German Evangelical Church declares that it sees, in recognition of these truths and in the rejection of these errors, the indispensable theological basis for the German Evangelical Church as a federation of Confessional Churches. It urges all who are able to accept its declaration to keep in mind these theological insights in their decisions regarding Church politics. It asks all whom it concerns to return to the unity of faith, love and hope.

For further reading

Arthur C. Cochrane, *The Church's Confession Under Hitler* (Philadelphia: Westminster, 1962).

Wolfgang Erlach, *And The Witnesses Were Silent: The Confessing Church and the Persecution of the Jews* (Lincoln: University of Nebraska Press, 2000).

Matthew D. Hockenos, *A Church Divided: German Protestants Confront the Nazi Past* (Bloomington: Indiana University Press, 2004).

6   Dietrich Bonhoeffer (1906–1945)

Bonhoeffer was a Lutheran pastor in Germany and a member of the Confessing Church (see "The Barmen Declaration" above) that defied the attempt to subordinate the church to the Nazi regime. He wrote his dissertation on ecclesiology, and the subject figures centrally in his writings after that. Bonhoeffer's ecclesiology is in stark contrast to those who (like Schleiermacher) begin with general experiential, psychological, or sociological categories, and explain the church's significance in those terms. For Bonhoeffer, one must begin with God's revelation in Christ. Indeed, Bonhoeffer identifies the church as the real body of Christ—a visible contrast to an unbelieving world: "the church of Jesus Christ is the place—that is the space—in the world where the reign of Jesus Christ over the whole world is to be demonstrated and proclaimed."[3] At the same time, the church is a "not yet" eschatological reality, especially given the church's sinfulness. The mediation of this visible body in the world is word and sacrament.

The Cost of Discipleship (1937)

Source: Geffrey B. Kelly, John D. Godsey (eds.), Barbara Green and Reinhard Krauss (trans.), *Dietrich Bonhoeffer Works*.

For the first disciples the bodily community with Jesus did not mean anything different or anything more than what we have today. Indeed, for us this community is even more definite, more complete, and more certain than it was for them, since we live in full community with the bodily presence of the glorified Lord. Our faith must become fully aware of the magnitude of this gift. The body of Jesus Christ is the ground of our faith and the source of its certainty; the body of Jesus Christ is the one and perfect gift through which

---

[3]   Dietrich Bonhoeffer, *Ethics* (Minneapolis: Fortress, 2000), p. 63.

we receive our salvation; the body of Jesus Christ is our new life. It is in the body of Jesus Christ that we are accepted by God from eternity. ...

The bond between Jesus and the disciples who followed him was a bodily bond. This was no accident but a necessary consequence of the incarnation. A prophet and teacher would not need followers, but only students and listeners. But the incarnate Son of God who took on human flesh does need a community of followers who not only participate in his teaching but also in his body. It is thus in the body of Christ that the disciples have community. They live and suffer in bodily community with Jesus. By being in community with the body of Jesus they are placed under the burden of the cross. For in that body they are all borne and accepted. ...

There is no community with Jesus Christ other than the community with his body! It is in this body alone that we are accepted and able to find salvation! The way we do gain a share in the community of the body of Christ is through the two sacraments of his body, that is, baptism and the Lord's Supper. ... The sacraments have their origin and goal in the body of Christ. Sacraments exist only because there is a body of Christ. There they begin and end. The word of proclamation alone is not sufficient to bring us into community with the body of Jesus Christ; the sacrament is necessary too. Baptism incorporates us as members into the unity of the body of Christ. The Lord's Supper keeps us in this community (κοινωνία) with Christ's body. ...

The body of Jesus Christ is identical with the new humanity which he has assumed. The body of Christ is his church-community. Jesus Christ at the same time is himself and his church-community (1 Cor. 12:12). Since Pentecost Jesus Christ lives here on earth in the form of his body, the church-community. Here is his body crucified and risen, here is the humanity he assumed. To be baptized therefore means to become a member of the church-community, a member of the body of Christ (Gal. 3:28; 1 Cor. 12:13). To be in Christ means to be in the church-community. But if we are in the church-community, then we are also truly and bodily in Jesus Christ. This insight reveals the full richness of meaning contained in the concept of the body of Christ.

Since the ascension, Jesus Christ's place on earth has been taken by his body, the church. The church is the present Christ himself. With this statement we are recovering an insight about the church which has been almost totally forgotten. While we are used to thinking of the church as an institution, we ought instead to think of it as a *person* with a body, although of course a person in a unique sense.

The church is one. All who are baptized arc "one in Christ" (Gal. 3:28; Rom. 12:5; 1 Cor. 10: 17). The church is "the human being per se." It is the *"new human being"* (καινὸς ἄνθρωπος). As such, the church was created through Christ's death on the cross. Here the hostility between Jews and Gentiles which had torn humanity apart is abolished, "in order that he might create in himself one new human being in place of the two, thus making peace" (Eph. 2:15).

The "new human being" is one, not many. Outside of the church, which is this new human being, there is only the old, internally divided human being.

The "new human being," which is the church, is "created according to the likeness of God in true righteousness and holiness and truth" (Eph. 4:24). The "new human being" is "being renewed in knowledge according to the image of its creator" (Col. 3:10). It is none other than Christ himself who is described here as the image of God. Adam was the first human being bearing the image of the creator. But he lost this image when he fell. Now a "second human being" a "last Adam," is being created in the image of God—Jesus Christ (1 Cor. 15:47). The "new human being" is thus at the same time Christ and the church. Christ is the new humanity in the new human being. Christ is the church. …

No one can become a new human being except by being within the church, that is, through the body of Christ. Whoever seeks to become a new human being individually cannot succeed. To become a new human being means to come into the church, to become a member of Christ's body. The new human being is not the single individual who has been justified and sanctified; rather, the new human being is the church–community, the body of Christ, or Christ himself. …

The unity between Christ and his body, the church, demands that we at the same time recognize Christ's lordship over his body. This is why Paul, in developing further the concept of the body, calls Christ the head of the body (Eph. 1:22; Col. 1:18; 2:19). The distinction is clearly preserved; Christ is the Lord. There are two events in salvation history, namely, Christ's ascension and his second coming, which make this distinction necessary; these events categorically rule out any idea of a mystical fusion between church-community and Christ. The same Christ who is present in his church-community will return from heaven. In both cases it is the same Lord and it is the same church; in both cases it is the very same body of the one who is present here and now, and the one who will return in the clouds. However, it makes a serious difference whether we are here or there. Thus, both the unity and the distinction are necessary aspects of the church. …

The church-community has, therefore, a very real impact on the life of the world. It gains space for Christ. For whatever is "in Christ" is no longer under the dominion of the world, of sin, or of the law. Within this newly created community, all the laws of this world have lost their binding force. This sphere in which brothers and sisters are loved with Christian love is subject to Christ; it is no longer subject to the world. The church-community can never consent to any restrictions of its service of love and compassion toward other human beings. For wherever there is a brother or sister, there Christ's own body is present; and wherever Christ's body is present, his church-community is also always present, which means I must also be present there.

All who belong to the body of Christ have been freed from and called out of the world. They must become visible to the world not only through the communal bond evident in the church-community's order and worship, but also through the new communal life among brothers and sisters in Christ. ...

Christians are to remain in the world, not because of the God-given goodness of the world, nor even because of their responsibility for the course the world takes. They are to remain in the world solely for the sake of the body of the Christ who became incarnate—for the sake of the church-community. They are to remain in the world in order to engage the world in a frontal assault. Let them "live out their vocation in this world" in order that their "unworldliness" might become fully visible. But this can take place only through visible membership in the church-community. The world must be contradicted within the world. That is why Christ became a human being and died in the midst of his enemies. It is for this reason—and this reason alone!—that slaves are to remain slaves, and Christians are to remain subject to authority. ...

The Christian community thus lives its own life in the midst of this world, continually bearing witness in all it is and does that "the present form of this world is passing away" (1 Cor. 7:31), that the time has grown short (1 Cor. 7:23), and that the Lord is near (Phil. 4:5). That prospect is cause for great joy to the church-community (Phil. 4:4). The world becomes too confining; all its hopes and dreams are set on the Lord's return. The community members still walk in the flesh. But their eyes are turned to heaven, from whence shall return the one whom they await. Here on earth, the church-community lives in a foreign land. It is a colony of strangers far away from home, a community of foreigners enjoying the hospitality of the host country in which they live, obeying its laws, and honoring its authorities. With gratitude it makes use of what is needed to sustain the body and other areas of earthly life. In all things the church-community proves itself to be honorable, just, chaste, gentle, quiet, and willing to serve. It demonstrates the love of its Lord to all people, but "especially for those of the family of faith" (Gal. 6:10; 2 Pet. 1:7). In suffering it is patient and joyful, taking pride in its tribulation. It lives its own life subject to a foreign authority and foreign justice. It prays for all earthly authority, thus rendering this authority the best service it can offer (1 Tim. 2:1). But it is merely passing through its host country. At any moment it may receive the signal to move on. Then it will break camp, leaving behind all worldly friends and relatives, and following only the voice of the one who has called it. It leaves the foreign country and moves onward toward its heavenly home.

Christians are poor and suffering, hungry and thirsty, gentle, compassionate and peaceable, persecuted and scorned by the world. Yet it is for their sake alone that the world is still preserved. They shield the world from God's judgment of wrath. They suffer so that the world can still live under God's forbearance. They are strangers and sojourners on this earth (Heb. 11:13; 13:14; 1 Pet. 1:1). They set their minds on things that are above, not on things that are of the earth (Col. 3:2). For their true life has not yet been revealed; it is still hidden with Christ in God (Col. 3:3). Here on earth, they only see the opposite of what they are to become. What is visible here is nothing but their dying—their hidden, daily dying to their old self, and their public dying before the world. They are still hidden even from themselves. The left hand does not know what the right hand is doing. As a visible church-community, their own identity remains completely invisible to them. They look only to their Lord. He is in heaven, and their life for which they are waiting is in him. But when Christ, their life, reveals himself, then they will also be revealed with him in glory (Col. 3:4).

Life Together (1939)

Source: Geffrey B. Kelly (ed.) and Daniel W. Bloesch (trans.), *Dietrich Bonhoeffer Works*.

Christian community means community through Jesus Christ and in Jesus Christ. There is no Christian community that is more than this, and none that is less than this. Whether it be a brief, single encounter or the daily community of many years, Christian community is solely this. We belong to one another only through and in Jesus Christ.

What does that mean? It means, *first*, that a Christian needs others for the sake of Jesus Christ. It means, *second*, that a Christian comes to others only through Jesus Christ. It means, *third*, that from eternity we have been chosen in Jesus Christ, accepted in time, and united for eternity. ...

The Christian community is not a spiritual sanatorium. Those who take refuge in community while fleeing from themselves are misusing it to indulge in empty talk and distraction, no matter how spiritual this idle talk and distraction may appear. In reality they are not seeking community at all, but only a thrill that will allow them to forget their isolation for a short time. It is precisely such misuse of community that creates the deadly isolation of human beings. Such attempts to find healing result in the undermining of speech and all genuine experience and, finally, resignation and spiritual death.

Whoever cannot be alone should beware of community. Such people will only do harm to themselves and to the community. Alone you stood before God when God called you. Alone you had to obey God's voice. Alone you had to take up your cross, struggle, and pray and alone you will die and give an account to God. You cannot avoid yourself, for it is precisely God who has singled you out. If you do not want to be alone, you are rejecting Christ's call to you, and you can have no part in the community of those who are called. ...

But the reverse is also true. *Whoever cannot stand being in community should beware of being alone.* You are called into the community of faith; the call was not meant for you alone. You carry your cross, you struggle, and you pray in the community of faith, the community of those who are called. You are not alone even when you die, and on the day of judgment you will be only one member of the great community of faith of Jesus Christ. If you neglect the community of other Christians, you reject the call of Jesus Christ, and thus your being alone can only become harmful for you.

For further reading

Dietrich Bonhoeffer, *Sanctorum Communio: A Theological Study of the Sociology of the Church*, Dietrich Bonhoeffer Works, 1 (Minneapolis: Fortress, 1998).
Renate Wind, *A Spoke in the Wheel: A Life of Dietrich Bonhoeffer*, trans. John Bowden (London: SCM Press, 1991).

7   William Temple (1881–1944)

Archbishop William Temple was one of the most significant of all Anglican church leaders and thinkers, and his context was that of an increasingly industrial society as well as a world at war. He worked vigorously on issues related to ecumenical unity and missions and also advocated for the church's responsibility for social justice as central to its nature and calling, as can be seen from this excerpt from his classic Christianity and Social Order. *In this particular excerpt we find his views on how the church should be involved in working for social and political change in the world along with his famous statement that "nine-tenths of the work of the Church in the world" is done outside the official system of the church. For Temple, the task of the church is to instill in its members Christian "principles" that will guide their social action at a concrete level. The church itself (acting corporately) should not prescribe in detail any particular social policies, even though its members, duly formed by the church, should exert what influence they can.*

Christianity and Social Order (1942)

Source: William Temple, *Christianity and Social Order*.

The Church never gets credit for the greater part of what it does. That does not very much matter, because credit (like merit in Lord Melbourne's dictum) is "only what one gentleman thinks of another gentleman"; and Christians are warned not to concern themselves about that. No doubt some people would attend more to the Church and therefore also to its Gospel if they knew all that it really does in the world; that would be a gain as far as it goes; but each heart must know its need before it finds the satisfaction of that need in Christ. It is not so much to gain for the Church the credit and influence to which it is entitled that I emphasize the importance of clear thinking about the way in which the Church does its work, but rather for the avoidance of confusion of thought tending to calamitous results in practice.

Nine-tenths of the work of the Church in the world is done by Christian people fulfilling responsibilities and performing tasks which in themselves are not part of the official system of the Church at all. For example, the abolition of the Slave Trade and, later, of Slavery itself, was carried through by Wilberforce and his friends in the inspiration of their Christian faith and by means of appeal to the Christian principles professed by their fellow-citizens. The far-reaching reform of our penal system in the interval between the two wars has been effected by a group of men who, being concerned with its administration, thought out the question how, on Christian principles, community ought to treat its own offenders. And apart from specific achievements like these there is the pervasive sweetening of life and of all human relationships by those who carry with them something of the Mind of Christ, received from Christian upbringing, from prayer and meditation, and from communion. No particular enterprises, nor all of them together, can compare in importance with the influence so exerted. To this extent they are justified who say that the task of the Church in face of social problems is to make good Christian men and women. That is by far its most important contribution. But (as I shall contend in a moment) it has others, less important and yet for their own purpose indispensable.

Next to the work of the Church done through its members in ordinary human relationships and in ordinary avocations, we may consider its work done through its members in their capacity as citizens shaping the political decisions which affect the national life and destiny. It is of crucial importance that the Church acting corporately should not commit itself to any particular policy. A policy always depends on technical decisions concerning the actual relations of cause and effect in the political and economic world; about these a Christian as such has no more reliable judgement than an atheist, except so far as he should be more immune to the temptations of self-interest. ... This refusal to adopt a particular policy is partly a matter of prudence, for the policy may turn out to be mistaken, as indeed every policy always turns out to have been less than perfectly adapted to the situation, and the Church must not be involved in its failure; still more is it a matter of justice, for even though a large majority of Christians hold a particular view, the dissentient minority may well be equally loyal to Christ and equally entitled to be recognized as loyal members of His Church. ... The Church is committed to the everlasting Gospel and to the Creeds which formulate it; it must never commit itself to an ephemeral programme of detailed action. ...

So we answer the question "How should the Church interfere?" by saying: In three ways—(1) its members must fulfil their moral responsibilities and functions in a Christian, spirit; (2) its members must exercise their purely civil rights in a Christian spirit; (3) it must itself supply them with a systematic statement of principles to aid them in doing these two things, and this will carry with it a denunciation of customs or institutions in contemporary life and practice which offend against those principles. ...

The method of the Church's impact upon society at large should be twofold. The Church must announce Christian principles and point out where the existing social order at any time is in conflict with them. It must then pass on to Christian citizens, acting in their civic capacity, the task of re-shaping the existing order in closer conformity to the principles. For at this point technical knowledge may be required and judgements of practical expediency are always required. If a bridge is to be built, the Church may remind the engineer that it is his obligation to provide a really safe bridge; but it is not entitled to tell him whether, in fact, his design meets this requirement; a particular theologian may also be a competent engineer, and, if he is, his judgement on this point is entitled to attention; but this is altogether because he is a competent engineer and his theological equipment has nothing whatever to do with it. In just the same way the Church may tell the politician what ends the social order should promote; but it must leave to the politician the devising of the precise means to those ends.

This is a point of first-rate importance and is frequently misunderstood. If Christianity is true at all it is a truth of universal application; all things should be done in the Christian spirit and in accordance with Christian principles. "Then," say some, "produce your Christian solution of unemployment." But there neither is nor could be such a thing. Christian faith does not by itself enable its adherent to foresee how a vast multitude of people, each one partly selfish and partly generous, and an intricate economic mechanism, will in fact be affected by a particular economic or political innovation—"social credit," for example. "In that case," says the reformer—or, quite equally, the upholder of the *status* quo—"keep off the turf. By your own confession you are out of place here." But this time the Church must say "Now; I cannot tell you what is the remedy; but I can tell you that a society of which unemployment (in peace time) is a chronic feature is a diseased society, and that if you are not doing all you can to find and administer the remedy, you are guilty before God." Sometimes the Church can go further than this and point to features in the social structure itself which are bound to be sources of social evil because they contradict the principles of the Gospel.

So the Church is likely to be attacked from both sides if it does its duty. It will be told that it has become "political" when in fact it has been careful only to state principles and point to breaches of them; and it will be told by advocates of particular policies that it is futile because it does not support these. If it is faithful to its commission it will ignore both sets of complaints, and continue so far as it can to influence all citizens and permeate all parties.

For further reading

Wendy Dackson, *The Ecclesiology of Archbishop William Temple (1881–1944)* (Lewiston, NY: Edwin Mellon Press, 2004).

John Kent, *William Temple: Church, State, and Society in Britain, 1880–1950* (Cambridge: Cambridge University Press, 1992).

William Temple, *The Church and its Teaching Today; being the William Belden Noble lectures delivered in the Memorial Church*, Harvard University, on December 17 and 18, 1935 (New York: Macmillan, 1936).

8   Henri de Lubac (1896–1991)

A French Jesuit priest, Henri de Lubac was one of the primary shapers of Roman Catholic ecclesiology in the twenty-first century and especially influential on the "communion ecclesiology" of Vatican II. De Lubac understood the church to be a universal and visibly inclusive church that was unyielding in its openness to the world, even in the face of totalitarian political regimes and in contrast to sectarian (and typically Protestant) ecclesiologies that would reduce the real church to some invisible subset of true believers. For de Lubac, the greatest heresy is schism—the loss of the whole in favor of this or that particularity. De Lubac's ecclesiology relies heavily on the notion of the church as a "mystery," and this shows up especially in his insistence that a Catholic is one who can hold various dimensions of truth in tension without selectively privileging one side of a paradox. The church is a universal mystery because it appeals to and includes the deepest dimensions of every human being.

Catholicism (1947)

Source: Henri de Lubac, *Catholicism: Christ and the Common Destiny of Man.*

The Church which is "Jesus Christ spread abroad and communicated" (Bossuet) completes—so far as it can be completed here below—the work of spiritual reunion which was made necessary by sin; that work which was begun at the Incarnation and was carried on up to Calvary. In one sense the Church is herself this reunion, for that is what is meant by the name of Catholic by which we find her called from the second century onward, and which in Latin as well as in Greek was for long bestowed upon her as a proper noun. Καθολικός, in classical Greek, was used by philosophers to indicate a universal proposition. Now a universal is a singular and is not to be confused with an aggregate. The Church is not Catholic because she is spread abroad over the whole of the earth and can reckon on a large number of members. She was already Catholic on the morning of Pentecost, when all her members could be contained in a small room, as she was when the Arian waves seemed on the point of swamping her; she would still be Catholic if tomorrow apostasy on a vast scale deprived her of almost all the faithful. For fundamentally Catholicity has nothing to do with geography or statistics. If it is true that it should be displayed over all the earth and be manifest to all, yet its nature is not material but spiritual. Like sanctity, Catholicity is primarily an intrinsic feature of the Church. ...

No more to St. Paul than to the other witnesses to the early faith is the Church a sort of "aeon," a transcendent hypostasis which really existed before the work of Christ in the world. But neither is she a mere federation of local assemblies. Still less is she the simple gathering together of those who as individuals have accepted the Gospel and henceforward have shared their religious life, whether in accordance with a plan of their own or as the occasion demanded, or even by following the instructions of the Master. Neither is she an external organism brought into being or adopted after the event by the community of believers. It is impossible to maintain either of these two extreme theses, as it is impossible to keep them entirely separate. Yet that is the vain endeavor of most Protestant theology. Paradoxically enough, on the other hand, it is precisely Protestant studies, completing and sometimes correcting Catholic work in the field of history or philology, that strengthen the traditional view on this important point. It emerges particularly that the primitive idea of the Church is in direct continuity with the Hebrew concept of "Qahal," a word translated in the Septuagint by Ἐκκλησία. "Qahal" does not mean a restricted group or a purely empirical gathering, but the whole people of God, a concrete reality which, however small it may seem outwardly, is yet always far greater than it appears.

The Greek word accepted from the Septuagint was suitable, too, because it emphasized another essential aspect of the Church. The man who hears the "glad tidings" and gives himself to Christ answers a call. Now by reason of the connection between the words (it does not appear in English) "to be called" is to be called to belong to the Church. The Ἐκκλησία that neither Paul nor any other of the first disciples ever imagined as an entirely invisible reality, but which they always understood as a mystery surpassing its outward manifestations, this Ἐκκλησία is in logical sequence to the κλητοι [called]: she convenes them and gathers them together for the Kingdom. She is a *convocatio* before being a *congregatio*. ...

In the interests of refuting such chaotic concepts as those which, see a divine Church only in a "Church of the saints," an entirely invisible society which is nothing but a pure abstraction, we must not fall into the contrary error. The Church "in so far as visible" is also an abstraction, and our faith should never make separate what God from the beginning has joined together: *sacramentum magnum in Christo et in ecclesia* [a great mystery in Christ and in the church]. Nor do we claim to prove this union by an explanation of it, for the mystery of the Church is deeper still, if that were possible, than the mystery of Christ, just as that mystery was more difficult to believe than the mystery of God, a scandal not only to the Jews and Gentiles, but also for too many Christians. *Avocamentum mentis, non firmamentum* [a disturbance for the mind, not a support]. For no one can believe in the Church, except in the Holy Spirit. That, at any rate, is not "to deify her visibility," as we are sometimes reproached with doing. We do not confuse the "institution of the Papacy, and the kingdom of God." We do not "attribute to the Church what belongs to God alone." We do not adore her. We do not believe in the Church in the same sense in which we believe in God, for the Church herself believes in God, and she is the "Church of God." All the more then do we reject Monophysitism in ecclesiology just as we do in Christology, but none the less strongly do we believe that dissociation of the divine and the human is in either case fatal. If necessary, the experience of Protestantism should serve us as sufficient warning. Having stripped it of all its mystical attributes, it acknowledged in the visible Church a mere secular institution; as a matter of course it abandoned it to the patronage of the state and sought a refuge for the spiritual life in an invisible Church, its concept of which had evaporated into an abstract ideal.

But the Church, the only real Church, the Church which is the Body of Christ, is not merely that strongly hierarchical and disciplined society whose divine origin has to be maintained, whose organization has to be upheld against all denial and revolt. That is an incomplete notion and but a partial cure for the separatist, individualist tendency of the notion to which it is opposed; a partial cure because it works only from without by way of authority, instead of effective union. If Christ is the sacrament of God, the Church is for us the sacrament of Christ; she represents him, in the full and ancient meaning of the term; she really makes him present. She not only carries on his work, but she is his very continuation, in a sense far more real than that in which it can be said that any human institution is its founder's continuation. The highly developed exterior organization that wins our admiration is but an expression, in accordance with the needs of this present life, of the interior unity of a living entity, so that the Catholic is not only subject to a power but is a member of a body as well, and his legal dependence on this power is to the end that he may have part in the life of that body. His submission in consequence is not an abdication, his orthodoxy is not mere conformity, but fidelity. It is his duty not merely to obey her orders or show deference to her counsels, but to share in a life, to enjoy a spiritual union. …

This makes it possible to understand why schism has always inspired the true believer with horror, and why from earliest times it has been anathematized as vigorously as heresy. For destruction of unity is a corruption of truth, and the poison of dissension is as baneful as that of false doctrine.

For further reading

Henri De Lubac, *The Motherhood of the Church* (San Francisco: Ignatius Press, 1971).
────── *The Church: Paradox and Mystery* (Staten Island, NY: Alba House, 1969)
────── *The Splendour of the Church* (New York: Sheed and Ward, 1956)
Dennis M. Doyle, "Henri de Lubac and the Roots of Communion Ecclesiology," *Theological Studies* 60 (1999), pp. 209–27.
Francisca Aran Murphy, "De Lubac, Ratzinger, and von Balthasar: A Communal Adventure in Ecclesiology," in Francisca Aran Murphy and Christopher Asprey (eds.), *Ecumenism Today: The Universal Church in the 21st Century* (Aldershot: Ashgate, 2008), pp. 45–80.
Hans Urs von Balthasar, *The Theology of Henri de Lubac: An Overview* (San Francisco: Communio Books, 1991).

9   "Here, O Lord, Your Servants Gather" (1958)

This hymn was written by Tokuo Yamaguchi (1900–1995), a Methodist minister, for the Fourteenth World Council of Christian Education Convention held in Tokyo, Japan in 1958. The text is based on John 14:6, in which Jesus is described as the "the way, the truth, and the life," and is a beautiful expression of the desire for ecclesial unity in the decade following World War II. The music of the hymn is worthy of attention though not included here. It was composed by Isao Koizumi (1907–1992) using Gagaku, a classical style of music used uniquely at the Japanese imperial court. This has led some hymnologists such as Carl Daw and C. Michael Hawn to suggest the possibility that the very music of the hymn be itself taken as an affirmation of the divinity of Christ rather than the emperor.

Source: The United Methodist Hymnal.

Here, O Lord, your servants gather, hand we link with hand;
looking toward our Savior's cross, joined in love we stand.
As we seek the realm of God, we unite to pray:
Jesus, Savior, guide our steps, for you are the Way.

Many are the tongues we speak, scattered are the lands,
yet our hearts are one in God, one in love's demands.
E'en in darkness hope appears, calling age and youth:
Jesus, teacher, dwell with us, for you are the Truth.

Nature's secrets open wide, changes never cease.
Where, oh where, can weary souls find the source of peace?
Unto all those sore distressed, torn by endless strife:
Jesus, healer, bring your balm, for you are the Life.

Grant, O God, an age renewed, filled with deathless love;
help us as we work and pray, send us from above
truth and courage, faith and power, needed in our strife:
Jesus, Master, be our Way, be our Truth, our Life.

10 Lesslie Newbigin (1909–1998)

Bishop J. E. Lesslie Newbigin spent almost 40 years in India as a missionary from the Church of Scotland, and was bishop of Madras from 1965 to 1974. Newbigin was also active in the global ecumenical movement. Few theologians have advocated for the church's essentially missionary character as ardently as Newbigin and few have connected that missionary character with its unity as convincingly and consistently as he did. Indeed, for Newbigin the church's unity and its missionary character presuppose one another. As can be seen from the excerpts here, Newbigin emphasized the congregational structure of the church within that missional and ecumenical enterprise. A church that seeks its unity or that carries out its mission primarily in denominational boardrooms cannot really be the "church for the world."

The Household of God (1953)

Source: Lesslie Newbigin, *The Household of God: Lectures on the Nature of the Church.*

The Church is the pilgrim people of God. It is on the move—hastening to the ends of the earth to beseech all men to be reconciled to God, and hastening to the end of time to meet its Lord who will gather all into one. Therefore the nature of the Church is never to be finally defined in static terms, but only in terms of that to which it is going. It cannot be understood rightly except in a perspective which is at once missionary and eschatological, and only in that perspective can the deadlock of our present ecumenical debate be resolved. But—and this is of vital importance—it will be a solution in which theory and practice are inseparably related, not one which can be satisfactorily stated in terms of theory alone. There is a way of bringing the eschatological perspective to bear upon our present perplexities which relieves them at no cost to ourselves, which allows us to rest content with them because in the age to come they will disappear. That is a radically false eschatology. The whole meaning of this present age between Christ's coming and His coming again is that in it the powers of the age to come are at work now to draw all men into one in Christ. When the Church ceases to be one, or ceases to be missionary, it contradicts its own nature. Yet the Church is not to be defined by what it is, but by that End to which it moves, the power of which now works in the Church, the power of the Holy Spirit who is the earnest of the inheritance still to be revealed. To say that the deadlock in the ecumenical debate will be resolved in a perspective which is missionary and eschatological is not true unless it is understood that that perspective means a new obedience to, and a new possession by, the Holy Spirit. It is a perspective inseparable from action, and that action must be both in the direction of mission and in that of unity, for these are but two aspects of the one work of the Spirit. ...

If we agree that the Church on earth is the visible body of those whom God has called into the fellowship of His Son, we have to ask—where is that body to be found? We know where it was on the day of Pentecost. It was there in Jerusalem. But where is it today? By what signs or works can a body rightly claim today to be the Church of God? We are all agreed that the Church is constituted by God's atoning acts in Christ Jesus—His incarnation, life, death, resurrection, ascension, His session at God's right hand and the gift of the Spirit. But how are we of the subsequent generations made participants in that atonement? *What is the manner of our ingrafting into Christ?* That is the real question with which we have to deal.

I think that there are three main answers to these questions, and these answers are embodied in great Christian communions which claim to be the Church.

The first answer is, briefly, that we are incorporated in Christ by hearing and believing the gospel. The second is that we are incorporated by sacramental participation in the life of the historically continuous Church. The third is that we are incorporated by receiving and abiding in the Holy Spirit.

The moment one has stated these three positions in this bald way, it is at once apparent that they are far from being mutually exclusive, that very few Christians would deny the truth of any of them, and that there is an infinite variety of combinations of and approximations to these three positions. Nevertheless I think that we can best approach our problem by isolating these three positions. Classical Protestantism, especially in its Lutheran form, of course ascribes an immense value to the sacraments. But the major emphasis is upon faith, and faith comes by hearing, and therefore the pulpit dominates the rest of the ecclesiastical furniture. It also knows and speaks of the work of the Holy Spirit but does so with reserve. It is shy of enthusiasm, and is reluctant to give a large place to the claims of "spiritual experience." Catholicism honours preaching and acknowledges the necessity of faith, but it finds the centre of religious life rather in the sacrament than in the sermon. It acknowledges a real operation of the Holy Spirit sanctifying the believer, but gives the decisive place rather to the continuous sacramental order of the Church. The third type—for which it is difficult to find a single inclusive name—acknowledges and values preaching and the sacraments, but judges them by their experienced effects, and is not interested in the question of historical continuity. All these three answers to the question can obviously make effective appeal to Scripture in support of the truth for which they contend. ... The distortions which have resulted from taking any one of these answers ... alone [is] the clue to the Church's nature.

"On Being the Church for the World" (1988)

Source: Lesslie Newbigin, "On Being the Church for the World," in G. Ecclestone (ed.), *The Parish Church? Explorations in the Relationship of the Church and the World*.

One possible definition of the Church which I think is worth thinking about, is that the Church is the provisional incorporation of humankind into Jesus Christ. Jesus Christ is the last Adam. All humankind is incorporated in Adam. We are all part of this natural human world. Jesus is the last Adam and the Church is the provisional incorporation of humankind into Christ. It is provisional in two senses: provisional in the sense that not all humankind is so incorporated; and provisional in the sense that those who are so incorporated are not yet fully conformed to the image of Christ. So the Church is a provisional body; it looks forward. It looks forward to the full formation of Christ in all its members, to the growth of its members in holiness to the stature of Jesus Christ. It also looks forward in the other sense, that it is only the provisional incorporation of what is in God's intention the whole of humanity.

That is however nonsense unless we deal with the actual realities of humanity. In talking about the world you have to talk about that segment of the world in which you are placed, and it is in relation to that segment of the world in which you are placed that the Church has to be recognizable as *for* that place. Certainly, the geographical definition of that segment may not be the only one that is relevant, although I think it is the fundamental one. There can be other possible definitions of the "place," but it is of the very essence of the Church that it is *for* that place, for that section of the world for which it has been made responsible. And the "for" has to be defined Christologically. In other words, the Church is *for* that place in a sense which is determined by the sense in which Christ is *for* the world. Now, one would need to go into a whole theology of the atonement to develop this, but obviously Christ on his cross is in one sense totally identified with the world, in another sense totally separated from the world. The cross is the total identification of Jesus with the world in all its sin but in that identification the cross is the judgement of the world, that which shows the gulf between God and his world, and we must always, in every situation, be wrestling with both sides of this reality: that the Church is *for* the world *against* the world; the Church is *against* the world *for* the world. The Church is for the human community in *that* place, *that* village, *that* city, *that* nation, in the sense which is determined by the sense in which Christ is for the world. And that must be the determining criterion at every point. …

I constantly hear people talking about "Kingdom issues" versus "Church issues." "Forget about the Church, all this ecclesiastical stuff which has nothing to do with God's will. On the last day, when the sheep and the goats are finally separated, they are all irrelevant questions. The important things are Kingdom issues: justice, peace, liberation." This has a certain element of truth in it. But if it's taken by itself, then the Church just becomes a crusader for liberation which is a very different thing. The Church cannot fulfil the Kingdom purpose that is entrusted to it—and certainly the Kingdom is the horizon for all our thinking: that God reigns and that the Church is sent into the world as a sign of the Kingdom—if it sees its role in merely functional terms. The Church is sign, instrument and foretaste of God's reign for that "place," that segment of the total fabric of humanity, for which it is responsible—a sign, instrument and foretaste for *that* place with its particular character. ...

Here I think the Orthodox have something to teach us. The Orthodox often criticize us in the Western Church for a too functional view of the Church, and I think they are right. The Orthodox have always stressed the point that the Church is first of all a communion in the Holy Spirit in the life of the triune God, so that you must define the Church in ontological terms and not just in functional terms. The Church is defined by what it is. It is already a sharing in the life of God. ... The first thing, therefore, is that the Church is a foretaste, and that means it will be different from the world. If it isn't, it's no good. Don't let us be afraid of the fact that the Church is different from the world, that the reality which we celebrate, which we share, which we rejoice in our worship is a reality which the world treats as an illusion. We must not evade that, or try to slide over it or make it seem less sharp.

But in so far as it is a foretaste, it can also be an instrument. It can be an instrument through which God's will for justice and peace and freedom is done in the world. That takes the Church out into the secular world with whatever is relevant to the real needs of that secular world. If that is not happening, how is the world going to know that the reality we talk about is true? ... The deeds without the words are dumb, they lack meaning. The two go together. And the Church, in so far as it is a foretaste of the reign of God, can also be an instrument of the reign of God, an instrument by which its justice is done. Not the only instrument of course. God has other instruments—the State is an instrument for God doing justice in the world. I think we have too much neglected this, that God has other instruments for the doing of His will in the world. But it is only the Church which can be the foretaste, the *arrabon* of the Kingdom.

Thirdly, a sign. The point of a sign is that it points to something that is not yet visible. ... The point of a sign is that it points to something which is real but not yet visible—which is not visible, not because it does not exist, but because it is over the horizon. Now the Church is a sign of the Kingdom, in so far as it is a foretaste. The Church is a sign of the Kingdom, pointing people to a reality which is beyond what we can see. And the necessary "other-worldliness" of the Church seems to me to be something that has to be absolutely held on to. We do not compete with all the other agencies in the world that are offering solutions to human problems here and now. We are not offering utopian illusions. We are pointing people to a reality which lies beyond history, beyond death. But we are erecting in this world, here and now, signs—credible signs—that make it possible for people to believe that that is the great reality and, therefore, to join us in going that way.

The Gospel in a Pluralistic Society (1989)

Source: Lesslie Newbigin, *The Gospel in a Pluralistic Society*.

The mission of the Church to all nations, to all human communities in all their diversity and in all their particularity, is itself the mighty work of God, the sign of the inbreaking of the kingdom. The Church is not so much the agent of the mission as the locus of the mission. It is God who acts in the power of his Spirit, doing mighty works, creating signs of a new age, working secretly in the hearts of men and women to draw them to Christ. When they are so drawn, they become part of a community which claims no masterful control of history, but continues to bear witness to the real meaning and goal of history by a life which—in Paul's words—by always bearing about in the body the dying of Jesus becomes the place where the risen life of Jesus is made available for others (2 Cor. 4:10).

It is impossible to stress too strongly that the beginning of mission is not an action of ours, but the presence of a new reality, the presence of the Spirit of God in power.

For further reading

George R. Hunsberger, *Bearing the Witness of the Spirit: Lesslie Newbigin's Theology of Cultural Plurality* (Grand Rapids: Eerdmans, 1998).
Lesslie Newbigin, *Foolishness to the Greeks* (Grand Rapids: Eerdmans, 1986).
——— *The Reunion of the Church* (London: SCM Press, 1948).
——— *A Word in Season: Perspectives on Christian World Missions* (Grand Rapids: Eerdmans, 1994).
Geoffrey Wainwright, *Lesslie Newbigin: A Theological Life* (New York: Oxford University Press, 2000).

11   Second Vatican Council (1962–1965)

No other doctrine was more central to the documents that emerged from the Second Vatican Council than ecclesiology. Of the 16 documents promulgated by the council, the two most important in this regard are the Dogmatic Constitution on the Church (Lumen gentium) *and the* Pastoral Constitution on the Church in the Modern World (Gaudium et spes)*, which have been excerpted here. In these documents, the council continues to affirm the primacy of the bishop of Rome and the hierarchical structure of the church, but the church is not to be understood either as* *merely a pyramidal institution on the one hand or a theological abstraction on the other. It is a dynamic and living organism, a mystical body, and a "communion." The origin, ongoing sustenance, and very form of the church is the Eucharistic meal that unites members of the church with one another and with Christ as his body. Christ is everywhere fully present in these Eucharistic bodies, but they are not self-sufficient and instead participate as one body in the unity of Christ through a reciprocal communion that is sacramentally received through the ministry of legitimate pastors. Vatican II also sought to recognize non-Catholic forms of belonging to the church and utilized the concept of "the people of God" as an "ecumenical bridge"[4] to do so. Thus, within this "people," non-Catholic Christians may be said to be "in communion" with the church (though that communion is imperfect). Indeed, even non-Christians may themselves be said to be "related" to the people of God. Vatican II affirmed the vocation and apostolate of the laity ("the common priesthood of the faithful") both in the church and in the world as well as a universal call to holiness. While* Lumen gentium *places more emphasis on doctrinal considerations,* Gaudium et spes *focuses on particular issues of relevance to the church's mission in and with the world, such as science and technology, economics, politics, human rights, industrialization, urbanization, and mass media. Theologically, the focus here is on the sacramental nature of the church as "the sign and instrument of intimate union with God and of the unity of the whole human race." No short set of excerpts from* Gaudium et spes *can do justice to the full range of the council's teaching on the nature and dignity of the human person, the social order, morality, social justice, and human activity in the world. The excerpts chosen focus on the relationship of the church to the world and the responsibility of the church in the world.*

Source: Austin Flannery, O.P. (ed.), *Lumen Gentium*, in *Vatican Council II: The Basic Sixteen Documents*.

Dogmatic Constitution on the Church (Lumen gentium)

Chapter 1   The mystery of the church
8. The one mediator, Christ, established and constantly sustains here on earth his holy church, the community of faith, hope and charity, as a visible structure through which he communicates truth and grace to everyone. But, the society equipped with hierarchical structures and the mystical body of Christ, the visible society and the spiritual community, the earthly church and the church endowed with heavenly riches, are not to be thought of as two realities. On the contrary, they form one complex reality comprising a human and a divine element. For this reason the church is compared, in no mean analogy, to the mystery of the incarnate Word. As the assumed nature, inseparably united to him, serves the divine Word as a living instrument of

---

⁴   Cardinal Joseph Ratzinger, "The Ecclesiology of Vatican II," in *L'Osservatore Romano: English Edition* (23 Jan. 2002), p. 5.

salvation, so, in a somewhat similar fashion, does the social structure of the church serve the Spirit of Christ who vivifies it, in the building up of the body (cf. Eph. 4:15).

This is the unique church of Christ which in the Creed we profess to be one, holy, catholic and apostolic, which our Savior, after his resurrection, entrusted to Peter's pastoral care (John 21:17), commissioning him and the other apostles to extend and rule it (cf. Matt. 28:18, etc.), and which he raised up for all ages as the pillar and mainstay of the truth (1 Tim. 3:15). This church, constituted and organized as a society in the present world, subsists in the Catholic Church, which is governed by the successor of Peter and by the bishops in communion with him. Nevertheless, many elements of sanctification and of truth are found outside its visible confines. Since these are gifts belonging to the church of Christ, they are forces impelling towards Catholic unity.

Chapter 2 The people of God

13. All women and men are called to belong to the new people of God. This people therefore, whilst remaining one and unique, is to be spread throughout the whole world and to all ages, in order that the design of God's will may be fulfilled: he made human nature one in the beginning and has decreed that all his children who were scattered should be finally gathered together as one (see John 11:52). It was for this purpose that God sent his Son, whom he appointed heir of all things (see Heb. 1:2), that he might be teacher, king and priest of all, the head of the new and universal people of God's sons and daughters. This, too, is why God sent the Spirit of his Son, the Lord and giver of life, who for the church and for each and every believer is the principle of their union and unity in the teaching of the apostles and communion, in the breaking of bread and prayer (see Acts 2:42).

The one people of God is accordingly present in all the nations of the earth, and takes its citizens from all nations, for a kingdom which is not earthly in character but heavenly. All the faithful scattered throughout the world are in communion with each other in the holy Spirit so that "he who dwells in Rome knows the Indians to be his members." Since the kingdom of Christ is not of this world (see John 18:36), in establishing this kingdom the church or people of God does not detract from anyone's temporal well-being. Rather it fosters and takes to itself, in so far as they are good, people's abilities, resources and customs. In so taking them to itself it purifies, strengthens and elevates them. The church, indeed, is mindful that it must gather in along with that King to whom the nations were given for an inheritance (see Ps. 2:8) and to whose city they bring gifts and offerings (see Ps. 71:10; Isa. 60:4–7; Rev. 21:24). The universality which adorns the people of God is a gift from the Lord himself whereby the catholic church ceaselessly and effectively strives to recapitulate the whole of humanity and all its riches under Christ the Head in the unity of his Spirit.

In virtue of this catholicity, each part contributes its own gifts to other parts and to the entire church, so that the whole and each of the parts are strengthened by the common sharing of all things and by the common effort to achieve fullness in unity. Hence, it is that the people of God is not only an assembly of different peoples, but in itself is made up of various ranks. This diversity among its members is either by reason of their duties—some exercise the sacred ministry for the good of their brothers and sisters; or it is due to their condition and manner of life, since many enter the religious state and, in tending to sanctity by the narrower way, stimulate their brothers and sisters by their example. Again, there are, legitimately, in the ecclesial communion particular churches which retain their own traditions, without prejudice to the Chair of Peter which presides over the entire assembly of charity, and protects their legitimate variety while at the same time taking care that these differences do not diminish unity, but rather contribute to it. Finally, between all the various parts of the church there is a bond of intimate communion whereby spiritual riches, apostolic workers and temporal resources are shared. For the members of the people of God are called upon to share their goods, and the words of the apostle apply also to each of the churches, "according to the gift that each has received, administer to it one another as good stewards of the manifold grace of God" (1 Pet. 4:10).

All are called to this catholic unity of the people of God which prefigures and promotes universal peace. And to it belong, or are related in different ways: the catholic faithful, others who believe in Christ, and finally all of humankind, called by God's grace to salvation.

14. This holy council, first of all, turns its attention to the catholic faithful. Relying on scripture and tradition, it teaches that this pilgrim church is required for salvation. Present to us in his body which is the church, Christ alone is mediator and the way of salvation. He expressly asserted the necessity of faith and Baptism (see Mark 16:16; John 3:5) and thereby affirmed at the same time the necessity of the church, which people enter through Baptism as through a door. Therefore, those could not be saved who refuse either to enter the church, or to remain in it, while knowing that it was founded by God through Christ as required for salvation.

Fully incorporated into the society of the church are those who, possessing the Spirit of Christ, accept its entire structure and all the means of salvation established within it and who in its visible structure are united with Christ, who rules it through the Supreme Pontiff and the bishops, by the bonds of profession of faith, the sacraments, ecclesiastical government, and communion. A person who does not persevere in charity, however, is not saved, even though incorporated into the church. Such people remain indeed in the bosom of the church, but only "bodily" not "in their hearts." All daughters and sons of the church should nevertheless remember that their exalted status is not to be ascribed to their own merits, but to the special grace of Christ. If they fail to respond in thought, word and deed to that grace, not only will they not be saved, they will be the more severely judged.

Catechumens who, moved by the holy Spirit, explicitly desire to be incorporated into the church, are by that very wish made part of it and with love and solicitude mother church already embraces them as her own.

15. The church has many reasons for knowing that it is joined to the baptized who are honored by the name of Christian, but do not profess the faith in its entirety or have not preserved unity of communion under the successor of Peter. For there are many who hold sacred scripture in honor as a rule of faith and of life, who display a sincere religious zeal, who lovingly believe in God the Father Almighty and in Christ, the Son of God and the Saviour. They are sealed by Baptism which unites them to Christ and they recognize and accept other sacraments in their own churches or ecclesiastical communities. Many of them possess the episcopate, celebrate the holy Eucharist and cultivate devotion to the Virgin Mother of God. There is furthermore a communion in prayer and other spiritual benefits. Indeed, there is a true union in the holy Spirit for, by his gifts and graces, his sanctifying power is active in them also and he has strengthened some of them even to the shedding of their blood. And so the Spirit stirs up desires and actions in all of Christ's disciples in order that all may be peacefully united, as Christ ordained, in one flock under one shepherd. Mother church never ceases to pray, hope and work that this may be achieved, and she exhorts her children to purification and renewal so that the sign of Christ may shine more brightly over the face of the church.

16. Finally, those who have not yet accepted the Gospel are related to the people of God in various ways. There is, first, that people to whom the covenants and promises were made, and from whom Christ was born in the flesh (see Rom. 9:4–5), a people in virtue of their election beloved for the sake of the fathers, for God never regret his gifts or his call (see Rom. 11:28–9). But the plan of salvation also includes those who acknowledge the Creator, first among whom are the Moslems: they profess to hold the faith of Abraham, and together with us they adore the one, merciful God, who will judge humanity on the last day. Nor is God remote from those who in shadows and images seek the unknown God, since he gives to everyone life and breath and all things (see Acts 17:25–8) and since the Savior wills everyone to be saved (see 1 Tim. 2:4). Those who, through no fault of their own, do not know the Gospel of Christ or his church, but who nevertheless seek God with a sincere heart, and, moved by grace, try in their actions to do his will as they know it through the dictates of their conscience—these too may attain eternal salvation. Nor will divine providence deny the assistance necessary for salvation to those who, without any fault of theirs, have not yet arrived at an explicit knowledge of God, and who, not without grace, strive to lead a good life. Whatever of good or truth is found amongst them is considered by the church to be a preparation for the Gospel and given by him who enlightens all men and women that they may at length have life. But very often, deceived by the Evil

One, people have lost their way in their thinking, have exchanged the truth of God for a lie and served the creature rather than the Creator (see Rom. 1:21, 25). Or else, living and dying in this world without God, they are exposed to ultimate despair. This is why, to procure the glory of God and the salvation of all of these people, the church, mindful of the Lord's command, "preach the Gospel to every creature" (Mark 16:15) takes great care to encourage the missions.

17. As he had been sent by the Father, the Son himself sent the apostles (see John 20:21) saying, "Go therefore and make disciples of all nations, baptizing them in the name of the Father, and of the Son, and of the holy Spirit, teaching them to observe all that I have commanded you; and see, I am with you all days even to the end of the world" (Matt. 28:19–20). The church has received from the apostles Christ's solemn command to proclaim the truth which saves, and it must carry it to the very ends of the earth (see Acts 1:8). Therefore, it makes the words of the apostle its own, "Woe to me if I do not preach the Gospel" (1 Cor. 9:16), and accordingly never ceases to send preachers of the Gospel until such time as the infant churches are fully established, and they can themselves continue the work of evangelization. For the church is driven by the holy Spirit to play its part in bringing to completion the plan of God, who has constituted Christ as the source of salvation for the whole world. By its proclamation of the Gospel, it draws its hearers to faith and the profession of faith, it prepares them for Baptism, snatches them from servitude to error, and incorporates them into Christ so that by love they may grow to full maturity in him. The effect of its activity is that whatever good is found sown in people's hearts and minds, or in the rites and customs of peoples, is not only saved from destruction, but is purified, raised up, and perfected for the glory of God, the confusion of the devil, and the happiness of humanity. All disciples of Christ are obliged to spread the faith to the best of their ability. However, while anyone can baptise those who believe, it is for the priests to complete the building up of the body by the Eucharistic sacrifice, thus fulfilling the words of god spoken by the prophet, "From the rising of the sun to its setting my name is great among the nations. And in every place there is a sacrifice, and there is offered to my name a clean offering" (Mal. 1:11). Thus the church both prays and works so that the fullness of the whole world may move into the people of God, the body of the Lord and the temple of the holy Spirit, and that in Christ, the head of all things, all honor and glory may be rendered to the Creator, the Father of the universe.

Pastoral Constitution on the Church in the Modern World (Gaudium et spes)

Solidarity of the church with the whole human family
1. The joys and hopes, the grief and anguish of the people of our time, especially of those who are poor or afflicted, are the joys and hopes, the grief and anguish of the followers of Christ as well. Nothing that is genuinely human fails to

find an echo in their hearts. For theirs is a community of people united in Christ and guided by the holy Spirit in their pilgrimage towards the Father's kingdom, bearers of a message of salvation for all of humanity. That is why they cherish a feeling of deep solidarity with the human race and its history.

An offer of service to humankind
3. Though proud of its discoveries and its power, humanity is often concerned about current developments in the world, about humanity's place and role in the universe, about the meaning of individual and collective endeavor, and finally about the destiny of nature and of humanity. And so the council, as witness and guide to the faith of all of God's people, gathered together by Christ, can find no more eloquent expression of this people's solidarity, respect and love for the whole human family, of which it forms part, than to enter into dialogue with it about all these various problems, throwing the light of the Gospel on them and supplying humanity with the saving resources which the church has received from its founder under the promptings of the holy Spirit. It is the human person that is to be saved, human society which must be renewed. It is the human person, therefore, which is the key to this discussion, each individual human person in her or his totality, body and soul, heart and conscience, mind and will.

This is the reason why this holy synod, in proclaiming humanity's noble destiny and affirming that there exists in it a divine seed, offers the human race the sincere cooperation of the church in fostering a sense of sisterhood and brotherhood to correspond to their destiny. The church is not motivated by earthly ambition but is interested in one thing only—to carry on the work of Christ under the guidance of the holy Spirit, who came into the world to bear witness to the truth, to save and not to judge, to serve and not to be served.

Mutual relationship of church and world
40. All we have said up to now about the dignity of the human person, the community of men and women, and the deep significance of human activity, provides a basis for discussing the relationship between the church and the world and the dialogue between them. The council now intends to consider the presence of the church in the world, and its life and activity there, in the light of what it has already declared about the mystery of the church.

Proceeding from the love of the eternal Father, the church was founded by Christ in time and gathered into one by the holy Spirit. It has a saving and eschatological purpose which can be fully attained only in the next life. But it is now present here on earth and is composed of women and men; they, the members of the earthly city, are called to form the family of the children of God even in this present history of humankind and to increase it continually until the Lord comes. Made one in view of heavenly benefits and enriched by them, this family has been "constituted and organized as a society in the present world" by Christ and "provided with means adapted to its visible and social union." Thus the church, at once "a visible organization and a spiritual community," travels the same journey as all of humanity and shares the same earthly lot with the world: it is to be a leaven and, as it were, the soul of human society in its renewal by Christ and transformation into the family of God.

That the earthly and the heavenly city penetrate one another is a fact open only to the eyes of faith; moreover, it will remain the mystery of human history, which will be harassed by sin until the perfect revelation of the splendor of the children of God. In pursuing its own salvific purpose not only does the church communicate divine life to humanity but in a certain sense it casts the reflected light of that divine life over all the earth, notably in the way it heals and elevates the dignity of the human person, in the way it consolidates society, and endows people's daily activity with a deeper sense and meaning. The church, then, believes that through each of its members and its community as a whole it can help to make the human family and its history still more human.

Furthermore, the Catholic Church deeply appreciates what other Christian churches and ecclesial communities have contributed and are contributing cooperatively to the realization of this aim. Similarly, it is convinced that there is a great variety of help that it can receive from the world in preparing the ground for the Gospel both from individuals and from society as a whole, by their talents and activity. The council will now outline some general principles for the proper fostering of mutual exchange and help in matters which are in some way common to the church and the world.

What the church offers to individuals
41. Contemporary women and men are in process of developing their personality and of increasingly discovering and affirming their rights. The church is entrusted with the task of manifesting to them the mystery of God, who is their final destiny; in doing so it discloses to them the meaning of their own existence, the innermost truth about themselves. The church knows well that God alone, whom it serves, can satisfy the deepest cravings of the human heart, for it can never be fully content with the world and what it has to offer. The church also realizes that men and women are continually being aroused by the Spirit of God and that they will never be utterly indifferent to religion—a fact confirmed by the experience of past ages and by a variety of evidence today. For people will always be keen to know, if only in a general way, what is the meaning of their life, their activity, their death. The very presence of the church recalls these problems to their minds. The most perfect answer to these questions is to be found in God alone, who created women and men in his own image and redeemed them from sin; and this answer is given in the revelation in Christ his Son who became man. To follow Christ the perfect human is to become more human oneself.

By this faith the church can keep the dignity of human nature out of the reach of changing opinions which, for example, either devalue the human body or glorify it. There is no human law so well fitted to safeguard the personal dignity and human freedom as is the Gospel which Christ entrusted to the church; for the Gospel announces and proclaims the freedom of the daughters and sons of God, it rejects all bondage resulting from sin, it scrupulously respects the dignity of conscience and its freedom of choice, it never ceases to encourage the employment of human talents in the service of God and humanity, and, finally, it commends everyone to the charity of all. This is nothing other than the basic law of the Christian dispensation. The fact that it is the same God who is at once saviour and creator, Lord of human history and of the history of salvation, does not mean that this divine order deprives creation, and humanity in particular, of their rightful autonomy; on the contrary, it restores and strengthens its dignity.

In virtue of the Gospel entrusted to it, the church proclaims human rights; it acknowledges and holds in high esteem the dynamic approach of today which is fostering these rights all over the world. But this approach needs to be animated by the spirit of the Gospel and preserved from all traces of false autonomy. For there is a temptation to feel that our personal rights are fully maintained only when we are free from every restriction of divine law. But this is the way leading to the extinction of human dignity, not its preservation.

What the church offers to society
42. The union of the human family is greatly consolidated and perfected by the unity which Christ established among the sons and daughters of God.

Christ did not bequeath to the church a mission in the political, economic, or social order: the purpose he assigned to it was religious. But this religious mission can be the source of commitment, direction, and vigor to establish and consolidate the human community according to the law of God. In fact, the church is able, indeed it is obliged, if times and circumstances require it, to initiate action for the benefit of everyone, especially of those in need, such as works of mercy and the like.

The church, moreover, acknowledges the good to be found in the social dynamism of today, especially in progress towards unity, healthy socialization, and civil and economic cooperation. The encouragement of unity is in harmony with the deepest nature of the church's mission, for it is "a sacrament—a sign and instrument, that is, of communion with God and of the unity of the entire human race." It shows to the world that social and exterior union comes from a union of hearts and minds, from the faith and love by which its own indissoluble unity has been founded in the holy Spirit. The impact which the church can have on modern society is due to an effective living of faith and love, not to any external power exercised by purely human means.

By its nature and mission the church is universal in that it is not committed to any one culture or to any political, economic or social system. Hence, it can be a very close bond between the various communities of people and nations, provided they trust the church and guarantee it true freedom to carry out its mission. With this in view the church calls upon its members and upon all people to put aside, in the family spirit of the children of God, all conflict between nations and races and to build up the internal strength of just human associations.

Whatever truth, goodness, and justice is to be found in past or present human institutions is held in high esteem by the council. In addition, the council declares that the church wants to help and foster these institutions insofar as this depends on it and is compatible with its mission. The church desires nothing more ardently than that it should develop in freedom in the service of all, under any regime which recognizes the basic rights of the person and the family, and the requirements of the common good.

What the church offers to human activity through its members
43. The council exhorts Christians, as citizens of both cities, to perform their duties faithfully in the spirit of the Gospel. It is a mistake to think that, because we have here no lasting city, but seek the city which is to come, we are entitled to evade our earthly responsibilities; this is to forget that because of our faith we are all the more bound to fulfil these responsibilities according to each one's vocation. But it is no less mistaken to think that we may immerse ourselves in earthly activities as if these latter were utterly foreign to religion, and religion were nothing more than the fulfilment of acts of worship and the observance of a few moral obligations. One of the gravest errors of our time is the dichotomy between the faith which many profess and their day-to-day conduct. As far back as the Old Testament the prophets vehemently denounced this scandal, and in the New Testament Christ himself even more forcibly threatened it with severe punishment. Let there, then, be no such pernicious opposition between professional and social activity on the one hand and religious life on the other. Christians who shirk their temporal duties shirk their duties towards his neighbor, neglect God himself, and endanger their eternal salvation. Let Christians follow the example of Christ who worked as a craftsman; let them be proud of the opportunity to carry out their earthly activity in such a way as to integrate human, domestic, professional, scientific and technical enterprises with religious values, under whose supreme direction all things are ordered to the glory of God.

It is to the laity, though not exclusively to them, that secular duties and activity properly belong. When therefore, as citizens of the world, they are engaged in any activity either individually or collectively, they will not be satisfied with meeting the minimum legal requirements but will strive to become truly proficient in that sphere. They will gladly cooperate with others working towards the same objectives. Let them be aware of what their faith demands of them in these matters and derive strength from it; let them not hesitate to take the initiative at the opportune moment and put their findings into effect. It is their task to cultivate a properly informed conscience and to impress the divine law on the affairs of the earthly city. For guidance and spiritual strength let them turn to the clergy; but let them realize that their pastors will not always be so expert as to have a ready answer to every problem, even every grave problem, that arises; this is not the role of the clergy: it is rather the task of lay people to shoulder their responsibilities under the guidance of Christian wisdom and with careful attention to the teaching authority of the church.

Very often their Christian vision will suggest a certain solution in some given situation. Yet it happens rather frequently, and legitimately so, that some of the faithful, with no less sincerity, will see the problem quite differently. Now if one or other of the proposed solutions is readily perceived by many to be closely connected with the message of the Gospel, they ought to remember that in those cases no one is permitted to identify the authority of the church exclusively with his or her own opinion. Let them, then, try to guide each other by sincere dialogue in a spirit of mutual charity and with a genuine concern for the common good above all.

The laity are called to participate actively in the entire life of the church; not only are they to animate the world with the spirit of Christianity, they are to be witnesses to Christ in all circumstances and at the very heart of the human community.

The task of directing the church of God has been entrusted to bishops and they, with their priests, are to preach the message of Christ in such a way that the light of the Gospel will shine on all activities of the faithful. Let all pastors of souls bear in mind that by their daily behavior and concerns they are presenting the face of the church to the world and that people judge from that the power and truth of the Christian message. By their words and example and in union with religious and with the faithful, let them show that the church with all its gifts is, by its presence alone, an inexhaustible source of all those virtues of which the modern world stands most in need. Let them prepare themselves by careful study to meet to enter into dialogue with the world and with people of all shades of opinion: let them have in their hearts above all these words of the council: "Since the human race today is tending more and more towards civil, economic and social unity, it is all the more necessary that priests should unite their efforts and combine their resources under the leadership of the bishops and the Supreme Pontiff and thus eliminate division and dissension in every shape or form, so that all humanity may be led into the unity of the family of God."

By the power of the holy Spirit the church is the faithful spouse of the Lord and will never fail to be a sign of salvation in the world; but it is by no means unaware that down through the centuries there have been among its members, both clerical and lay, some who were disloyal to the Spirit of God. Today as well, the church is not blind to the discrepancy between the message it proclaims and the human weakness of those to whom the Gospel has been entrusted. Whatever is history's judgment on these shortcomings, we cannot ignore them and we must combat them assiduously, lest they hinder the spread of the Gospel. The church also realizes how much it needs the maturing influence of centuries of past experience in order to work out its relationship to the world. Guided by the holy Spirit the church ceaselessly exhorts her children "to purification and renewal so that the sign of Christ may shine more brightly over the face of the church."

What the church receives from the modern world
44. Just as it is in the world's interest to acknowledge the church as a social reality and a driving force in history, so too the church is not unaware how much it has profited from the history and development of humankind. It profits from the experience of past ages, from the progress of the sciences, and from the riches hidden in various cultures, through which greater light is thrown on human nature and new avenues to truth are opened up. The church learned early in its history to express the Christian message in the concepts and languages of different peoples and tried to clarify it in the light of the wisdom of their philosophers: it was an attempt to adapt the Gospel to the understanding of all and the requirements of the learned, insofar as this could be done. Indeed, this kind of adaptation and preaching of the revealed word must ever be the law of all evangelization. In this way it is possible to create in every country the possibility of expressing the message of Christ in suitable terms and to foster vital contact and exchange between the church and different cultures. Nowadays when things change so rapidly and thought patterns differ so widely, the church needs to step up this exchange by calling upon the help of people who are living in the world, who are expert in its organizations and its forms of training, and who understand its mentality, in the case of believers and non believers alike. With the help of the holy Spirit, it is the task of the whole people of God, particularly of its pastors and theologians, to listen to and distinguish the many voices of our times and to interpret them in the light of God's word, in order that the revealed truth may be more deeply penetrated, better understood, and more suitably presented.

The church has a visible social structure, which is a sign of its unity in Christ: as such it can be enriched, and it is being enriched, by the evolution of social life, not as if something were missing in the constitution which Christ gave the church, but in order to understand this constitution more deeply, express it better, and adapt it more successfully to our times. The church acknowledges gratefully that, both as a whole and in its individual sons and daughters, it has been helped in various ways by people of all classes and conditions. Whoever contributes to the development of the human community on the level of family, culture, economic and social life, and national and international politics, according to the plan of God, is also contributing in no small way to the community of the church insofar as it depends on things outside itself. The church itself also recognizes that it has benefited and is still benefiting from the opposition of its enemies and persecutors.

For further reading

Bonaventure Kloppenburg, *Ecclesiology of Vatican II* (Chicago: Franciscan Herald Press, 1982).

Matthew L. Lamb and Matthew Levering (eds.), *Vatican II: Renewal within Tradition* (Oxford: Oxford University Press, 2008).

René Latourelle, *Vatican II: Assessment and Perspectives: Twenty-Five Years After (1962–1987)*, 3 vols. (New York: Paulist Press, 1987).

K. McNamara (ed.), *Vatican II: The Constitution on the Church. A Theological and Pastoral Commentary* (London: Geoffrey Chapman, 1968).

Cardinal Joseph Ratzinger, "The Ecclesiology of Vatican II," *L'Osservatore Romano: English Edition* (23 Jan. 2002), p. 5.

12   Basil Christopher Butler (1902–1986)

Bishop B. C. Butler was a convert to Catholicism from the Church of England, and became a Benedictine monk, biblical scholar, and theologian who played a formative role in the Second Vatican Council. Butler was one of the council's chief proponents and expositors in the years that followed it. The excerpts here elaborate on the value of the council's "communion ecclesiology" as its approach to unity and ecumenical relations.

"Ecumenism" (1966)

Source: Basil Christopher Butler, *The Theology of Vatican II: The Sarum Lectures 1966.*

We seem, driven to say that the Church, existing in its integral fullness in the Catholic Church, exists also, by self-transcendence, in bodies out of communion with the Catholic Church. We shall mean by "out of communion" that they do not enjoy "perfect communion"; but we shall admit that they have with us, and we with them, a communion which is very real, which can increase, and which is ontologically ordered, by the elements which constitute it, towards perfect communion. Our resulting ecclesiology may lack something of the clarity and definiteness of views associated with the name of Bellarmine; but it will have gained in richness and nuance, and in recognition of the mysteriousness of Christianity, not easily framed in precise human language. Perhaps we could say, with a distinguished Orthodox theologian, "We know where the Church is; it is not for us to judge and say where the Church is not."

Our examination of the decree has shown that the notion of "communion," while fully traditional, is yet flexible. In this respect it has a great advantage, for the ecumenical dialogue, over the description of the Church as "a society." A society is something whose edges are essentially sharp. You belong to it so long as you recognise and are recognised, in a juridical sense, by its governing authority; otherwise, you do not belong to it. Communion, by contrast, exists wherever there is common possession, whether of material or spiritual riches. There is a primordial communion between all men through their possession of a common specific (and rational) nature. There is a closer communion between men of a single culture or single political system. There is a certain communion between all who recognise the existence of a holy creator God. But there is obviously a much greater "communion" between all those who acknowledge Jesus Christ as the redeemer of mankind. And this is still more true of Christians who, having been truly baptised, are thereby marked with a common seal of incorporation into Christ—a sealing which we believe to be indelible in this life. On the other hand, since all must agree that Christ gave a total endowment of spiritual means to his Church, there must remain a marked difference between forms of Christian communion based on the common sharing of only part of this totality and a "perfect communion" in the totality of the Sacred Tradition.

It may be almost superfluous to enlarge upon the value, for ecumenical dialogue, of such an ecclesiology of communion. Its importance is that it approaches the whole question of the Church and her nature as visible on earth, from a basis which does not presuppose, on the part of those taking part in the dialogue, an acceptance of the belief that the perfect communion exists on earth—or that it is identical with the Roman Catholic Church. Just as it enables Catholics to recognise other Christian bodies as genuinely Christian communions, linked with the Catholic Church by all that is held in common between them, so it enables non-Catholics to acknowledge the Catholic Church as a Christian communion, closely linked to them by the same constitutive elements. Behind this common agreement, or rather beyond it, there remains, of course, disagreement about the actual existence here and now or the identification, of the perfect communion. But if ecumenical dialogue is directed towards visible Christian unity, it is implied that a perfect communion either *can* exist on earth, or at least is the ideal which must govern ecumenical endeavour. The Catholic, like the eastern Orthodox, in holding that what can exist does exist, and has a divine guarantee of perpetual existence, can claim that he holds to a "realised" eschatological conception of the Church. But he can respect and co-operate, in thought and practice, with those who hope from the future for what he believes God has guaranteed in the present.

For further reading

Basil Christopher Butler, *The Church and Unity* (London: Geoffrey Chapman, 1979).
—— *The Idea of the Church* (Baltimore: Helicon Press, 1963).
Anne Therese Flood, "B. C. Butler's Developing Understanding of Church: An Intellectual Biography" (Ph.D. Thesis: Catholic University of America, 1981).

13 Martin Luther King Jr. (1929–1968)

Martin Luther King Jr. was a Baptist pastor, scholar, organizer, orator, and activist who inspired the movement for civil rights in the United States. The church was central to his movement and he frequently addressed the church—both the black church and white church—in calling on Christians to form a nonviolent movement that would appeal to the moral conscience of the nation. For King, the church is that place where equality is learned, cultivated, and modeled before the world. The work of the church could not be separated from the work of social reform, therefore. Rather, the church is, as he described it during the Selma march, "the place you go from."

"The Answer to a Perplexing Question" (1962–1963)

Source: Clayborn Carson (ed.), *The Papers of Martin Luther King, Jr.*

[A lopsided theology that over-emphasizes human depravity] has often led to a purely other-worldly religion. It has caused many churches to ignore the "here" and emphasize only the "yonder." By stressing the utter hopelessness of this world and emphasizing the need for the individual to concentrate his efforts on getting his soul prepared for the world to come, it has ignored the need for social reform, and divorced religion from life. It sees the Christian gospel as only concerned with the individual soul. Recently a church was seeking a new minister and the pulpit committee listed several qualifications that he should possess. The first qualification was "He must be able to preach the true gospel and not talk about social issues." This emphasis has lead to a dangerously irrelevant church. It is little more than a country club where people assemble to hear and speak pious platitudes. …

If the church is to be worthy of its name it must become the fountainhead of a better social order. It must seek to transform not only individual lives, but also the social situation. It must be concerned not only about individual sin but also about social situations that bring to many people anguish of spirit and cruel bondage.

For further reading

Lewis Baldwin, *The Voice of Conscience: The Church in the Mind of Martin Luther King, Jr.* (Oxford: Oxford University Press, 2010).
Michael Battle, *The Black Church in America: African American Christian Spirituality* (Malden, MA: Blackwell, 2006).
Andrew Billingsley, Mighty Like a River: The Black Church and Social Reform (New York: Oxford University Press, 1999).
C. Eric Lincoln and Lawrence H. Mamiya, *The Black Church in the African American Experience* (Durham, NC: Duke University Press, 1990).

14   M. M. Thomas (1916–1996)

A prolific theologian and member of the Mar Thoma Orthodox Church, Madathiparampil Mammen Thomas wrote and was active during the transition from colonial to post-colonial India. Thomas's ecclesiology is thoroughly contextualized by the revolutionary impulses of his time and the challenge facing the church to be truly international not merely in terms of quantitative expansion but in terms of its character in relation to other religious faiths as well as secular movements seeking independence and human dignity.

Towards a Theology of Contemporary Ecumenism (1947–1975)

Source: M. M. Thomas, *Towards a Theology of Contemporary Ecumenism: A Collection of Addresses to Ecumenical Gatherings (1947–1975).*

It is evident that, as Dr. J. H. Oldham used to insist, a return to God should mean a return to politics; that a recovery of the mission of the Church requires a concern for identification with the peoples who are involved in the revolutionary struggles to change existing power-structures so they can express their human dignity through real participation in the total life of society.

This approach presupposes that the work of Christ and his Kingdom is discernible in the secular social and political revolutions of our time, and that the Church's function is to discern it and witness to it and (to use the words of the Report of the Division of Ecumenical Action) to participate in "God's work in a changing world." (*Work Book*, p. 25).[5] Of course, this presupposition is still violently disputed in certain theological circles and the counter-affirmation is made that any attempt to "discern the activity of the Spirit in the emergence of free nations and international solidarities, in undertakings where Christians

---

[5]   All parenthetical citations used by Thomas that appear in this excerpt refer to documents from the World Council of Churches General Assembly in Uppsala, 1968.

and non-Christians cooperate in seeking justice or peace, in the new social structure created by the technological revolution" is to posit "new divine revelations" other than Christ, and that the signs· and anticipation of the Kingdom are to be discerned "only" in the life and mission of the Church (*Draft Statements*, p. 10). In a rejoinder; it may be conceded that the Church has a special function as the sacramental sign or anticipation of the Kingdom, but this cannot justify the circumscribing of the signs and anticipations of the Kingdom within the Church. It is in circles where Christ and his Kingdom are seen as operating exclusively within the Church, that the Church falls into the idolatry of institutionalism and the perverse ideology of Christendom, both of which make it incapable of discerning the Divine Judgment on itself and the illuminations of Christ and his will mediated through world events. In such a theological context, there is no point in a dialogue between the Church and the world, only proclamation of the Word is valid—perhaps no point in a dialogue between theology and social science as a means of understanding man and social reality. It seems to me that a neat and absolute division between salvation history and secular history has done no good to theology.

It may not be out of place to point out here that the Church, directly through its preaching and teaching or indirectly through the influence of cultural values informed by Christian preaching and teaching, has played no small part in creating the spiritual ferment underlying the revolutions of our time. So if the Church is defined as including not only the institution, but also its extensive influence, we could make a strong case for saying that even where the Church as an institution is rejected, its mission has provided the ferment for the humanism which has produced signs and anticipations of the Kingdom in the revolutions of our time. When the Geneva World Conference says that "the discernment by Christians of what is just and unjust, human and inhuman in the complexities of political and economic change, is a discipline exercised in continual dialogue with biblical resources, the mind of the Church through history and today, and the best insights of social scientific analysis" (*Official Report*, p. 201), it is not looking at "the complexities of political and economic change" as a new revelation, but as part of the continuing work of the living Jesus Christ to awaken man to his true humanity, promised in Christ, and needing the discipline of the Gospel for its fulfilment.

Salvation and Humanism (1971)

Source: M. M. Thomas, *Salvation and Humanism: Some Crucial Issues of the Theology of Mission in Contemporary India.*

Ultimately, however, the dialogue between Christianity and Secularism at the inter-faith level acquires its evangelistic significance only within the context of an active co-operation between them in the humanisation of the structures of society and state. Dr. Hromadka used to speak of the problem of the credibility of the gospel; that is, the problem of believing the Christian affirmation that the gospel is a more adequate basis for humanisation. In his opinion it was dependent upon the Church being there where the action is, participating in the protest against dehumanising conditions of life, and in the political struggle for social justice and personal dignity, alongside the secularist. Participation is the presupposition of dialogue. And the form of the Church and its congregational life oriented to mission to secular man should be such as to make this participation effective. Probably for a long period, participation may well be in silence, without the noise of dialogue, to live down the unholy past of Christianity and to create confidence. Silence is necessary in many situations. Of course, this is a period of listening and learning; and it is also a waiting in expectancy, for sooner or later the dialogic situation creates a dialogic movement which, under God who is ever in dialogue with man, may also become evangelistic.

The form of the Church is a question of radical importance in this secular age. It is evident that the process of secularisation has destroyed, or is in fact destroying, in all lands, whatever integration had existed at the institutional level among Religion, Society and State, so that the idea and ideal of Christendom have no more validity. The Church no longer controls society and politics—which was the characteristic of the long Constantinian era. In this setting the danger is that the Church will become one minor department of life, a private affair of individuals who care, with no creative, prophetic or redemptive word to the larger areas of public life. This would be denying the very core of the essence of the Church which is its message that all things are to be summed up in Christ. But this rather exclusively individualist piety is not the only alternative to the idea of Christendom. The idea of the Church as the Suffering Servant of society and state has taken shape through the life and witness of the Confessing Church in Germany. Hitler would have gladly allowed the Church to take care of the disembodied souls of men if only it would leave the secular affairs to his control. The Confessing Church was not prepared to accept that narrow role but took the role of the Suffering Servant, concerned with the totality of personal and social existence, but expressing this concern without power but in witness and service. Harvey Cox has pointed out certain aspects of the form and meaning of the Church as God's avant-garde and as cultural exorcist in the emerging secular city.

In this connection it is necessary for us in India to consider whether the pattern of the Christian religious community obtaining here is of any value at all for the new shape of the Church. I have already indicated elsewhere that it has little value. For two reasons. *First*, it is in some sense an attempt to take control of the total life of Christians in the same way as Christendom did, that is, by controlling their lives through institutional authority. This will become more and more impossible with secularisation, with Christians finding their various social needs and urges met by a plurality of secular groupings. *Second*, because it isolates the Church from other religious communities by communalism, i.e. by making the Christian community one self-regarding religious community among many such religious communities; and it is hard if not impossible to distinguish between the Church which is the open servant of all men and the communally oriented Christian Community, conscious of its minority status. We have to find a more proper form for the Church in India than the very unsatisfactory form of an Indian religious community. The goal should be its capacity to witness to Christ as Saviour, Servant and Perfector of all men not merely as isolated individuals, but as persons in and with their various secular and religious group-ties and longing for fuller life and expressing it in categories of thought and life characteristic of the different groupings. We need a new pattern of combining Christian self-identity and secular solidarity with all men.

Risking Christ for Christ's Sake (1987)

Source: M. M. Thomas, *Risking Christ for Christ's Sake: Towards an Ecumenical Theology of Pluralism.*

The nature of the church has been the central subject of consideration in Christian ecumenism through the years. The church has always been defined in relation to God's purpose for the whole of humanity—either in terms of God's mission of salvation to an alienated humanity or, more recently, as "the sign and sacrament" of an already ontologically existing unity or a historical "coming unity" of humanity (Vatican II and Uppsala 1968). These formulations remain valid. But the discernment of faith-responses to Christ outside the church and the need for Christians to be in dialogical partnership with others in the witness to the kingdom to come call for a redefinition of the different levels and forms of koinonia-in-Christ in history and the relation between them in Christian living and the Christian mission of humanization and salvation. This is an important ecumenical task for our generation.

We shall continue to speak of the community of those openly acknowledging the crucified and risen Jesus as the Christ and gathered round the Lord's Table and the exposition of the word of God and scattered for witness and service, as the *church*, the "structured nucleus" of the people of Christ. But we have also to acknowledge a larger "unstructured stream" of koinonia-in-Christ or communion in the Messiah in human history, which is spiritually continuous and discontinuous with it. …

The "lamb slain" who is "on the throne" at the End is present "from the foundation of the world" (Rev. 13:8). Despite demons of self-righteousness and self-aggression the cross or the self-emptying redemptive love of God revealed in Jesus has been the central dynamic of all history. "The light shines in darkness and the darkness has not overcome it" (John 1:5). John V. Taylor goes even further when he sees the principle of the cross, of life through self-sacrifice, present and at work side by side with the principle of self-aggression, in the whole creation process, including that of nature and society. He says: "The free obedience of Jesus, his dying for us all and his rising again, are both history and universal reality." It is the crucified and risen Jesus who is our evidence that "we are citizens of a forgiven universe," and that being-in-Christ is the "primary and essential condition of man's existence." This is clearly declared in the New Testament hymns of creation in John 1, Colossians 1, and Hebrews 1, and in the creeds where "all things" are seen as having been created through Christ and by him, and as subsisting in him and oriented towards him. Such a universal presence of Christ also posits the possibility and the reality of people being saved "not by relating only to that historical life, death and resurrection in which the pattern was made plain, once for all, but by relating also to the pattern wherever it emerges" in the tissue of historical existence—not merely religious existence, but just human existence, religious or secular, and not only in contemporary history, but in the whole history of humanity. This is what gives validity to all our talk of the Unknown Christ, Anonymous Christianity and the latent church. But the historical cross remains the clue, the criterion for discerning the stirrings and positive responses of faith to the universal cross. And therefore, as Schillebeeckx says, they are "the initial stage—something which of its nature requires to grow to completion" in the acknowledgment of the dialectic between the historical and the universal in Jesus Christ.

This means that several kinds of implicit faith-response to Christ, without explicit acknowledgement of Jesus as the Christ, could well be included in the wider koinonia-in-Christ. As in these examples. The pattern of secular self-giving love and forgiveness, with an openness to the realm of transcendent forgiveness. A faith in the holy with the expectation of a divine mediation of love or the atonement of a suffering Messiah. A recognition of the person of Jesus as the ultimate pattern of the Messiah to come. The experience of mystic union where there is a recognition of mutual indwelling between human persons and the divine person. The self-commitment to the cause of creating a community of persons on earth envisaged as faith overcoming death. And more.

C. F. Andrews, writing to Tambaram 1938, said that the mission of the church involved "not merely to quicken those who are dead in trespasses but also to welcome with joy his radiant presence in those who have seen from afar his glory." The church's recognition of and dialogue with this wider koinonia-in-Christ are spiritually necessary for both. On the one hand, it will save the church from the kind of spiritual egoism which arrogates to itself the right to decide who belongs to the messianic people, and it can bring to the church an awareness of hitherto unexplored insights and facets of life in the Holy Spirit. On the other, through the encounter with the Person of Jesus Christ, commitments to the universal Christ-principle and the way of the cross could escape the danger of being perverted into legalism and used as instruments of self-justification. ...

Now to sum up. If the New Humanity in Christ is to transcend Christianity, other religions, and atheistic ideologies, it must transform them all from within, and it can then take new and diverse forms in them. Thus unity in Christ has to be seen as resulting from inner reform and should accommodate diversity. It seems to also envisage three levels of koinonia-in-Christ: first, the koinonia of the eucharistic community of the church, itself a unity of diverse peoples acknowledging the *Person* of Jesus as the Messiah; second, a larger koinonia of dialogue among people of different faiths inwardly being renewed by their acknowledgment of the ultimacy of the *pattern* of suffering servanthood as exemplified by the crucified Jesus; third, a still larger koinonia of those involved in the power-political struggle for new societies and a world community based on secular or religious anthropologies *informed by* the agape of the cross. The spiritual tension between them seems to be essential for the health of all of them and for the development of a Christology, Christian mission and forms of church life more adequate for and relevant to our pluralistic age.

The theology of religious pluralism is indeed an ecumenical issue of great importance—and of great consequences—in our time.

For further reading

Sathianathan Clarke, "M. M. Thomas (1916–1996)," in Don H. Compier and Joerg Rieger (eds.), *Empire and the Christian Tradition: New Readings of Classical Theologians* (Minneapolis: Fortress, 2007), pp. 423–37.

George R. Hunsberger, "Conversion and Community: Revisiting the Lesslie Newbigin–M. M. Thomas Debate," *The International Bulletin of Missionary Research* 22/3 (July 1998), pp. 112–17.

M. M. Thomas, *The Church's Mission and Post-Modern Humanism: A Collection of Essays and Talks, 1992–1996* (Delhi: Christava Sahitya Samithi and the Indian SPCK, 1996).

M. M. Thomas et.al. *Some Theological Dialogues*, Indian Christian Thought, 14 (Madras: Christian Literature Society, 1977).

15   John Howard Yoder (1927–1997)

At the end of the twentieth century, as Christendom continued to wane in Europe and North America, new ways of thinking about the relationship of the church to its surrounding social order began to surface. John Howard Yoder, an Anabaptist historian, theologian, and ethicist, was influential in articulating the relevance of a "free church" or "believer's church" ecclesiology for a post-Christendom, post-Constantinian context that emphasized the moral nonconformity and visible distinctiveness of the church both from the world and for the world. For Yoder, obedience to the lordship of Christ demands a radical shift in loyalties such that the claims of Caesar (or other powers that would demand our ultimate loyalty) are relativized if not displaced altogether, especially when it comes to the use of violence. From the standpoint of the biblical witness, the locus of historical meaning is not in society (which the church is then responsible for reforming) nor is it in the subjectivity of the individual (who is then called to an awareness of her own inner guilt and forgiveness), but rather in the church as a new and unprecedented form of social reconciliation and wholeness that is the very shape of the salvation God is working in the world. The church is the miracle of a new humanity that embodies through its practices in the world the coming reign of God, already made present in Christ.

Source: John Howard Yoder, *The Royal Priesthood*, ed. Michael G. Cartwright.

"The Otherness of the Church" (1961)

For the early church, "church" and "world" were visibly distinct yet affirmed in faith to have one and the same lord. This pair of affirmations is what the so-called Constantinian transformation changes (I here use the name of Constantine merely as a label for this transformation, which began before A.D. 200 and took over 200 years; the use of his name does not mean an evaluation of his person or work). The most pertinent fact about the new state of things after Constantine and Augustine is not that Christians were no longer persecuted and began to be privileged, nor that emperors built churches and presided over ecumenical deliberations about the Trinity; what matters is that the two visible realities, church and world, were fused. There is no longer anything to call "world"; state, economy, art, rhetoric, superstition, and war have all been baptized.

It is not always recognized in what structural connection this change, in itself self-evident, stands with a new distinction that now arose. It was perfectly clear to men like Augustine that the world had not become Christian through its compulsory baptism. Therefore, the doctrine of the invisibility of "the true church" sprang up in order to permit the affirmation that on some level somewhere the difference between belief and unbelief, i.e., between church and world, still existed. But this distinction had become invisible, like faith itself. Previously Christians had known as a fact of experience that the church existed but had to believe against appearances that Christ ruled over the world. After Constantine one knew as a fact of experience that Christ was ruling over the world but had to believe against the evidence that there existed "a believing church." Thus the order of redemption was subordinated to that of preservation, and the Christian hope turned inside out. …

The Constantinian approach has thereby shown itself to be incapable, not accidentally but constitutionally, of making visible Christ's lordship over church and world. The attempt to reverse the New Testament relationship of church and world, making faith invisible and the Christianization of the world a historic achievement with the institutional forms, was undertaken in good faith but has backfired, having had the sole effect of raising the autonomy of unbelief to a higher power. ... Those who have refused to learn from the New Testament must now learn from history; the church's responsibility to and for the world is first and always to be the church. The short-circuited means used to "Christianize" "responsibly" the world in some easier way than by the gospel have had the effect of dechristianizing the Occident and demonizing paganism. ...

The awareness of the visible reality of the world leads to two scandalous conclusions. The first is that Christian ethics is for Christians. Since Augustine this has been denied; the first criterion for an ethical ideal for the laity is its generalizability. From Kant's rigorous formulation of this criterion to the lay application in questions like, "What would happen if we were all pacifists like you?" the presupposition is universal that the right will have to apply as a simple performable possibility for a whole society. Thus the choice is between demanding of everyone a level of obedience and selflessness that only faith and forgiveness make meaningful (the "puritan" alternative) and lowering the requirements for everyone to the level where faith and forgiveness will not be needed (the medieval alternative). This dilemma is *not* part of the historical situation; it is an artificial construction springing from a failure to recognize the reality of the world.

The second scandalous conclusion is that there may well be certain functions in a given society which that society in its unbelief considers necessary and which the unbelief renders necessary, in which Christians will not be called to participate. This was self evident in the early Christian view of the state; that it had to be rejected later becomes less and less self-evident the longer we live and learn.

This view of the church commends itself exegetically and theologically. Contrary to the opposing view, it refuses to accept pragmatic grounds for deciding how Christians should relate themselves to the world. And yet after saying this we observe that this biblical approach is in fact the most effective. The moral renewal of England in the eighteenth century was the fruit not of the Anglican establishment but of the Wesleyan revival. The Christianization of Germanic Europe in the Middle Ages was not achieved by the "state church" structure, with an incompetent priest in every village and an incontinent Christian on every throne, but by the orders, with the voluntaristic base, the demanding discipline, the mobility, and the selectivity as to tasks that characterize the "free-church" pattern. What moral tone there is in today's Germany is due not to the state-allied church and the church-allied political parties but to the bootleg *Brüderschaften* of the Barmen Confession.

This makes it clear that the current vogue of the phrase "responsible society" in ecumenical circles is a most irresponsible use of terms. Even if we let pass the intentional ambiguity that makes society both the subject and the object of the responsibility, and the further confusion caused by the hypostatizing of "society," there remains a fundamental misdefinition, furthered by a misreading of socio-ethical history. It continues to work with the Constantinian formulation of the problem, as if the alternatives were "responsibility" and "withdrawal." The body of thought being disseminated under this slogan is a translation into modern terms of the two ancient axioms: that the most effective way for the church to be responsible for society is for it to lose its visible specificity while leavening the lump; and that each vocation bears in itself adequately knowable inherent norms. Thus we are invited to repeat the mistake of the Reformation, and that just as the time when the younger churches, themselves in an essentially pre-Constantinian position, need to be helped to think in other terms than those of the *corpus christianum* framework that has already dechristianized Europe.

Christ's victory over the world is to be dated not A.D. 311 or 312 but A.D. 29 or 30. That church will partake most truly of his triumph that follows him most faithfully in that warfare whose weapons are not carnal but mighty. The church will be most effective where it abandons effectiveness and intelligence for the foolish weakness of the cross in which are the wisdom and the power of God. The church will be most deeply and lastingly responsible for those in the valley of the shadow if it is the city set on the hill. The true church is the *free* church.

How then do we face deconstantinization? If we meet it as just another turn of the inscrutable screw of providence, just one more chance to state the Constantinian position in new terms, then the judgment that has already begun will sweep us along in the collapse of the culture for which we boast that we are responsible. But if we have an ear to hear what the Spirit says to the churches, if we let ourselves be led out of the inferiority complex that the theologies of the Reformation have thus far imposed on free church thought, if we discover as brethren in a common cause the catacomb churches of East Germany and the *Brüderschaften* of West Germany, if we puncture the "American dream" and discover that even in the land of the God-trusting post office and the Bible-believing chaplaincy we are in the same essentially missionary situation, the same minority status as the church in Sri Lanka or Colombia; if we believe that the free church, and not the "free world," is the primary bearer of God's banner, the fullness of the One who fills all in all, if we face deconstantinization not as just another dirty trick of destiny but as the overdue providential unveiling of a pernicious error; then it may be given to us, even in the twentieth century, to be the church. For what more could we ask?

"A People in the World" (1969)

In every direction we might follow in exposition, *the distinctness of the church of believers is prerequisite to the meaningfulness of the gospel message.* If what is called "the church" is the religious establishment of a total society, then the announcement that God has created human community is redundant, for the religiously sanctioned community is identical with the given order. The identification of the church with a given society denies the miracle of the new humanity in two ways: on the one hand by blessing the existing social unity and structure that is a part of the fallen order rather than a new miracle, and on the other hand by closing its fellowship to those of the outside or the enemy class or tribe or people or nation. If any concept of meaningful mission is to remain in this context, it must be transmuted to the realm of subjectivity, calling a few individuals to a depth of "authenticity" that separates them from their brethren.

Pragmatically it is self-evident that there can be no procedure of proclamation without a community, distinct from the rest of society, to do the proclaiming. Pragmatically it is just as clear that there can be no evangelistic call addressed to a person inviting him or her to enter into a new kind of fellowship and learning, if there is not such a body of persons, again distinct from the totality of society, to whom to come and from whom to learn. But this congruence between the free, visible existence of the believers' church and the possibility of valid missionary proclamation is not a merely pragmatic or instrumental one. It is founded deeply in the nature of the gospel itself. If it is not the case that there are in a given place people of various characters and origins who have been brought together in Jesus Christ, then there is not in that place the new humanity and in that place the gospel is not true. If on the other hand, this miracle of new creation has occurred, then all the verbalizations and interpretations whereby this body communicates to the world around it are simply explications of the fact of its presence. …

The political novelty that God brings into the world is a community of those who serve instead of ruling, who suffer instead of inflicting suffering, whose fellowship crosses social lines instead of reinforcing them. This new Christian community in which the walls are broken down not by human idealism or democratic legalism but by the work of Christ is not only a vehicle of the gospel or only a fruit of the gospel; it is the good news. It is not merely the agent of mission or the constituency of a mission agency. This is the mission.

For further reading

J. Alexander Sider, *To See History Doxologically: History and Holiness in John Howard Yoder's Ecclesiology* (Grand Rapids: Eerdmans, 2011).

Alain Epp Weaver, "After Politics: John Howard Yoder, Body Politics, and the Witnessing Church," *Review of Politics* 61/4 (1999), pp. 637–73.

Nigel Wright, *Disavowing Constantine: Mission, Church and the Social Order in the Theologies of John Howard Yoder and Jurgen Moltmann* (Carlisle: Paternoster, 2000).

John Howard Yoder, *Body Politics: Five Practices of the Christian Community before the Watching World* (Scottdale, PA: Herald Press, 1992).

———— *The Christian Witness to the State* (Newton, KS: Faith and Life Press, 1964).

———— "How H. Richard Niebuhr Reasoned: *A Critique of Christ and Culture*," in Glen H. Stassen, D. M. Yeager, and John Howard Yoder, *Authentic Transformation: A New Vision of Christ and Culture* (Nashville: Abingdon, 1996), pp. 31–90.

———— *The Jewish–Christian Schism Revisited*, ed. Michael G. Cartwright and Peter Ochs (Grand Rapids: Eerdmans, 2003).

16   World Council of Churches

Any number of documents could be provided as an introduction to the various ways the World Council of Churches (formally established in 1948) has taken up ecclesiological questions, including those that deal with faith, order, unity, baptism, Eucharist, ministry, liturgy, evangelism, mission, social justice, education, and more. The Third Assembly of the WCC, which gathered in New Delhi, India in 1961, made major statements on the unity of the church and incorporated the World Missionary Council. One of the notable documents to come out of the Assembly was The Church for Others and the Church for the World: A Quest for Structures for Missionary Congregations. *The document deals with the question of how the church engages a world where God is already present and attempts to cast the church's missionary existence in terms of a center that lies outside itself so that there is an important sense in which "the world sets the agenda" for the church's mission.*

"The Church for Others" (1967)

Source: World Council of Churches, "The Church for Others," in *The Church for Others: Two Reports on the Missionary Structure of the Congregation*.

Rethinking the relationship of church and world

In the past it has been customary to maintain that God is related to the world through the Church. When we sharpen this view into a formula the sequence would be: God–Church–world. This has been understood to mean that God is primarily related to the Church and only secondarily to the world by means of the Church. Further, it has been held that God relates himself to the world through the Church in order to gather everyone possible from the world into the Church. God, in other words, moves through the Church to the world. We believe that the time has come to question this sequence and to emphasize an alternative. According to this alternative the last two items in God–Church–world should be reversed, so that it reads instead God–world–Church. That is, God's primary relationship is to the world, and it is the world and not the Church that is the focus of God's plan. According to the bible, God is the creator and so all creation is his concern. He may use people; he may use individuals, but always it is the whole cosmos that occupies his attention. According to the fourth gospel, "God loved the *world* so much that he gave his only Son. … It was not to judge the world that God sent his Son into the world, but that through him the world might be saved" (John 3:16–17). According to Paul, "God was in Christ reconciling the *world* to himself" (2 Cor. 5:19). The Church lives through God's dealing with the world.

The old sequence of God–Church–world further tends to falsify the biblical account of the way God works in the world: it leads one to think that God always initiates change from inside out, from inside the Church to the "outsiders" in the world. But God often spoke to Israel through his actions in outside events, e.g. through the actions of a Cyrus or of the Babylonians taking the Hebrews into exile. Further, there is a danger of confining God's activity to the Church—his activity in the world being no more than that of the Church itself—so God is refashioned in the image of a residential deity and the world is left apparently bereft of the divine presence, which is enshrined within and reserved exclusively for the Church.

How then are we to define the relationship between the Church and the world? Again we must distinguish between models that have been adopted in the past and the emphasis that is required today. In former times the Church was viewed as the ark, perilously afloat amidst the turbulent seas of this world; outside the safety of this vessel mankind is going down to destruction and the only safety is to be dragged from the deep into the ecclesiastical ship. Or again, the Church has been seen as an armed camp and individual Christian soldiers are members of the army of the Lord of hosts set in the midst of active enemies. From time to time Christians sally forth from their palisades to rescue from the hostile environment as many as they can. It has to be admitted that some support for these pictures, describing the relationship of Church and world in terms of implacable enmity, may appear to be given by certain New Testament passages. "Do not unite yourselves with unbelievers; they are no fit mates for you. What has righteousness to do with wickedness? … Come away and leave them, separate yourselves." (2 Cor. 6:14, 17, quoting Isa. 52:11). "Religion which is without stain or fault," according to James, "is to keep oneself untarnished by the world" (1:27).

Ex-centric position of the church

But the Church has to be seen as a segment of the world, and thinking about the Church should always begin by defining it as part of the world, albeit one which confesses the universal Lordship of Christ. This apparent contradiction—it would be better to call it tension—between defining the relationship of Church and world in terms of hostility or in terms of virtual identity, is itself reflected in the New Testament. On the one hand Christians are a community of strangers and pilgrims whose citizenship is in heaven, and yet on the other hand they are to be the salt of the earth and the light of the world. We may say that the Church is only required to be separate in order to be prepared for engagement, that is, the Church exists for the world. It is called to the service of mankind, of the world. This is not election to privilege but to serving engagement. The Church lives in order that the world may know its true being. It is *pars pro toto*; it is the first fruits of the new creation. But its centre lies outside itself; it must live "ex-centredly." It has to seek out those situations in the world that call for loving responsibility and there it must announce and point to *shalom*. This ex-centric position of the Church implies that we must stop thinking from the inside towards the outside. But this is still the main train of thought in missionary thinking. The apostolate is conceived as a repetition outside of what happens inside, as an extension of the pastorate. We continue to think in this way, although there is sufficient evidence that in so doing we shall never touch people beyond the fringes of Church life. Moreover, this movement from the alleged centre to the periphery will, more often than not, distort and pervert mission into propaganda, into the attempt to make man in *our* Christian image and after our ecclesiastical likeness. There is yet another corollary. The view that the Church has a central position carries with it the illusion that we already possess the institutions and structures we require. On the contrary we have to recognize that they all have to be scrutinized and tested in terms of their relevance to the needs of modern men. …

A church for the world
We have to recognize that the churches have developed into "waiting churches" into which people are expected to come. Its inherited structures stress and embody this static outlook. One may say that we are in danger of perpetuating "come-structures" instead of replacing them by "go-structures." One may say that inertia has replaced the dynamism of the Gospel and of participation in the mission of God. …

But to speak of the need for "go-structures" does not mean just crossing frontiers, leaving the "church" area and entering the "world" area. To speak of "going" is to give up all idea of self-aggrandizement; it means refusing to engage in proselytism; it means adopting the pattern of the messianic life—the form of the servant—without concern for success in terms of church membership and church activities. Because in our missions we participate in the mission of God, we should expect, in confident hope, that people will find new, perhaps unprecedented, forms to express their obedience to God. "The seed you sow is not the body that shall be, but a naked grain. … God clothes it with the body of his choice" (1 Cor. 15:37–8). It may well be (in fact it has happened very often) that the new body of God's choice will suffer a premature death because of the missionary's impatience to incorporate those who have accepted the faith into the old body. Frequently this impatience is an indication of proselytization, which is the very opposite of mission. The proselytizing Church conceives itself to be the mediating centre of salvation; it expects men to emigrate from the world into the ecclesiastical structure. Against this one must plead for freedom that the new communities, which may arise as a fruit of mission, should have full opportunity to form their own lives.

The world provides the agenda
Moreover, in seeking new forms of missionary presence, they must be allowed to emerge from the interplay of the Gospel and the contemporary situation, as Christians seek to be obedient to the Christ who is both the content of the Gospel and the Lord of the world. The obedience of the churches require that they obtain a clear picture of the actual situation, so that the Gospel may reach the poor and so that they may serve where the hungry and thirsty, the naked and the imprisoned are. This commission of the churches is pluralistic in character—that is, it is always concrete. The message and structures of the churches can only be formulated with respect to the immense variety of actual realities amidst which we live. Hence it is the world that must be allowed to provide the agenda for the churches.

For further reading

Lesslie Newbigin, "Comments on the Church, the Churches and the World Council of Churches," *Ecumenical Review* 3/3 (1951), pp. 253–4.
Jean Tillard "An Ecclesiology of Councils of Churches," *Mid-Stream* 22 (1983), pp. 188–98.
Lukas Vischer, "Councils—Instruments of Ecclesial Communion" *Ecumenical Review* 24/1 (1972), pp. 79–87
W. A. Visser't Hooft (ed.), *The New Delhi Report: The Third Assembly of the World Council of Churches, 1961* (New York: Association Press, 1962).

17 Hans Küng (1928–)

Hans Küng is a Roman Catholic theologian who has written extensively on the church but also had his permission to teach Catholic theology removed by the Vatican because of his attack on papal infallibility in 1970. Küng's work has been consistently ecumenical, especially seeking common ground between Protestants and Catholics, while also being global in outlook so that ecumenism stretches beyond Christian communions. Küng was a consultant to Vatican II and his work expresses a concern that more attention be given to the charismatic constitution, giftedness, and structure of the church rather than its bureaucratic or institutional structure.

The Church (1967)

Source: Hans Küng, *The Church*, trans. Ray Ockenden and Rosaleen Ockenden.

Distortions of the image of the church
The Church as the object of faith: let us try to reach a deeper understanding of this idea by analyzing more precisely why we believe *the* Church, rather than *in* the Church.

To say that we do not believe *in* the Church means that the Church is not God. The Church as a fellowship of believers is, in spite of everything positive that can be said about it, neither God nor a god-like being. Of course, the believer is convinced that God works in the Church and in the work of the Church. But God's work and the Church's are neither identical nor overlapping, there is indeed a fundamental distinction between them. God remains God. His work can never be superseded, made superfluous or redundant, by what he has already effected. The Church, however, is and remains something created. It is therefore not omniscient and omnipotent, not self-sufficient and autonomous, not eternal and sinless. It is not the source of grace and truth, it is not Lord, redeemer and judge, and there can be no question of idolizing it. The Church is the often threatened and endangered fellowship of the faithful and the obedient, which lives from God and for God, which places all its trust in him, which believes in God.

To say that we do not believe *in* the Church means that *we* are the Church. As the fellowship of believers the Church is in no way different from us. It is not a Gnostic collective person, whom we can see to be separate from us. *We* are the Church, and we *are* the Church. And if we are the Church, then the Church is a fellowship of those who seek, journey and lose their way, of the helpless, the anguished and the suffering, of sinners and pilgrims. If *we* are the Church, then the Church is a sinful and pilgrim Church, and there can be no question of idealizing it. It is the fellowship of those who hear and believe, who make their pilgrimage through darkness and uncertainty, completely dependent on God's grace and truth, forgiveness and deliverance, putting their whole trust in God: as such this fellowship cannot be said to believe in itself.

To say that we believe *the* Church, however, means that it is from God's grace and through faith that the Church lives. A community that does not believe is not the Church. The Church does not exist of itself but in the actual men who believe. Just as there can be no country without people, no body without limbs, so there can be no Church without believers. The Church does not spring simply from God's ordinance but from the decision which is required of the men who must form the Church, the radical decision for God and his reign. This decision is faith. …

The church as the creation of the Spirit

The Spirit is God's eschatological gift with which the community, and the individual who is incorporated into the community through baptism, is blessed in the last days. ... For Paul there can be no new eschatological existence at all without the Spirit. If there is no Spirit, it does not mean that the community lacks its missionary commission, but that there is no community at all. ... The Spirit is ... the earthly presence of the glorified Lord. In the Spirit Christ becomes Lord of his Church, and in the Spirit the resurrected Lord acts both in the community and in the individual. The power of his resurrection is more than a power of ecstasy and miracle; it produces a new creation. The Spirit opens up for the believer the way to the saving action of God in Christ. ... The Spirit makes the believer a part of Christ's body. It is he who creates the unity of the body, which consists of many members, with different gifts of the Spirit (cf. 1 Cor. 12).

The church is one

The existing common ecclesial reality must be recognized: In Christ we are already united—in spite of the conflicting multiplicity of Churches. We know this by faith; the unity of the Church is a unity in faith. In him all Churches, whatever their disagreements among themselves, acknowledge the *one* Lord and at the same time in the *one* Spirit, his Spirit, the *one* Father, his Father. In him all Churches possess the one Gospel, his good news, however differently they may interpret it. And if these Churches baptize validly in his name—which is not in dispute—in which ecclesia are the baptized incorporated if not in his, the one ecclesia, of which body are they members if not the one body of Christ? And if these Churches also validly celebrate the Lord's Supper—which is only disputed in a few cases (with justice?)—what body do they receive and in what body are they united, if not in his, the one body? Is there not therefore much in common in the different faiths and hopes of the Churches, so much more in common than there is separating them? Cannot the love in the different Churches rise above, if it cannot obliterate the differences in faith? Thus the different Churches should not search for the unity of the Church as though it had never been found, but on the broad basis of the unity which has already been found, which has indeed been given to us. The unity of the Church is not merely a goal, but is the foundation of necessary work for unity. It is not, in fact, without reason that the different Christian Churches call themselves *Churches*. And it is precisely because all Christian Churches are Churches that they are faced with the task of the unity of the Church through faith in Christ. ...

The church is holy

The need for reform in the Church, for which it always has ample grounds, given that the Church is human and sinful, does not arise from any kind of opportunistic or transient reason, such as an enthusiasm for progress, the desire for modernity, an automatic conformism, fear of temporal powers and so on. It arises primarily from the demands made in the Gospel by the Lord of the Church, the call to metanoia, to new faith, to new righteousness, holiness and freedom, to new life. Church reforms are not called for simply by the whim of the Church or Church leaders. They are a continuing task and opportunity given by the Lord of the Church. Reform is a way in which the Church fulfills the will of God, following in the footsteps of Christ with its eye on the coming of the kingdom. There will always be opposition. Uncommitted indifference, an illusionary view of the Church's situation, ecclesiastical self-satisfaction, a lazy traditionalism, an apologetic attitude, a superficial, narrow or secularized ecclesiology, defeatism and lack of hope—these will always exist. But genuine distress at the permanently unreformed Church, heartfelt prayers that the Church may be delivered from evil, committed and constructive criticisms of the Church, zeal for the Lord and active love—these are the sources of a continually revived readiness for reform.

... Church reform must be a positive reforming of the Church in accordance with its nature. If it is a real reform, it will never spend itself in purely negative acts of abolition, rejection and prohibition. It will be a positive re-forming and re-expression of its nature. The word "renewal" is often better than the word "reform", precisely because it emphasizes this positive and creative aspect. Genuine Church reform is not the same as *revolution.* It does not aim at a violent upheaval, it is not doctrinaire, fanatical or loveless in its quest of what is new. While aiming at what is new and better, it is concerned about the continuity of historical development; it is not innovation but *renewal.* Genuine Church reform is on the other hand not the same as *restoration.* It does not aim at a contented continuation of an old system, but courageously breaks with old systems in order to find greater truth. Instead of restoring old forms, it looks for new forms fitted to the age; instead of insisting with fresh intensity on the rigid observation of laws and ordinances, canons and codes, it seeks to renew the inner life of institutions and constitutions. While retaining a sense of tradition, genuine reform is concerned with finding the new and creative forms demanded by the present time; it is not restoration, but again *renewal.*

It is not enough, as we have seen, to effect an inner reform of the heart which neglects the reform of structures, institutions and constitutions. Equally, a purely external reform, abolishing abuses and merely patching up the old structures, institutions and constitutions, is of no avail. What is constantly necessary is a creative reform of conditions and structures, which, far from destroying the nature of the Church, gives it new and credible form. True, what God himself through Christ in the Spirit has instituted and constituted in the Church has a share in the holiness of God himself and needs no reform. But what men themselves have instituted and constituted in the Church is conditioned by human imperfections and sinfulness and is in constant need of reform. Since, however, nature and historical form cannot properly be separated, there are no irreformable areas in the Church; at most there are irreformable constants. There is no stone, no cloister in the building of the Church which does not need reforming again and again; but the constructional formula which is the key to the whole must not be contravened. The only measure for renewal in the Church is the original Gospel of Jesus Christ himself; the only concrete guide is the apostolic Church. The credibility of the Church depends crucially on its constantly undertaking new reforms and renewing itself afresh. An unreformed Church will fail to convince. Drawing on the forgiveness which has been granted to her, the Church must help to renew both individual and community, and so demonstrate that it is a holy Church.

"Which Church Has a Future?" (2001)

Source: Hans Küng, *The Catholic Church: A Short History*, trans. John Bowden.

Four conditions need to be met if the church is to have a future in the third millennium.

1. It must not turn backward and fall in love with the Middle Ages or the time of the Reformation or the Enlightenment, but be a church rooted in its Christian origin and concentrated on its present tasks.
2. It must not be patriarchal, fixated on stereotyped images of women, exclusively male language, and predetermined gender roles, but be a church of partnership, which combines office and charism and accepts women in all church ministries.
3. It must not be narrowly confessional and succumb to confessional exclusiveness, the presumption of officialdom, and the refusal of communion, but be an ecumenically open church, which practices ecumenism inwardly and finally follows up many ecumenical statements with ecumenical actions like the recognition of ministries, the abolition of all excommunications, and complete Eucharistic fellowship.
4. It must not be Eurocentric and put forward any exclusivist Christian claims and show a Roman imperialism, but be a tolerant universal church which has respect for the truth that is always greater, and therefore also attempt to learn from the other religions and leave an appropriate autonomy to the national, regional, and local churches.

For further reading

Veli-Matti Kärkkäinen, "Hans Küng: Charismatic Ecclesiology," in *An Introduction to Ecclesiology: Ecumenical, Historical & Global Perspectives* (Downers Grove, IL: InterVarsity Press, 2002), pp. 103–12.

Hans Küng, *The Catholic Church: A Short History*, trans. John Bowden (New York: Random House, 2003).

———— *On Being a Christian* (Garden City, NY: Doubleday, 1976).
———— *Structures of the Church* (New York: Thomas Nelson, 1964).
Corneliu C. Simut, *A Critical Study of Hans Küng's Ecclesiology* (New York: Palgrave Macmillian, 2008).

18   Alexander Schmemann (1921–1983)

Protopresbyter Alexander Schmemann was an influential Russian Orthodox theologian and expert on Orthodox liturgy, history, and theology who was also a helpful interpreter of Orthodox liturgy both to Orthodox and non-Orthodox Christians. In the following excerpt, Schmemann outlines some of the distinctive features of an Orthodox approach to ecclesiology.

"Ecclesiological Notes" (1967)

Source: Alexander Schmemann, "Ecclesiological Notes," *St. Vladimir's Seminary Quarterly* 11/1 (1 Jan. 1967).

1. One of the greatest "ecumenical" difficulties the Orthodox Church has is that her thought forms and "terms of reference" are different from those of the West. … In our own "sources"—the Fathers, the Councils, the Liturgy— we do not find any formal definition of the Church. This is not because of any lack of ecclesiological interest and consciousness, but because the Church (in the Orthodox approach to her) does not exist, and therefore cannot be defined, apart from the very content of her life. The Church, in other terms, is not an "essence" or "being" distinct, as such, from God, man, and the world, but is the very reality of *Christ in us* and *us in Christ*, a new mode of God's presence and action in His creation, of creation's life in God. She is God's gift and man's response and appropriation of this gift. She is union and unity, knowledge, communion and transfiguration. And, since apart from the "content" the "form" has no meaning, … Orthodox ecclesiology rather than precise definitions or forms, conditions and modalities, is an attempt to present an *icon* of the Church as *life in Christ*—an icon which to be adequate and true must draw on all aspects and not only on the institutional ones of the Church. For the Church is an *institution*, but she is also a *mystery*, and it is mystery that gives meaning and life to institution and is, therefore, the object of ecclesiology.

2. Such an attempt must probably begin with the Church as *new* creation. Orthodox ecclesiology traditionally sees the beginning of the Church in paradise and her life as the manifestation of the Kingdom of God. … Thus the basic dimensions of Orthodox ecclesiology are cosmic and eschatological.

On the one hand, in Christ, the Incarnate Son of God, the new Adam, creation finds not only redemption and reconciliation with God, but also its fulfillment. Christ is the Logos, the Life of all life, and this life, which was lost because of sin, is restored and communicated in Christ, in His incarnation, death, resurrection, and glorification, to man and through him to the whole creation. Pentecost, the descent of the Holy Spirit, the giver of life, is not a mere establishment of an institution endowed with specific powers and authorities. It is the inauguration of the new age, the beginning of life eternal, the revelation of the kingdom which is "joy and peace in the Holy Spirit." The Church is the continuing presence of Pentecost as power of sanctification and transfiguration of all life, as *grace* which is knowledge of God, communion with Him and, in Him, with all that exists. The Church is creation as renewed by Christ and sanctified by the Holy Spirit.

But, on the other hand, the kingdom which Christ inaugurates and the Holy Spirit fulfills is *not of this world*. "This world," by rejecting and condemning Christ, has condemned itself; no one, therefore, can enter the Kingdom without in a real sense dying to the world, i.e. rejecting it in its self-sufficiency, without putting all faith, hope, and love in the "age to come," in the "day without evening" which will dawn at the end of time. "You are dead and your life is hid with Christ in God" (Col. 3:3). This means that although the Church abides in the world, her real life is a constant expectation and anticipation of the world to come, a preparation for it, a passage into reality which in this world can be experienced only as future, as promise and token of things yet to come. The fruits of the Spirit (joy, peace, holiness, vision, knowledge) are real, but their reality is that of the joy which a traveler has when at the end of a long journey he finally sees the beautiful city where he is going—into which, however, he must yet enter. The Church reveals and truly bestows now the Kingdom which is to come, and creation becomes new when it dies to itself as "this world" and becomes thirst and hunger for the consummation for all things in God.

3. It is the mystery of the Church as new creation in its two dimensions—the cosmic and eschatological—that reveals to us the meaning and structure of the Church as *institution*. The nature of the institution can be termed *sacramental*, and this means not only a given or static inter-dependence between the visible and the invisible, nature and grace, the material and the spiritual, but also, and primarily, the dynamic essence of the Church as passage from the old into the new, from this world into the world to come, from the kingdom of nature into the Kingdom of Grace. The Church, as visible society and organization, belongs to this world; it is truly a part of it. And she must belong to it because she is "instituted" to represent and to stand for the world, to assume the whole creation. It belongs thus to the very "institution" of the Church to be a people, a community, a family, an organization, a nation, a hierarchy; to assume, in other words, all the natural forms of human existence in the world, in time and space. She is an organic continuity with the whole of human life, with the totality of human history. She is the *pars pro toto* of the whole creation. Yet she is all this in order to reveal and manifest the true

meaning of creation as fulfillment in Christ, to announce to the world its end and the inauguration of the Kingdom. The "institution" is thus the sacrament of the Kingdom, the means by which the Church always becomes what she is, always fulfills herself as the One, Holy, Catholic, and Apostolic Church, as the Body of Christ and the Temple of the Holy Spirit, as the new life of the new creation. The basic act of this fulfillment, and therefore the true "form" of the Church, is the Eucharist: the sacrament in which the Church performs the passage, the *passover*, from this world into the Kingdom, offers in Christ the whole creation to God, seeing it as "heaven and earth full of His glory," and partakes of Christ's immortal life at His table in His Kingdom. ...

5. In this world the One, Holy, Catholic, and Apostolic Church manifests itself as a plurality of churches, each one of which is both a part and a whole. It is a part because only in unity with all churches and in obedience to the universal truth can it be the Church; yet it is also a whole because in each church, by virtue of her unity with the One, Holy, Catholic, and Apostolic Church, the whole Christ is present, the fullness of grace is given, the catholicity of new life is revealed. The visible unity of all churches as the One, Holy, Catholic, and Apostolic Church is expressed and preserved in the unity of faith, the unity of sacramental structure, and the unity of life. The unity of faith has its norm and content in the universal tradition. The unity of sacramental structure is preserved through the apostolic succession, which is the visible and objective continuity of the Church's life and order in time and space. The unity of life manifests itself in the active concern of all churches for each other and of all them together for the Church's mission in the world.

6. The organ of unity in the Church is the episcopate. "The Church is in the Bishop." This means that in each church the personal ministry of the bishop is to preserve the fullness of the Church, i.e., her identity and continuity with the One, Holy, Catholic, and Apostolic Church; to be the teacher of the universal traditions; the offerer of the Eucharist which is the sacrament of unity; and the pastor of the people of God on its pilgrimage to the Kingdom. By virtue of his consecration by other bishops and of his belonging to the universal episcopate, he *represents*, he makes present and unites his church to all churches and *represents* all other churches, and therefore the whole Church, to his own church. In him each church is thus truly a part of the whole Church and the whole Church is truly present in each church. In the Orthodox tradition, the unity of the episcopate, and especially the organ of this unity, a synod or council of bishops, is the supreme expression of the Church's teaching and pastoral function the inspired mouth of the whole Church. But, "The Bishop is in the Church," and this means that neither one bishop nor the episcopate as a whole are above the Church. ... It is rather the bishop's complete identification with and his total obedience to the *consensus Ecclesiae*, to her teaching, life, and holiness, as well as his organic unity with the people of God, that makes the bishop the teacher and the guardian of the truth. For in the Church no one is without the Holy Spirit, and according to

the Encyclical of Eastern Patriarchs, the preservation of the truth is entrusted to the whole people of the Church. Thus the Church is both hierarchical and conciliary, and the two principles are not only not opposed to each other but are in their interdependence essential for the full expression of the mystery of the Church. ...

9. The Church is both in *statu patriae* [having arrived in heaven] and in *statu viae* [journeying]. As "Christ in us," as the manifestation of the Kingdom and the sacrament of the age to come, her life is already filled with the "joy and peace of the Holy Spirit," and it is this paschal joy that she expresses and receives in worship, in the holiness of her members, and in the communion of the saints. As "we in Christ," she is in pilgrimage and expectation, in repentance and struggle. And above everything else, she is mission, for her belonging to the world to come, the joy that in Christ has entered the world, and the vision of the transfigured world are given to her so that she may in this world witness to Christ and may save and redeem in Him the whole creation.

For further reading

John Meyendorff, *The Orthodox Church: Its Past and Its Role in the World Today*, rev. edn. (Crestwood, NY: St. Vladimir's Seminary Press, 1996).
Alexander Schmemann, *The Eucharist: Sacrament of the Kingdom* (Crestwood, NY: St. Vladimir's Seminary Press, 1987).
———— *For the Life of the World: Sacraments and Orthodoxy* (Crestwood, NY: St. Vladimir's Seminary Press, 1997).
Timothy Ware, *The Orthodox Church*, rev. edn. (New York: Penguin Books, 1997).

19   Juan Luis Segundo (1925–1996)

Juan Luis Segundo, from Uruguay, was one of the earliest and most erudite voices of what came to be known as "liberation theology." He was far more concerned with the liberating purpose and function of the church in the world and in history than in abstract definitions of the nature of the church. The grace of God and the possibility of humanizing love toward one another are, according to Segundo, universally present throughout the world. The significance of the church as a particular people, therefore, is not to serve as the exclusive bearer of salvation, but as the community of those "who know" this and who share the message of this possibility to the world. The church can be described as the "consciousness of humanity" and "humanity arriving at full awareness of what is taking place in it." It is a particular and historical sign of what is always and everywhere available to all. Rather than attempt to be a religion of the masses through its own quantitative spread throughout the world, the church is called to be a creative minority in the world—a vanguard that makes explicit the way that the love of God is at work in history. The church's task is to embody the love of God by working to transform the world through efforts of humanization and liberation.

The Community Called Church (1968)

Source: Juan Luis Segundo, *The Community Called Church*, trans. John Drury.

When we read the Gospel and the rest of the New Testament, we encounter two lines of thought regarding how salvation is obtained. … One line of thought shows salvation to be conditioned by particular, specific means (which only some people seem to possess). The second line shows salvation in its absolutely universal dimension.

Here we need only recall two central texts dealing with these two lines of thought. They are not the only texts we could cite but they are the most well known. They lead the way for a whole series of other passages spread throughout the New Testament. The first text is in Saint Mark's Gospel (16:15–16). Christ has risen from the dead and he is telling his apostles about the kingdom of God. He tells them: "Go into the whole world and preach the gospel to the whole creation. He who believes and is baptized will be saved; but he who does not believe will be condemned." Here we have a very clear line of thought about salvation, in which salvation appears to be conditioned by the fact of entering the Church through faith and baptism, through faith in Christ's preaching, and through the sacrament which makes one a part of the Church. Salvation is attributed to this. …

On the other hand, we find that another line of thought appears in an equally central spot in the Gospel where Christ talks about the last days. He is telling his apostles about the last judgment that God will pass on humanity. How is God going to look at the whole of human history in order to decide whether people are to be saved or condemned?

His reply is in Matthew's Gospel (25:31–46), and we are all familiar with the passage. The key factor in the judgment that the incarnate God will pass on all humanity is this: What did you do for me when I was hungry, thirsty, alone, and mistreated? And eternal life will be awarded to those who showed true love, that is, to those who truly aided the God-made-man. We are talking here about actions which merit God himself as a fair recompense (note Christ's "because"!); thus they are divine, supernatural actions, and yet they are required of all men and can be found in them.

Precisely to resolve this difficulty, Christ chose to add an essential aspect to his picture of the judgment: the general surprise. On the scene are people who never saw him, people who passed through history before his coming, people who did not know him during their lifetime either personally or through his Church. So the vast majority of human beings will ask the question that Christ puts on their lips: Lord, when did we see you and succor you, when did we pass you by? His answer is that it matters little that they never met him. The merit of the things they did for other human beings, invested with love, reaches the God who is brother of all and brings them to eternal life.

In other words, the merit that human beings see in mutual love, self-giving, and solidarity is only a shadowy indication of what these attitudes really contain, what they themselves will discover when God passes judgment on them, and what is already known by those who have received from God the revelation of this central mystery concerning humanity. So here we have a second line of thought regarding salvation, which is intimately related to the universal dimension of the Church. … The Church cannot arrive on the scene too late for humanity's salvation because all men are going to be judged by the same criterion: mutual love. The new community called Church does not seem to bring in any decisive element that was lacking before. The judge will pose the same questions to both Christians and non-Christians: What did you do for your brother? What did you do for my brother? But if this response gets us out of one problem, it drops us into another. We must now justify the importance and necessity of this particular community which is fashioned by faith and the sacraments and which has been placed in history by Christ and closely tied up with salvation.

Let us put this another way. The universal reality of the Church and her particular reality seem to be opposed to each other in the same way that the two lines of thought on salvation are. One line of thought attributes salvation to a universal factor such as love; the other attributes it to a particular factor such as entry and permanent membership in the ecclesial community. …

What distinguishes the Christian in his judgment portrait? The answer is obvious. Only one thing does: the Christian will not be surprised by the criterion used to judge all men. He will not ask the Lord: When did I see you? For if he is a believer, he is so precisely because he has accepted the revelation of this universal plan which culminates in the last judgment. The Christian is he *who already knows*. This, undoubtedly, is what distinguishes and defines him.

Let us put this in more general terms, Through Christ, God gave every man the possibility of loving others, and he joined all men and every individual in solidarity; he thus put love in everyone's hands as the divine instrument of salvation. This possibility is as vast and as ancient as humanity itself. It does not date from A.D. 1 or 30. Nor is it limited by the historical limits of the ecclesial community. Through Christ, it reaches all men. The more traditional strains of theology have always echoed these perspectives: The redemptive work of Christ, carried out within history, goes beyond the limits of time and dominates the whole unfolding development of the universe—both its past and its future.

But there is something that begins with Christ and that moves out solely toward the future: namely, the revelation of this plan that suffuses all time. The Christian is not the only one to enter into this plan. But he is the one who knows it. He knows the plan because he has received not only redemption but also revelation. …

The Mystical Christ (i.e., the Church as a particular reality) and the Cosmic Christ (the Church as a universal reality) are inseparable aspects of the one and only Christian reality. They differ only in terms of faith and the sacraments (visible signs and awareness of the Christian mystery); they do not differ at all in salvation content. Both are inseparable, as are the sacramental sign and the grace signified, as are the historical Christ (who is particular and visible) and his universal salvation mystery. The paschal Christ is the Mystical Christ and the Cosmic Christ at the same time. The Church, as a particular reality, is the conscious and visible sign of the presence of Christ the Savior in the heart of each human being.

For further reading

Mary Kaye Nealen, *The Poor in the Ecclesiology of Juan Luis Segundo* (New York: Peter Lang, 1992).
Juan Luis Segundo, *Theology and the Church: A Response to Cardinal Ratzinger and a Warning to the Whole Church* (San Francisco: Harper & Row, 1987).

20   James Cone (1938–)

In 1969 James Cone published Black Theology and Black Power, *in which the experience of African Americans became the hermeneutical lens for addressing theological and social questions in the USA. One of the primary features of the book was its contextual identification of the work of Christ with the Black Power movement of the late 1960's, a movement that emphasized black solidarity, activism, and pride and drew as much (or more) religiously from Malcolm X as it did from Martin Luther King Jr. Notably, Cone's book gave central attention to the nature and mission of the church, providing a penetrating critique of both the white church and the black church in relation to the meaning of the Christian gospel in light of the experience of African Americans.*

Black Theology and Black Power (1969)

Source: James H. Cone, *Black Theology and Black Power*.

What is the Church and its relationship to Christ and Black Power? The Church is that people called into being by the power and love of God to share in his revolutionary activity for the liberation of man. ...

The Church of Christ is not bounded by standards of race, class, or occupation. It is not a building or an institution. It is not determined by bishops, priests, or ministers as these terms are used in their contemporary sense. Rather, the Church is God's suffering people. It is that grouping of men who take seriously the words of Jesus: "Blessed are you when men revile you and persecute you and utter all kinds of evil against you falsely on my account" (Matt. 5:11). The call of God constitutes the Church, and it is a call to suffering. … "Where Christ is, there is the Church." Christ is to be found, as always, where men are enslaved and trampled under foot; Christ is found suffering with the suffering; Christ is in the ghetto—there also is his Church. The Church is not defined by those who faithfully attend and participate in the 11:00 A.M. Sunday worship. As Harvey Cox says: "The insistence by the Reformers that the church was 'where the word is rightly preached and the sacraments rightly administered' will simply not do today."[6] It may have been fine for distinguishing orthodoxy from heresy, but it is worthless as a vehicle against modern racism. We must therefore be reminded that Christ was not crucified on an altar between two candles, but on a cross between two thieves. He is not in our peaceful, quiet, comfortable suburban "churches," but in the ghetto fighting the racism of churchly white people. …

The white church has not merely failed to render services to the poor, but has failed miserably in being a visible manifestation to the world of God's intention for humanity and in proclaiming the gospel to the world. It seems that the white church is not God's redemptive agent but, rather, an agent of the old society. It fails to create an atmosphere of radical obedience to Christ. Most church fellowships are more concerned about drinking or new buildings or Sunday closing than about children who die of rat bites or men who are killed because they want to be treated like men. The society is falling apart for want of moral leadership and moral example, but the white church passes innocuously pious resolutions and waits to be congratulated. …

If there is any contemporary meaning of the Antichrist (or "the principalities and powers"), the white church seems to be a manifestation of it. It is the enemy of Christ. …

The existence of *the* Church is grounded exclusively in Christ. And in twentieth-century America, *Christ means Black Power!* It is certainly the case that the major institutional black churches have not caught the spirit of Black Power. They have, for the most part, strayed from their calling, seeking instead to pattern their life after white models. The divinely appointed task of proclaiming freedom and equality was abandoned in the ungodly pursuit of whiteness. Joseph Washington puts it graphically: "Heretofore, the function of the Negro Church has been that of a haven. In effect it has served as a cut-rate outlet, selling itself for quantity rather than quality, offering cheap white medicine in colored doses of several hours of relief for a week-long headache."[7] The only hope for the black church is to repent by seeking the true mission of Christ in the world.

It is clear that there are creative possibilities in the black church which seem to be absent in its white counterpart. The black church has a heritage

---

[6] Harvey Cox, *The Secular City* (New York: Macmillan, 1965), p. 145.

[7] Joseph Washington, *The Politics of God* (Boston: Beacon Press, 1967), p. 209.

of radical involvement in the world. This past is a symbol of what is actually needed in the present. The white American Church has no history of obedience; and without it, it is unlikely that it will ever know what radical obedience to Christ means. Since it is identified with the structure of power, it will always be possible for it to hedge and qualify its obedience to Christ. Also, being white in soul and mind, the white church must make a "special" effort in order to identify with the suffering of the oppressed, an effort which is almost inevitably distorted into plantation charity. To follow the line of least resistance means that it cannot be for Christ. It seems that the major white church institutions have followed that course so long that the probability is slight that they can free themselves from the structures of power in this society.

The black church, on the other hand, by virtue of being black, is automatically a part of the unwanted. It knows the meaning of rejection because it was rejected. All the black church has to do is to accept its role as the sufferer and begin to follow the natural course of being black. In so doing, it may not only redeem itself through God's Spirit, but the white church as well. The black church, then, is probably the only hope for renewal or, more appropriately, revolution in organized Christianity. It alone has attempted to be recognizably Christian in a hostile environment. It alone, being victimized by color, has championed the cause of the oppressed black people. Black churchmen are in a position to reaffirm this heritage, accepting the meaning of blackness in a white society and incorporating it into the language and work of the gospel. Speaking a true language of black liberation, the black church must teach that, in a white world bent on dehumanizing black people, Christian love means giving no ground to the enemy, but relentlessly insisting on one's dignity as a person. Love is not passive, but active. It is revolutionary in that it seeks to meet the needs of the neighbor amid crumbling structures of society. It is revolutionary because love may mean joining a violent rebellion.

For further reading

Dale Andrews, *Practical Theology for Black Churches: Bridging Black Theology and African American Folk Religion* (Louisville: Westminster John Knox, 2002).

James H. Cone, *A Black Theology of Liberation* (Philadelphia: J. B. Lippincott, 1970).

——— *For My People: Black Theology and the Black Church* (Maryknoll, NY: Orbis, 1984).

——— *Speaking the Truth: Ecumenism, Liberation, and Black Theology* (Grand Rapids: Eerdmans, 1986).

Jamie T. Phelps, O.P., "Communion Ecclesiology and Black Liberation Theology," *Theological Studies* 61 (2000), pp. 672–99.

21   Gustavo Gutíerrez (1928–)

Gustavo Gutíerrez, a Dominican priest from Peru, wrote the groundbreaking and widely influential A Theology of Liberation: History, Politics, Salvation *in 1971. The book asked what it means to be the church in the Latin American context of crushing poverty and social injustice, and concluded that the church's mission is to denounce injustice and side with the poor and the oppressed. There is only one history, for Gutíerrez, not one that is profane and the other sacred. The redemptive work of Christ takes place in all of history and underlies all of human existence. The church's task is to serve as a sacrament and revelation of that universal salvation.*

"The Church: Sacrament of History" (1971)

Source: Gustavo Gutíerrez, *A Theology of Liberation*, trans. and ed. Sister Caridad Inda and John Eagleson.

Because the Church has inherited its structures and its lifestyle from the past, it finds itself today somewhat out of step with the history which confronts it. But what is called for is not simply a renewal and adaptation of pastoral methods. It is rather a question of a new ecclesial consciousness and a redefinition of the task of the Church in a world in which it is not only *present*, but of which it *forms a part* more than it suspected in the past. In this new consciousness and redefinition, intraecclesial problems take a second place.

Universal sacrament of salvation

The unqualified affirmation of the universal will of salvation has radically changed the way of conceiving the mission of the Church in the world. It seems clear today that the purpose of the Church is not to save in the sense of "guaranteeing heaven." The work of salvation is a reality which occurs in history. This work gives to the historical becoming of humankind its profound unity and its deepest meaning. It is only by starting from this unity and meaning that we can establish the distinctions and clarifications which can lead us to a new understanding of the mission of the Church. …

Vatican II was able to set forth the outlines of a new ecclesiological perspective. And it did this almost surprisingly by speaking of the Church as a sacrament. This is undoubtedly one of the most important and permanent contributions of the Council. The notion of sacrament enables us to think of the Church within the horizon of salvific work and in terms radically different from those of the ecclesiocentric emphasis. The Council itself did not place itself totally in this line of thinking. Many of the texts still reveal the burden of a heavy heritage; they timidly point to a way out from this turning in of the Church on itself, without always accomplishing this. But what must be emphasized is that in the midst of the Council itself, over which hovered an ecclesiocentric perspective, new elements arose which allowed for a reflection which broke with this perspective and was more in accord with the real challenges to the Christian faith of today. ...

To call the Church the "visible sacrament of this saving unity" (*Lumen gentium*, no. 9) is to define it in relation to the plan of salvation, whose fulfillment in history the Church reveals and signifies to the human race. A visible sign, the Church imparts to reality "union with God" and "the unity of all humankind" (*Lumen gentium*, no. 1). The Church can be understood only in relation to the reality which it announces to humankind. Its existence is not "for itself," but rather "for others." Its center is outside itself, it is in the work of Christ and his Spirit. It is constituted by the Spirit as "the universal sacrament of salvation" (*Lumen gentium*, no. 48); outside of the action of the Spirit which leads the universe and history towards its fullness in Christ, the Church is nothing. Even more, the Church does not authentically attain consciousness of itself except in the perception of this total presence of Christ and his Spirit in humanity. The mediation of the consciousness of the "other"—of the world in which this presence occurs—is the indispensable precondition of its own consciousness as community–sign. Any attempt to avoid this mediation can only lead the Church to a false perception of itself—to an ecclesiocentric consciousness.

Through the persons who explicitly accept his Word, the Lord reveals the world to itself. He rescues it from anonymity and enables it to know the ultimate meaning of its historical future and the value of every human act. But by the same token the Church must turn to the world, in which Christ and his Spirit are present and active; the Church must allow itself to be inhabited and evangelized by the world. It has been said for this reason that a theology of the Church in the world should be complemented by "a theology of the world in the Church." This dialectical relationship is implied in the emphasis on the Church as sacrament. This puts us on the track of a new way of conceiving the relationship between the historical Church and the world. The Church is not a non-world; it is humanity itself attentive to the Word. It is the People of God which lives in history and is orientated toward the future promised by the Lord. ...

As a sacramental community, the Church should signify in its own internal structure the salvation whose fulfillment it announces. Its organization ought to serve this task. As a sign of the liberation of humankind and history, the Church itself in its concrete existence ought to be a place of liberation. A sign should be clear and understandable. If we conceive of the Church as a sacrament of the salvation of the world, then it has all the more obligation to manifest in its visible structures the message that it bears. Since the Church is not an end in itself, it finds its meaning in its capacity to signify the reality in function of which it exists. Outside of this reality the Church is nothing; because of it the Church is always provisional; and it is towards the fulfillment of this reality that the Church is oriented: this reality is the Kingdom of God which has already begun in history.

In Latin America the world in which the Christian community must live and celebrate its eschatological hope is the world of social revolution; the Church's task must be defined in relation to this. Its fidelity to the Gospel leaves it no alternative: the Church must be the visible sign of the presence of the Lord within the aspiration for liberation and the struggle for a more human and just society. Only in this way will the message of love which the Church bears be made credible and efficacious.

For further reading

Gustavo Gutiérrez, "Community: Out of Solitude," in *We Drink From Our Own Wells* (Maryknoll, NY: Orbis, 1983), pp. 128–35.
———— "The Liberating Mission of the Church," in *The Truth Shall Make You Free: Confrontations*, trans. Matthew J. O'Connell (Maryknoll, NY: Orbis, 1986), pp. 141–72.
James B. Nickoloff, "Church of the Poor: The Ecclesiology of Gustavo Gutiérrez," *Theological Studies* 54 (1993), pp. 512–35.

22   Jürgen Moltmann (1926–)

Jürgen Moltmann is well known as the twentieth century's theologian "of hope." A native of Germany, Moltmann was among the soldiers captured and held by British forces as a prisoner of war during World War II. It was at that time that he became a Christian, and upon his return to Germany began to develop a post-war theology with hope as its guiding principle. Moltmann describes the church as a "pilgrim people" that resists accommodation by its surrounding culture and is instead subject to Christ's lordship, empowered by the spirit toward the future in openness and hope, and oriented by its messianic identity to be a people for the world.

The Church in the Power of the Spirit (1975)

Source: Jürgen Moltmann, *The Church in the Power of the Spirit: A Contribution to Messianic Ecclesiology*, trans. Margaret Kohl.

The church, Christendom and Christianity understand their own existence and their tasks in history in a messianic sense. Their life is therefore determined by anticipation, resistance, self-giving and representation. Everything that they are and do cannot be legitimated through themselves but must continually be legitimized by the Messiah and the messianic future, so that through their profession of faith, their existence and their influence, people, religions and societies are opened up for the truth of what is to come and their powers are activated for life. The church in the power of the Spirit is not yet the kingdom of God, but it is its anticipation in history. Christianity is not yet the new creation, but it is the working of the Spirit of the new creation. Christianity is not yet the new mankind but it is its vanguard, in resistance to deadly introversion and in self-giving and representation for man's future. The provisional nature of its messianic character forces the church to self-transcendence over is social and historical limitations. Its historical finality gives it certainty in still uncertain history, and joy in the pains over its resistance. In provisional finality and in final provisionality the church, Christendom and Christianity witness to the kingdom of God as the goal of history in the midst of history. In this sense the church of Jesus Christ is *the people of the kingdom of God*. ...

The church lives in the history which finds its substantiation in the resurrection of the crucified Christ and whose future is the all-embracing kingdom of freedom. The living remembrance of Christ directs the church's hope towards the kingdom, and living hope in the kingdom leads back to the inexhaustible remembrance of Christ. The present power of this remembrance and this hope is called "the power of the Holy Spirit," for it is not of their own strength, reason and will that people believe in Jesus as the Christ and hope for the future as God's future. It is true that people believe and hope with all their strength, reason and will. But the certainty of faith and the assurance in hope is joined by the consciousness that in these we are already living in indestructible fellowship with God. It is not faith that makes Jesus the Christ; it is Jesus as the Christ who creates faith. It is not hope that makes the future into God's future; it is this future that wakens hope. Faith in Christ and hope for the kingdom are due to the presence of God in the Spirit. The church understands the tension between faith and hope as the history of the Spirit that makes all things new. Its fellowship with Christ is founded on the experience of the Spirit which manifests Christ, unites us with him and glorifies him in men. Its fellowship in the kingdom of God is founded on the power of the Spirit, which leads it into truth and freedom. It is when the church, out of faith in Christ and in hope for the kingdom, sees itself as the messianic fellowship that it will logically understand its presence and its path in the presence and the process of the Holy Spirit.

For further reading

Richard Bauckham, "Ecclesiology," *The Theology of Jürgen Moltmann* (London: T. & T. Clark, 1995), pp. 119–50.

23   Oscar Romero (1917–1980)

When Oscar Romero was appointed archbishop of San Salvador in 1977, El Salvador was in the midst of revolution and upheaval. Though he was initially welcomed by the government, the military, and the wealthy—and likewise viewed as a disappointment to progressive priests committed to liberation theology—he underwent a conversion to the poor and to the struggle for liberation the more he witnessed repression, torture, social injustice, and persecution of the church, including assassinations of the priests in his archdiocese. He was assassinated in 1980 while celebrating mass. Romero was outspoken not only about poverty, injustice, and violence, but about the church's mission to be in solidarity with the poor, the persecuted, and the violated. The following excerpts include a range of speeches, sermons, and radio addresses given during his life.

Source: James R. Brockman, S.J. (ed. and trans.), *Oscar Romero: The Violence of Love*.

For the church, the many abuses of human life, liberty, and dignity are a heartfelt suffering. The church, entrusted with the earth's glory, believes that in each person is the Creator's image and that everyone who tramples it offends God. As holy defender of God's rights and of his images, the church must cry out. It takes as spittle in its face, as lashes on its back, as the cross in its passion, all that human beings suffer, even though they be unbelievers. They suffer as God's images. There is no dichotomy between man and God's image. Whoever tortures a human being, whoever abuses a human being, whoever outrages a human being, abuses God's image, and the church takes as its own that cross, that martyrdom (31 December 1977).

God wants to save us in a people. He does not want to save us in isolation. And so today's church more than ever is accentuating the idea of being a people. The church therefore experiences conflicts, because it does not want a mass; it wants a people. A mass is a heap of persons, the drowsier the better, the more compliant the better. The church rejects communism's slander that it is the opium of the people. It has no intention of being the people's opium. Those that create drowsy masses are others. The church wants to rouse men and women to the true meaning of being a people. A people is a community of persons where all cooperate for the common good (15 January 1978).

Everyone who struggles for justice, everyone who makes just claims in unjust surroundings, is working for God's reign, even though not a Christian. The church does not comprise all of God's reign; God's reign goes beyond the church's boundaries. The church values everything that is in tune with its struggle to set up God's reign. A church that tries only to keep itself pure and uncontaminated would not be a church of God's service to people. The authentic church is one that does not mind conversing with prostitutes and publicans and sinners, as Christ did—and with Marxists and those of various political movements—in order to bring them salvation's true message (3 December 1978).

A church that suffers no persecution but enjoys the privileges and support of the things of earth—beware!—is not the true church of Jesus Christ (11 March 1979).

The church is not an opposition party. The church is a force of God in the people, a force of inspiration so that the people may forge their own destiny. The church does not want to impose political or social systems. It must not. That is not its field of competence. Rather, the church invokes the freedom of peoples not to have a single standard imposed on them, but for individuals to be allowed to further through their skills and technology what the people deserves, what they thinks it wants—as the architect of its own destiny, free to choose its own way to achieve the destiny that God points out to it (10 June 1979).

I repeat what I told you once before when we feared we might be left without a radio station: God's best microphone is Christ, and Christ's best microphone is the church, and the church is all of you. Let each one you, in your own job, in your own vocation—nun, married person, bishop, priest, high school or university student, day laborer, wage earner, market woman—each one in your own place live the faith intensely and feel that in your surroundings you are a true microphone of God our Lord (27 January 1980).

For further reading

James R. Brockman, *The Word Remains: A Life of Oscar Romero* (Maryknoll, NY: Orbis, 1989).
Oscar Romero, *Voice of the Voiceless: The Four Pastoral Letters and Other Statements* (Maryknoll, NY: Orbis, 1985).

24   Leonardo Boff (1938–)

The experience of base Christian communities had a significant impact on the ecclesiological reflection arising from Latin America (especially Brazil) in the latter part of the twentieth century. Base communities arose in response to a shortage of priests by empowering laypersons to lead their communities in evangelization, reflection on scripture, pastoral care, and community organizing. For Brazilian liberation theologian Leonardo Boff, "the church comes into being as church when people become aware of the call to salvation in Jesus Christ, come together in community, profess the same faith, celebrate the same eschatological liberation, and seek to live the discipleship of Jesus Christ."[8] In his book Church, Charism, and Power, *Boff holds out base communities as a new model of church that is vastly different from more institutional forms that preceded it. This new church, born at the margins of society and as a "church of the poor," is at the same time not new, but rather a revival of primitive Christianity. In response to his book, the Vatican Congregation for the Doctrine of the Faith, led by Cardinal Joseph Ratzinger (who would later become Pope Benedict XVI) silenced Father Boff and sent him a "Notification" of his errors, in which he was accused of relativizing the church and "a profound misunderstanding of the Catholic faith on the church of God in the world" (11 March 1985).*

---

[8]   Leonardo Boff, *Ecclesiogenesis: The Base Communities Reinvent the Church* (Maryknoll, NY: Orbis, 1986), p. 11.

"Ecclesiogenesis: The New Church Born of the Old" (1981)

Source: Leonardo Boff, *Church: Charism and Power*, trans. Andrea Reily Rocha, Rachel Vogelzang, and Bryan Stone.

Based on a meditation on the gospels and a theological reading of the signs of the times, a significant part of the institutionalized Church has understood the challenges that are posed to the Christian faith and tried to respond to them responsibly. One can see, little by little, the rise of a new Church, conceived in the heart of the old: *comunidades de base* [base communities], on the peripheries of the cities, a Church of the poor, made up of the poor, in which bishops, priests, and members of religious orders have immersed themselves in the lives of the marginalized, centers of evangelism led by laypeople, and so forth. It is a Church that has definitively renounced political power, in which the central axis now resides in the idea of the Church as People-of-God, a pilgrim people, open to the historic journey of humanity, who participate in all the risks and rejoice in each small victory, with a deep sense of following Jesus Christ, identified with the poor, the rejected, and the disinherited of the earth. This Church is being built day by day while opening itself to new ministries that respond to the needs of the community, ministries that are directed toward the totality of human life and not just liturgical space and gestures. It is a Church immersed in the working world and living in the heart of the secular world with the meaning and the inaudible joy of resurrection.

We are witnessing today a true ecclesiogenesis precisely where the institutional structure shows visible signs of weariness and brokenness. The gospel is not bound to one classic and consecrated articulation, inherited from a glorious institutionalized past. It is again being lived out as a movement that creates for itself structures more adequate for our times, avoiding the polemics of the old Church, without the grumbling and pharisaical spirit of those who believe they possess a more vital and genuine Christianity. This new Church understands that it does not exist for itself; its function is to be a sign of Christ for the world and a space where the Spirit is explicitly at work. The sign does not exist for itself, but for others. It is *of* Christ *for* the world. Because it never judges itself to be complete, but always in the process of becoming that which it ought to be, that is, the sacrament of Christ and of the Spirit, it bubbles up dynamically from within, creative, self-critical, with a heart sufficiently sensitive to recognize already in the world the presence of the Risen One and of his grace, even before the gospel is announced.

This new Church, like all the renewal movements, emerges on the periphery. Only here is there the possibility of true creativity and liberty in the face of power. Faith is born and manifested by personal witness; it is neither supported nor nurtured by the institution. Because of this, a purity and evangelical authenticity is made possible that cannot be formed from within the institution, given its preoccupation with assuring itself and with its demanding bureaucracy that requires time for conserving, expanding, justifying, and defending itself.

Clearly the old Church will look with a certain degree of suspicion on the new Church at the periphery along with the gospel freedom it has embraced. It will see in it a competitor and label it a parallel Church with a parallel magisterium and a lack of obedience and loyalty towards the Center! The new Church will need to develop intelligent strategies and tactics: it cannot allow itself to be drawn into the Center's game of condemnation and suspicion. The new Church must be gospel-focused, understanding that the institution is a power that is only able to use a language that does not put its own power at risk and that will always fear any distance from the behavior dictated by the Center, viewing it as disloyalty. Understanding all this, the new Church must be faithful to its path and loyally disobedient. It will need to search for a profound loyalty to the demands of the gospel. It will need to listen to the voice of the Center as it questions the truth of its interpretation of the gospel. As it exercises this kind of critical thinking and is deeply convinced of its path, the new Church will need to have the courage to be disobedient in the Lord and in the gospel to the demands of the Center, with neither anger nor complaint, but in a deep adherence to the desire to be faithful to the Spirit that we presume exists also in the Center. The essential basic communion must be preserved. This gospel purity is a provocation for the Center itself to awake to the Spirit that cannot be channeled according to human interests. The openness to communion with all, even if this means the possibility of a break that could destroy unity and love, and which could lead to isolation, persecution, and condemnation by the Center, is the guarantee of Christian authenticity inspired by the gospel.

For further reading

"Base-Level Ecclesial Communities (CEBs), the Parish, and the Local Church" from "Puebla: The Final Document," in John Eagleson and Philip Scharper (eds.), *Puebla and Beyond: Documentation and Commentary* (Maryknoll, NY: Orbis, 1979), pp. 210–14.

Congregation for the Doctrine of the Faith, "Instruction on Certain Aspects of the 'Theology of Liberation' " (Vatican City, 6 August 1984), *Origins* 14 (13 Sept. 1984), pp. 193–204.

Leonardo Boff, *Ecclesiogenesis: The Base Communities Reinvent the Church* (Maryknoll, NY: Orbis, 1986).

Harvey Cox, *The Silencing of Leonardo Boff: The Vatican the Future of World Christianity* (Bloomington, IN: Meyer Stone Books, 1988).

25 Stanley Hauerwas (1940–)

Stanley Hauerwas is one of the most influential, even if iconoclastic, shapers of Christian ethics and ecclesiology at the turn of the twenty-first century. Hauerwas emphasizes the story-formed nature of the Christian community, but even more importantly the way that particular story—narrated through the stories of Israel, Christ, and the church—produces a people capable of offering a distinctive and nonviolent witness to the God of Jesus in an increasingly post-Christendom world. For Hauerwas the primary task of the church is to be the church so that the world can know what it is and can encounter through the church a foretaste of God's peaceable reign.

"The Servant Community: Christian Social Ethics" (1983)

Source: Stanley Hauerwas, *The Peaceable Kingdom: A Primer in Christian Ethics.*

Christian ethics would be unintelligible if it did not presuppose the existence and recognizability of communities and corresponding institutions capable of carrying the story of God.

The most general name we give that community is church, but there are other names for it in the history of Christianity. It is "the way," the body of Christ, people of God, and a plethora of images that denote the social reality of being Christian and what it means to be a distinctive people formed by the narrative of God. We should remember that the name "church" is no less an image than "people of God." In fact, one of the issues in theology is which images of the church are primary or controlling for the others.

Thus, the claim that there is no ethic without a qualifier itself implies that a Christian ethic is always a social ethic. Indeed, the notion that one can distinguish between personal and social ethics distorts the nature of Christian convictions, for Christians refuse to admit that "personal" morality is less a community concern than questions of justice, etc. "Personal" issues may, of course, present different kinds of concern to the community from those of justice, but they are no less social for being personal.

At a general level there is much to be said for the contention that every ethic is a social ethic. The self is fundamentally a social self. We are not individuals who come into contact with others and then decide our various levels of social involvement. ... Our individuality is possible only because we are first of all social beings. After all, the "self" names not a thing, but a relation. I know who I am only in relation to others, and, indeed, who I am is a relation with others.

But the claim that Christian ethics is a social ethic is even stronger than those now commonplace observations about the self's sociality. ... The content of Christian ethics involves claims about a kingdom. Therefore, the first words about the Christian life are about a life together, not about the individual. This kingdom sets the standard for the life of the church, but the life of the kingdom is broader than even that of the church. For the church does not possess Christ; his presence is not confined to the church. Rather, it is in the church that we learn to recognize Christ's presence outside the church.

The church is not the kingdom but the foretaste of the kingdom. For it is in the church that the narrative of God is lived in a way that makes the kingdom visible. The church must be the clear manifestation of a people who have learned to be at peace with themselves, one another, the stranger, and of course, most of all God. There can be no sanctification of individuals without a sanctified people. We need examples and masters, and if we are without either, the church cannot exist as a people who are pledged to be different from the world.

Therefore we see that contained in the claim that there is no ethic without a qualifier—a claim that at the beginning seemed to be primarily a methodological one—is a strong substantive assumption about the status and necessity of the church as the locus for Christian ethical reflection. It is from the church that Christian ethics draws its ethical substance and it is to the church that Christian ethical reflection is first addressed. Christian ethics is not written for everyone but for those people who have been formed by the God of Abraham, Isaac, Jacob, and Jesus. Therefore Christian ethics can never be a minimalistic ethic for everyone, but must presuppose a sanctified people wanting to live more faithful to God's story.

The fact that Christian ethics begins and ends with a story requires a corresponding community existing across time. The story of God as told through the experience of Israel and the church cannot be abstracted from those communities engaged in the telling and the hearing. As a story it cannot exist without a historic people, for it requires telling and remembering if it is to exist at all. God has entrusted his presence to a historic and contingent community which can never rest on its past success, but must be renewed generation after generation. That is why the story is not merely told but embodied in a people's habits that form and are formed in worship, governance, and morality.

Therefore the existence of Israel and the church [is] not accidentally related to the story but [is] necessary for our knowledge of God. You cannot tell the story of God without including within it the story of Israel and the church. So it is not so odd that as part of the creed we affirm that we believe in the One Holy Catholic and Apostolic Church. We believe in the church in the sense that we know that it is not finally our creation, but exists only by God's calling of people. Moreover, it is only through such a people that the world can know that our God is one who wills nothing else than our good. To be sure, the church is often unfaithful, but God refuses to let that unfaithfulness be the last word. God creates and sustains a peaceable people in the world, generation after generation. …

But surely in matters of social ethics there must be moral generalities anchored in our social nature that provide the basis for common moral commitment and action. Surely in social ethics we should downplay the distinctively Christian and emphasize that we are all people of good will as we seek to work for a more peaceable and just world for everyone.

Yet that is exactly what I am suggesting we should not do. I am in fact challenging the very idea that Christian social ethics is primarily an attempt to make the world more peaceable or just. Put starkly, the first social ethical task of the church is to be the church—the servant community. Such a claim may well sound self-serving until we remember that what makes the church the church is its faithful manifestation of the peaceable kingdom in the world. As such, the church does not have a social ethic; the church is a social ethic.

The church is where the stories of Israel and Jesus are told, enacted, and heard, and it is our conviction that as a Christian people there is literally nothing more important we can do. But the telling of that story requires that we be a particular kind of people if we and the world are to hear the story truthfully. That means that the church must never cease from being a community of peace and truth in a world of mendacity and fear. The church does not let the world set its agenda about what constitutes a "social ethic," but a church of peace and justice must set its own agenda. It does this first by having the patience amid the injustice and violence of this world to care for the widow, the poor, and the orphan. Such care, from the world's perspective, may seem to contribute little to the cause of justice, yet it is our conviction that unless we take the time for such care neither we nor the world can know what justice looks like.

By being that kind of community we see that the church helps the world understand what it means to be the world. For the world has no way of knowing it is the world without the church pointing to the reality of God's kingdom. ... Therefore the first social task of the church—the people capable of remembering and telling the story of God we find in Jesus—is to be the church and thus help the world understand itself as world. That world, to be sure, is God's world, God's good creation, which is all the more distorted by sin because it still is bounded by God's goodness. For the church to be the church, therefore, is not anti-world, but rather an attempt to show what the world is meant to be as God's good creation.

We must remember that the "world" as that opposed to God is not an ontological designation. Thus, "world" is not inherently sinful; rather, its sinful character comes from its own free will. The only difference between church and world is the difference between agents. ... Therefore, calling for the church to be the church is not a formula for a withdrawal ethic, nor is it a self-righteous attempt to flee from the world's problems. Rather, it is a call for the church to be a community which tries to develop the resources to stand within the world witnessing to the peaceable kingdom and thus rightly understanding the world. The gospel is a political gospel. Christians are engaged in politics, but it is a politics of the kingdom that reveals the insufficiency of all politics based on coercion and falsehood and finds the true source of power in servanthood rather than domination.

This is not to imply that the church is any less a human community than other forms of human association. Just as in other institutions, the church draws on and requires patterns of authority that derive from human needs for status, belonging, and direction. The question is not whether the church is a natural institution, as it surely is, but how it shapes that "nature" in accordance with its fundamental convictions. "Nature" provides the context for community but does not determine its character.

The church therefore is a polity like any other, but it is also *unlike* any other insofar as it is formed by a people who have no reason to fear the truth. They are able to exist in the world without resorting to coercion to maintain their presence. That they are such depends to a large extent on their willingness to move—they must be "a moveable feast." For it is certain that much of the world is bound to hate them for calling attention to what the world is. They cannot and should not wish to provoke the world's violence, but if it comes they must resist even if that resistance requires them to leave one place for another. For as Christians we are at home in no nation. Our true home is the church itself, where we find those who, like us, have been formed by a savior who was necessarily always on the move.

For further reading

Stanley Hauerwas, "In Defense of Cultural Christianity," in *Sanctify Them in the Truth: Holiness Exemplified* (Nashville: Abingdon, 1998), pp. 157–73.
———— "On Being a Church Capable of Addressing a World at War: A Pacifist Response to the United Methodist Bishops' Pastoral In Defense of Creation," in *The Hauerwas Reader*, ed. John Berkman and Michael Cartwright (Durham, NC: Duke University Press, 2001), pp. 426–58.
———— "The Sanctified Body," in *Sanctify Them in the Truth*, pp. 77–91.
———— "A Story-Formed Community: Reflections on Watership Down" in *A Community of Character: Toward A Constructive Christian Social Ethic* (Notre Dame: University of Notre Dame Press, 1981), pp. 9–35.
———— "What Could it Mean for the Church to be Christ's Body?" in *In Good Company: The Church as Polis* (Notre Dame: University of Notre Dame Press, 1995), pp. 19–31. Stanley Hauerwas and William Willimon, *Resident Aliens: Life in the Christian Colony* (Nashville: Abingdon, 1989).
John B. Thomson, *The Ecclesiology of Stanley Hauerwas: A Christian Theology of Liberation* (Aldershot: Ashgate, 2003).

26   John Zizioulas (1931–)

The Orthodox ecclesiology of John Zizioulas was worked out from within a full-blown ontology of what it means to be a person in Greek philosophy and patristic theology. An individual becomes a person only in communion; indeed, God's very existence is communion. At the same time, "every form of communion which denies or suppresses the person is inadmissible." Christ is not merely a historical individual in the past whom the church follows; Christ is constitutionally corporate. The church participates in him and shares his life Eucharistically. Indeed the church becomes the church through Eucharistic communion. This distinctive relationship between the "one" and the "many" in Orthodox thought can also be expressed in the relationship between the bishop and the congregation through whom the bishop is constituted as its head.

Being as Communion (1985)

Source: John D. Zizioulas, *Being as Communion: Studies in Personhood and the Church.*

The Church is not simply an institution. She is a "mode of existence," *a way of being*. The mystery of the Church, even in its institutional dimension, is deeply bound to the being of man, to the being of the world and to the very being of God. ... From the fact that a human being is a member of the Church, he becomes "an image of God," he exists as God himself exists, he takes on God's "way of being." This way of being is not a moral attainment, something that man *accomplishes*. It is a way of *relationship* with the world, with other people and with God, an event of *communion*, and that is why it cannot be realized as the achievement of an *individual*, but only as an *ecclesial* fact. ...

The eucharistic community makes the Church eschatological. It frees it from the causality of natural and historical events, from limitations which are the result of the individualism implied in our natural biological existence. It gives it the taste of eternal life as love and communion, as the image of the being of God. The eucharist, as distinct from other expressions of ecclesial life is unthinkable without the gathering of the whole Church in one place, that is, without an event of *communion*; consequently, it manifests the Church not simply as something instituted, that is, historically *given*, but also as something *con-stituted*, that is constantly realized as an event of free communion, prefiguring the divine life and the Kingdom to come. In ecclesiology, the polarization between "institution" and "event" is avoided thanks to a correct understanding of the eucharist: Christ and history give to the Church her being which becomes *true being* each time that the Spirit con-stitutes the eucharistic community as Church. In this way, the eucharist is not a "sacrament," something parallel to the divine word: it is the eschatologization of the historical word, the voice of the historical Christ, the voice of the Holy Scripture which comes to us, no longer simply as "doctrine" through history, but as life and *being* through the *eschata*. It is not the sacrament completing the word, but rather the word becoming flesh, the risen Body of the Logos. ...

Christ's existence is applied to our historical existence not *in abstracto* or individualistically, but in and through a *community*. This community is formed from out of ordinary existence, through a radical conversion from individualism to personhood in baptism. As death and resurrection in Christ, baptism signifies the decisive passing of our existence from the "truth" of individualized being into the truth of personal being. The resurrectional aspect of baptism is therefore nothing other than *incorporation into the community*. The existential truth arising from baptism is simply the truth of personhood, the truth of communion. A new birth (ἀναγέννησις) is required for this, simply because birth by normal procreation ... is for created beings a cause of individualization and is thus a birth of beings destined to death. Eternal life needs the new birth of baptism as a "birth in the Spirit," just as Christ's own birth was "in the Spirit," so that each baptized person can himself become "Christ," his existence being one of communion and hence of true life.

For further reading

Dennis M. Doyle, *Communion Ecclesiology: Vision and Versions* (Maryknoll, NY: Orbis, 2000).
Nicholas M. Healy, "Ecclesiology and Communion," *Perspectives in Religious Studies* 31/3 (2004), pp. 273–90.
Vladimir Lossky, "Concerning the Third Mark of the Church: Catholicity," in John H. Erickson (ed.), *The Image and Likeness of God* (Crestwood, NY: St. Vladimir's Seminary Press, 1985), pp. 169–82.
Jean-Marie Tillard, O.P., *Church of Churches: The Ecclesiology of Communion* (Collegeville, MN: The Liturgical Press, 1992).
John D. Zizioulas, *Communion and Otherness* (New York: T. & T. Clark, 2006).

27   Rosemary Radford Ruether (1936–)

A pioneering Roman Catholic feminist theologian, Rosemary Radford Ruether offered radical critiques of the church but also traced constructively the theology and practice of a new feminist vision of the church in the form of "women-church." The women-church movement had formal beginnings in the early 1980s, and gathered women and men who affirmed the full incorporation of women into the life and decision-making of the church through a transformation of the church and not merely an admission into the ranks of an existing church or clergy defined by patriarchy. That incorporation might take a variety of forms and stages, including feminist liturgical base communities that represent "liberated zones" where new models of being the church could be practiced.

Women-Church (1985)

Source: Rosemary Radford Reuther, *Women-Church: Theology and Practice of Feminist Liturgical Communities.*

Women-Church represents the first time that women collectively have claimed to be church and have claimed the tradition of the exodus community as a community of liberation from patriarchy. This means that patriarchy is rejected as God's will. It is rejected as the order of creation or as a reflection of biological nature. Patriarchy is named as a historically contrived social system by which the "fathers"—that is, ruling-class males—have used power to establish themselves in a position of domination over women and also over dependent classes in the family and society. Ruling-class males have built social structures and systems of cultural justification to assure that they would monopolize the cultural, economic, and political power of the society. Others are forbidden access to this power and are confined to auxiliary status as physical laborers in production and reproduction, while the ruling males own and command the fruits of this labor.

Women-Church means not only that women have rejected this system and are engaged in efforts to escape from it, but that they are doing so collectively. ...

Thus the first step in forming the feminist exodus from patriarchy is to gather women together to articulate then own experience and communicate it with each other. Women assure each other that they really are not crazy, that they really have been defined and confined by systemic marginalization of their human capacities. They develop words and analysis for the different aspects of this system of marginalization, and they learn how to recognize and resist the constant messages from patriarchal culture that try to enforce their acquiescence and collaboration with it. Distressing as it may seem to males who imagine themselves sympathetic to feminism, this process of consciousness raising must necessarily have a separatist stage. Women have to withdraw from male-dominated spaces so they can gather together and [define] their own experience.

The need for a period of withdrawal from men and communication with each other is essential for the formation of the feminist community, because women, more than any other marginalized group, have lacked a critical culture of their own. Repressed ethnic and racial groups retained remnants of cultures prior to their conquest. They have also developed subcultures of resistance in modes of talk, song, and dance. Precisely because of women's isolation from each other, separated by patriarchal family structures, their deprivation of education, and even of speech, their cultural colonization by an education that incorporates them into a language that they have not defined, but which defines them as inferior and auxiliary to a male dominated world, women need separate spaces and all-female gatherings to form the critical culture that can give them an autonomous ground from which to critique patriarchy. ...

Women-Church is the Christian theological expression of this stage of feminist collectivization of women's experience and the formation of critical culture. It means that women delegitimize the theological myths that justify the *ecclesia* of patriarchy and begin to form liturgies to midwife their liberation from it. They begin to experience the gathering of liberated women as a redemptive community rooted in a new being. They empower themselves and are empowered by this liberated Spirit upon which they are grounded (the two are not contradictory, since one empowers oneself authentically only by being empowered by the Spirit that grounds one) to celebrate this new community, to commune with it, and to nurture themselves and be nurtured in the community of liberated sisterhood.

How Women-Church might be transcended in a redemptive community of both men and women liberated from patriarchy remains to be seen. I assume that it should happen as the fulfillment and culmination of a process in which Women-Church is one stage. One can see this begin to happen as women shape a sufficiently clarified critical culture so that some men feel compelled to try to understand it on its own terms and not simply to try to ridicule or repress it. What is required for the development of a new cohumanity of men and women liberated from patriarchy is that men begin to critique their own dehumanization by patriarchy and form their critical culture of liberation from it in a way that truly complements the feminist exodus and allows the formation of real dialogue. I assume the name for this liberated humanity would then no longer be "Women-Church," but simply "Church"; that is, the authentic community of exodus from oppression that has been heralded by the traditions of religious and social liberation but, until now, corrupted by reversion to new forms of the *ecclesia* of patriarchy. ...

Women-Church means neither leaving the church as a sectarian group, nor continuing to fit into it on its terms. It means establishing bases for a feminist critical culture and celebrational community that have some autonomy from the established institutions. It also means sharing this critical culture and sense of community with many women who are working within existing churches but who gather, on an occasional or regular basis, to experience the feminist vision that is ever being dimmed and limited by the parameters of the male-dominated institution. It means some women might worship only in alternative feminist liturgies; others might do so on a regular basis, while continuing to attend liturgies in traditional parishes into which they seek to inject something of this alternative; and some women might enter into these experiences only occasionally, such as at annual gathering of women pastors or feminist retreats, where women worship and celebrate their community together in the context of these occasional communities. ...

As Women-Church we claim the authentic mission of Christ, the true mission of Church, the real agenda of our Mother–Father God who comes to restore and not to destroy our humanity, who comes to ransom the captives and to reclaim the earth as our promised Land. We are not in exile, but the Church is in exodus with us. God's Shekinah, Holy Wisdom, the Mother-face of God has fled from the high thrones of patriarchy and has gone into exodus with us. She is with us as we flee from the smoking altars where women's bodies are sacrificed, as we cover our ears to blot out the inhuman voice that comes forth from the idol of patriarchy.

As Women-Church we are not left to starve for the words of wisdom, we are not left without the bread of life. Ministry too goes with us into exodus. We learn all over again what it means to minister, not to lord over, but to minister to and with each other, to teach each other to speak the words of life. Eucharist comes with us into exodus. The waters of baptism spring up in our midst as the waters of life, and the tree of life grows in our midst with fruits and flowers. We pluck grain and make bread; harvest grapes and make wine. And we pass them around as the body and blood of our new life, the life of the new humanity that has been purchased by the bloodly struggles of our martyrs, by the bloodly struggle of our brother Jesus, and of Perpetua and Felicitas, and of all the women who were burned and beaten and raped, and of Jean Donovan and Maura Clarke and Ita Ford and Dorothy Kazel, and of the women of Guatemala, Honduras, El Salvador, and Nicaragua who struggle against the leviathan of patriarchy and imperialism. This new humanity has been purchased by their blood, by their lives, and we dare to share the fruits of their victory together in hope and faith that they did not die in vain. But they have risen, they are rising from the dead. They are present with us as we share this sacrament of the new humanity, as we build together this new earth freed from the yoke of patriarchy.

We are Women-Church, not in exile, but in exodus. We flee the thundering armies of Pharaoh. We are not waiting for a call to return to the land of slavery to serve as alter girls in the temples of patriarchy. No! We call our brothers also to flee from the temples of patriarchy. ... We call our brothers to join us in exodus from the land of patriarchy, to join us in our common quest for that promised land where there will be no more war, no more burning children, no more violated women, no more discarded elderly, no more rape of the earth. Together, let us break up that great idol and grind it into powder; dismantle the great Leviathan of violence and misery who threatens to destroy the earth, plow it into the soil, and transform it back into the means of peace and plenty, so that all the children of earth can sit down together at the banquet of life. ...

All the functions of church—the repentance by which we enter it, the Eucharist by which we commune with it, and the ministry by which we mutually empower it—are simply expressions of entering and developing a true human community of mutual love. The greatest possible distortion of church is to identify it with an ecclesiastical superstructure that distorts our true nature and has been created by competitive and oppressive hierarchicalism. The whole concept of ministry as an ordained caste, possessing powers ontologically above nature and beyond the reach of the people, must be rejected. Instead, ministry must be understood as the means by which the community itself symbolizes its common life to itself and articulates different aspects of its need to empower and express that common life.

If we understand clericalism as the expropriation of ministry, sacramental life, and theological education from the people, then women-church—and indeed all base Christian communities—are engaged in a revolutionary act of reappropriating to the people what has been falsely expropriated from us. We are reclaiming sacramental life as the symbol of our own entry into and mutual empowerment within the redemptive life, the authentic human life or original blessing upon which we stand naturally when freed from alienating powers. Theological education and teaching are our own reflections on the meaning of reclaiming our authentic life from distortion. Ministry is the active praxis of our authentic life and the building of alternative bases of expression from which to challenge the systems of evil.

For further reading

Susan Abraham and Elena Procario-Foley (eds.), *Frontiers in Catholic Feminist Theology* (Minneapolis: Fortress, 2009).

Mary E. Hunt, "Spiral Not Schism: Women-Church as Church," *Religion and Intellectual Life* 7 (Fall, 1989), pp. 82–92.

Rosemary Radford Ruether, "The Call of Women in the Church," in Virginia Ramey Mollenkott (ed.), *Women of Faith in Dialogue* (New York: Crossroad, 1987), pp. 77–88.

———— *Catholic Does Not Equal the Vatican: A Vision for Progressive Catholicism* (New York: The New Press, 2008).

———— *Sexism and God-talk: Toward a Feminist Theology* (Boston: Beacon Press, 1993).

———— "Women-Church: Emerging Feminist Liturgical Communities," in Norbert Greinacher and Norbert Mette (eds.), *Popular Religion* (Edinburgh: T. & T. Clark, 1986), pp. 52–9.

28   George A. Lindbeck (1923–)

Lindbeck's "post-liberal" theology rejects the (liberal) notion that religious doctrines are expressions of common human experiences, capable of being understood and evaluated in abstraction from the distinct forms of life, or cultures in which they arise and make sense. Lindbeck advocates for a "cultural-linguistic" approach to doctrine in which the church is precisely that distinct form of life in which Christian doctrine is made intelligible. He proposes an "Israel-like view of the church" in which Israel and the church as the messianic extension of Israel to the Gentiles are together a particular people through whom God intends to save the world. It is this very peoplehood, moreover, rather than some private or personal experience mediated by this people, that is the salvation God offers to the world.

"The Church" (1988)

Source: George A. Lindbeck, "The Church," in *Keeping the Faith: Essays to Mark the Centenary of Lux Mundi*, ed. Geoffrey Wainwright.

The early Christians were a Jewish sect. They believed in a crucified and resurrected Messiah who authorized them, some of them believed, to welcome the uncircumcised into their fellowship, but this did not diminish their desire to maintain their legitimacy as Jews. All the categories they possessed for their communal self-understanding were derived from the Hebrew Scriptures (usually, to be sure, in the Greek Septuagint version). These were their only inspired text, and they interpreted it as Jews. It was natural that they should understand their communities as *ekklesia*, as *qahal*, the assembly of Israel in the new age. (For once philology and etymology cohere with broader historical considerations.) Thus the story of Israel was their story. They were that part of the people of God who lived in the time between the times after the messianic era had begun but before the final coming of the kingdom. Whatever is true of Israel is true of the Church except where the differences are explicit.

Four heuristic guidelines for reading the New Testament references to the Church are suggested by this historical background. First, as befits those who thought of themselves as a people, early Christian communal self-understanding was narrative shaped. The Church, in other words, was fundamentally identified and characterized by its story. Images such as "body of Christ" or the traditional marks of "unity, holiness, catholicity and apostolicity" cannot be first defined and then used to specify what was and what was not "church." The story was logically prior. It determined the meaning of images, concepts, doctrines and theories of the Church rather than being determined by them. Just as the story of the Quakers is more fundamental than descriptions such as "church of the poor" or "church of the wealthy" (for they have been both), and the story of the French is more fundamental than "monarchy" or "republic" (for France has been both), so it is also in the case of the Church.

A corollary of this priority of story was that "church" ordinarily referred to concrete groups of people, not to something transempirical. An invisible Church is as biblically odd as an invisible Israel. Stories of the biblical realistic-narrative type can only be told of agents and communities of agents acting and being acted upon in a space-time world of contingent happenings. Thus to say that it was empirical churches in all their actual or potential messiness of which exalted concepts and images such as "holy" and "bride of Christ" were predicated is an analytic implicate of the primacy of narrative. For the early Christians, in the second place, Israel's history was their only history.

They did not yet have the New Testament or later church history as sources, Israel's history, to be sure, was seen through the prism of Christ, and this made a profound difference; but yet, to repeat, the Hebrew Scriptures were the sole ecclesiological textbook. The only inspired stories available to the Church for its self-understanding were the stories of Israel.

A third rule is an extension of this second one. Not only was Israel's story the early Christians' only communal story but it was the whole of that story which they appropriated. It was not only the favorable parts, such as the Old Testament accounts of faithful remnants, which they applied to themselves. All the wickedness of the Israelites in the wilderness could be theirs. They might rebel, as did Korah or perish for fornication, as did three and twenty thousand in the desert (1 Cor. 10:5–10). These happenings, Paul tells his readers, are types (*tupoi*) written for our admonition (v. 11). As of old, judgment continues to begin in the house of the Lord (1 Pet. 4:17), and the unfaithful Church can be severed from the root no less than the unbelieving synagogue (Rom. 11:21). It can, like Eve, yield to the wiles of the serpent and lose its virginal purity (2 Cor. 11:1–4). One can imagine early Christians going on in more extreme situations, such as later developed, to say of the bride of Christ what Ezekiel said of the betrothed of Jahweh (Ezek. 16:23): she can be a whore worse than the heathen. As was earlier noted, when the New Testament is silent we need to turn to the Hebrew Scriptures, the ecclesiological text par excellence, to discover how the early Christians thought about the Church.

In opposition to most later exegesis, therefore, the relation of Israel's history to that of the Church in the New Testament was not that of shadow to reality or promise to fulfillment or type to antitype. Jesus Christ alone is the antitype or fulfillment. He is depicted as the embodiment of Israel (e.g. "Out of Egypt have I called my son," Matt. 2:15), and the Church is the body of Christ. Thus Israel's story, transposed into a new key through Christ, becomes prototypical for the history of the Church which is its continuation rather than its fulfillment.

From this it follows, in the fourth place, that Israel and the Church were one people for the early Christians. There was no breach in continuity. A new age had begun, but the story continued and therefore also the people which it identified. The French remain French after the revolution, the Quakers remain Quakers after becoming wealthy, and Israel remains Israel even when transformed by the arrival of the eschaton in Christ. The Church is simply Israel in the time between the times. The continuity of the story and the identity of the people are unbroken.

Discontinuity and nonidentity are problems in the New Testament, not for the Church per se, but for unbelieving Jews on the one hand and gentile Christians on the other. The apostle Paul says of the first group in Romans 11 that they have been cut off, but that this can happen does not differentiate them from Christians. Churches also, as we have already noted, can be severed from the root. They can, in the even more vigorous language of Revelation, be spewed forth, expectorated (Rev. 3:16). Yet when this occurs, it does not alter the identity of the people of the promise. "The gifts and the call of God are irrevocable" (Rom. 11:29). Unbelieving Jewry will ultimately be restored. Furthermore, post-biblical Judaism which has not heard the gospel (and how can it hear in view of Christian persecution?) lives theologically before Christ and cannot be equated with the unbelieving Jewry of which Paul speaks. Nothing in his account prevents us from saying that the synagogue, like remnants in ancient Israel, is at times more faithful to God's will and purposes than are unfaithful churches. In any case, in the one New Testament writing in which the problem is directly addressed, Judaism after Christ is as inalienably embraced as the Church in the continuous overarching story of the single people, consisting of faithful remnants and unfaithful masses, which stretches from the patriarchal period to the last days.

So strong was this sense of uninterrupted peoplehood that the only available way to think of gentile Christians was, in Krister Stendahl's phrase, as "honorary Jews." The uncircumcised, "alienated from the commonwealth of Israel," have become "fellow citizens ... of the household of God," "fellow heirs, [fellow] members of the same body, and [fellow] partakers of the promise" (Eph. 2:11, 19; 3:6). This inclusion of the Gentiles is represented in Ephesians as the most wondrous aspect of the work of Christ. Where there were two, there is now one, the new man in Christ (Eph. 2:11–3:11), the beginnings of the new humanity, the third race of which the early fathers spoke. Thus has begun the gathering of all humankind into God's people, the promised ascent of the nations to worship in Zion, the crowding of the Gentiles into the heavenly Jerusalem. But Zion does not change identity: the twelve apostles are commemorated on the foundations of the walls of the New Jerusalem, but its gates are marked with the names of the twelve tribes (Rev. 21:12). The inclusion of the uncircumcised in the covenant with Abraham by means of the new covenant in Christ did not, for the earliest Christians, constitute the formation of a different people but rather the enlargement of the old.

From this perspective, not only the enlargement of the people but also its other special features are functions of life in the new age, not changes in identity. Who and what the people is becomes more fully manifest now that the Messiah has come. The bride of Yahweh is the bride and body of Christ. The Spirit is now offered and may be poured out on all flesh as it was not before (Acts 2:17–21). Thus the *ab initio* trinitarian calling, constituting and empowering of God's people stands revealed. It is a new epoch of unheard-of possibilities and actualities, not a New Israel, which begins at Pentecost. ...

The Church's story, understood as continuous with Israel's, tells of God doing in this time between the times what he has done before: choosing and guiding a people to be a sign and witness in all that it is and does, whether obediently or disobediently, to who and what he is. Both God's mercy and God's judgment are manifest in the life of this people as nowhere else.

This is what the narrative is about. By remembering that this is the subject matter, we can identify the Church in the 20th no less than in the 1st century. It is true that the Church looks very different in these two periods, but then so did Israel in the wilderness, under judges and kings, and in exile. The encoded historical data vary, and so do the descriptive results, but the identifying code is the same and therefore also the identified people.

The referential force of this narrative code can be analyzed into distinct aspects. First, the identity and being of the Church rests on God's election, not on its faithfulness. Second, as an implicate of this, the elect communities are stamped by objective marks which are both blessing and curse depending on how they are received. Eating and drinking, Paul reminds us, can be unto judgment (1 Cor. 11:29) and not only life, and the same applies to circumcision and baptism, the *shema* and the *apostolicum*. Even when the sacraments are spiritualized, as by Quakers, the profession that the Christ spoken of in Scripture is the Lord can be a publicly unmistakable brandmark of the group's election. Third, election is communal. Individuals are elect by virtue of visible membership in God's people. Last, the primary mission of this chosen people is to witness to the God who judges and who saves, not to save those who would otherwise be damned (for God has not confined his saving work exclusively to the Church's ministrations). It testifies to this God whether or not it wills to do so, whether it is faithful or unfaithful. The final consummation which has begun in Christ is proleptically present in this people as nowhere else, but so also is the eschatological judgment (1 Pet. 4:17; cf. Amos 3:2; Jer. 25:29).

The Church thus identified sounds Catholic in its comprehensiveness, Calvinist in the unconditionality of its chosenness, and Lutheran in its possibilities of unfaithfulness while remaining genuinely the Church; but the total effect, not surprisingly, is more Jewish than anything else. This is true, first, in reference to those who are designated individually and communally as part of the Church. The Church consists of those, whether atheists or believers, reprobate or regenerate, who are stamped with the marks of membership in elect communities. Baptism may be easier to ignore than circumcision (though secular Israelis are adept at doing so), but God remembers. Nor does communal degeneracy erase election. The Amhara and the Falasha in Ethiopia may resemble the animist tribes which surround them, but if one admits they are Christian and Jewish respectively, one is obligated to accept them as fully parts, even if defective parts, of the elect people. Similarly, the apartheid churches of South Africa are no less churches than the black ones they oppress, just as 16th-century Catholics and Protestants were part of the same elect people as the Anabaptists whom they jointly slaughtered, and just as the Gush Emmunim and Peace Now advocates, not to mention the warring sects of whom Josephus tells, are and were fully Jewish. To put this point in the terminology of the social sciences, the people of God consists of cultural–linguistic groupings that can be meaningfully identified by ordinary sociological and historical criteria as Christian or Jewish (even though their chosenness, needless to say, is known only to faith). This is what is meant biblically and, in the present perspective, theologically by a people.

For further reading

George A. Lindbeck, *The Church in a Postliberal Age*, ed. James J. Buckley (Grand Rapids: Eerdmans, 2002).

29   Elisabeth Schüssler Fiorenza (1938–)

Elisabeth Schüssler Fiorenza is a pioneering Catholic feminist theologian, historian, and biblical scholar who has written extensively on feminist interpretation of scripture and the role of women in the church. In 1982 she proposed that "Women are Church and have always been Church," and this has been a starting point and central thesis of her work in ecclesiology. She uses the phrase "ekklēsia of women" as a way of pulling together a variety of movements, strategies, and thinking that assert the full participation of women in and as the church and that undertake a critique and overthrow of patriarchal privilege and exclusion. The following excerpt outlines the hermeneutical, re/constructive, and political dimensions of that term.

"Daughters of Vision and Struggle" (1990)

Source: Elisabeth Schüssler Fiorenza, *Discipleship of Equals: A Critical Feminist Ekklēsia-logy of Liberation*.

1. The expression "*ekklēsia* of women" is a *hermeneutical* way and a linguistic means to communicate that women are church. When Christian feminists speak of "the church," we often tacitly assume that women are here and the church is there, an entity totally different from us. Since church has for so long been identified with the male hierarchy, church has become synonymous with patriarchal, hierarchical structures not only in the media but also in the minds of many Christians. Yet theologically the patriarchal hierarchy may not be identified with "institutional" church—as though the church as an institution could only be patriarchal. Conversely, it is not just the male hierarchy that makes the church patriarchal. If this were the case we would only need to replace men with women. Rather, patriarchy affects every aspect of church. Thus if women insist that "we are church and always have been church," we must also recognize that women have been and still are "collaborators" of the patriarchal church. The expression "*ekklēsia* of women" is thus not a term exclusive of men but a linguistic means to lift into public consciousness that women are church.

In addition, the expression *"ekklēsia* of women" also seeks to envision and to create a theoretical and practical space where women can articulate a different vision of church, theology, and religion from a feminist vantage point—one that can replace the dominant androcentric "commonsense" mindset into which we all have been socialized. It seeks to create an intellectual, symbolic, and spiritual universe that is not just gynocentric, but feminist-centric. The vision of the *ekklēsia* of women focuses on the empowerment of women because women as church have been excluded from the interpretation of the world and of the divine. It seeks to enable women to find their own theological voices and to become visible as church.

2. Hence the expression *"ekklēsia* of women" has *constructive and reconstructive* aims. It seeks to recover women's heritage as church. If the oppression of a people is total because it has neither an oral nor a written history, then the reconstruction of such a history of suffering and resurrection, of struggle and survival, is an important means to empower women and other nonpersons. It can correct the deformation of our historical consciousness that has eliminated women's and other nonpersons' victimizations and struggles from our ecclesial memory. I have attempted to articulate such a feminist theological reconstruction of the discipleship of equals in the first centuries of the church as a heritage and memory for women-church. Other feminist historical and theological studies have done so for different periods of Christian history. However, the attempt to reconstruct the heritage of women-church must not succumb to apologetic patriarchal interests. Nor should it be done over and against its sociocultural political contexts. Rather its "dialogic imagination" (Pui Lan Kwok) must reconstruct women's history as church as one element of women's religious-cultural heritage.

3. The expression *"ekklēsia* of women" also seeks to name a *political* reality. The Greek word *ekklēsia* means the democratic decision-making assembly of free citizens. The *ekklēsia* of women seeks to create an alternative vision and reality of church that is not patriarchal. It does not position this vision and reality on the margins of the patriarchal church but in the center of it. Like ivy it seeks to envelop the patriarchal ecclesial weeds and to replace them one by one with a different praxis. Hence women-church is not an end in itself but has as its goal to make experientially available here and now the well-being and inclusivity of the *basileia,* of God's intended world. It is not dialectically related to the institutional church as exodus-liberation church; rather it seeks to replace patriarchal institutional ecclesial power with a practice of church that sustains the creative tension between leadership and community, local and national, regional and global, diverse particularity and "common ground." Women-church is constitutive of church, regenerating and transforming the patriarchal church into the discipleship of equals.

The *ekklēsia* of women is also not identical with the feminist movements in biblical religions. Rather, it becomes tangible reality in the feminist struggles to end religious and societal patriarchal relationships of domination and exclusion. It is not one feminist group within biblical religions but seeks to inspire them for concerted action. It seeks to articulate a "common ground" for the ingathering of the dispersed "powers of the weak" in divergent liberation struggles. These powers are embodied in different feminist strategies: in being at home and in rootedness, in ecclesial leadership, in intellectual, theological, and spiritual work, in the ritual power of naming the divine in women's image, in the power of interpretation, reconstruction, decision making, and transformation.

The *ekklēsia* of women does not delineate feminist movements in biblical religion as "liberated zones" but understands them to be deeply steeped in patriarchal relations of domination. Its spirituality and vision does not deny the entanglement of feminists in patriarchy but calls for constant *metanoia* — conversion. Its spirituality not only articulates visions of liberation but also names the "deadly" dangers and failures threatening feminist movements in religion. Such failures include: psychologism, which does not allow for any critical debate, but infantilizes women by "mothering" them; anti-intellectualism, which understands serious intellectual work as male and therefore unfeminine; collectivism, which neither recognizes nor respects creative leadership but usurps it by manipulating groups; horizontal violence, which thrashes strong women who refuse to remain feminine victims; guilt-tripping and confessionalism, which repeat the litany of patriarchy's sins without ever doing any thing about them; exclusivism, which insists on women-church as the gathering of the truly true feminists and which dehumanizes men as evil; dogmatism, which draws its boundaries in doctrinal terms instead of welcoming diversity of gifts and visions.

Facing increasing patriarchal repression in society and church, the *ekklēsia* of women must develop a politics and spirituality for survival and change. We need a spirituality that understands fear, co-optation, betrayal, male violence, and feminist burn-out in political-theological terms. Feminist retreats, liturgies, and rituals should not move us "beyond anger," encouraging us to deny our pain. Rather they should renew our vision, energy, and *exousia* (power). We must keep alive the burning indignation at the destructive powers of patriarchy in women's lives — an indignation that fuels the courage and faith necessary in the struggle for survival and liberation. Only if we keep this holy anger alive will we sustain the courage and love that is necessary to work for the conversion and transformation of the patriarchal church into the discipleship of equals.

The diverse women's movements in the churches must come together as the public forum and alliance of the *ekklēsia* of women. As a "rainbow" discipleship of equals we can voice and celebrate our differences because we have as a "common ground" our commitment to the liberation struggle and vision of God's *basileia*, God's intended world and community of well-being for all. We are not the first to engage in this struggle for ending societal and ecclesiastical patriarchy. Nor are we alone in it. A "great cloud of witnesses" surrounds us and has preceded us throughout the centuries in the *ekklēsia* of women. We derive hope and courage from the memory of our foremothers and their struggles for survival and dignity, from the remembrance of our foresisters who have resisted patriarchal dehumanization and violence in the power of the Spirit.

For further reading

Susan Abraham, "Justice as the Mark of Catholic Feminist Ecclesiology," in *Frontiers in Catholic Feminist Theology: Shoulder to Shoulder* (Philadelphia: Fortress, 2009), pp. 193–214.

Rosemary P. Carbine, " 'Artisans of a New Humanity': Re-Visioning the Public Church in a Feminist Perspective," in *Frontiers in Catholic Feminist Theology*, pp. 173–92.

Elizabeth T. Groppe, "Women and the *Persona* of Christ: Ordination in the Roman Catholic Church," in *Frontiers in Catholic Feminist Theology*, pp. 153–72.

Elisabeth Schüssler Fiorenza, *In Memory of Her: A Feminist Theological Reconstruction of Christian Origins*, 2nd edn. (London: SCM Press, 1993).

30   Bénézet Bujo (1940–)

Father Bujo is a Catholic theologian from the former Zaire whose writings seek to advance an indigenous theology that arises out of African social traditions and values and that speaks to Africans in their own context. In the particular African cultural context addressed by Bujo, life is a unity and the entire community is animated and united by a life force whose source is God. Ancestors are not merely those who leave behind a set of customs and laws but also those with whom the community, or clan, is in a mystical communion. Ancestors continue to exercise influence on the community while the community, by honoring them and following their wisdom, receive the strength, health, and life that God imparts through them. Jesus, says Bujo, is the "proto-ancestor," the one who founds, accompanies, and imparts life to the clan that is gathered around the table with him in the ancestral (Eucharistic) meal.

African Theology in its Social Context (1992)

Source: Bénézet Bujo, *African Theology in its Social Context*, trans. John O'Donohue.

The African concept of Jesus as Proto-Ancestor in no way contradicts the teaching of the New Testament. It is not of course that we are treating Jesus as an ancestor in any crudely biological sense. When we regard him as the ancestor *par excellence*, we mean that we find in him the one who begets in us a mystical and supernatural life.

In offering us fullness of life, Jesus offers to the people of Africa true development. After the traumas of the slave-trade and colonialism, and now the horrors of the refugee situation, the African people are searching for a new identity. Jesus Christ is our Proto-Ancestor for today, our modern Moses who will lead us through today's problems of oppression and poverty to the waters of life. In giving himself as food to those who believe in him, he becomes the life-giving grace which flows into all his descendants, the true "life-force" which Africa has always been seeking. Today the African community, clan or nation, can only develop by participating in the proto-life of Jesus, as we may call it; at the same time individuals can only help their communities to grow when they remain grounded in Jesus, the living sap which is the unique source of life for the whole Mystical Body.

When we try to construct an ecclesiology from this point of view, we see that the Eucharist as the proto-ancestral meal must be the foundation-stone of a Church which is truly African. A Church constructed on such a basis can have important prophetic consequences for the whole social and community life of modern Africa. … At the Last Supper, Jesus shared bread and wine with the apostles in anticipation of his death, filling them with what had been entrusted to him by the Father, that they might find the courage to go on living and announce to the coming generation the life-giving memory and the vital power of their Lord. This memory was sealed by the death and resurrection of Jesus, which bestowed once and for all on the apostles, and on all the disciples of Jesus, the intensified proto-ancestral life-force, strengthened by the Spirit of the Crucified and Risen One. The apostles and disciples were no longer afraid to proclaim the good news and to continue the mission of their Master.

The ecclesiological model we are proposing is evidently pneumatological. … It was through that dynamic force, which is the Spirit, that the Father raised the Son from the dead. It is this same joyful vital power, uniting Father and Son, and constituting the inner strength of the Trinity, which now creates a new community of initiated "clan" members. The Son, raised from the dead to a new life by the power of the Spirit, is, by that same power, constituted as Proto-Ancestor. He is now the source of that power. Together with the Father, he gives in abundance the vitality which he shares with the Father, and that vitality leads the community as Church to fullness of life and eschatological completion.

For further reading

Marthinus Daneel, "The Church as Healing and Liberating Institution," in *African Earthkeepers: Wholistic Interfaith Mission* (Maryknoll, NY: Orbis, 2004), pp. 137–63.

Joseph Healey and Donald Sybertz, "Church as the Extended Family of God," in *Towards an African Narrative Theology* (Maryknoll, NY: Orbis, 1996), pp. 104–67.

Aidan G. Msafiri, "The Church as a Family Model: Its Strengths and Weaknesses," in Emmanuel Katongole (ed.), *African Theology Today* (Scranton: University of Scranton Press, 2002), pp. 85–98.

J. N. K. Mugambi and L. Magesa (eds.), *The Church in African Christianity: Innovative Essays in Ecclesiology* (Nairobi: Initiatives Publishers, 1978).

Mercy Oduyoye, *Beads and Strands: Reflections of an African Woman on Christianity in Africa* (Maryknoll, NY: Orbis, 2004).

—— "The Household of God: Studies in Ecclesiology," in *African Women's Theology* (Cleveland, OH: Pilgrim Press, 2002), pp. 78–89.

Cephas N. Omenyo, "Essential Aspects of African Ecclesiology: The Case of the African Independent Church," *PNEUMA: The Journal of the Society for Pentecostal Studies* 22/2 (2000), pp. 231–48.

31 Wolfhart Pannenberg (1928–)

Pannenberg is a German theologian who has focused on epistemological questions in dialogue with the sciences, philosophy, and history. Here, in an excerpt, from his Systematic Theology, *many of those same epistemological concerns surface as he emphasizes the function of the church as an anticipatory sign of God's reign pointing beyond itself to the future inbreaking of the divine mystery of salvation. The church, therefore, is not an end in itself, but always a partially broken and partially illuminating revelation of the reconciliation God intends for the whole world.*

"The Church and the Kingdom of God" (1993)

Source: Wolfhart Pannenberg, *Systematic Theology*, trans. G. W. Bromiley.

The church ... is nothing apart from its function as an eschatological community and therefore as an anticipatory sign of God's coming rule and its salvation for all humanity. By its very nature, then, the Christian mission has transcended the boundaries of the Jewish people, and the particularity of its institutions, in order to become the church of Jews and Gentiles united by faith in the appearing of Jesus as the inbreaking of a new humanity that will be consummated in the future of God.

The structure of this sign includes the fact that sign and thing differ. A sign points beyond itself to the thing signified. It is thus essential to the function of the sign that we should distinguish them. We must not equate the thing with the sign in its weakness. Only by this distinction can the thing signified be, in a certain sense, present by way of the sign. This is how the church relates to the kingdom of God. The church must distinguish itself from the future fellowship of men and women in the kingdom of God in order that it may be seen to be a sign of the kingdom by which its saving future is already present for people in their own day. If the church fails to make this distinction clearly, then it arrogates to itself the finality and glory of the kingdom, but by the poverty and all too human character of its own life it also makes the Christian hope incredible. As Jesus in his earthly proclamation humbly distinguished himself from the Father and the future of his kingdom, so the church must distinguish its own existence from the future of the kingdom of God. Only in the spiritual poverty and humility of this self-distinction is it the place at which, by the power of the Holy Spirit, the eschatological future of God's lordship is already present and at work for human salvation. Only as it renounces exclusive claims for its own specific form can it plainly be a sign of the universality of the kingdom of God and an instrument of the reconciliation of human beings with one another and with God, transcending all the differences that separate people from one another and from the God of Israel. This is why the nature of the church's existence as a sign has always come out especially clearly in times of suffering and persecution.

For further reading

Stanley J. Grenz, "Sacramental Spirituality, Ecumenism, and Mission to the World: Foundational Motifs of Pannenberg's Ecclesiology," *Mid-Stream* 30/1 (1991), pp. 20–34.
Wolfhart Pannenberg, *The Church* (Philadelphia: Westminster, 1983).
———— *Ethik und Ekklesiologie* (Gottingen: Vandenhoeck & Ruprecht, 1977).
———— "The Kingdom of God and the Church," in *Theology and the Kingdom of God* (Philadelphia: Westminster, 1969), pp. 72–101.

32   Letty M. Russell (1929–2007)

Letty Russell was a widely respected and influential Presbyterian feminist theologian, pastor, and ecumenist. In Church in the Round, *Russell took on the challenge of developing a feminist ecclesiology using the domestic images of table, household, and kitchen, but turning them into powerful and liberating metaphors of an inclusive, justice-seeking, and egalitarian church. For Russell, some of the most important work the church does is tending its boundaries — not in an effort to preserve a fixed identity, but to daringly open itself to others as a community of invitation and hospitality.*

Church in the Round (1993)

Source: Letty M. Russell, *Church in the Round: Feminist Interpretation of the Church*.

The need for a feminist interpretation of the church has been recognized by Christian feminists for some time. Whenever one's paradigm or perspective on reality shifts, everything has to be thought through from this new perspective. Using a prism of feminist advocacy of the full humanity of *all* women together with men leads to critique, reconstruction, and reinterpretation of all the Christian traditions. ...

In presenting this particular feminist interpretation of the church, I describe the church as a community of Christ, bought with a price, where everyone is welcome. It is a *community of Christ* because Christ's presence, through the power of the Spirit, constitutes people as a community gathered in Christ's name (Matt. 18:20; 1 Cor. 12:4–6). This community is *bought with a price* because the struggle of Jesus to overcome the structures of sin and death constitutes both the source of new life in the community and its own mandate to continue the same struggle for life on behalf of others (1 Cor. 6:20; Phil. 2:1–11). It is a community *where everyone is welcome* because it gathers around the table of God's hospitality. Its welcome table is a sign of the coming feast of God's mended creation, with the guest list derived from the announcements of the Jubilee year in ancient Israel (Luke 14:12–14). ...

This feminist critical principle of interpretation needs to be applied to interpretation of the church as well as of scripture. *The critical principle of feminist ecclesiology is a table principle.* It looks for ways that God reaches out to include all those whom society and religion have declared outsiders and invites them to gather round God's table of hospitality. The measure of the adequacy of the life of a church is how it is connected to those on the margin, whether those the NRSV calls "the least of these who are members of my family" are receiving the attention to their needs for justice and hope (Matt. 25:40).

The authority for the table principle is the gospel understanding of the household or commonwealth of God. Jesus' preaching is constantly directed toward the invitation of those who are the rejected ones of society, those on the margin, to share the feast of God's new household (Luke 19:1–10). Jesus' message is that all persons are created by God and are welcome in God's household. ...

Discussion of tradition and ecclesiology from a feminist perspective is most definitely a way of talking back to a community whose self-understanding has been shaped in all its aspects of tradition from a patriarchal paradigm of authority as domination. The shift to the metaphor of church in the round is one way of talking back because it reconfigures the paradigm of what evokes assent from the image of the household ruled by a patriarch to one of a household where everyone gathers around the common table to break bread and to share table talk and hospitality. All are welcome to participate in the table talk because in that way they become participants in their own journey of faith and struggle for the mending and liberation of creation. …

[With regard to] communities of faith and struggle and [to] the many and various ways they are connected to movements and to the Christian tradition, we perhaps can discern a few clues for feminist liberation ecclesiologies from the witness of these groups to the possibility of new life, of resurrection in the church.

First, from them, and from countless others like them, we have learned that the missionary nature of the church as it participates in God's sending and liberating work in the world requires a justice connection. There is no way to be an advocate for partnership beyond patriarchy without working for justice. Kitchen table solidarity requires that persons and their communities share in the struggle for full humanity and human dignity for all people, and especially those too poor and powerless even to think beyond the need to find some food for the family gathering.

Second, we have seen over and over again that the witness of the church is rooted in a life of hospitality when bounded communities who have sought to gain identity behind their particular walls of tradition find themselves broken open by the gospel invitation of hospitality to the stranger in their midst. Communities of hospitality become a living invitation to God's welcome table and, in turn, are developed by those who have found a new openness and welcome in the gospel message.

Last, we can see from our discussion of feminist and liberation communities that the life of the church involves the nurture of spirituality of connection. It practices the presence and connection to God and to the people on the margins of society through the study of the Bible and its interpretation and celebration in the round table community of Christ. In such settings there is an opportunity for life to come together in a way that both transcends and includes the bits and pieces that make up the struggle for wholeness, freedom, and full humanity.

For further reading

Serene Jones, "Church: Graced Community," in *Feminist Theory and Christian Theology: Cartographies of Grace* (Minneapolis: Fortress, 2000), pp. 153–76.

Pui-lan Kwok, "Women and the Church," in *Asian Feminist Theology* (Cleveland, OH: Pilgrim Press, 2000), pp. 98–112.

Letty M. Russell, *Just Hospitality: God's Welcome in a World of Difference*, ed. J. Shannon Clarkson and Kate M. Ott (Louisville: Westminster John Knox, 2009).

Natalie Watson, *Introducing Feminist Ecclesiology* (Cleveland, OH: Pilgrim Press, 2002).

—————— "Feminist Ecclesiology," in Gerard Mannion and Lewis Mudge (eds.), *The Routledge Companion to the Christian Church* (New York: Routledge, 2008), pp. 461–75.
Pamela Dickey Young, *Re-Creating the Church: Communities of Eros* (New York: Continuum, 2000).

33 Delores S. Williams (1934–)

One of the earliest and most influential womanist theologians, Delores Williams reinterpreted classical Christological and soteriological themes of the Christian story through the lens of African American women's struggle for survival and quality of life in her book Sisters in the Wilderness. *At the conclusion of the book she turns to the question of the black church, and while describing it as invisible, at the same time states eloquently narrates its powerful role in the lives of African-Americans, both men and women.*

"The Black Church Invisible" (1993)

Source: Delores S. Williams, *Sisters in the Wilderness: The Challenge of Womanist God-Talk.*

The black church does not exist as an institution. Regardless of sociological, theological, historical and pastoral attempts, the black church escapes precise definition. As many discussions of it as there are, there will be that many (and more) different definitions. Some believe it to be rooted deeply in the soul of the community memory of black folk. Some believe it to be the core symbol of the four-hundred-year-old African-American struggle against white oppression with God in the struggle providing black people with spiritual and material resources for survival and freedom. Others believe it to be places where black people come to worship God without white people being present.

I believe the black church is the heart of hope in the black community's experience of oppression, survival struggle and its historic efforts toward complete liberation. It cannot be tampered with or changed by humans to meet human expectations and goals. The black church cannot be made respectable because it is already sacralized by the pain and resurrection of thousands upon thousands of victims. It cannot be made elite because it is already classless. In America it came first to the community of slaves. It cannot be made racial because it is too real for false distinctions. It cannot be made more male than female because it is already both, equally. It cannot be made heterosexist because it is a "homo-hetero" amalgam. It cannot be made political because it is perfect justice.

We cannot confine the black church to one special location because it can move everywhere faster than a bird in flight, faster than a rocket soaring, faster than time—but slowly enough to put spiritual songs in our burdened souls—slowly enough to put love in our broken lives—slowly enough to bring moments of liberation to our troubled people.

The black church is invisible, but we know it when we see it: our daughters and sons rising up from death and addiction recovering and recovered; our mothers in poverty raising their children alone, with God's help, making a way out of no way and succeeding; Harriet Tubman leading hundreds of slaves into freedom; Isabel, the former African-American slave, with God's help, transforming destiny to become Sojourner Truth, affirming the close relation between God and woman; Mary McLeod Bethune's college starting on a garbage heap with one dollar and fifty cents growing into a multimillion dollar enterprise; Rosa Parks sitting down so Martin Luther King, Jr., could stand up. The black church is invisible, but we know it when we see oppressed people rising up in freedom. It is community essence, ideal and real as God works through it in behalf of the survival, liberation and positive, productive quality of life of suffering people.

It has neither hands nor feet nor form, but we know when we feel it in our communities as neither Christianity, nor Islam, nor Judaism, nor Buddhism, nor Confucianism, nor any human-made religion. Rather, it comes as God-full presence to our struggles quickening the heart, measuring the soul and bathing life with the spirit from head to toe. It comes as moral wisdom in the old folks saying, "You give out one lemon, God gonna give you a dozen back!" It comes as folk-analysis in the old people claiming, "White folks and us both Christians, but we ain't got the same religion." It comes as folk-faith nevertheless believing that *"all* God's children got wings to soar." The black church gave us spiritual songs and blues and gospel and rap and a singing way to justice, fighting. It is invisible, but we know when we see, hear and feel it quickening the heart, measuring the soul and bathing life with the spirit in time.

For further reading

Karen Baker-Fletcher, *My Sister, My Brother: Womanist and Xodus God-Talk* (Maryknoll, NY: Orbis, 1997)
Cheryl Townsend Gilkes, *If It Wasn't for the Women: Black Women's Experience and Womanist Culture in Church and Community* (Maryknoll, NY: Orbis, 2001).

34   Miroslav Volf (1941–)

Miroslav Volf is a Croatian-born theologian whose efforts at developing a contemporary free-church ecclesiology build on the legacy of early Baptist theologian John Smyth in ecumenical dialogue with Roman Catholic, Orthodox, and feminist theologies. Ecclesial participation, for Volf, is nothing less than participation in the life of the triune God, who indwells believers, establishing a communion with them and among them and thereby transforming them into an anticipation of God's new creation. In keeping with the ecclesiology of Smyth, the nature of the church as a covenanted congregation, or assembly, is accentuated as is the importance of faith and obedience. Volf goes on to emphasize the charismatic constitution of the church, and his approach has had strong resonances with theologians in the Pentecostal and charismatic traditions.

After Our Likeness: The Church as the Image of the Trinity (1998)

Source: Miroslav Volf, *After Our Likeness: The Church as the Image of the Trinity*.

What is the church?

The future of the church in God's new creation is the mutual personal indwelling of the triune God and of his glorified people, as becomes clear from the description of the new Jerusalem in the Apocalypse of John (Rev. 21:1–22:5). ... Such participation in the communion of the triune God, however, is not only an object of hope for the church, but also its present experience, "We declare to you what we have seen and heard so that you also may have fellowship with us; and truly our fellowship *is* with the Father and with his Son Jesus Christ" (1 John 1:3). Faith in this proclaimed "life," life that was with the Father and appeared in this world in an audible and tangible fashion (see 1 John 1:1, 4), establishes communion between believers and the triune God and thus also among believers themselves. Present participation in the trinitarian *communio* through faith in Jesus Christ anticipates in history the eschatological communion of the church with the triune God. ...

Wherever the Spirit of Christ, which as the eschatological gift anticipates God's new creation in history (see Rom. 8:23; 2 Cor. 1:22; Eph. 1:14), is present in its *ecclesially constitutive* activity, there is the church. The Spirit unites the gathered congregation with the triune God and integrates it into a history extending from Christ, indeed, from the Old Testament saints, to the eschatological new creation. This Spirit-mediated relationship with the triune God and with the entire history of God's people—a history whose center resides in Jesus' own proclamation of the reign of God, in his death and in his resurrection—constitutes an assembly into a church. ...

The church as an assembly

The church is first of all an *assembly*: "where two or three are *gathered* in my name, I am there among them" (Matt. 18:20). In his book *Versammelte Gemeinde*, Otto Weber correctly designates the church a "visible assembly of visible persons at a specific place for specific action." Doubtless, however, the life of the church is not exhausted in the act of assembly. Even if a church is not assembled, it does live on as a church in the mutual service its members render to one another and in its common mission to the world. The church is not simply an act of assembling; rather, it assembles at a specific place (see 1 Cor. 14:23). It is the *people* who in a specific way assemble at a specific place. In its most concentrated form, however, the church does manifest itself concretely in the act of assembling for worship, and this is constitutive for its ecclesiality. ...

The church and the confession of faith
A church is an assembly, but an assembly is not yet a church. An indispensable condition of ecclesiality is that the people assemble *in the name of Christ*. Gathering in the name of Christ is the precondition for the presence of Christ in the Holy Spirit, which is itself constitutive for the church: "where two or three are gathered *in my name*, I am among them."

Two conditions of ecclesiality emerge from the church's status as a congregation assembled in the *name* of Christ. The first is the *faith* of those who are thus assembled. The church is essentially *communio fidelium*, whatever else it may be beyond this. Without faith in Christ as Savior, there is no church. Certainly, the church does not stand or fall with the faith of every individual member. "It existed before the individual came to faith, and it will remain even if certain individuals fall away from faith." This is so, however, not because the church would somehow also exist above the *communio fidelium*, but because the individual standing in faith does not constitute the entire church. The church exists even if I do not believe; yet without at least someone believing, there can be no church, and in this sense the existence of the church is bound to the faith of its members in Christ as their Savior and Lord. (This does not turn the church into a human accomplishment, since faith itself is not a human accomplishment.)

The second condition of ecclesiality associated with assembling in the *name* of Christ is the *commitment* of those assembled to allow their own lives to be determined by Jesus Christ. Radicalizing the Calvinist tradition, the Free Churches originally took as their point of departure the assertion that faith without fruit is dead; where there is no fruit, there is no true faith, and where there is no true faith, neither is there a church.

For further reading

Ralph Del Colle, "Communion and the Trinity: The Free Church Ecclesiology of Miroslav Volf—A Catholic Response," *PNEUMA: The Journal of the Society for Pentecostal Studies* 22/2 (2000), pp. 303–27.

Curtis W. Freeman, "Where Two or Three Are Gathered: Communion Ecclesiology in the Free Church," *Perspectives in Religious Studies* 31/3 (2004), pp. 259–72.

James William McClendon, *Systematic Theology*, vol. 2: *Doctrine* (Nashville: Abingdon, 1994), pp. 327–453.

35   Elizabeth A. Johnson (1941–)

Elizabeth Johnson is a Roman Catholic theologian who works in the area of systematic, ecological, and feminist theology. In her book Friends of God and Prophets *she provides a feminist theological reading of the "communion of saints," a concept that has always been closely connected to ecclesiology in Christian history (as, for example, the* Apostles' Creed*). Johnson traces the way the Christian veneration of saints early on implied a companionship of equals and friends that in a post-Constantinian era morphed into a system of patronage marked by a hierarchy of clients and patrons. Johnson seeks to recover the earlier model as a way of reviving the importance of saints for an inclusive, egalitarian church in which all persons are valued and holy.*

Friends of God and Prophets (1999)

Source: Elizabeth A. Johnson, *Friends of God and Prophets: A Feminist Theological Reading of the Communion of Saints.*

The communion of saints comprises all living persons of truth and love. The point to emphasize is "all": all Christians as well as all persons of good will. While the term itself springs from the experience of grace within the church, the communion of saints does not limit divine blessing to its own circle. Within human cultures everywhere, Spirit-Sophia calls every human being to fidelity and love, awakening knowledge of the truth and inspiring deeds of compassion and justice. The friends of God and prophets are found in every nation and tongue, culture and religion, and even among religion's cultured despisers. Indeed, where human participation in divine holiness disappears the opposite appears—barbarity, cruelty, murder, and unspeakable despair. At its most elemental, then, the communion of saints embraces all women and men who hear Holy Wisdom's call and follow her path of righteousness: "whoever finds me finds life" (Prov. 8:35). ...

The communion of saints is comprised first of all of the current generation of living Christians who respond to the promptings of the Spirit and follow the way of Jesus in the world. In the circumstances of their own historical time and place, these women and men try to be faithful friends and courageous prophets, taking seriously the invitation to love God and neighbor and pouring good purpose into their lives. Some work anonymously in fidelity to duty; others speak loudly in the assembly; some risk the wrath of the powerful by engaging in structural analysis and action on behalf of justice, for the poor and for women; others are the powerful converted to their responsibility; still others perform miracles of nonviolence in bringing about peace; some bountifully nurture and nourish young life; others show the way in nurturing and healing the oppressed self; still others lead the way in caring for the earth; some compassionately tend the sick and the dying; others are artisans of new visions, new images, new designs for society; some know the pleasures of sexual expression; others experience their sexuality as the locus of violation; some fulfill a particular mission or office in the church; many more live "ordinary lives," growing in love through the complex interactions of their work, play, and relationships; some are well-off; many more are numbered among the poor who struggle for bread; some know success; many others are broken by suffering, both personal and political; some clearly make God attractive; others wrestle with demons that obscure the immediacy of divine presence. Any combination of the above situations is possible; the diversity of circumstances is amazing.

This *communio sanctorum* participates in the holiness of Sophia-God, whose kindly, people-loving spirit fills the world, pervading everything and holding all things together. The symbol itself originates when Christians recognize this corporate sharing in grace that marks themselves and others, and rise up in appreciation of the blessing. Since for Christian faith the one God graciously relates to the world in a triune gift of self-communication through incarnation and grace, we use this threefold pattern to describe the foundational relation to the Holy One without which there would be no communion of saints. ...

Saints on earth have access to the company of saints in heaven through memory and hope. Memory is meant here in the sense of *anamnesis*, an effective remembering that makes something genuinely past to be present and active in the community today. A remembered event becomes a living force in history when it is recalled and narrated; in the very retelling power comes forth to change the horizon of our days and offer new possibilities of existence. The primary *anamnesis* of the Christian community occurs in the sacramental action of the Eucharist, where the community makes memorial of Jesus' death and resurrection in such a way that it becomes a living, transforming reality in the lives of those who celebrate it. Christian remembrance of the saints is linked to this action, making present the creative struggle and witness of so many who themselves participated in this paschal mystery. Retelling their story brings the subversive, encouraging, and liberating power of their love and witness into the present generation.

Lamentably, the exclusion of women from the public culture of the church has resulted in an official memory that has erased a good part of the history of women's discipleship, giving to the communion of saints a largely male face both in heaven and on earth. This erasure has never been wholly effective, however, and feminist hermeneutical methods now bring to light women and the contributions they have made in licit and illicit ways. For ecclesial practices of memory to be liberating to women, to poor women, to women of color, to lay women, to married women everywhere, deliberate attention must be turned to their stories. Their absence must be noticed, missed, criticized, and corrected. It is not just a matter of adding women to what remains a patriarchal master narrative. The challenge, rather, is to reshape the church's memory so as to reclaim an equal share in the center for women and thereby transform the community.

The prevailing relationship among members of this company of the living and the dead that crosses centuries is fundamentally mutual and egalitarian. This interpretation retrieves the biblical insight that the people as a whole are holy, as well as its affirmation of each person's equal standing in a political as well as spiritual sense: "There is no longer Jew or Greek, there is no longer slave or free, there is no longer male and female; for all of you are one in Christ Jesus" (Gal. 3:28). It also reclaims the intuition of the early Christian centuries that the martyrs are splendid companions in the following of Christ. This relational pattern runs counter to the later image of a spiritual hierarchy of patrons and petitioners, with saints in heaven in the role of powerful intercessors and nonsaints on earth asking for their aid. Shaped according to the Roman system of patronage, this construal understands God to be a powerful monarch whom a little person dares not approach directly. Saints dwell in the heavenly court, some closer to the throne than others, and can present the needs of their devotees with greater certainty of success. This patronage model has been rendered moot by deep theological shifts, not least the gospel depiction of Jesus' ministry to the poor and marginalized that embodies divine compassion for the most godforsaken with an overwhelming freedom and graciousness, calling all to a place around the table. It also falters in the light of feminist theological analysis that reveals it to be projection of patriarchal structures into heaven. By contrast, the saints alive in God are sisters and brothers who accompany the current generation on the path of discipleship. In this companionship paradigm, differences between persons are not erased but neither are they the occasion for relating as superior to inferior. Rather, because each person is truly called to the one holiness and gifted by the Spirit with a unique talent, all come together as companions along the way. … Rather than be caught in an elitist structure, the saints in heaven and on earth become partners in memory and hope.

For further reading / viewing

Babette's Feast, dir. Gabriel Axel (Nordisk Film, 1987) [film].

Peter Brown, *The Cult of the Saints: Its Rise and Function in Latin Christianity* (Chicago: University of Chicago Press, 1981).

Romano Guardini, *The Saints in Christian Life* (Philadelphia: Chilton Books, 1966).

Elizabeth A. Johnson, *She Who Is: The Mystery of God in Feminist Theological Discourse* (New York: Crossroad, 1996).

Michael Perham, *The Communion of Saints* (London: Alcuin Club and SPCK, 1980).

36   Amos Yong (1965–)

*Conservative estimates are that by the end of the twentieth century a quarter of a
billion people (one out of eight Christians) worldwide were adherents of Pentecostalism
and of charismatic Christianity more generally—with most of these Christians, it is
important to note, living in developing countries throughout the world. As vibrant
and widespread as Pentecostalism is, however, relatively little attention has been given
to a Pentecostal ecclesiology, with far more focus placed on the experience and gifts
of the Spirit, Trinitarian doctrine, and on the practices of mission and evangelism. In
his book* The Spirit Poured Out on All Flesh, *Amos Yong, a Pentecostal theologian,
rethinks the four classic marks of the church (unity, holiness, catholicity, and
apostolicity) in dialogue with Roman Catholic sources such as Yves Congar and from
a pneumatological perspective. In doing so, he demonstrates the way these marks are
to be understood as eschatological indicators produced by the work of the Holy Spirit.
The following excerpt demonstrates the significance of this perspective for the mark
of unity.*

The Spirit Poured Out on All Flesh (2005)

Source: Amos Yong, *The Spirit Poured Out on All Flesh: Pentecostalism and the Possibility
of Global Theology.*

Pentecostals certainly would affirm the unity of the church. They would deny,
however, that any one episcopate constitutes that unity. … Because ecclesial
unity is experienced in the fellowship of those who confess Jesus as Lord by
the Holy Spirit (cf. 1 Cor. 12:3), such unity is eschatological but also supremely
particularistic, perhaps even sacramental.

Pentecostal sacramentality should *not* be considered in the classic sense,
whereby salvation is mediated through the priesthood, through baptism, or
through the (other) sacraments. Rather, insofar as Pentecostals are convinced
that the Spirit who resides within and presides over the church is the same
Spirit who anointed Jesus of Nazareth and that the Spirit is truly encountered
and manifest palpably and tangibly in the lives of individuals who constitute
the church—for example, through tongues, healings, the shout, and the
dance—the Spirit's reality is mediated through the particularly embodied
experiences of the community of saints. There is therefore a unique sort of
Pentecostal sacramentality at work, an experiential and incarnational logic
that acknowledges the Spirit's being made present and active through the
materiality of personal embodiment and congregational life.

But more important, Pentecostal sacramentality means that the unity of the
church comes about through the eschatological work of the Spirit. The word
made flesh and the Spirit breathing and making the Word real in and through
the community of saints together constitute the one work of the triune God.
Such an account of ecclesial unity as both spiritual and embodied undergirds

the Pentecostal notion of unity in diversity. This is not, however, for diversity's sake but for the sake of the reconciliation of a broken creation. ...

This paradigm of unity-in-diversity as reconciliation emerges from the pneumatic and charismatic intuitions derived from the Pentecostal experience. The Pentecostal experience at Azusa Street, which overcame gender, ethnic, racial, and socioeconomic barriers present in American life at the turn of the twentieth century, simply reembodied the eschatological outpouring of the Spirit on the day of Pentecost and in the life of the early church. The Pentecostal experience, then and now, brings sons and daughters together with menservants and maidservants—no small feat for a world ruled by patriarchy. It binds Samaritans, Ethiopians, and other Gentiles together with Jews—again, a major achievement in a world of ethnic and racial hostilities. It reconciles into one body the haves and have-nots through various means, whether it be the securing of justice (Zacchaeus in Luke 19:1–10), the redistribution of goods (Barnabas in Acts 4:36–7; the widows in Acts 6:1), or the affirmation of the ministry of the well-to-do among those less well off (Dorcas in Acts 9:36–43; Lydia in Acts 16:13–15). The case of the Ethiopian eunuch is particularly noteworthy here (Acts 8:27–39). Not only does the inclusion in the body of Christ of this high-ranking foreign official cut across ethnic, socioeconomic, and political lines; it also emphatically demarginalizes those who for physical reasons were barred from the assembly (cf. Deut. 23:1; Isa. 56:3–5).

Though beginning among the variously marginalized of American society, Pentecostalism was and is driven by a convergence of a diversity of perspectives and experiences brought about by the eschatological work of the Spirit of God. Those who have continued in obedience to the Spirit's leading and have been sensitive to the church's calling toward unity have also recognized the ecumenical potential of Pentecostal-charismatic spirituality and participated in the reconciling work of the Spirit through the later charismatic-renewal movements. But given human fallibility and sinfulness, even the unity of Pentecostal faith and experience was insufficient to keep the movement from splintering into innumerable factions. Ongoing repentance and acts of reconciliation have been and should continue to be normative.

All of this does not deny that Pentecostals affirm spiritual over institutional or structured unity. Yet such spiritual unity is not devoid of concrete manifestations across the spectrum of Christian life; it is, rather, a unity that includes reconciliation and healing. And such unity is to be experienced in the Spirit, who brings those otherwise separated together in Jesus Christ in anticipation of the eschatological union before the throne of God. ...

It could be argued that the universality of the Pentecostal community is due in part to the fact that Pentecostalism is first and foremost an ecumenical experience and spirituality rather than an organized network of institutions. The ties that bind Pentecostals together around the world are their experiences of Jesus in the power of the Spirit. It is not that Pentecostals are not concerned about Christian unity. Rather, Pentecostals experience Christian unity precisely through the universality of the Spirit's presence and activity, which enable the confession of Jesus' lordship amidst the peculiarly Pentecostal congregations and liturgies.

For further reading

Simon Chan, *Liturgical Theology: The Church as Worshipping Community* (Downers Grove, IL: InterVarsity Press, 2006).

———— "Mother Church: Toward a Pentecostal Ecclesiology," *PNEUMA: The Journal of the Society for Pentecostal Studies* 22/2 (2000), pp. 177–208.

M. L. Hodges, *A Theology of the Church and Its Mission: A Pentecostal Perspective* (Springfield, MO: Gospel Publishing House, 1977).

Veli-Matti Kärkkäinen, "The Church as the Fellowship of Persons: An Emerging Pentecostal Ecclesiology of Koinonia," *PentecoStudies* 6/1 (2007), pp. 1–15.Steven J. Land, *Pentecostal Spirituality: A Passion for the Kingdom* (Sheffield: Sheffield Academic Press, 1993).

Miroslav Volf, *After Our Likeness: The Church as the Image of the Trinity* (Grand Rapids: Eerdmans, 1998).

For Further Reading

Note: The following list is in addition to the suggestions already included after each excerpt.

Gillian T. W. Ahlgren, *The Human Person and the Church* (Maryknoll, NY: Orbis, 1999).

Wallace M. Alston Jr., *The Church of the Living God* (Louisville: Westminster John Knox, 2002).

Gilberte Baril, *The Feminine Face of the People of God: Biblical Symbols of the Church as Bride and Mother* (Collegeville, MN: The Liturgical Press, 1992)

Donald Bloesch, *The Church: Sacraments, Worship, Ministry, Mission* (Downers Grove, IL: InterVarsity Press, 2005).

Carl E. Braaten, *Mother Church: Ecclesiology and Ecumenism* (Minneapolis: Fortress, 1998).

Stephen Brachlow, *The Communion of Saints: Radical Puritan and Separatist Ecclesiology, 1570–1625* (Oxford: Oxford University Press, 1988).

Michael L. Budde and Robert W. Brimlow, *The Church as Counterculture* (Albany: State University of New York Press, 2000).

——— *Christianity Incorporated: How Big Business is Buying the Church* (Grand Rapids: Brazos, 2002).

William T. Cavanaugh, *Torture and Eucharist: Theology, Politics, and the Body of Christ* (Oxford: Blackwell, 1998).

——— *Theopolitical Imagination* (London: T. & T. Clark, 2002).

Henry Chadwick, *The Church in Ancient Society: From Galilee to Gregory the Great* (Oxford: Oxford University Press, 2001).

Rodney Clapp, *A Peculiar People: The Church as a Post-Christian Society* (Downers Grove, IL: InterVarsity Press, 1996).

Raymond F. Collins, *The Many Faces of the Church: A Study in New Testament Ecclesiology* (New York: Crossroad, 2003).

Bernard Cooke, *Ministry to Word and Sacrament* (Philadelphia: Fortress, 1980).

Sally Cunneen, *Mother Church: What the Experience of Women is Teaching Her* (Mahwah, NJ: Paulist Press, 1991)

Dennis Doyle, *Communion Ecclesiology: Visions and Versions* (Maryknoll, NY: Orbis, 2000).

Avery Dulles, *Models of the Church*, exp. edn. (New York: Doubleday, 2002)

Gillian R. Evans, *The Church and the Churches: Towards an Ecumenical Ecclesiology* (Cambridge: Cambridge University Press, 1994).

Norma Cook Everist (ed.), *The Difficult but Indispensable Church* (Minneapolis: Augsburg Fortress, 2002).

Eileen M. Fagan, *An interpretation of Evangelization: Jon Sobrino's Christology and Ecclesiology in Dialogue* (San Francisco: Catholic Scholars Press, 1998).

Douglas B. Farrow, *Ascension and Ecclesia: On the Significance of the Doctrine of the Ascension for Ecclesiology* (Grand Rapids: Eerdmans, 1999).

John Fuellenbach, *Church: Community for the Kingdom* (Maryknoll, NY: Orbis, 2002).

Mary McClintock Fulkerson, *Places of Redemption* (Oxford: Oxford University Press, 2007).

Richard R. Gaillardetz, *Ecclesiology for a Global Church* (Maryknoll, NY: Orbis, 2008).

Eddie Gibbs and Ryan K. Bolger, *Emerging Churches: Creating Christian Community in Postmodern Cultures* (Grand Rapids: Baker, 2005).

Cheryl Townsend Gilkes, *If it Wasn't For the Women* (Maryknoll, NY: Orbis, 2001).

Robin Gill, *Churchgoing and Christian Ethics* (Cambridge: Cambridge University Press, 1999).

——— *The "Empty" Church Revisited* (Aldershot: Ashgate, 2003).

Romano Guardini, *The Church of the Lord: On the Nature and Mission of the Church* (Chicago: Henry Regnery, 1966).

Darrell L. Guder (ed.), *Missional Church: A Vision for the Sending of the Church in North America* (Grand Rapids: Eerdmans, 1998).

Colin Gunton and Daniel Hardy, *On Being the Church: Essays on the Christian Community* (Edinburgh: T. & T. Clark, 1989).

James M. Gustafson, *Treasure in Earthen Vessels: The Church as a Human Community* (Chicago: University of Chicago Press, 1976).

Roger Haight, *Christian Community in History*, 3 vols. (New York: Continuum, 2004–2008).

Douglas John Hall, *Confessing the Faith: Christian Theology in a North American Context* (Minneapolis: Fortress, 1998).

Nicholas M. Healy, *Church, World, and the Christian Life: Practical-Prophetic Ecclesiology* (Cambridge: Cambridge University Press, 2000).

Michael J. Himes, *Ongoing Incarnation: Johann Adam Möhler and the Beginnings of Modern Ecclesiology* (New York: Crossroad, 1997).

Peter C. Hodgson, *Revisioning the Church: Ecclesial Freedom in the New Paradigm* (Minneapolis: Fortress, 1988).

Michael S. Horton, *People and Place: A Covenant Ecclesiology* (Louisville: Westminster John Knox, 2008).

Wes Howard-Brook, *The Church Before Christianity* (Maryknoll, NY: Orbis, 2001).

George Hunsberger and Craig Van Gelder (eds.), *The Church Between Gospel and Culture* (Grand Rapids: Eerdmans, 1996).

Mark Husbands and Daniel J. Treier (eds.), *The Community of the Word: Toward an Evangelical Ecclesiology* (Downers Grove, IL: InterVarsity Press, 2005).

Reinhard Hütter, "Ecclesial Ethics, the Church's Vocation, and Paraclesis," *Pro Ecclesia* 2/4 (Fall, 1993), pp. 433–50.

——— *Suffering Divine Things: Theology as Church Practice* (Grand Rapids: Eerdmans, 2000).

——— "The Church," in James J. Buckley and David S. Yeago (eds), *Knowing the Triune God: The Work of the Spirit in the Practices of the Church* (Grand Rapids: Eerdmans, 2001), pp. 23–48.

Eric G. Jay, *The Church: Its Changing Image through Twenty Centuries* (Atlanta: John Knox, 1980).

Michael Jinkins, *The Church Faces Death: Ecclesiology in a Postmodern Context* (Oxford: Oxford University Press, 2002).

Luke Timothy Johnson, *Scripture and Discernment: Decision-Making in the Church* (Nashville: Abingdon, 1996).

Charles Cardinal Journet, *The Theology of the Church* (San Francisco: Ignatius Press, 2004).

Veli-Matti Kärkkäinen, *An Introduction to Ecclesiology. Ecumenical, Historical & Global Perspectives* (Downers Grove, IL: InterVarsity Press, 2002).

Walter Kasper, *Theology and Church* (New York: Crossroad, 1989).

Joseph A. Komonchak, *Foundations in Ecclesiology* (Boston: Boston College Lonergan Workshop, 1995).

Hans Küng, *Structures of the Church* (New York: Thomas Nelson, 1964).

Gordon W. Lathrop, *Holy People: A Liturgical Ecclesiology* (Minneapolis: Fortress, 1999).

Richard Lennan, *The Ecclesiology of Karl Rahner* (New York: Oxford University Press, 1997).

Gerhard Lohfink, *Jesus and Community* (Philadelphia: Fortress, 1984).

——— *Does God Need the Church? Toward a Theology of the People of God* (Collegeville, MN: The Liturgical Press, 1999).

Gerard Mannion, *Ecclesiology and Postmodernity: Questions for the Church in Our Time* (Collegeville, MN: The Liturgical Press, 2007).

Gerard Mannion and Lewis Mudge (eds.), *The Routledge Companion to the Christian Church* (New York: Routledge, 2008).

Vincent Martin, *A House Divided: The Parting of the Ways Between Synagogue and Church* (New York: Paulist Press, 1995).

Paul S. Minear, *Images of the Church in the New Testament* (Louisville: Westminster John Knox, 1970).

Lewis S. Mudge, *Rethinking the Beloved Community: Ecclesiology, Hermeneutics, Social Theory* (Geneva and Lanham, MD: WCC Publications and University Press of America, 2000).

H. Richard Niebuhr, *The Social Sources of Denominationalism* (New York: World Publishing, 1957).

——— *"The Responsibility of the Church for Society" and Other Essays* (Louisville: Westminster, 2008).

Christopher O'Donnell, *Ecclesia: A Theological Encyclopedia of the Church* (Collegeville, MN: The Liturgical Press, 1996).

Thomas Franklin O'Meara, O.P., "Philosophical Models in Ecclesiology," *Theological Studies* 39/1 (1978), pp. 3–21.

Martyn Percy, *Power and the Church: Ecclesiology in an Age of Transition* (London: Cassell, 1998).

Norman Pittenger, *The Pilgrim Church and the Easter People* (Wilmington, DE: Michael Glazier, 1987).

Bernard P. Prusak, *The Church Unfinished: Ecclesiology Through the Centuries* (Mahwah, NJ: Paulist Press, 2004).

Ephraim Radner, *The End of the Church: A Pneumatology of Christian Division in the West* (Grand Rapids: Eerdmans, 1998).

——— *Hope Among the Fragments* (Grand Rapids: Brazos, 2004).

Thomas P. Rausch, *Towards a Truly Catholic Church: An Ecclesiology for the Third Millennium* (Collegeville, MN: The Liturgical Press, 2005).

R. R. Reno, *In the Ruins of the Church: Sustaining Faith in an Age of Diminished Christianity* (Grand Rapids: Brazos, 2002).

Herwi Rikhof, *The Concept of Church: A Methodological Inquiry into the Use of Metaphors in Ecclesiology* (London: Sheed & Ward, 1981).

Alan J. Roxburgh, *The Missionary Congregation, Leadership, & Liminality* (Harrisburg, PA: Trinity Press International, 1997).

The Rutba House, *School(s) for Conversion: 12 Marks of a New Monasticism* (Eugene, OR: Cascade, 2005).

Edward Schillebeeckx, *Ministry: Leadership in the Community of Jesus* (New York: Crossroad, 1981).

——— *Church: The Human Story of God* (New York: Crossroad, 1994).

Jon Sobrino, *The True Church and the Poor* (Maryknoll, NY: Orbis, 1984).

——— "The Economics of Ecclesia: A Poor Church is a Church Rich in Compassion," in David Batstone (ed.), *New Visions For the Americas: Religious Engagement and Social Transformation* (Minneapolis: Fortress, 1993), pp. 83–100.

C. S. Song, *Jesus the Crucified People* (Minneapolis: Fortress, 1996).

John Stackhouse, *Evangelical Ecclesiology: Reality or Illusion?* (Grand Rapids: Baker Academic, 2003).

Carl F. Starkloff, "Church as Structure and Communitas: Victor Turner and Ecclesiology," *Theological Studies* 58 (1997), pp. 643–8.

Francis A. Sullivan, S.J., *The Church We Believe In: One, Holy, Catholic, and Apostolic* (Mahwah, NJ: Paulist Press, 1988).

George H. Tavard, *The Church, Community of Salvation: An Ecumenical Ecclesiology* (Collegeville, MN: The Liturgical Press, 1992)

Gesa Elsbeth Thiessen, *Ecumenical Ecclesiology: Unity, Diversity and Otherness in a Fragmented World.* (New York: T. & T. Clark, 2009).

Susan Brooks Thistlewaite, *Metaphors for the Contemporary Church* (Cleveland, OH: Pilgrim Press, 1983).

Dave Tomlinson, *The Post-Evangelical* (Grand Rapids: Zondervan, 2003).
Keith Ward, *Religion and Community* (Oxford: Oxford University Press, 2000).
Brent Webb-Mitchell, *Christly Gestures: Learning to Be Members of the Body of Christ* (Grand Rapids: Eerdmans, 2003).

Index